D0919743

Penguin Education X75

Monopoly and Competition

Penguin Modern Economics Readings

General Editor
B. J. McCormick

Advisory Board
K. J. W. Alexander
R. W. Clower
G. R. Fisher
P. Robson
J. Spraos
H. Townsend

Monopoly and Competition

Selected Readings

Edited by Alex Hunter

Penguin Books

Penguin Books Ltd, Harmondsworth,
Middlesex, England,
Penguin Books Inc., 7110 Ambassador Road,
Baltimore, Md 21207, U.S.A.
Penguin Books Australia Ltd, Ringwood,
Victoria, Australia,

First published 1969
This selection © A. Hunter, 1969
Introduction and notes © A. Hunter, 1969

Made and printed in Great Britain by
Cox & Wyman Ltd, London, Reading and Fakenham
Set in Monotype Times

Contents

The theory of economics does not furnish a body of settled conclusions immediately applicable to policy. It is a method rather than a doctrine, an apparatus of the mind, which helps its possessor to draw correct conclusions.

John Maynard Keynes

The world will always be governed by self interest. We should not try to stop this; we should try to make the self interest of cads a little more coincident with that of decent people.

Samuel Butler

Introduction

The monopoly problem, or how to maintain and restore competition, is one of the classics of economic science. It has held a position of fluctuating but always considerable importance ever since Adam Smith, the founder of economics, made his famous remark: 'People of the same trade seldom meet together, even for merriment and diversion, but the conversation ends in a conspiracy against the public or in some contrivance to raise prices.' The famous, or infamous, 'Gary dinners', at which the members of the U.S.A. steel industry discussed their market problems (see Reading 12), is the kind of thing he had in mind.

Needless to say the problem is still with us. True, attempts at control through statute, as distinct from the common law, were not made until relatively recently. The U.S.A., pioneer in the field, passed the *Sherman Act* in 1890; but it was a little-used instrument before the 1930s New Deal era. In Europe there were few enactments before 1939; the majority came after World War II. This tardiness is particularly true of Britain where, despite frequent commissions and committees on trusts, combines and restrictions of competition, no attempt to establish statutory control was made prior to the 1948 *Monopolies and Restrictive Practices (Inquiry and Control) Act* – and this itself was a tentative reconnaissance along lines of surveillance rather than control.

At this point in time there would seem to be little need to assert the importance of studies in monopoly and competition. The American code has been extended from the old *Sherman Act* to include the *Clayton Act* and the *Federal Trade Commission Act* (1914). Britain has its very effective *Restrictive Trade Practices Act* of 1956 and the *Resale Prices Act* of 1964. In Europe practically every country has its code on restrictive business practices. Canada has its *Combines Investigation Act*, New Zealand its *Trade Practices Act 1958–61* and Australia has its *Trade Practices Act 1965*. In the Common Market countries, signatories to the Rome Treaty have at their disposal articles 85 and 86, and the regulations thereof, which control restrictive trade practices and monopolization activities.

It is apparent that governments are in no doubt of the practical importance of the issues involved in monopoly and competition.

On the other hand, academic economists have, from time to time, argued explicitly or implicitly against statutory control of combines, cartels, shipping conferences, orderly marketing arrangements and the like. They have suggested that many of the criticisms of monopolistic and restrictive activities were grounded in envy and frustration rather than a concern for the public interest. To a certain extent this was true of the initiation of the U.S.A. *Sherman Act*. Another claim was that restrictions of competition are often necessary. They are techniques required to curb ruinous competition caused by excess capacity during trade cycles. The experiences of the inter-war depression in Britain and elsewhere gave some temporary support to this view. A more radical, less pragmatic interpretation – common at the end of the nineteenth century – saw the phenomena of monopoly and restrictions of competition as merely steps in the continuing evolution of capitalist private enterprise. Either they had a function and survived; or the need for them passed and they disappeared. This sort of thinking reappears in the twentieth century in Schumpeter's writing on the subject. He was prepared to take the logic of what may be called the social Darwinists' theory further and assert that monopolization or restriction of competition often are legitimate forms of insurance for business men – to cover the commercial risks associated with the initiation of a new product, material or business. He also held that large monopolistic companies were frequently misunderstood. Properly viewed, he said, they are creators of the original ideas, the superior technology, and the new products which are the core of increasing material welfare in industrial societies. In any event, leaving aside their technical and commercial leadership, competition of the kind they offered – based not on price but on successful innovation – was more effective than any of the free competition ideas of orthodox economics (see Reading 4). One must admit that again there are substantial grounds for these points of view.

However, while economists will concede that not all monopolies and restrictive agreements are *ipso facto* bad, neither are they disposed to say that control or surveillance over them is redundant or damaging. Even Schumpeter was prepared to say that his argument did 'not amount to a case against state regulation'. He asked for 'rational as distinct from vindictive regulation' by public authorities. He had the U.S.A. 'trust-busting' code in mind when stating the matter this way. The U.S.A. code is more doctrinaire than most – even dogmatic. Outside of the U.S.A., on the other hand, most statutory controls recently established attempt to be rational in the sense he meant. They are devised to select, and give conditional approval of, the beneficial elements in a monopoly or restrictive practice. Legislators are nowadays prone to be pragmatic, rather than dogmatic, on monopoly-competition issues. They instruct judges, broadly speaking, to see all sides of the question – a procedure which can lead, unfortunately, to creating more problems than it solves.

If one examines contemporary circumstances one finds fresh reasons for a careful consideration of the monopoly-competition problem. We are witnessing a continuous and spontaneous merger movement, in the U.S.A. mainly in the 1950s but in Britain and Europe in the 1960s, comparable with the great mergers of the end of the nineteenth century which determined in large degree the structure of modern industrial economies today (see Reading 6); and which were the occasion for the introduction of the anti-trust laws of the U.S.A. Also, it is significant, and thought-provoking, that larger and larger mergers are now actively being encouraged by governments not merely in Germany and Japan, the homes of the semi-official combine, but also in Britain, traditionally the repository of *laissez faire* and free competition.

Furthermore, mergers do not nowadays stop at national borders. Consider the rise of the international corporation in such industries as petroleum, chemicals, man-made fibres, automobiles, agricultural machinery, electrical goods, electronics, computers and data-processing machinery, aircraft and mining for ferrous, non-ferrous and precious minerals. It is possible to claim, on good evidence, that such companies are the main vehicles of an international dissemination of superior technology and commercial know-how such as has never before been witnessed. But there are other, possibly disturbing sides to the picture. The same companies may control a sales turnover greater than the national

11

product of a moderate-sized European country. Frequently their activities dominate the employment and investment picture of a developing country. They make arrangements to develop one foreign market – leaving others to their competitors. Their investment decisions throughout the world not only influence the flow of capital internationally – they can visibly affect the allocation of resources between countries. And, of course, their market behaviour helps set the tone in matters of competition or collusion.

There are signs that existing statutory machinery cannot cope with these new phenomena. Most acts, after all, are designed to handle restrictive agreements in which the benefit and detriments, while not ideal material from a judicial point of view (see Reading 8), at least can be handled by intelligent men. Similarly, while monopolies may throw up some intransigent points, the dangers of leaving market control of an industry which is subject to neither internal nor external competition in the hands of one enterprise, are obvious; and the responsibility for appropriate action difficult to evade. But what of the complex phenomena of oligopoly? Can one confidently maintain there will normally be some elements of 'workable competition' (see Reading 5) because each of the large firms of the group is free to compete through the quality of its products, through research, by means of better technology or by superior distribution and merchandising technique? When does the sales promotion technique of the oligopolist (see the *Household Detergents* case in Reading 14), or competing research efforts to find a different and more attractive formula for pharmaceuticals, begin to be a waste of resources? When does parallel pricing behaviour become collusion – instead of a camouflage for intensive competition (see *American Tobacco* in Reading 12).

Mergers offer even more inscrutable problems to judges and commissioners. What individual is sufficiently talented to gaze into his crystal ball and accurately determine whether a particular new industry structure will successfully hold its own in foreign markets (and will not at the same time take advantage of its predominance in the domestic market to arrange its prices there)? Who can be certain that the assurances of a publishing proprietor, not to interfere with the editorial freedom of the merged newspaper (see Reading 14), are worth anything after an interval of a few years? And where is the solid evidence that economies of scale, greater efficiency, more rational research and superior innovation will be the result of merger? Would not the determined managers of smaller companies find their way past these problems anyway? And is it not better to have available a variety of management decisions – not just one or two – in order to have available a wider range of adjustment techniques to market and technological uncertainties of the future?

A reading of some reports suggests the disquieting thought that, frequently, judges and commissioners are not masters of the material they examine. The 'cellophane' case (*duPont de Nemours*, Reading 12), and others in the U.S.A. jurisdiction, suggest the idea that it is useless, even undesirable, to interfere in order to break down large dominant enterprises. Such judgements may be correct – and often are in law – but it is not entirely clear on what economic grounds they are right. In Britain, some reports of the Monopolies Commission on mergers (Reading 14) appear to reflect the commissioners' feelings of helplessness in the face of an inevitable and unstoppable trend towards greater concentration of industry – not conviction that they are economically justifiable.

Perhaps there is less need for concern than some of these trends appear to indicate. It is arguable, *à la* social Darwinism, that the new forms of industry structure must be superior in some substantial sense to flourish as they do. This is not a completely reassuring thought. Another idea: the dominant firm may not always remain dominant in the market. Monopoly power, as Galbraith interestingly suggests (Reading 7), may generate its own monopsonistic opposition on the other side of the market. Thus the traditional equilibria of small-scale competition is replaced by a more visible – but vulnerable – bargaining power. A reassurance: Schumpeter and Galbraith may be correct in maintaining that inventions and innovations are no longer the natural terrain of the individual. Access to large funds, and the organization of complex, integrated teams for science-based research and development, may be the surer and more rapid route to economic growth. Another reassurance: although concentration of industry removes some of the flexibility in policy conferred by a number of different managements, the giant company may contain within its organization a variety of alternative opinions and strategies which, tested against one another over the committee table, are as good or better than the institutions of the market place.

Possibly our modern industrial economies are halfway, or more than halfway, on a journey between the nineteenth-century *laissez-faire* framework and Burnham's 'managerial' society; and it may follow that, not only are we examining the phenomena of monopoly, oligopoly and merger from the wrong point of view, but the statutory tools we employ are already obsolete.

Obviously, the issues surrounding the monopoly-competition problem are not purely economic. It is an area of political economy – to use the older and here more appropriate label for the discipline – which attracts more than the normal share of reformist doctrine, political opportunism and fair-play sentiment which then become compounded and confused with fundamental questions of economic and social organization. Thus it is important to bear constantly in mind, when attempting to gauge the mixture of competition and monopoly appropriate to a particular country, that there are two broad categories of objective involved: (1) economic-efficiency objectives which are concerned with obtaining the optimal allocation of resources at any given point in time, yet at the same time securing a series of decisions on organization and investment matters which will keep the economy close to the path of rapid economic growth; and (2) political objectives or value judgements associated with the kind of society we wish to have.

The first set of objectives is difficult enough to secure. But there are, at least, some agreed techniques, measurements and professional talent available for the task. On the second set of objectives, agreement – by definition – is beyond reach; settlement, or compromise, to be accomplished through the machinery of government and political pressure groups, is possible. But it may well be difficult to secure since few of the interested parties are fully aware of what they want from industrial society; and many more are unaware that the debate is, inexorably, in progress before their eyes.

The economist is more-than-average competent in the handling of value judgements, and distinguishing them for other people, since he is trained to segregate the economic from the non-economic not only in terms of objectives but also of language, data and technique. On the other hand, he has no special authority in this area. He cannot validly speak for others – only try to interpret what they may want. Summarizing these facts: he may be a guide, but he should not be a mentor.

In this volume of readings Part One indicates the progress of the more important developments in theory. The reader will quickly detect that economic theory does not come to any definitive conclusions. Substantially it offers a method of thought – or, more precisely, several partially conflicting methods of thought – to assist in reaching conclusions. Part Two brings out the pragmatic and manipulative techniques of economists – their selective applications of theories or models to the problem in hand. This is particularly true of the readings on workable competition, resale price maintenance and the measurement of monopoly power. The reading on countervailing power, on the other hand, is not merely an application of established ideas – it contains a substantially new thought on how to look at certain developments of industrial society. Part Three examines the particular difficulties involved in applying what are essentially economic-organizational concepts through a process of law. The language of the lawyers is different; and the framework of legislation and law throws up some subtle barriers against the correct translation of ideas. Part Four quotes from judgements on restrictions of competition and on monopoly situations and practices.

The decisions reached are not always what an economist would wish for. However, we should be surprised that any sensible judgements are found from the chaos of facts and argument presented to a court on issues of monopoly and competition; and pleasantly surprised that they bear a definable relationship to the economic ideas buried in the words of the relevant statute.

Part One The Theoretical Framework

Despite the great political and social significance of monopoly, it has never occupied a secure niche in the corpus of economic theory. Early economists, impressed by the predominance of free competition and small-scale enterprise, regarded monopolies as isolated phenomena. The growth, in the U.S.A., Britain and Germany, of large combines in chemicals, petroleum, explosives, distilling, cement, iron and steel, did not stimulate examination of large size as such. Instead economists attacked the monopoly-competition problem obliquely. Elegant analyses, stressing the necessary intermingling of monopoly and competition elements in business life, emerged. 'Monopolistic competition' thus became a useful tool in the explanation of the monopoly elements conferred by reputation, location or sales promotion leading to the establishment of successful brand images. It could also explain why competition could create static (as opposed to transitional or dynamic) excess capacity as epitomized by the phrase: 'too many pharmacists in the High Street'. But the significance of oligopoly was somewhat overlooked; and large size of business – as a contributor to or a detractor from economic welfare – did not receive satisfactory treatment. What emerged instead were analyses of monopoly elements as comprehensive and tenacious misallocations of resources over the whole economy. A generation of left-wing economists, made cynical by the failure of private-enterprise, were only too willing to conceive of large businesses as price and output manipulators adding to the vicissitudes of unemployment and depression. Only Schumpeter saw beyond the narrowness of the static concept. He pointed out that large companies, although often involved in price and output cartels, were more frequently than not the creators of new materials, new technologies, new products and new markets. His message was that economic growth, or the generation of economic welfare in terms of material goods, was closely associated with technological success, the large size of companies and even, quite frequently, restrictions of competition.

1 J. K. Galbraith

The Development of Monopoly Theory

Excerpt from J. K. Galbraith, 'Monopoly and the concentration of economic power', chapter 3 in H. S. Ellis (ed.), *A Survey of Contemporary Economics*, American Economic Association and Blakiston, 1948, pp. 99–103.

Excluding only the issues associated with fiscal policy and the level and stability of employment, no problem attracted more attention from economists during the 'thirties than that of monopoly. As usual, the sources of this interest are traceable in part to ideas and in part to circumstance. Several years before the depression started, certain long-held and vital assumptions concerning the structure of the typical market were undergoing re-examination. The results became apparent at a time when economists everywhere were looking for an interpretation of the current crisis in capitalist society. A retrospect on monopoly, in its theoretical and applied aspects, properly begins, therefore, with a review of the ideas which accounted for the original revival of interest. It is appropriately followed by a consideration of the effect of these ideas as they were carried into the world of policy and politics. [...]

The first influential new step in the field of ideas was the publication in 1926 by Piero Sraffa of his now famous article, 'The laws of returns under competitive conditions' (1). Subject to qualifications, the tendency at the time Mr Sraffa's article appeared was to recognize the limiting case of monopoly, but to assume, in general, a rule of competition. Competition was not assumed to be perfect. Those already in the business might variously obstruct the entry of newcomers. Or entry might be rendered difficult by the prestige associated with trademarks and trade names. Imperfect knowledge of opportunities might interfere. Decreasing costs were deemed an especially serious handicap for the newcomer, who, because he was new, was likely to be small. If large scale and accompanying requirements in capital and organization brought substantial economies, the small newcomer was faced with an organic handicap. Nevertheless, these barriers, though widely recognized, were conventionally assumed to be of secondary effect. They were frictions that muddied and at times diverted but did not check the great underlying current which was toward a competitive equilibrium. Given that equilibrium, there was a presumption, again subject to many dissenting voices, that economic resources would be employed with maximum efficiency and the product so distributed as to maximize satisfactions. Sraffa attacked the assumption that the 'frictions' were in fact a secondary and fugitive phenomenon. He argued they were stable and indeed cumulative and yielded a solution consistent not with a competitive, but a monopolistic equilibrium. He argued that monopoly, not free competition, was the more appropriate assumption in market theory.

In 1932–3 Mrs Robinson (2) and Professor Chamberlin (3) produced the two books that were to become the texts for the revived interest in monopoly. The first leaned heavily on Sraffa; the second has a more independent genesis. Both had a prompt and enthusiastic reception. This is not difficult to explain. For years there had been marked discontent with the accustomed assumptions and the standard analysis of competitive and monopolized markets. Discussion and teaching had too long centred on what, too obviously, were limiting cases. Even (or perhaps especially) students were reluctant to accept the results as descriptive of the real world. The new work had the great advantage, from the viewpoint of marketability, of adding something new to something old, and of adding almost precisely what the customers wanted. Both books were solidly in the tradition of Marshallian partial equilibrium analysis; and in the United States and the United Kingdom this had become not only an utterly respectable but an all but impregnable tradition in economic thought. The inhabitants of this citadel, although never too hospitable to strangers, were bound to accept old inhabitants armed with familiar weapons even though they used these weapons in a seemingly dangerous way. Both Professor Chamberlin and Mrs Robinson offered an organized, intellectually palatable approach to the middle ground between monopoly and competition – an obvious antidote to the existing uneasiness. In this respect their contribution was sharply distinguished from that of Marshall, J. M. Clark, and others who had delved but

briefly into this intermediate area, from that of teachers who had
warned their students that the old categories were inadequate,
and from that of Cournot, Edgeworth, and Bowley who, at
most, had offered a smattering of mostly improbable solutions
to mostly improbable situations.

In retrospect the most important contribution of Professor
Chamberlin and Mrs Robinson was to emancipate the analysis of
markets from the inadequate categories of competition (impaired
by sundry frictions) and single-firm monopoly. Almost at once
duopoly, oligopoly, and the purposeful differentiation of products
became accredited and very useful categories in market analysis.

This liberalization of market categories was more important than
the theory that explored them. Professor Chamberlin did make a
notable refinement in the existing concept of competition. Where
previously competition had often been loosely identified by the
terms of rivalry in the market – conditions of entry, the energy
and knowledge of participants, and the like – he, in effect, derived
its character from the competitive equilibrium it was assumed to
bring about. The concept of 'pure' competition was thereby
confined to markets where the demand for the product of the individual seller was infinitely elastic at the ruling price. This was a
good deal more rigorous than existing definitions; it had, as I
shall argue presently, important practical consequences.

Both Professor Chamberlin and Mrs Robinson also made the
marginal revenue curve a standard tool of market analysis and
Professor Chamberlin's theory of monopolistic competition –
of competition between numerous sellers differentiated by location, personality, or physical or psychic differences in their
product – brought the vast phenomenon of merchandising and
advertising within the scope of theoretical analysis. For the purposes of the present essay, however, it was the area of failure
rather than achievement of the new work that is of prime significance. Without much doubt the dominant market of modern
capitalism is not one made up of many sellers offering either
uniform or differentiated products. Rather it is a market of few
sellers, that is oligopoly. Apart from consumers' goods, the
counterpart of few buyers associated with many or few sellers
is also a common phenomenon. Where sellers are few the product is automatically identified with its vendor and hence there

is always a measure of differentiation – the elasticity of substitution between products of a few sellers can never be quite perfect. But the ruling characteristic is the fewness of the sellers.

In dealing with small numbers or oligopoly, Professor Chamberlin, who went farthest with the problem on a general theoretical level, did little more than resurrect the engaging but largely irrelevant novelties of Cournot and Edgeworth. This was a failure of prime importance – one that economists were, on the whole, slow to recognize. The failure was inevitable. Success, by familiar standards, implied a determinate solution. One certain fact about oligopoly (and its counterpart on the buyer's side of the market) is that the entire market solution can be altered unilaterally by any single participant. This is at once the simplest and the most critical distinction between oligopoly and pure competition. It also means that the methodological device by which the competitive market has been analysed, that is, laying down general assumptions about the group response of numerous individuals to common stimuli, is inadmissible. Rather the assumptions must be sufficiently comprehensive to cover the behavior pattern of each participant in the market. Even though it is assumed that each participant seeks to maximize his return, the possible individual behavior patterns and resulting market solutions are almost infinitely numerous, and the assumption that all individuals will seek maximum pecuniary return (as distinct from non-pecuniary prestige, expression of individuality, etc.) is questionable. Edgeworth and Cournot and, in that tradition, Chamberlin, merely derived the market solution that followed from two or three out of a near infinity of possible behavior combinations. It follows that they were not offering a theory of duopoly or oligopoly but displaying a few samples. Little progress has been made to an analysis of oligopoly by this route and little could be expected.

The importance of oligopoly in the world as it exists was highlighted, almost simultaneously with the appearance of Professor Chamberlin's and Mrs Robinson's books, by Berle and Means's mammoth study of the modern corporation (4). This study was also launched well prior to the Great Depression; its inspiration, Professor Berle stated in the preface, was the Wall Street boom and the attendant pyramiding of 'industrial oligarchies'. But it was not Professor Berle's interesting and erudite study of the changing property rights of the individual security holder but Gardiner C. Means's statistics on the industrial predominance of the nation's 200 largest non-financial corporations that captured popular attention. These, he estimated, had combined assets at the beginning of 1930 of $81 billion, or about half of all assets owned by corporations. Although open to challenge as to detail, his calculations buttressed his contention that 'the principles of duopoly have become more important than those of free competition'. The book had a popular as well as academic audience and the figure of '200' became a magic symbol in subsequent investigations of economic power.

The new market categories, plus the evidence of Berle and Means and of the scholar's own eyes as to the need for them, set the stage for the revived interest in monopoly and its allied issues. One must also emphasize the *esprit* which Chamberlin's and Robinson's works gave to students of the field. Even though they substituted a new set of frustrations for the old ones, the new ones were welcome. It has been suggested that 'the most revolutionary feature of the monopolistic competition theories [was] the unprecedented pace at which they conquered their audience'(5). Neither Chamberlin nor Robinson was destroyed and redestroyed as was Keynes a few years later. Their most effective critic, Professor Schumpeter, centered his attacks not on the validity of their analysis *per se* but more generally on the notion that it much affected the assessment of capitalist reality.[1] Rarely in economics have ideas had such an enthusiastic and uncritical welcome.

1. See Reading 4.

References
1. P. SRAFFA, 'The laws of returns under competitive conditions', *Economic Journal*, vol. 36, 1926, pp.535–50.
2. J. ROBINSON, *Economics of Imperfect Competition*, London, 1933.
3. E. H. CHAMBERLIN, *The Theory of Monopolistic Competition*, Harvard University Press, Cambridge, Mass., 1932.
4. A. A. BERLE and G. C. MEANS, *The Modern Corporation and Private Property*, Macmillan, New York, 1934.
5. R. TRIFFIN, *Monopolistic Competition and General Equilibrium Theory*, Harvard University Press, Cambridge, Mass., 1940, p.17.

2 K. W. Rothschild

Price Theory and Oligopoly

Excerpt from K. W. Rothschild, 'Price theory and oligopoly', *Economic Journal*, vol. 57, 1947, pp. 299–320.

[. . .]

This change in price theory [the introduction of monopolistic and imperfect competition] meant a great advance in so far as it included a vast number of cases in the main theoretical body, which were formerly regarded as 'exceptions' and had to be explained by additional factors. At the same time, with its greater scope, price theory lost some of the simplicity and determinateness which it possessed under the competitive approach. With the consideration of product differentiation, price discrimination, and advertising, 'industry', 'commodity', 'cost' and 'price' lost their exactly definable meanings, and it seemed as if the new theory would no longer be able to offer any exact solution of an 'equilibrium price'. This in itself need not be very tragic if the loss in simple determinateness is compensated by a greater relevance of the theory. Nevertheless the strong tradition of price theory centering round a definite long-term 'equilibrium price' made any idea of indeterminateness so abhorrent to the 'father', and even more to the 'mother', of imperfect competition theory[1] that most of their analysis was centered on those cases where determinate solutions in the mechanistic–biological sense could be most easily achieved. That is, their typical case deals with the market situation characterized by many small producers, product differentiation and free entry, which sets very definite limits to the freedom of action of the individual firm. A determinate solution is achieved by making the impersonal market forces the very powerful factor, and restricting the independent action of the firm to an adjustment to these forces - an adjustment which will be unique

1. See Reading 1.

on the basis of profit maximization (and survival in the case of the marginal firm).

This is, of course, a very important addition to the perfect competition model, and a useful frame of reference when we try to explain price in many of the present-day markets, particularly in retailing, but also in some small-scale industries. But, again, what can be regarded as the established body of 'monopolistic competition theory' does not cover the whole field of price formation. In particular, it badly neglects the case where a small number of powerful firms compete with each other, the action of each exerting a marked influence on the position of all the others, and each of them not only adjusting itself passively to a 'given' market situation, but capable of actively changing that market situation. This neglect of duopoly and oligopoly problems is the more regrettable as recent investigations have shown that oligopoly is by no means an exception, but that the most typical case in industry is probably monopolistic competition, with a considerable admixture of oligopoly (1). Indeed, the reader of the classics of monopolistic competition must be left with the impression that the problem of monopoly with which our society is faced is predominantly created by the small grocer down the street rather than by the big steel firms. [. . .]

To say that duopoly and oligopoly problems have been neglected does not mean that there have not been frequent attempts towards their theoretical solution. But it seems to the writer that these attempts – in contrast to much of the descriptive literature on this subject – have been hampered by being too much influenced by the models of perfect and monopolistic competition, and 'pure' monopoly. Yet neither of these theories can be expected to form a sound basis for the study of duopoly and oligopoly prices.

On the whole, we can divide the theories dealing with duopoly and oligopoly into two groups (2): those presenting a determinate solution and those stressing the indeterminateness of the problem. The determinate solution, in turn, can be reached in two ways. Either it is assumed that the oligopolists do not take into account the effects of their action on the policy of their rivals, as in the famous Cournot and Bertrand solutions; or these effects are recognized, but a determinate solution is reached with the help of additional assumptions. The first type of approach is absolutely valueless, because it only solves the oligopoly problem by removing from the analysis its most essential differentiating aspect: the oligopolists' consciousness of their interdependence.

Those who take into account this interdependence are free from this fundamental mistake. But in spite of this, their theories do not advance much towards a better explanation of reality, because in their desire to reach determinate solutions within the traditional framework of price theory they adopt additional assumptions which are too artificial.[2] In particular, these theories are all based on the assumption that the oligopolists – while recognizing that their price activities will call forth reactions from their rivals – acquiesce in the permanent nature of the industry's structure. But since it is doubtless one of the distinguishing characteristics of duopoly and oligopoly that the rival firms can *actively* influence and change the market situation, these theories, too, fail to provide a theoretical framework for the interpretation of reality (3).

In a certain way, therefore, the writers who stressed the indeterminateness of the problem made an important step in the right direction. For they recognized that the reduction of producers to a small number meant that the market situation was no longer the 'natural' price determining force of perfect competition theory nor the strictly limiting price environment of monopolistic competition. They realized that under such conditions the firms become active agents which have the power to change those very market factors on which the determinate theories had to rely for their solution.

But while thus the increasing acceptance of the indeterminateness of the problem was an advance towards a more realistic treatment of the subject, it was also a retreat from the former belief that price theory could be sufficiently developed to deal with all possible market phenomena. Indeed, the majority of these writers, once they have shown the inadequacy of the determinate solutions, take up an almost nihilistic attitude towards the theory

2. 'The unreal atmosphere which surrounds our current theories of oligopoly may be ascribed to the fact that the assumptions are too often chosen for their analytical convenience, rather than for their actual relevance to the real world of today' (R. Triffin [4] p. 78).

of duopoly and oligopoly. They may, like Chamberlin, just add a short list of 'uncertainties' to an artificial, determinate solution; or they may deny the possibility of a general theory covering industry under oligopolistic conditions and substitute for it voluminous case-studies describing the behaviour pattern of particular industries; or they may just view oligopolistic industry as a chaotic mess where practically anything may happen, and about which economic analysis has very little to say.

But, surely, the recognition of indeterminateness should have been only the first step towards building up a more adequate price theory for duopoly and oligopoly conditions. For the statement that there is no determinate solution to the problem can only be a relative one. It can only mean that the question cannot be suitably solved *within the framework of existing price theory*, just as the question of the monopolistic competition price could not have been suitably solved with the industrial demand and supply curves of perfect competition theory. But there can be no absolute and inherent indeterminateness in this problem, any more than in any other of the questions facing natural or social science. It has been said quite rightly:

No doubt, there is a sense in which the solution is always determinate; it all depends on the number of variables that are considered. But it is clear that the variables that would have to be added to determine the solution might be of a very different type from the ones generally used by pure economics of the equilibrium brand. Such considerations as financial backing, political influence, prestige psychology, optimistic or pessimistic slant, enterprise or routine-like attitude in business, etc. may well play an overwhelming role in determining the solution. (4, p.71).

Economists have on the whole shied away from this problem of drawing up a wider and different framework which could deal with the oligopolistic cases, because the concepts and methods used for the other market situations would be of little use. In particular, the influence of analogies drawn from mechanics and biology – so fruitful in the fields of perfect and monopolistic competition respectively – must be discarded when we deal with powerful active agents like duopolists and oligopolists. If analogies have to be used (and they may be of considerable heuristic value), then they will have to be drawn from those spheres where writers deal with moves and counter-moves, with struggles for power and position – in short, from books dealing with the general aspects of politics, and military strategy and tactics.

This is by no means a new discovery. Not only has a military terminology found increasing acceptance in price theory (for example, economic warfare, price strategy, aggressive and non-aggressive price policies), but both theoretical and descriptive economists have pointed out the appropriateness of comparing oligopolistic price behaviour with this field of human activity. Thus, Professor Pigou, in his *Economics of Welfare*, refers to the resemblance between the mutual bluff under oligopolistic conditions and a game of chess. Speaking of the motives influencing the actions of big corporations, Berle and Means come to the conclusion that 'it is probable that more could be learned regarding them by studying the motives of an Alexander the Great, seeking new worlds to conquer, than by considering the motives of a petty tradesman of the days of Adam Smith.' The matter is put still more definitely in an article by Nourse:

While, of course, the conditioning environment imposes rigorous limitations on the price administrator's freedom of action in a capitalist society dedicated to 'free enterprise', he devises and implements business plans in ways broadly similar to those of military command. A general must operate within the limitations of the terrain on which he fights and of the personnel and material at his disposal – to say nothing of meteorological conditions. But at the same time, much depends too on the strategy which he and the high command devise and the specific tactics by which he and his officers seek to carry it out. It seems appropriate, therefore, to discuss price policy in terms of business strategy and tactics. (5, p.205).

But while thus the need for a new methodological and conceptual framework for oligopolistic price theory is clearly recognized, no attempt is made to lay the foundation for such a theory. Nourse, in particular, after stating the necessity of a new approach in the clear way illustrated by the above quotation, largely spoils his case by urging more research into the thinking, prejudices, etc., of the entrepreneur in order to make possible a more proper analytical treatment of price policy. But, surely, the peculiarities of price behaviour under oligopolistic conditions are not due to any peculiarities in the psychology of duopolists and oligopolists, but to the different economic environment in which they work. By all means let us have more research into the psychology of the businessman in all the various market situations, but the *distinguishing* feature of oligopolistic price theory cannot lie in additional psychological investigations, but in the provision of a framework which will show the actions of a 'normal' businessman under the specific conditions of an oligopolistic environment (6).

The oligopoly-theorist's classical literature can neither be Newton and Darwin, nor can it be Freud; he will have to turn to Clausewitz's *Principles of War*.[3] There he will not only find numerous striking parallels between military and (oligopolistic) business strategy, but also a method of a *general* approach which – while far less elegant than traditional price theory – promises a more realistic treatment of the oligopoly problem. To write a short manual on the *Principles of Oligopolistic War* would be a very important attempt towards a new approach to this aspect of price theory; and the large amount of descriptive material that has been forthcoming in recent years should provide a sufficient basis for a start. [. . .]

3. An abridged translation of Clausewitz's *On War*, edited by Anatol Rapoport, is available in Pelican Classics [ed.].

References
1. R. L. HALL and C. J. HITCH, 'Price theory and business behaviour', *Oxford Economic Papers*, May 1939.
2. E. H. CHAMBERLIN, *The Theory of Monopolistic Competition*, Harvard University Press, Cambridge Mass., 1932, chapter 3 and Appendix A.
3. R. F. KAHN, 'The problem of duopoly', *Economic Journal*, vol. 47, 1937, p. 17.
4. R. TRIFFIN, *Monopolistic Competition and General Equilibrium Theory*, Harvard University Press, Cambridge, Mass., 1940.
5. E. G. NOURSE, 'The meaning of price policy', *The Quarterly Journal of Economics*, February 1941.
6. J. VON NEUMANN and O. MORGENSTERN, *Theories of Games and Economic Behaviour*, Princeton University Press, 1944.

3 A. Hunter

Welfare Analysis and Monopoly

Excerpt from chapter 2 of A. Hunter, *Competition and the Law*, Allen &
Unwin, London, 1966.

Despite the ambitious scope of welfare economics the actual techniques developed turn out to be surprisingly concentrated on one
aspect of economic efficiency – on the problem of resource allocation towards a particular distribution of consumer preferences.
Thus, economic efficiency, as defined by welfare economics, takes
on a rather narrow meaning. It is not, and in the nature of the
analysis cannot be, concerned with such efficiency factors as affect
the rate of technological change in industry, the rate of innovation,
the importance of large units in promoting economies of scale,
productivity methods, etc., etc. Thus, as we shall see, many monopoly elements emerge in the welfare analysis primarily as obstacles
to an otherwise tidy and logically developed system of adjustments.
Their possible contribution to economic efficiency and welfare, in
senses other than the allocative, are simply by-passed by the theory.

The concept of the optimum is the starting point of welfare
analysis. Historically it is a concept which originated with Pareto
but was resuscitated for economic theory more recently, by Lerner
and Hicks in particular. The optimum is defined as a situation
in which the distribution of consumer goods (including leisure)
is such that it is impossible to reallocate goods, by means of some
reorganization of prices and factors, without making at least one
person worse off: and in which production arrangements (including the substitution of present for future goods) are such that it is
impossible to reallocate inputs without diminishing the output
of at least one commodity already in production. By itself this
conceptual framework is too general to have operational meaning.
But, since 1939 specially, the more recent developments in welfare
theory have been concerned to derive the conditions which give
content to the concept (1 and 2).

A. Hunter

Aptly named by Hicks the 'marginal conditions', they set out the requirements for any arrangement of the economy to conform to one of the Paretian optima (6). Thus the most efficient distribution of commodities to consumers occurs when the marginal rate of substitution between any two products is the same for every pair of individuals who consume both. The proper allocation of inputs requires that the marginal technical rates of substitution between any pair of factors is the same for any two firms using both to produce the same product; that the marginal rate of transformation between any factor and any product must be the same for any pair of firms, etc. All the conditions can be summarized in the general requirements that the marginal rates of substitution between commodities be the same for every pair of individuals who consume them; that all marginal technical rates of transformation be the same for every pair of commodities; and that all equivalent rates of substitution and transformation be equal to one another. For the application of welfare theories to pricing policy and industrial reorganization the principal 'rule' which emerges from the marginal conditions is the well-known one that price should be equal to marginal cost.[1]

In principle, any arrangement of the economy which can conform to the marginal conditions will provide a Paretian optimum (leaving aside divergences between marginal private and social costs such as may arise from external economies of scale). However, the welfare world remains remarkably hypothetical in terms of possible organizations. In practice, only one highly formal market structure succeeds in meeting the requirements. This, of course, is the perfect (or sometimes pure) competition model. The achievement of this model is the consequence of a well-known property inherent in the relationships of perfectly competitive market situations. In such markets the price of the commodity bought and sold cannot vary with the quantities transacted

1. It should be noted that the analysis of welfare in terms of the marginal conditions does not produce *the* social optimum. There is an infinite range of positions which can satisfy the Paretian optimum requirements (best exhibited by considering the range of points along the contract curve of an Edgeworth box diagram). Strictly speaking, each Paretian optimum position is sub-optimal; and the intervention of a value judgement on income distribution and other matters, to decide which is the social optimum, is required.

31

by individual buyers or sellers. By definition, no one individual or unit is large enough to affect the price. Therefore consumers and producers can maximize their advantage by each taking his line of consumption or production to the point where price equals the marginal rate of substitution or transformation for the goods under consideration. And, since the price of each commodity or factor in perfect markets is the same for all individuals and units, there are consequently equilibrating adjustments throughout all inputs and outputs which make the relevant marginal rates of substitution and transformation equal to one another because adjusted to the common and uniform set of prices.

The deductions to be made on monopoly elements of all kinds in this pattern of relationships are startling and sweeping. Monopoly, oligopoly, imperfections due to product differentiation, collective restrictions on price and output – all of them dislocate the system of equal corresponding rates of substitution and transformation for goods and factors because they upset the uniformity of price within each market. Thus (i) the existence of commodities which among consumers have varying degrees of demand elasticity and varying prices as between firms means that the corresponding marginal rates of substitution will not necessarily be the same. (ii) For input markets the existence of different degrees of monopoly among suppliers affects factor prices and therefore the corresponding marginal technical rates of substitution of factors one for another are not necessarily equal. And (iii) in product markets the varying monopoly power of firms ensures that corresponding marginal rates of transformation of factors into products are not necessarily equal. In brief, any departure from perfect competition constitutes, by definition, a net loss in economic efficiency.

Although it is the only example of a feasible practical operation of the Paretian optimum and, it is generally agreed, occurs rather infrequently, the influence of the perfect competition model on welfare thought is remarkable. Among welfare economists there is at work a powerful disposition to favour market situations which are perfect; or to identify and classify market structures in terms of divergences from the model ('imperfections of competition') despite the now rather obvious truism that the allocative efficiency induced by perfect competition conditions is not the only or even the most significant source of economic efficiency or welfare. Some economists go further, specifically or by implication: for them not only does perfect competition happen to satisfy the Paretian optimum; the stronger conclusion is reached that only perfect competition among competitive market structures can meet the optimum requirements and therefore should be implemented (5) as far as possible (7).

In this connexion it is interesting to note how the content of the term 'competition' has changed although the prejudice in its favour has not altered greatly. For the classical economists competition meant the achievement and maintenance of economic freedom – the abolition of internal regulations in trade, the removal of tariffs and the erosion of the economic and political power of the landed gentry. For them competition was freedom to encroach – an exercise in the dynamics of social change rather than a machine for allocative efficiency. Marshall also was more interested in what he termed the Freedom of Industry and Enterprise and the economic forces governing the growth and decay of firms. True, he was at the same time responsible for the introduction of many ideas which led to more rigorous definitions of what is meant by competitive markets. But it is significant that the relevant theorems were confined to footnotes and mathematical appendices; and his text, basically, continues to deal with competition in terms of economic rivalry rather than analytical properties. The emergence of the imperfect competition schools of thought of the 1920–30s marked a sharp change of approach.

Competition had now become in texts specifically 'perfect' competition: that is, an analytical system containing the properties of perfect market structures and therefore implications concerning divergences from it. The great contribution of the imperfect competition school here was to demonstrate the ubiquity of monopoly elements in almost all market situations. But in addition they become crusaders. The classicists' strong feeling in favour of the 'hidden hand' of competition, with its optimal distribution of resources assumption, was now transferred to perfect competition (12). Only a short step was required to develop theorems demonstrating the 'wastes of competition' (11); another short step brought in the idea of a 'degree of monopoly' (4), and yet another gave the marginal conditions of welfare economics. Thus welfare economists were the fortunate inheritors of a tradition favouring more rigorous and exact thinking where it could be developed. They saw and appreciated this. What they did not see was that they also inherited a prejudice which transferred emotive characteristics to a term which could have and should have remained neutral.[2]

It is not surprising therefore that when the structure of industry throws up economic units large, relative to their market outlets, the welfare economist's position has led him to propose either public operation of certain large-scale types of enterprise (to permit the application of a price-equal-marginal-cost rule); or comprehensive intervention in industry by means of subsidy and/or taxation to secure the same result. It is possible to find merit in the first of these proposals although few, after debate and reflection on the matter, would now consider applying the marginal-cost price rule without considerable qualifications (3); and fewer still would take the extreme view that it be applied in all circumstances regardless of the incidence of losses. Very little can be said in favour of the second set of proposals for comprehensive subsidization and taxation over all the 'imperfectly competitive' forms in the economy to bring about a price equal to marginal cost situation (7); or a price proportional (10) to marginal cost on some suggestions for 'second best' solutions. Yet, on occasion, such schemes have been proposed in order to reproduce in our disorderly oligopolistic and monopolistic world some facsimile of perfectly competitive conditions. Fortunately, so obviously formidable were the administrative problems of such schemes that they never were in danger of being taken seriously.

It is difficult to explain satisfactorily the extent to which the perfect competition concepts (refined by welfare economics) have influenced the present structure of microeconomic theory and thinking on policy matters. For anyone who doubts that this is a

2. It is worth footnoting that E. H. Chamberlin (11, chapter 5) was cautious and drew only limited welfare conclusions from his version of the theory. Mainly he stressed a strong tendency to 'excess capacity' in the competitive framework. But he was careful also to bring out the *positive* welfare advantages of product differentiation from the consumer's point of view. Joan Robinson was altogether more radical in her conclusions; and in chapter 27 of her book (12) was one of the first theorists to adumbrate the type of welfare approach which emphasizes the virtues of perfect competition.

serious matter inspection of the contents of the majority of accepted micro-economics textbooks for elementary and intermediate classes will convince him. The central argument of such texts – allegedly explaining the processes of competition – is made up of a presentation of the properties of the perfect competition model followed by an extensive analysis of the allocative efficiency of such market structures. Then, an account of the characteristics of monopolistic competition, oligopoly, monopoly, etc., is given along the same lines emphasizing their divergence from the perfect competition terms, their failure to allocate properly or fully exploit available resources. Were this a pedagogic exercise occupying one-half or one-third of micro-economic exposition little harm could ensue. But so frequently the elucidation of competition in terms of welfare economics takes up seven-eighths or more of the available text; and the possibility that judgement on the desirability of oligopolistic and monopolistic structures rests on criteria other than their allocative efficiency occupies only a summary chapter or so. In some cases a paragraph or two suffices. Students of economics are taken a long way along a blind alley (for the sake of systematic exposition presumably) and become steeped in terminology which, with its discussions of divergences from a hypothetical norm, scarcely rises above scholastic jargon. One tragic aspect of the problem is that, usually, the more precise and scientific the style of the text and the more the treatment relies on formal geometry or mathematics the greater the devotion to this 'systematic exposition' *à la* perfect competition. The texts by Scitovsky (8) and Henderson and Quandt (9) illustrate this point admirably. [. . .]

It is possible to present more specific, constructive criticisms than those mentioned so far rejecting the analytical approach of welfare economics to monopoly. There are several sets of arguments to be considered briefly. Some of these find defects in the welfare analysis even on static grounds. Others employ growth and development theories of capitalist society to display serious inconsistencies between theory and fact.

One fundamental cause of error is that 'the degree of monopoly' as measured in applications of the welfare model to imperfect competition is entirely a function of the elasticity of demand curves for the products of firms. Thus, on the usual price-theory reasoning, a falling demand curve leads to a price determination higher than long-run marginal cost; and to a plant size smaller than that which corresponds to the minimum point of the long-run average-cost curve. Several monopoly factors may give rise to this falling demand curve phenomenon. But it is to be noted that some of them have substantial or even unanswerable reasons for their existence.

First, the most ubiquitous 'cause' of monopoly in this sense is product differentiation. Outside of certain unusual market situations every firm is selling a different product. In so far as this is the factor at work then less-than-infinite elasticities of demand are a direct consequence of the consumer's desire for and acceptance of variety, convenience, etc. There is a welfare problem in this situation. More varieties of retailing outlets than are necessary to satisfy consumer tastes may come into existence – the well-known phenomenon of 'excess capacity'. There may therefore be a case for standardizing on a smaller range of products or distribution points. But so far welfare economics has not come up with any satisfactory criteria of standardization. It seems likely to remain one of a numerous category of problems subject to the value judgements of society but without society necessarily taking any action on the matter.[3]

However, one thing is certain. It is not possible to argue that product differentiation should be eliminated for the sake of resource allocation. Variety and convenience are welfare features which are the subject of active demands of consumers. If, as a result, perfectly competitive prices and outputs are not selected this is just too bad for allocative efficiency. One monopoly element at least is inevitable and is indeed a genuine component of welfare.[4]

3. The excess capacity problem induced by variety may seem a trivial example of monopoly. In one sense it is. Yet an excessive number of varieties of a well-used product – say cars or antibiotics – can mean a number of uneconomical production runs. And an excessive number of grocers or chemists shops can constitute a formidable misallocation of resources. The first problem remains, for a democratic society, fundamentally insoluble because it involves interference with individual choices. The second problem has some remedy through competition. The abolition of resale price maintenance can induce sufficient competition in distribution to eliminate some substantial sources of excess capacity.

4. It is curious how this fundamental obstacle to the general application of welfare analysis is overlooked persistently despite some early caustic

Second, pure oligopoly (large size of productive unit treated in isolation from associated product differentiation features) must also be regarded as in some degree or other inevitable. Certainly, industrial structures of this type cannot be written off simply on account of their failure to allocate properly. The usual application of welfare analysis proceeds by comparing the price-output adjustments of oligopoly and monopoly with that of perfect competition in order to bring out their inability to reach an optimum size of production flow or to make price equal to marginal costs (9). Without going into the now more fashionable dynamics of growth and performance of the two models it is easy enough, on static grounds, to point out a defect in this type of comparison. It proceeds as though comparing like with like. But it is now generally accepted that highly concentrated structures are likely to have much lower unit costs of production than the same industries would have under perfect or pure competition. Large units came into existence mainly where the technology and integration of the industry permits large size. And naturally lower size will not be developed except where substantially lower unit costs hold out the prospect of profitable rates of return on large investments required. Thus we have no difficulty in comprehending why, on the one hand, steel-making, oil-refining, railways and industrial chemicals are organized in massively concentrated industries (some basic chemicals, for example, cannot be produced in significant quantities at all except by using very large-scale processes); and why, on the other hand, dairy farming, hairdressing, accountancy and motor repairing remain in closer approximation to perfect or pure competition conditions. Hence, given that lower absolute costs of production are associated with oligopolistic and monopolistic industries on account of superior technology and organization, the welfare exercise involved in comparing resource allocation properties of different industrial structures is completely irrelevant and quite misleading.

Third, the treatment in welfare analysis of certain modes of competition calls for adverse comment. What are essentially competi-

comment by Hicks and Little. (See A. Hunter 'Product differentiation and welfare economics', *Quarterly Journal of Economics*, vol. 69, pp. 533–52, and the references therein.)

tive activities are converted into monopolistic blemishes by the logic of the welfare system. For example, the development of imperfect and monopolistic theories might have been expected to bring improvement by calling attention to a range of competitive adjustments via quality improvement, service, packaging and labelling, sales-promotion and advertisement. However, in the event, these adjustments were either quietly ignored or quickly assimilated into welfare analysis, in a familiar manner, not as activities so much as elements conditioning the system into deviations away from the perfect competition norm. Hence, advertisement expenditures add to the costs of production and, to that extent, raise them above that likely to be experienced under perfect competition. While the net effect of product differentiation and sales promotions of all kinds is to lower the elasticity of demand curves and thus induce higher prices, lower than optimum outputs, misallocation of factors, etc., into the competitive system.

It is difficult to reconcile this account of competitive behaviour with ordinary usage. The businessman naturally regards all product differentiation and sales promotion activities as competitive in character. Fundamentally they are competitive, not only in the ordinary business sense, but also in any reasonable appreciation of the economic meaning of the word. Along with price adjustment variations of product supply the main avenues open to producers to maintain their market position or encroach upon that of their competitors. Further, with respect to the dynamic characteristics of an economy – the introduction of new goods, superior technology and higher productivity – product differentiation and sales expenditure are a *sine qua non* of competitive effort. The labelling of fundamental competitive behaviour as 'monopolistic' – almost a reversal of the ordinary meaning of the word – provides yet one more of those irritating verbal paradoxes which, not only are confusing to laymen, but also inhibit constructive thought in the application of theory to competition and monopoly. [. . .]

References
1. K. BOULDING, 'Welfare economics', in B. E. Haley (ed.), *A Survey of Contemporary Economics*, Irwin, 1952.
2. E. J. MISHAN, 'A survey of welfare economics, 1939–59', *Economic Journal*, vol. 70, 1960, pp. 197–265.

3. I. M. D. LITTLE, *A Critique of Welfare Economics*, 2nd edn, Oxford University Press, 1957.
4. A. P. LERNER, 'The concept of monopoly and the measurement of monopoly power', *Review of Economic Studies*, June, 1934, pp. 157–75.
5. A. P. LERNER, *The Economics of Control*, McGraw-Hill, 1944.
6. J. R. HICKS, 'Foundations of welfare economics', *Economic Journal*, vol. 49, 1939, pp. 549–52.
7. M. W. REDER, *Studies in the Theory of Welfare Economics*, Columbia University Press, 1947.
8. T. SCITOVSKY, *Welfare and Competition*, Allen & Unwin, 1952.
9. J. M. HENDERSON, and R. E. QUANDT, *Microeconomic Theory*, McGraw-Hill, 1958.
10. R. F. KAHN, 'Some notes on ideal output', *Economic Journal*, vol. 45, 1935, pp. 1–35.
11. E. H. CHAMBERLIN, *Theory of Monopolistic Competition*, Harvard University Press, 1932.
12. J. ROBINSON, *Economics of Imperfect Competition*, Macmillan, 1933.

4   J. A. Schumpeter

The Dynamics of Competition and Monopoly

Excerpt from J. A. Schumpeter, *Capitalism, Socialism and Democracy*, Allen & Unwin, London, 1947, chapters 7 and 8.

The Process of Creative Destruction

The theories of monopolistic and oligopolistic competition and their popular variants may in two ways be made to serve the view that capitalist reality is unfavorable to maximum performance in production. One may hold that it always has been so and that all along output has been expanding in spite of the secular sabotage perpetrated by the managing bourgeoisie. Advocates of this proposition would have to produce evidence to the effect that the observed rate of increase can be accounted for by a sequence of favorable circumstances unconnected with the mechanism of private enterprise and strong enough to overcome the latter's resistance. However, those who espouse this variant at least avoid the trouble about historical fact that the advocates of the alternative proposition have to face. This avers that capitalist reality once tended to favor maximum productive performance, or at all events productive performance so considerable as to constitute a major element in any serious appraisal of the system; but that the later spread of monopolist structures, killing competition, has by now reversed that tendency.

First, this involves the creation of an entirely imaginary golden age of perfect competition that at some time somehow metamorphosed itself into the monopolistic age, whereas it is quite clear that perfect competition has at no time been more of a reality than it is at present. Secondly, it is necessary to point out that the rate of increase in output did not decrease from the nineties from which, I suppose, the prevalence of the largest-size concerns, at least in manufacturing industry, would have to be dated; that there is nothing in the behavior of the time series of the total output to suggest a 'break in trend'; and, most important of all, that the modern standard of life of the masses evolved during the period of relatively unfettered 'big business'. If we list the items that enter the modern workman's budget and from 1899 on observe the course of their prices not in terms of money but in terms of the hours of labor that will buy them – that is, each year's money prices divided by each year's hourly wage rates – we cannot fail to be struck by the rate of the advance which, considering the spectacular improvement in qualities, seems to have been greater and not smaller than it ever was before. If we economists were given less to wishful thinking and more to the observation of facts, doubts would immediately arise as to the realistic virtues of a theory that would have led us to expect a very different result. Nor is this all. As soon as we go into details and inquire into the individual items in which progress was most conspicuous, the trail leads not to the doors of those firms that work under conditions of comparatively free competition but precisely to the doors of the large concerns – which, as in the case of agricultural machinery, also account for much of the progress in the competitive sector – and a shocking suspicion dawns upon us that big business may have had more to do with creating that standard of life than with keeping it down.

The conclusions alluded to at the end of the preceding chapter are in fact almost completely false. Yet they follow from observations and theorems that are almost completely true. Both economists and popular writers have once more run away with some fragments of reality they happened to grasp. These fragments themselves were mostly seen correctly. Their formal properties were mostly developed correctly. But no conclusions about capitalist reality as a whole follow from such fragmentary analyses. If we draw them nevertheless, we can be right only by accident. That has been done. And the lucky accident did not happen.

The essential point to grasp is that in dealing with capitalism we are dealing with an evolutionary process. It may seem strange that anyone can fail to see so obvious a fact which moreover was long ago emphasized by Karl Marx. Yet that fragmentary analysis which yields the bulk of our propositions about the functioning of modern capitalism persistently neglects it. Let us restate the point and see how it bears upon our problem.

Capitalism, then, is by nature a form or method of economic change and not only never is but never can be stationary. And this evolutionary character of the capitalist process is not merely due to the fact that economic life goes on in a social and natural environment which changes and by its change alters the data of economic action; this fact is important and these changes (wars, revolutions, and so on) often condition industrial change, but they are not its prime movers. Nor is this evolutionary character due to a quasi-automatic increase in population and capital or to the vagaries of monetary systems of which exactly the same thing holds true. The fundamental impulse that sets and keeps the capitalist engine in motion comes from the new consumers' goods, the new methods of production or transportation, the new markets, the new forms of industrial organization that capitalist enterprise creates.

As we have seen in the preceding chapter, the contents of the laborer's budget, say from 1760 to 1940, did not simply grow on unchanging lines but they underwent a process of qualitative change. Similarly, the history of the productive apparatus of a typical farm, from the beginnings of the rationalization of crop rotation, plowing and fattening to the mechanized thing of today – linking up with elevators and railroads – is a history of revolutions. So is the history of the productive apparatus of the iron and steel industry from the charcoal furnace to our own type of furnace, or the history of the apparatus of power production from the overshot water wheel to the modern power plant, or the history of transportation from the mailcoach to the airplane. The opening up of new markets, foreign or domestic, and the organizational development from the craft shop and factory to such concerns as U.S. Steel illustrate the same process of industrial mutation – if I may use that biological term – that incessantly revolutionizes the economic structure *from within*, incessantly destroying the old one, incessantly creating a new one. This process of creative destruction is the essential fact about capitalism. It is what capitalism consists in and what every capitalist concern has got to live in. This fact bears upon our problem in two ways.

First, since we are dealing with a process whose every element takes considerable time in revealing its true features and ultimate effects, there is no point in appraising the performance of that process *ex visu* of a given point of time; we must judge its performance over time, as it unfolds through decades or centuries. A system – any system, economic or other – that at *every* given point of time fully utilizes its possibilities to the best advantage may yet in the long run be inferior to a system that does so at *no* given point of time, because the latter's failure to do so may be a condition for the level or speed of long-run performance.

Second, since we are dealing with an organic process, analysis of what happens in any particular part of it – say, in an individual concern or industry – may indeed clarify details of mechanism but is inconclusive beyond that. Every piece of business strategy acquires its true significance only against the background of that process and within the situation created by it. It must be seen in its role in the perennial gale of creative destruction; it cannot be understood irrespective of it or, in fact, on the hypothesis that there is a perennial lull.

But economists who, *ex visu* of a point of time, look for example at the behavior of an oligopolist industry – an industry which consists of a few big firms – and observe the well-known moves and countermoves within it that seem to aim at nothing but high prices and restrictions of output are making precisely that hypothesis. They accept the data of the momentary situation as if there were no past or future to it and think that they have understood what there is to understand if they interpret the behavior of those firms by means of the principle of maximizing profits with reference to those data. The usual theorist's paper and the usual government commission's report practically never try to see that behavior, on the one hand, as a result of a piece of past history and, on the other hand, as an attempt to deal with a situation that is sure to change presently – as an attempt by those firms to keep on their feet, on ground that is slipping away from under them. In other words, the problem that is usually being visualized is how capitalism administers existing structures, whereas the relevant problem is how it creates and destroys them. As long as this is not recognized the investigator does a meaningless job. As soon as it is recognized, his outlook on capitalist practice and its social results changes considerably.

The first thing to go is the traditional conception of the *modus operandi* of competition. Economists are at long last emerging from the stage in which price competition was all they saw. As soon as quality competition and sales effort are admitted into the sacred precincts of theory, the price variable is ousted from its dominant position. However, it is still competition within a rigid pattern of invariant conditions, methods of production and forms of industrial organization in particular, that practically monopolizes attention. But in capitalist reality as distinguished from its textbook picture, it is not that kind of competition which counts but the competition from the new commodity, the new technology, the new source of supply, the new type of organization (the largest-scale unit of control for instance) – competition which commands a decisive cost or quality advantage and which strikes not at the margins of the profits and the outputs of the existing firms but at their foundations and their very lives. This kind of competition is as much more effective than the other as a bombardment is in comparison with forcing a door, and so much more important that it becomes a matter of comparative indifference whether competition in the ordinary sense functions more or less promptly; the powerful lever that in the long run expands output and brings down prices is in any case made of other stuff.

It is hardly necessary to point out that competition of the kind we now have in mind acts not only when in being but also when it is merely an ever-present threat. It disciplines before it attacks. The businessman feels himself to be in a competitive situation even if he is alone in his field or if, though not alone, he holds a position such that investigating government experts fail to see any effective competition between him and any other firms in the same or a neighbouring field and in consequence conclude that his talk, under examination, about his competitive sorrows is all make-believe. In many cases, though not in all, this will in the long run enforce behaviour very similar to the perfectly competitive pattern.

Many theorists take the opposite view which is best conveyed by an example. Let us assume that there is a certain number of retailers in a neighborhood who try to improve their relative position by service and 'atmosphere' but avoid price competition and stick as to methods to the local tradition – a picture of stagnating routine. As others drift into the trade that quasi-equilibrium is indeed upset, but in a manner that does not benefit their customers. The economic space around each of the shops having been narrowed, their owners will no longer be able to make a living and they will try to mend the case by raising prices in tacit agreement. This will further reduce their sales and so, by successive pyramiding, a situation will evolve in which increasing potential supply will be attended by increasing instead of decreasing prices and by decreasing instead of increasing sales.

Such cases do occur, and it is right and proper to work them out. But as the practical instances usually given show, they are fringe-end cases to be found mainly in the sectors furthest removed from all that is most characteristic of capitalist activity. Moreover, they are transient by nature. In the case of retail trade the competition that matters arises not from additional shops of the same type, but from the department store, the chain store, the mail-order house and the supermarket which are bound to destroy those pyramids sooner or later. Now a theoretical construction which neglects this essential element of the case neglects all that is most typically capitalist about it: even if correct in logic as well as in fact, it is like *Hamlet* without the Danish prince.

Monopolistic Practices

What has been said so far is really sufficient to enable the reader to deal with the large majority of the practical cases he is likely to meet and to realize the inadequacy of most of those criticisms of the profit economy which, directly or indirectly, rely on the absence of perfect competition. Since, however, the bearing of our argument on some of those criticisms may not be obvious at a glance, it will be worth our while to elaborate a little in order to make a few points more explicit.

1. We have just seen that, both as a fact and as a threat, the impact of new things – new technologies for instance – on the existing structure of an industry considerably reduces the long-run scope and importance of practices that aim, through restricting output, at conserving established positions and at maximizing the profits accruing from them. We must now recognize the further fact that restrictive practices of this kind, as far as they are effective, acquire a new significance in the perennial gale of creative destruction, a significance which they would not have in a stationary

state or in a state of slow and balanced growth. In either of these cases restrictive strategy would produce no result other than an increase in profits at the expense of buyers except that, in the case of balanced advance, it might still prove to be the easiest and most effective way of collecting the means by which to finance additional investment. But in the process of creative destruction, restrictive practices may do much to steady the ship and to alleviate temporary difficulties. This is in fact a very familiar argument which always turns up in times of depression and, as everyone knows, has become very popular with governments and their economic advisers – witness the N.R.A. While it has been so much misused and so faultily acted upon that most economists heartily despise it, those same advisers who are responsible for this invariably fail to see its much more general rationale.

Practically any investment entails, as a necessary complement of entrepreneurial action, certain safeguarding activities such as insuring or hedging. Long-range investing under rapidly changing conditions, especially under conditions that change or may change at any moment under the impact of new commodities and technologies, is like shooting at a target that is not only indistinct but moving – and moving jerkily at that. Hence it becomes necessary to resort to such protecting devices as patents or temporary secrecy of processes or, in some cases, long-period contracts secured in advance. But these protecting devices which most economists accept as normal elements of rational management[1] are only special cases of a larger class comprising many others which most economists condemn although they do not differ fundamentally from the recognized ones.

If for instance a war risk is insurable, nobody objects to a firm's collecting the cost of this insurance from the buyers of its products. But that risk is no less an element in long-run costs, if there are no facilities for insuring against it, in which case a price strategy aiming at the same end will seem to involve unnecessary restriction and to be productive of excess profits. Similarly, if a patent cannot be

1. Some economists, however, consider that even those devices are obstructions to progress which, though perhaps necessary in capitalist society, would be absent in a socialist one. There is some truth in this. But that does not affect the proposition that the protection afforded by patents and so on is, in the conditions of a profit economy, on balance a propelling and not an inhibiting factor.

secured or would not, if secured, effectively protect, other means may have to be used in order to justify the investment. Among them are a price policy that will make it possible to write off more quickly than would otherwise be rational, or additional investment in order to provide excess capacity to be used only for aggression or defense. Again, if long-period contracts cannot be entered into in advance, other means may have to be devised in order to tie prospective customers to the investing firm.

In analysing such business strategy *ex visu* of a given point of time, the investing economist or government agent sees price policies that seem to him predatory and restrictions of output that seem to him synonymous with loss of opportunities to produce. He does not see that restrictions of this type are, in the conditions of the perennial gale, incidents, often unavoidable incidents, of a long-run process of expansion which they protect rather than impede. There is no more of paradox in this than there is in saying that motor cars are travelling faster than they otherwise would *because* they are provided with brakes.

2. This stands out most clearly in the case of those sectors of the economy which at any time happen to embody the impact of new things and methods on the existing industrial structure. The best way of getting a vivid and realistic idea of industrial strategy is indeed to visualize the behavior of new concerns or industries that introduce new commodities or processes (such as the aluminum industry) or else reorganize a part or the whole of an industry (such as, for instance, the old Standard Oil Company).

As we have seen, such concerns are aggressors by nature and wield the really effective weapon of competition. Their intrusion can only in the rarest of cases fail to improve total output in quantity or quality, both through the new method itself – even if at no time used to full advantage – and through the pressure it exerts on the pre-existing firms. But these aggressors are so circumstanced as to require, for purposes of attack and defense, also pieces of armour other than price and quality of their product which, moreover, must be strategically manipulated all along so that at any point of time they seem to be doing nothing but restricting their output and keeping prices high.

On the one hand, largest-scale plans could in many cases not materialize at all if it were not known from the outset that competition will be discouraged by heavy capital requirements or lack of experience, or that means are available to discourage or checkmate it so as to gain the time and space for further developments. Even the conquest of financial control over competing concerns in otherwise unassailable positions or the securing of advantages that run counter to the public's sense of fair play – railroad rebates – move, as far as long-run effects on total output alone are envisaged, into a different light: they *may* be methods for removing obstacles that the institution of private property puts in the path of progress. In a socialist society that time and space would be no less necessary. They would have to be secured by order of the central authority.

On the other hand, enterprise would in most cases be impossible if it were not known from the outset that exceptionally favorable situations are likely to arise which if exploited by price, quality and quantity manipulation will produce profits adequate to tide over exceptionally unfavorable situations provided these are similarly managed. Again this requires strategy that in the short run is often restrictive. In the majority of successful cases this strategy just manages to serve its purpose. In some cases, however, it is so successful as to yield profits far above what is necessary in order to induce the corresponding investment. These cases then provide the baits that lure capital on to untried trails. Their presence explains in part how it is possible for so large a section of the capitalist world to work for nothing; in the midst of the prosperous twenties just about half of the business corporations in the United States were run at a loss, at zero profits, or at profits which, if they had been foreseen, would have been inadequate to call forth the effort and expenditure involved.

Our argument however extends beyond the cases of new concerns, methods and industries. Old concerns and established industries, whether or not directly attacked, still live in the perennial gale. Situations emerge in the process of creative destruction in which many firms may have to perish that nevertheless would be able to live on vigorously and usefully if they could weather a particular storm. Short of such general crises or depressions, sectional situations arise in which the rapid change of data that is characteristic of that process so disorganizes an industry for the time being as to inflict functionless losses and to create avoidable unemployment. Finally, there is certainly no point in trying to conserve obsolescent industries indefinitely: but there is a point in trying to avoid their coming down with a crash and in attempting to turn a rout, which may become a center of cumulative depressive effects, into orderly retreat. Correspondingly there is, in the case of industries that have sown their wild oats but are still gaining and not losing ground, such a thing as orderly advance.[2]

All this is of course nothing but the tritest common sense. But it is being overlooked with a persistence so stubborn as sometimes to raise the question of sincerity. And it follows that, within the process of creative destruction, all the realities of which theorists are in the habit of relegating to books and courses on business cycles, there is another side to industrial self-organization than that which these theorists are contemplating. 'Restraints of trade' of the cartel type as well as those which merely consist in tacit understandings

2. A good example illustrative of this point – in fact of much of our general argument – is the post-war history of the automobile and the rayon industry. The first illustrates very well the nature and value of what we might call 'edited' competition. The bonanza time was over by about 1916. A host of firms nevertheless crowded into the industry afterwards, most of which were eliminated by 1925. From a fierce life and death struggle three concerns emerged that by now account for over 80 per cent of total sales. They are under competitive pressure inasmuch as, in spite of the advantages of an established position, an elaborate sales and service organization and so on, any failure to keep up and improve the quality of their products or any attempt at monopolistic combination would call in new competitors. Among themselves, the three concerns behave in a way which should be called corespective rather than competitive: they refrain from certain aggressive devices (which, by the way, would also be absent in perfect competition); they keep up with each other and in doing so play for points at the frontiers. This has now gone on for upwards of fifteen years and it is not obvious that if conditions of theoretically perfect competition had prevailed during that period, better or cheaper cars would now be offered to the public, or higher wages and more or steadier employment to the workmen. The rayon industry had its bonanza time in the twenties. It presents the features incident to introducing a commodity into fields fully occupied before and the policies that impose themselves in such conditions still more clearly than does the automobile industry. And there are a number of other differences. But fundamentally the case is similar. The expansion in quantity and quality of rayon output is common knowledge. Yet restrictive policy presided over this expansion at each individual point of time.

about price competition may be effective remedies under conditions of depression. As far as they are, they may in the end produce not only steadier but also greater expansion of total output than could be secured by an entirely uncontrolled onward rush that cannot fail to be studded with catastrophes. Nor can it be argued that these catastrophes occur in any case. We know what has happened in each historical case. We have a very imperfect idea of what might have happened, considering the tremendous pace of the process, if such pegs had been entirely absent.

Even as now extended however, our argument does not cover all cases of restrictive or regulating strategy, many of which no doubt have that injurious effect on the long-run development of output which is uncritically attributed to all of them; and even in the cases our argument does cover, the net effect is a question of the circumstances and of the way in which and the degree to which industry regulates itself in each individual case. It is certainly as conceivable that an all-pervading cartel system might sabotage all progress as it is that it might realize, with smaller social and private costs, all that perfect competition is supposed to realize. This is why our argument does not amount to a case against state regulation. It does show that there is no general case for indiscriminate 'trust-busting' or for the prosecution of everything that qualifies as a restraint of trade. Rational as distinguished from vindictive regulation by public authority turns out to be an extremely delicate problem which not every government agency, particularly when in full cry against big business, can be trusted to solve. But our argument, framed to refute a prevalent *theory* and the inferences drawn therefrom about the relation between modern capitalism and the development of total output, only yields another *theory*, that is, another outlook on facts and another principle by which to interpret them. For our purpose that is enough. For the rest, the facts themselves have the floor.

3. Next, a few words on the subject of rigid prices which has been receiving so much attention of late. It really is but a particular aspect of the problem we have been discussing. We shall define rigidity as follows: a price is rigid if it is less sensitive to changes in the conditions of demand and supply than it would be if perfect competition prevailed (1 and 2).

Quantitatively, the extent to which prices are rigid in that sense depends on the material and the method of measurement we select and is hence a doubtful matter. But whatever the material or method, it is certain that prices are not nearly as rigid as they seem to be. There are many reasons why what in effect is a change in price should not show in the statistical picture; in other words, why there should be much spurious rigidity. I shall mention only one class of them which is closely connected with the facts stressed by our analysis.

I have adverted to the importance, for the capitalist process in general and for its competitive mechanism in particular, of the intrusion of new commodities. Now a new commodity may effectively bring down the pre-existing structure and satisfy a given want at much lower prices per unit of service (transportation service for instance), and yet not a single recorded price need change in the process; flexibility in the relevant sense may be accompanied by rigidity in a formal sense. There are other cases, not of this type, in which price reduction is the sole motive for bringing out a new brand while the old one is left at the previous quotation – again a price reduction that does not show. Moreover, the great majority of new consumers' goods – particularly all the gadgets of modern life – are at first introduced in an experimental and unsatisfactory form in which they could never conquer their potential markets. Improvement in the quality of products is hence a practically universal feature of the development of individual concerns and of industries. Whether or not this improvement involves additional costs, a constant price per unit of an improving commodity should not be called rigid without further investigation.

Of course, plenty of cases of genuine price rigidity remain – of prices which are being kept constant as a matter of business policy or which remain unchanged because it is difficult to change, say, a price set by a cartel after laborious negotiations. In order to appraise the influence of this fact on the long-run development of output, it is first of all necessary to realize that this rigidity is essentially a short-run phenomenon. There are no major instances of long-run rigidity of prices. Whichever manufacturing industry or group of manufactured articles of any importance we choose to investigate over a period of time, we practically always find that in the long run prices do not fail to adapt themselves to technological progress – frequently they fall spectacularly in response to it – unless prevented from doing so by monetary events and policies or, in some cases, by autonomous changes in wage rates which of course should be taken into account by appropriate corrections exactly as should changes in quality of products. And our previous analysis shows sufficiently why in the process of capitalist evolution this must be so.

What the business strategy in question really aims at – all, in any case, that it can achieve – is to avoid seasonal, random and cyclical fluctuations in prices and to move only in response to the more fundamental changes in the conditions that underlie those fluctuations. Since these more fundamental changes take time in declaring themselves, this involves moving slowly by discrete steps – keeping to a price until new relatively durable contours have emerged into view. In technical language, this strategy aims at moving along a step function that will approximate trends; and that is what genuine and voluntary price rigidity in most cases amounts to. In fact, most economists do admit this, at least by implication. For though some of their arguments about rigidity would hold true only if the phenomenon were a long-run one – for instance most of the arguments averring that price rigidity keeps the fruits of technological progress from consumers – in practice they measure and discuss primarily cyclical rigidity and especially the fact that many prices do not, or do not promptly fall in recessions and depressions. The real question is therefore how this short-run rigidity may affect the long-run development of total output. Within this question, the only really important issue is this: prices that stay up in recession or depression no doubt influence the business situation in those phases of the cycles; if that influence is strongly injurious – making matters much worse than they would be with perfect flexibility all round – the destruction wrought each time might also affect output in the subsequent recoveries and prosperities and thus permanently reduce the rate of increase in total output below what it would be in the absence of those rigidities. Two arguments have been put forth in favor of this view.

In order to put the first into the strongest possible light, let us assume that an industry which refuses to reduce prices in recession goes on selling exactly the same quantity of product which it would sell if it had reduced them. Buyers are therefore out of pocket by the amount to which the industry profits from the rigidity. If these buyers are the kind of people who spend all they can and if the industry or those to whom its net returns go does not spend the increment it gets but either keeps it idle or repays bank loans, then total expenditure in the economy may be reduced thereby. If this happens, other industries or firms may suffer and if thereupon they restrict in turn, we may get a cumulation of depressive effects. In other words, rigidity may so influence the amount and distribution of national income as to decrease balances or to increase idle balances or, if we adopt a popular misnomer, savings. Such a case is conceivable. But the reader should have little difficulty in satisfying himself that its practical importance, if any, is very small.

The second argument turns on the dislocating effects price rigidity may exert if, in the individual industry itself or elsewhere, it leads to an additional restriction of output, that is to a restriction greater than that which must in any case occur during depression. Since the most important conductor of those effects is the incident increase in unemployment – unstabilization of employment is in fact the indictment most commonly directed against price rigidity – and the consequent decrease in total expenditure, this argument then follows in the tracks of the first one. Its practical weight is considerably reduced, although economists greatly differ as to the extent, by the consideration that in the most conspicuous cases price rigidity is motivated precisely by the low sensitiveness of demand to short-run price changes within the practicable range. People who in depression worry about their future are not likely to buy a new car even if the price were reduced by 25 per cent, especially if the purchase is easily postponable and if the reduction induces expectations of further reductions.

Quite irrespective of this however, the argument is inconclusive because it is again vitiated by a *ceteris paribus* clause that is inadmissible in dealing with our process of creative destruction. From the fact, so far as it is a fact, that at more flexible prices greater quantities could *ceteris paribus* be sold, it does not follow that either the output of the commodities in question, or total output and hence employment, would actually be greater. For inasmuch as we may assume that the refusal to lower prices strengthens the position of the industries which adopt that policy either by increasing their revenue or simply by avoiding chaos in their markets – that is to say, so far as this policy is something more than a mistake on their part – it may make fortresses out of what otherwise might be centers of devastation. As we have seen before, from a more general standpoint, total output and employment may well keep on a higher level with the restrictions incident to that policy than they would if depression were allowed to play havoc with the price structure. In other words, under the conditions created by capitalist evolution, perfect and universal flexibility of prices might in depression further unstabilize the system, instead of stabilizing it as it no doubt would under the conditions envisaged by general theory. Again this is to a large extent recognized in those cases in which the economist is in sympathy with the interests immediately concerned, for instance in the case of labor and of agriculture; in those cases he admits readily enough that what looks like rigidity may be no more than regulated adaptation.

Perhaps the reader feels some surprise that so little remains of a doctrine of which so much has been made in the last few years. The rigidity of prices has become, with some people, the outstanding defect of the capitalist engine and – almost – the fundamental factor in the explanation of depressions. But there is nothing to wonder at in this. Individuals and groups snatch at anything that will qualify as a discovery lending support to the political tendencies of the hour. The doctrine of price rigidity, with a modicum of truth to its credit, is not the worst case of this kind by a long way.

4. Another doctrine has crystallized into a slogan, viz. that in the era of big business the maintenance of the value of existing investment – conservation of capital – becomes the chief aim of entrepreneurial activity and bids fair to put a stop to all cost-reducing improvement. Hence the capitalist order becomes incompatible with progress.

Progress entails, as we have seen, destruction of capital values in the strata with which the new commodity or method of production competes. In perfect competition the old investments must be adapted at a sacrifice or abandoned: but when there is no perfect competition and when each industrial field is controlled by a few big concerns, these can in various ways fight the threatening attack on their capital structure and try to avoid losses on their capital accounts: that is to say, they can and will fight progress itself.

So far as this doctrine merely formulates a particular aspect of restrictive business strategy, there is no need to add anything to the argument already sketched in this chapter. Both as to the limits of that strategy and as to its functions in the process of creative destruction, we should only be repeating what has been said before. This becomes still more obvious if we observe that conserving capital values is the same thing as conserving profits. Modern theory tends in fact to use the concept present net value of assets (= capital values) in place of the concept of profits. Both asset values and profits are of course not being simply conserved but maximized.

But the point about the sabotage of cost-reducing improvement still calls for comment in passing. As a little reflection will show, it is sufficient to consider the case of a concern that controls a technological device – some patent, say – the use of which would involve scrapping some or all of its plant and equipment. Will it, in order to conserve its capital values, refrain from using this device when a management not fettered by capitalist interests such as a socialist management could and would use it to the advantage of all?

Again it is tempting to raise the question of fact. The first thing a modern concern does as soon as it feels that it can afford it is to establish a research department every member of which knows that his bread and butter depends on his success in devising improvements. This practice does not obviously suggest aversion to technological progress. Nor can we in reply be referred to the cases in which patents acquired by business concerns have not been used promptly or not been used at all. For there may be perfectly good reasons for this; for example, the patented process may turn out to be no good or at least not to be in shape to warrant application on a commercial basis. Neither the inventors themselves nor the investigating economists or government officials are unbiased judges of this, and from their remonstrances or reports we may easily get a very distorted picture.[3]

3. Incidentally, it should be noticed that the kind of restrictive practice under discussion, granted that it exists to a significant extent, would not be without compensatory effects on social welfare. In fact, the same critics who talk about sabotage of progress at the same time emphasize the *social* losses

But we are concerned with a question of theory. Everyone agrees that private and socialist managements will introduce improvements if, with the new method of production, the total cost per unit of product is expected to be smaller than the prime cost per unit of product with the method actually in use. If this condition is not fulfilled, then it is held that private management will not adopt a cost-reducing method until the existing plant and equipment is entirely written off, whereas socialist management would, to the social advantage, replace the old by any new cost-reducing method as soon as such a method becomes available, that is without regard to capital values. This however is not so.[4]

Private management, if actuated by the profit motive, cannot be interested in maintaining the values of any given building or machine any more than a socialist management would be. All that private management tries to do is to maximize the present net value of total assets which is equal to the discounted value of expected net returns. This amounts to saying that it will always adopt a new method of production which it believes will yield a larger stream of future income per unit of the corresponding stream of future outlay, both discounted to the present, than does the method actually in use. The value of past investment, whether or not paralleled by a bonded debt that has to be amortized, does not enter at all except in the sense and to the extent that it would have to enter into the calculation underlying the decisions of a socialist management. So far as the use of the old machines saves future costs as compared with the immediate introduction of the new methods, the remainder of their service value is of course an element of the decision for both the capitalist and the socialist manager: otherwise bygones are bygones for both of them and any attempt to conserve the value of past investment would con-

---

incident to the pace of capitalist progress, particularly the unemployment which that pace entails and which slower advance might mitigate to some extent. Well, is technological progress too quick or too slow for them? They had better make up their minds.

4. It should be observed that even if the argument were correct, it would still be inadequate to support the thesis that capitalism is, under the conditions envisaged, 'incompatible with technological progress'. All that it would prove is, for some cases, the presence of a lag of ordinarily moderate length in the introduction of new methods.

flict as much with the rules following from the profit motive as it would conflict with the rules set for the behavior of the socialist manager.

It is however not true that private firms owning equipment the value of which is endangered by a new method which they also control – if they do not control it, there is no problem and no indictment – will adopt the new method only if total unit cost with it is smaller than prime unit cost with the old one, or if the old investment has been completely written off *according to the schedule decided on before the new method presented itself.* For if the new machines when installed are expected to outlive the rest of the period previously set for the use of the old machines, their discounted remainder value as of that date is another asset to be taken account of. Nor is it true, for analogous reasons, that a socialist management, if acting rationally, would always and immediately adopt any new method which promised to produce at smaller total unit costs or that this would be to the social advantage.

There is however another element which profoundly affects behavior in this matter and which is being invariably overlooked. This is what might be called *ex ante* conservation of capital in expectation of further improvement. Frequently, if not in most cases, a going concern does not simply face the question whether or not to adopt a definite new method of production that is the best thing out and, in the form immediately available, can be expected to retain that position for some length of time. A new type of machine is in general but a link in a chain of improvement and may presently become obsolete. In a case like this it would obviously not be rational to follow the chain link by link regardless of the capital loss to be suffered each time. The real question then is at which link the concern should take action. The answer must be in the nature of a compromise between considerations that rest largely on guesses. But it will as a rule involve some waiting in order to see how the chain behaves. And to the outsider this may well look like trying to stifle improvement in order to conserve *existing* capital values. Yet even the most patient of comrades would revolt if a socialist management were so foolish as to follow the advice of the theorist and to keep on scrapping plant and equipment every year.

5. I have entitled this section as I did because most of it deals with the facts and problems that common parlance associates with monopoly, or monopolistic practice. So far I have as much as possible refrained from using those terms in order to reserve for a separate section some comments on a few topics specifically connected with them. Nothing will be said however that we have not already met in one form or another.

(a) To begin with, there is the term itself. Monopolist means single seller. Literally therefore anyone is a monopolist who sells anything that is not in every respect, wrapping and location and service included, exactly like what other people sell; every grocer, or every haberdasher, or every seller of 'Good Humors' on a road that is not simply lined with sellers of the same brand of ice cream. This however is not what we mean when talking about monopolists. We mean only those single sellers whose markets are not open to the intrusion of would-be producers of the same commodity and of actual producers of similar ones or, speaking slightly more technically, only those single sellers who face a given demand schedule that is severely independent of their own action as well as of any reactions to their action by other concerns. The traditional Cournot-Marshall theory of monopoly as extended and amended by later authors holds only if we define it in this way and there is, so it seems, no point in calling anything a monopoly to which that theory does not apply.

But if accordingly we do define it like this, then it becomes evident immediately that pure cases of long-run monopoly must be of the rarest occurrence and that even tolerable approximations to the requirements of the concept must be still rarer than are cases of perfect competition. The power to exploit at pleasure a given pattern of demand – or one that changes independently of the monopolist's action and of the reactions it provokes – can under the conditions of intact capitalism hardly persist for a period long enough to matter for the analysis of total output, unless buttressed by public authority, for instance, in the case of fiscal monopolies. A modern business concern not *so* protected – that is, even if protected by import duties or import prohibitions – and yet wielding that power (except temporarily) is not easy to find or even to imagine. Even railroads and power and light concerns had first to create the demand for their services and, when they had done so, to defend their market against competition. Outside the field of public utilities, the position of a single seller can in general be conquered – and retained for decades – only on the condition that he does not behave like a monopolist. Short-run monopoly will be touched upon presently.

Why then all this talk about monopoly? The answer is not without interest for the student of the psychology of political discussion. Of course, the concept of monopoly is being loosely used just like any other. People speak of a country's having a monopoly of something or other even if the industry in question is highly competitive and so on. But this is not all. Economists, government agents, journalists and politicians in this country obviously love the word because it has come to be a term of opprobrium which is sure to rouse the public's hostility against any interest so labeled. In the Anglo-American world monopoly has been cursed and associated with functionless exploitation ever since, in the sixteenth and seventeenth centuries, it was English administrative practice to create monopoly positions in large numbers which, on the one hand, answered fairly well to the theoretical pattern of monopolist behavior and, on the other hand, fully justified the wave of indignation that impressed even the great Elizabeth.

Nothing is so retentive as a nation's memory. Our time offers other and more important instances of a nation's reaction to what happened centuries ago. That practice made the English-speaking public so monopoly-conscious that it acquired a habit of attributing to that sinister power practically everything it disliked about business. To the typical liberal bourgeois in particular, monopoly became the father of almost all abuses – in fact, it became his pet bogey. Adam Smith, thinking primarily of monopolies of the Tudor and Stuart type, frowned on them in awful dignity. Sir Robert Peel – who like most conservatives occasionally knew how to borrow from the arsenal of the demagogue – in his famous epilogue to his last period of office that gave so much offense to his associates, spoke of a monopoly of bread or wheat, though English grain production was of course perfectly competitive in spite of protection. And in this country monopoly is being made practically synonymous with any large-scale business.

(b) The theory of simple and discriminating monopoly teaches that, excepting a limiting case, monopoly price is higher and monopoly output smaller than competitive price and competitive output. This is true provided that the method and organization of production – and everything else – are exactly the same in both cases. Actually however there are superior methods available to the monopolist which either are not available at all to a crowd of competitors or are not available to them so readily; for there are advantages which, though not strictly unattainable on the competitive level of enterprise, are as a matter of fact secured only on the monopoly level, for instance, because monopolization may increase the sphere of influence of the better, and decrease the sphere of influence of the inferior, brains,[5] or because the monopoly enjoys a disproportionately higher financial standing. Whenever this is so, then that proposition is no longer true. In other words, this element of the case for competition may fail completely because monopoly prices are not necessarily higher or monopoly outputs smaller than competitive prices and outputs would be at the levels of productive and organizational efficiency that are within the reach of the type of firm compatible with the competitive hypothesis.

There cannot be any reasonable doubt that under the conditions of our epoch such superiority is as a matter of fact the outstanding feature of the typical large-scale unit of control, though mere size is neither necessary nor sufficient for it. These units not only arise in the process of creative destruction and function in a way entirely different from the static schema, but in many cases of decisive importance they provide the necessary form for the achievement. They largely create what they exploit. Hence the usual conclusion about their influence on long-run output would be invalid even if they were genuine monopolies in the technical sense of the term.

Motivation is quite immaterial. Even if the opportunity to set

5. The reader should observe that while, as a broad rule, that particular type of superiority is simply indisputable, the inferior brains, especially if their owners are entirely eliminated, are not likely to admit it and that the public's and the recording economists' hearts go out to them and not to the others. This may have something to do with a tendency to discount the cost or quality advantages of quasimonopolist combination that is at present as pronounced as was the exaggeration of them in the typical prospectus or announcement of sponsors of such combinations.

monopolist prices were the sole object, the pressure of the improved methods or of a huge apparatus would in general tend to shift the point of the monopolist's optimum toward or beyond the competitive cost price in the above sense, thus doing the work – partly, wholly, or more than wholly – of the competitive mechanism,[6] *even if restriction is practiced and excess capacity is in evidence all along.* Of course if the methods of production, organization and so on are not improved by or in connexion with monopolization as is the case with an ordinary cartel, the classical theorem about monopoly price and output comes into its own again. So does another popular idea, viz. that monopolization has a soporific effect. For this, too, it is not difficult to find examples. But no general theory should be built upon it. For, especially in manufacturing industry, a monopoly position is in general no cushion to sleep on. As it can be gained, so it can be retained only by alertness and energy. What soporific influence there is in modern business is due to another cause that will be mentioned later.

(c) In the short run, genuine monopoly positions or positions approximating to monopoly are much more frequent. The grocer in a village on the Ohio may be a true monopolist for hours or even days during an inundation. Every successful corner may spell monopoly for the moment. A firm specializing in paper labels for beer bottles may be so circumstanced – potential competitors realizing that what seem to be good profits would be immediately destroyed by their entering the field – that it can move at pleasure on

6. The Aluminum Company of America is not a monopoly in the technical sense as defined above, among other reasons because it had to build up its demand schedule, which fact suffices to exclude a behavior conforming to the Cournot-Marshall schema. But most economists call it so and in the dearth of genuine cases we will for the purposes of this note do the same. From 1890 to 1929 the price of the basic product of this single seller fell to about 12 per cent, or, correcting for the change in price level (B.L.S. index of wholesale prices), to about 8·8 per cent. Output rose from 30 metric tons to 103,400. Protection by patent ceased in 1909. Argument from costs and profits in criticism of this 'monopoly' must take it for granted that a multitude of competing firms would have been about equally successful in cost-reducing research, in the economical development of the productive apparatus, in teaching new uses for the product and in avoiding wasteful breakdowns. This is, in fact, being assumed by criticism of this kind; that is, the propelling factor of modern capitalism is being assumed away.

a moderate but still finite stretch of the demand curve, at least until the metal label smashes that demand curve to pieces.

New methods of production or new commodities, especially the latter, do not *per se* confer monopoly, even if used or produced by a single firm. The product of the new method has to compete with the products of the old ones and the new commodity has to be introduced, that is, its demand schedule has to be built up. As a rule neither patents nor monopolistic practices avail against that. But they may in cases of spectacular superiority of the new device, particularly if it can be leased like shoe machinery: or in cases of new commodities, the permanent demand schedule for which has been established before the patent has expired.

Thus it is true that there is or may be an element of genuine monopoly gain in those entrepreneurial profits which are the prizes offered by capitalist society to the successful innovator. But the quantitative importance of that element, its volatile nature and its function in the process in which it emerges put it in a class by itself. The main value to a concern of a single seller position that is secured by patent or monopolistic strategy does not consist so much in the opportunity to behave temporarily according to the monopolist schema, as in the protection it affords against temporary disorganization of the market and the space it secures for long-range planning. Here however the argument merges into the analysis submitted before.

6. Glancing back we realize that most of the facts and arguments touched upon in this chapter tend to dim the halo that once surrounded perfect competition as much as they suggest a more favorable view of its alternative. I will now briefly restate our argument from this angle.

Traditional theory itself, even within its chosen precincts of a stationary or steadily growing economy, has since the time of Marshall and Edgeworth been discovering an increasing number of exceptions to the old propositions about perfect competition and, incidentally, free trade, that have shaken that unqualified belief in its virtues cherished by the generation which flourished between Ricardo and Marshall – roughly, J. S. Mill's generation in England and Francesco Ferrara's on the Continent. Especially the propositions that a perfectly competitive system is ideally economical of resources and allocates them in a way that is optimal with respect to a given distribution of income – propositions very relevant to the question of the behavior of output – cannot now be held with the old confidence (3).

Much more serious is the breach made by more recent work in the field of dynamic theory (Frisch, Tinbergen, Roos, Hicks and others). Dynamic analysis is the analysis of sequences in time. In explaining why a certain economic quantity, for instance a price, is what we find it to be at a given moment, it takes into consideration not only the state of other economic quantities at the same moment, as static theory does, but also their state at preceding points of time, and the expectations about their future values. Now the first thing we discover in working out the propositions that thus relate quantities belonging to different points of time is the fact that, once equilibrium has been destroyed by some disturbance, the process of establishing a new one is not so sure and prompt and economical as the old theory of perfect competition made it out to be: and the possibility that the very struggle for adjustment might lead such a system farther away from instead of nearer to a new equilibrium. This will happen in most cases unless the disturbance is small, In many cases, lagged adjustment is sufficient to produce this result.

All I can do here is to illustrate by the oldest, simplest and most familiar example. Suppose that demand and *intended* supply are in equilibrium in a perfectly competitive market for wheat, but that bad weather reduces the crop below what farmers intended to supply. If price rises accordingly and the farmers thereupon produce that quantity of wheat which it would pay them to produce if that new price were the equilibrium price, then a slump in the wheat market will ensue in the following year. If now the farmers correspondingly restrict production, a price still higher than in the first year may result to induce a still greater expansion of production than occurred in the second year. And so on (as far as the pure logic of the process is concerned) indefinitely. The reader will readily perceive, from a survey of the assumptions involved, that no great fear need be entertained of ever higher prices, and ever greater outputs, alternating till doomsday. But even if reduced to its proper proportions, the phenomenon suffices to show up glaring weaknesses in the mechanism of perfect competition. As soon as this is realized much of the optimism that used to grace the practical implications of the theory of this mechanism passes out through the ivory gate.

But from our standpoint we must go further than that.[7] If we try to visualize how perfect competition works or would work in the process of creative destruction, we arrive at a still more discouraging result. This will not surprise us, considering that all the essential facts of that process are absent from the general schema of economic life that yields the traditional propositions about perfect competition. At the risk of repetition I will illustrate the point once more.

Perfect competition implies free entry into every industry. It is quite true, within that general theory, that free entry into all industries is a condition for optimal allocation of resources and hence for maximizing output. If our economic world consisted of a number of established industries producing familiar commodities by established and substantially invariant methods and if nothing happened except that additional men and additional savings combine in order to set up new firms of the existing type, then impediments to their entry into any industry they wish to enter would spell loss to the community. But perfectly free entry into a *new* field may make it impossible to enter it at all. The introduction of new methods of production and new commodities is hardly conceivable with perfect – and perfectly prompt – competition from the start. And this means that the bulk of what we call economic progress is incompatible with it. As a matter of fact, perfect competition is and always has been temporarily suspended

7. It should be observed that the defining feature of dynamic theory has nothing to do with the nature of the economic reality to which it is applied. It is a general method of analysis rather than a study of a particular process. We can use it in order to analyse a stationary economy, just as an evolving one can be analysed by means of the methods of statics ('comparative statics'). Hence dynamic theory need not take, and as a matter of fact has not taken, any special cognizance of the process of creative destruction which we have taken to be the essence of capitalism. It is no doubt better equipped than is static theory to deal with many questions of mechanism that arise in the analysis of that process. But it is not an analysis of that process itself, and it treats the resulting individual disturbances of given states and structures just as it treats other disturbances. To judge the functioning of perfect competition from the standpoint of capitalist evolution is therefore not the same thing as judging it from the standpoint of dynamic theory.

whenever anything new is being introduced – automatically or by measures devised for the purpose – even in otherwise perfectly competitive conditions.

Similarly, within the traditional system the usual indictment of rigid prices stands all right. Rigidity is a type of resistance to adaptation that perfect and prompt competition excludes. And for the kind of adaptation and for those conditions which have been treated by traditional theory, it is again quite true that such resistance spells loss and reduced output. But we have seen that in the spurts and vicissitudes of the process of creative destruction the opposite may be true; perfect and instantaneous flexibility may even produce functionless catastrophes. This of course can also be established by the general dynamic theory which, as mentioned above, shows that there are attempts at adaptation that intensify disequilibrium.

Again, under its own assumptions, traditional theory is correct in holding that profits above what is necessary in each individual case to call forth the equilibrium amount of means of production, entrepreneurial ability included, both indicate and in themselves imply net social loss and that business strategy that aims at keeping them alive is inimical to the growth of total output. Perfect competition would prevent or immediately eliminate such surplus profits and leave no room for that strategy. But since in the process of capitalist evolution these profits acquire new organic functions – I do not want to repeat what they are – that fact cannot any longer be unconditionally credited to the account of the perfect competitive model, so far as the secular rate of increase in total output is concerned.

Finally, it can indeed be shown that, under the same assumptions which amount to excluding the most characteristic features of capitalist reality, a perfectly competitive economy is comparatively free from waste and in particular from those kinds of waste which we most readily associate with its counterpart. But this does not tell us anything about how its account looks under the conditions set by the process of creative destruction.

On the one hand, much of what without reference to those conditions would appear to be unrelieved waste ceases to qualify as such when duly related to them. The type of excess capacity for example that owes its existence to the practice of 'building ahead of demand' or to the practice of providing capacity for the cyclical peaks of demand would in a regime of perfect competition be much reduced. But when all the facts of the case are taken into consideration, it is no longer correct to say that perfect competition wins out on that score. For though a concern that has to accept and cannot set prices would, in fact, use all of its capacity that can produce at marginal costs covered by the ruling prices, it does not follow that it would ever have the quantity and quality of capacity that big business has created and was able to create precisely because it is in a position to use it 'strategically'. Excess capacity of this type may – it does in some and does not in other cases – constitute a reason for claiming superiority for a socialist economy. But it should not without qualification be listed as a claim to superiority of the perfectly competitive species of capitalist economy as compared with the 'monopoloid' species.

On the other hand, working in the conditions of capitalist evolution, the perfectly competitive arrangement displays wastes of its own. The firm of the type that is compatible with perfect competition is in many cases inferior in internal, especially technological, efficiency. If it is, then it wastes opportunities. It may also in its endeavors to improve its methods of production waste capital because it is in a less favorable position to evolve and to judge new possibilities. And, as we have seen before, a perfectly competitive industry is much more apt to be routed – and to scatter the bacilli of depression – under the impact of progress of external disturbance than is big business. In the last resort, American agriculture, English coal mining, the English textile industry are costing consumers much more and are affecting *total* output much more injuriously than they would if controlled, each of them, by a dozen good brains.

Thus it is not sufficient to argue that because perfect competition is impossible under modern industrial conditions – or because it always has been impossible – the large-scale establishment or unit of control must be accepted as a necessary evil inseparable from the economic progress which it is prevented from sabotaging by the forces inherent in its productive apparatus. What we have got to accept is that it has come to be the most powerful engine of that progress and in particular of the long-run expansion of total

J. A. Schumpeter

output not only in spite of, but to a considerable extent through, this strategy which looks so restrictive when viewed in the individual case and from the individual point of time. In this respect, perfect competition is not only impossible but inferior, and has no title to being set up as a model of ideal efficiency. It is hence a mistake to base the theory of government regulation of industry on the principle that big business should be made to work as the respective industry would work in perfect competition. And socialists should rely for their criticisms on the virtues of a socialist economy rather than on those of the competitive model.

References
1. D. D. HUMPHREY, 'The nature and meaning of rigid prices, 1890–1933', *Journal of Political Economy*, October 1937.
2. E. S. MASON, 'Price inflexibility', *Review of Economic Statistics*, May 1938.
3. R. F. KAHN, 'Some notes on ideal output', *Economic Journal*, March 1935.

Part Two Applied Theory and Measurement

Despite Schumpeter's reminders of the welfare-conferring
characteristics of large size and monopolistic power, we have
no definitive statement of principle in this area of thought.
Economists are properly appreciative of economies of scale,
and the importance of adequate finance for technological
research and economic innovation: but they are equally
aware of the dangers of foreclosure of entry into an industry,
and of arbitrary pricing, the empire-building propensities of
businessmen and the risk of simple stagnation where no
competition is there to stimulate. In their search for the safer
principle, economists tend to hold to a presumption in favour
of competition. Competition, as well as being more appropriate
to an open society, insures against the possibility of massive
error in a monolithic industry organization. Where there are
a number of minds at work, resources are never all committed
to one course of action: and there is always scope for one part
of the industry to experiment and adjust. Hence the theory, or
technique, of workable competition – a pragmatic view of
what kind of applications of competitive theory best fit the
conditions of the market economy. Freedom of entry into
industry, independent action on the part of each market rival,
and a reasonable number of competitors, are the main criteria
of those who, in a practical way, wish to preserve free
competition. There is one other device which can preserve a
balance. As Galbraith shows, a monopolistic situation can
generate a monopsonistic reaction on the other side of the
market: and if 'countervailing power' does not arise
naturally it can be artificially stimulated. In the distribution
of consumer goods, which absorbs about one-third of their retail

value, the practice of resale price maintenance can eliminate one of the most effective forms of economic adjustment – price competition. Yamey analyses the dangers of this very simple and effective restriction of competition.

5 The U.S.A. Attorney General's Committee on Anti-Trust Laws

Workable Competition

Excerpt from chapter 7 of *The Report of the Attorney General's Nationa Committee to Study Anti-Trust Laws*, U.S. Government Printing Office, Washington, 1955.

[. . .]

In seeking to clarify economic concepts which may be of use to the law in the analysis of market forces, a central preliminary task is to define the circumstances under which competition theoretically becomes 'effective' from the economic point of view, in preventing a concern or a group of concerns acting in concert from having 'effective' monopoly power. For this purpose, the issues center on 'effective' or 'workable' competition or its absence.

The concept of 'workable' or 'effective' competition can perhaps best be described as the economists' attempt to identify the conditions which could provide appropriate leads for policy in assuring society the substance of the advantages which competition should provide. It is a kind of economist's 'rule of reason' – not, of course, to be confused with the legal rule of reason, but analogous to it in the sense that it is also an acknowledgement of the inevitability of the exercise of human judgement and discretion in classifying different forms of economic behavior.

The basic characteristic of effective competition in the economic sense is that no one seller, and no group of sellers acting in concert, has the power to choose its level of profits by giving less and charging more. Where there is workable competition, rival sellers, whether existing competitors or new or potential entrants into the field, would keep this power in check by offering or threatening to offer effective inducements, so long as the profits to be anticipated in the industry are sufficiently attractive in comparison with those in other employment, when all risks and other deterrents are taken into account. The result would be to force the seller who sought to increase his profits above this level by employing a high-price, limited-output monopoly policy either to give it up, or to lose ground to his rivals at a rate sufficient to reduce his profits, thus defeating his policy. In an effectively competitive market, the individual seller cannot control his rivals' offerings, and those offerings set narrow limits on his discretion as to price and production. He must, in the light of his own costs, adjust his offerings to a market scale of prices for offerings of different quality or attractiveness. In the moderately long run, he must accept market prices determined by changes in supply and demand beyond any effect which may be attributable to his own change in price or output. These market conditions inflict penalties on high costs or poor services. To bring this result about, it is necessary that rivals be free in fact to compete by lower prices and better service or products and selling activities, if they can achieve low enough costs to enable them to do so: and that no seller have power to limit this freedom of his rivals, and thus escape the pressures and penalties which effective competition imposes.

The market pressures which effective competition imposes upon each seller derive from the self-interested rivalry of his competitors. The essential character of this rivalry is to promote the competitor's economic interest by offering buyers inducements attractive enough to cause them to deal with him, in free bargaining, and in the face of inducements offered by his rivals. The inducements consist of quantity, quality, time and place of delivery, incidental services, selling effort and price. The chief enabling condition is efficient operation. The rivalry may take the form of trying to enlarge one's share of the market by offering something more attractive than one's competitors, or to avoid a reduction of one's share of the business by offsetting the superior attractions of rivals' offers. In other words, competition includes both aggressive and defensive tactics.

Competitive rivalry in a given business situation may or may not be capable of developing enough force to deny any one seller or group of sellers acting in concert effective power to control the price they will charge, and other conditions of sale. Whether this condition is achieved normally depends on the character of the market. Active competition, for example, may involve initial moves by one competitor, the responses of the buyers, and the further responses of rival sellers. In some cases, the distinction between effective and ineffective competition may depend in part upon the speed of these responses, both the absolute and relative speed, and the certainty or uncertainty of buyers' responses and rivals' responses. The character of these responses may be affected not only by the aggressiveness and business policies of the rival sellers and buyers, but by their number, relative size and the nature of their expectations.

The market pressures of effective competition can be, and should properly be, quite severe. The firm rendering service inferior to that of its rivals would be seriously handicapped; and a firm maintaining superiority over its rivals has a prospect of increasing its volume of trade progressively at their expense so long as it can maintain this superiority. The penalties of unsuccessful competition may take the form of either a positive shrinkage or a failure to expand, and may be viewed in a short-term or a long-run perspective. It is ordinarily poor business policy, to attempt to squeeze out the utmost profit that can be made in a single year, at least where other firms can enter the field, or where substitute goods or services are at all available. In an effectively competitive market, if one seller is shortsighted enough to attempt this, others will grow at his expense. The law need not concern itself with good managerial practice in this regard since it is sufficiently assured by the market itself, provided the conditions of market rivalry are sufficiently free, active, and healthy.

Definition of 'The Market'

In evaluating the market forces which together would characterize effective competition, the rivalry of close substitutes which may, for other purposes, be classified as belonging in other industries has, in varying degree, the same kind of effect as that of competing producers of the same or differentiated products or services classified within the same industry. Technical advance has often made the rivalry of close substitutes quite effective. But this general fact says nothing about the effectiveness of competition in any given market. It emphatically does not mean that public policy can afford to be indifferent to the elimination of competition within the industry. In the interest of rivalry that extends to all buyers and all uses, competition among rivals within the industry is always important.

For purposes of economic analysis, the 'market' is the sphere of competitive rivalry within which the crucial transfer of buyers' patronage from one supplier of goods or services to another can take place freely. The boundaries of an 'industry' or 'market' will often be uncertain and controversial, and a definition appropriate in one case may be inappropriate in another. For our purposes, a market is an economic relationship among sellers and buyers, whose boundaries are not necessarily defined by geographical area alone, nor by conventional product classifications. To ascertain whether a firm or group of firms acting in concert has monopoly power, the 'market' should include all firms whose production has so immediate and substantial an effect on the prices and production of the firms in question that the actions of the one group cannot be explained without direct and constant reference to the other. One should include in a market all firms whose products are in fact good and directly available substitutes for one another in sales to some significant group of buyers, and exclude all others. Where the products of different industries compete directly as alternatives for the same use, the market for that class of products should include the rival goods supplied by different industries. One should combine into one market two or more products (or two or more areas) if an appreciable fall in the price of one product (or in one area) will promptly lead to a relatively large diversion of purchasers from the other product (or area). The appropriate market area may be international, national, regional or local.

Tests of Performance

The economists' distinction between 'effective monopoly' and 'effective competition' does not turn on whether the industry in question is progressively managed or technologically advanced, nor on its policies with regard to wages, profits or high- or low-price programs. Effective competition is not a matter of the motives or policies of businessmen. The ultimate question in distinguishing 'effective monopoly' from 'effective competition' is whether the pressures of the market situation are such as tend of themselves to

bring about the main beneficial effects which constitute the economic reasons why we try to maintain competition in our economy.

The process of adjusting the employment of resources to the
pressures and demands of a workably competitive market is one
of the chief means through which the diffusion of the benefits of
competition takes place. In the long run, effective competition,
implying the expansion (or contraction or withdrawal) of existing
firms, or the entry of new ones, would reduce (or raise) the profit
for a representative firm with respect to any particular product
or service towards the point where bringing forth the supply earns
no more than could be earned in alternative employments of the
capital, labor, and management involved. The long-run tendency
of effective competition to equalize the attractiveness of investment
throughout the economy operates as among industries, as among
the firms in any given industry, and within the business firm itself,
which is guided by the relative profitability of the various products
which it makes or can make. However, beyond the broadest
identification of trends, industrywide profit averages have significance only in measuring the comparative pull of different industries in their competition for capital – that is, the comparative
profit and risk prospects of different industries. For firms, not industries, are the units through which economic decisions are made.
The constant and often severe – and properly severe – pressure of
competition to drive rates of profit throughout the economy
towards minimum levels is consistent with continuingly high rates
of return for firms with better-than-average location, resources,
efficiency or rate of innovation. Where firms produce more than
one product, cost allocation may afford only a crude and imperfect guide to the relative profitableness of different products,
and business policy may diverge from such indications as it does
give. But a considerable check on such divergence may come from
the competition of rival firms which differ in their product-mix.
And the general force of competition in this direction, even if
deferred by imperfect knowledge and foresight, is of unquestioned
importance in multi-product industries.

The impact of effective competition on profits throughout the
economy, and thus on the flow of capital to alternative uses, is one
of its most important functions. However, it is altogether normal
in a competitive economy that a given industry or group of firms

in an industry, each acting independently, can earn extremely high (or low) profits at any given time, and over considerable periods of time. For such profits are the signals through which a market economy attracts capital and other resources to more productive uses, and drives them out of less productive uses.

For these reasons reduction of costs and moderation of profits, like other tests of 'progressive' performance in industry, do not prove the existence, nor their absence the lack, of effective competition. The rate of technical progress, and the level of profit in a firm or an industry, can reflect many forces other than the presence or absence of effective competition. In some cases, in conjunction with other more material facts, they may be considered to furnish collateral or corroborative evidence of the nature and significance of competitive forces in the industry.

In terms of progress, a young industry, or one in process of exploiting recent basic or significant improvement inventions or scientific discoveries, might make a better showing than an older and more mature industry, although the latter might be more competitive. Regardless of whether it is competitive or monopolistic, an industry with declining demand might show a very low rate of profit. On the other hand, a monopolistic industry, with dynamic management and active research, might perform better, for example, in the sense of cost reductions, than a fairly competitive branch of industry which is inferior in these characteristics. Our public policy, however, is founded on the economically sound assumption that competition will on the average result in much more progressiveness and efficiency than monopoly.

Summary of Factors Bearing on Identification of Workable Competition

What aspects of the market situation are significant in determining whether or not it is effectively competitive from the economic point of view? The short-hand legal definition of monopoly – 'power ... to raise prices or to exclude competition when it desired to do so' – focuses directly on the ultimate economic elements of the problem. The economic definition of workable competition concentrates on the effective limits it sets on the power of a seller, or group of sellers acting in concert, over their price.

That power cannot normally be retained for long without natural or imposed limitations on the opportunity for entry or growth of rivals. Restriction on the entry of rival firms is an integral part of the economic as it is of the legal definition of monopoly power, for competitive results are often less likely in a market where entry is not reasonably free. The factors listed below are considered some of the more important in summing up the economic aspects of workable competition. They indicate some of the types of information that may be used in determining whether from an economic standpoint, effective competition exists. Of the 10 factors enumerated, the first 3 are the most general. But all the factors are in varying degrees elements of market situations which bear directly on the presence or absence of effective competition, in the sense in which that term is used in this section, that is, a seller's power over his own price.

Several members emphasize that the first three factors are not only more general but overwhelmingly more important. Freedom of entry is basic but the ultimate test of freedom of entry is the appearance of new rivals; and independence of action of rivals is also basic but independence is highly correlated with the number of rivals – so the number (and relative size) of firms is especially strategic. The minor and equivocal information provided by the other factors should not obscure this broad verdict of economic analysis.

(1) *A Number of Effective Competitive Sellers: The Issue of Relative Size*

The number and relative strength of firms necessary to effective competition cannot be compressed into a formula. The answer to the question depends also on other factors, including those hereafter discussed, so that a given number of firms might be compatible with effective competition in one industry and not in another. Size in the abstract is meaningless. Whatever significance it has exists only in relation to a particular market. Absolute size, as measured by number of employees, or dollars of assets, or similar formulae, has no significance in determining the presence or absence of workable competition. The interrelation and relative importance in different situations of the various factors bearing on the presence or absence of effective competition have not yet been fully isolated and measured by economics. However, where firms are few in number, special study would usually be needed to determine whether an industry were workably competitive.

For effective competition, in the economic sense, to exist, there should be that degree of self-interested independent rivalry in any given market that exists where there is no one firm or group of firms acting in concert which have effective monopoly power, as heretofore defined. By this we mean that no one firm or group of firms acting in concert could hold for long the power to choose its level of profits by giving less and charging more, or to exclude the entry into the market of alternate sources of supply.

Unless numbers are already large in a given market, a reduction of numbers may involve some reduction of competition, although not necessarily a lessening to the point of 'effective' monopoly. Where genuine economies of large scale operations, or other considerations (including the capacity to innovate), permit only very small numbers of sellers, added vigilance is indicated as to other requisites of effective competition.

Effective competition may be affected not only by the total number of sellers: their relative size and strength must also be considered. This does not mean that close equality of size among the various firms is essential for workable competition to exist, but only that the rivalry should not depend entirely upon sellers who are so weak or inefficient as to exist by sufferance. For such firms are not independent, and are not properly counted among the number of effectively competitive sellers; and as the number of independent sellers reaches unity, the market obviously reaches monopoly. The presence in any market of a unit much stronger than the others is a factor to be closely examined for its bearing on the workably competitive character of that market, and on the issue of whether any firm in fact exists only by sufferance, but by itself is not indicative of the absence of workable competition.

Where the number of sellers is large, each one of them faces an impersonal market with a market price which he can take or leave. He can do little to affect total supply or to raise the market price.

When sellers are few, each producing a significant share of total market supply, each seller is aware of the fact that any substantial change in his price or his production will have an appreciable effect upon total market supply and market price, and will tend to elicit responsive changes in the prices and outputs of his rivals. Hence there is a mutual awareness rather than an impersonal market relationship. Where such a market is isolated from competitive pressures, the possibility of successful collusion is greater, to detect it is harder, and its rewards may be more immediate and tempting. Hence there is need for vigilance in scrutinizing such industries, without prejudging whether in fact any type of conspiracy exists. When sellers are few, even in the absence of conspiracy, the market itself may not show many of the characteristics of effective competition, and in fact may not be effectively competitive in the economic sense.

(2) *Opportunity for Entry*

From the economic point of view, relative freedom of opportunity for entry of new rivals is a fundamental requisite for effective competition in the long run. Without this condition, it is idle to expect effective competition. The entry and withdrawal of firms, whether new firms or existing firms from other market areas, or other industries, or other stages of production and marketing, is the basic mechanism of the market for achieving its economic results. The cost of entry into the competitive area should not be impracticably high. This does not imply an absolute criterion for ease of entry in terms of a given number of dollars. Nor does it deny recognition to the fact that as a practical matter, the size of minimum adequate investment capital and other factors may make the entry of new firms into even a competitive industry a relatively slow or hazardous process. But it does mean that under prevailing conditions as to the availability of capital, an attempt by existing firms to raise prices considerably above the competitive norm would make it profitable and practicable for new firms or existing borderline firms to invade the field. In economic terms, this means that conditions of cost for a new firm should not be excessively higher, at least after a reasonable period of initial development, than conditions of cost for an existing member of the industry. In many cases, of course, the new firm may start with the cost advantage of being able to use the most advanced available techniques.

Reasonable opportunity for outsiders with requisite skill to enter

79

the market may appear dispensable, for if there are a sufficient number of competitors, and they compete vigorously, what purpose would be served by additional numbers? But if energetic and imaginative rivals cannot enter, the boldest and most rewarding innovations may be excluded.

New firms entering an industry may not all survive. Some may be weeded out in the competitive struggle, sometimes indeed after making their contribution either to pricing or to business methods. But reasonable opportunity for entry is needed if there is to be assurance of a sufficient number of sellers to maintain effective competition and thus prevent markets from evolving gradually into a state of monopolistic stability. The exclusion of new rivals may be a major impairment of competition in itself and the power to exclude rivals is usually associated with the power to eliminate rivalry between those already in the industry.

(3) *Independence of Rivals*

A primary condition of workable competition in an economic sense is that there be genuine independence on the part of the business units in an industry, so that each firm pursues its own individual advantage. In industries with numerous sellers, concerted action is difficult to achieve without relatively visible machinery of cooperation. Where there are only a limited number of sellers, however, concerted action can be subtle and informal, and sometimes difficult to detect. In all industries, it is normal for sellers to try to take the reactions of rivals into account in determining their own competitive policies; where there are few sellers it may be easier to forecast such reactions. This may or may not impair competition, depending on whether or not the initiator of a competitive move can expect to retain an improved market position after his rivals have responded. Fewness of sellers does not necessarily lead to mutual interdependence of policies, but it may do so.

(4) *Predatory Preclusive Practices*

There should be no predatory preclusive tactics, such that their natural effect would be to enable the user to eliminate rivals without regard to their efficiency, or at least to place them under serious handicaps irrelevant to their efficiency. It should be noted as a practical matter that predatory competition in this sense can usually only be waged where a considerable degree of market power already exists, or where an attempt is being made to use a long purse in order to destroy or coerce rivals. Such conduct is regarded therefore as symptomatic either of monopoly or the intent to monopolize, or both, although it may not be necessary for those possessing market power in high degree to use such methods in order to gain or to keep monopolistic advantages from their position. Conversely, the accusation of 'predatory' or 'cutthroat' practices often turns out on examination not to stem from the abuse of significant degrees of market power, but from the uncomfortably active pressures of competition itself. Only by examining the facts, including the market, is it possible to answer these important questions, among others: whether the low prices or other alleged predatory acts were temporary and for the purpose of destroying or coercing rivals; or whether they were undertaken to meet competition, or to increase profits under high level production at low cost, or for some equally proper competitive purpose; whether the profit-seeking interests of the company under attack would have been served by predatory or oppressive tactics; and so forth. These facts bear not on the justification for predatory conduct – there is none – but on the issue of whether such conduct exists.

(5) *Rate of Growth of the Industry or Market*

The speed with which an industry is growing is not a direct economic indicator of the state of competition within it. An industry may be actually in decline and yet be actively effectively competitive. For example, an industry may decline because the demand for its products is declining and yet there may still be competitive rivalry for shares of the remaining market. Rate of growth, however, is often important in determining the significance to be attached to other factors, and particularly to numbers and reasonable opportunity for entry.

The rate of growth or expansion of a market can, for example, strongly color the significance to competition of the number and relative size of the firms, and alter the effectiveness of barriers to entry. The expected rate of growth of the industry affects the attitudes and expectations of firms in the industry, the attractiveness of the industry to outside firms, and the possibility of maintaining positions of market power without severe restrictions on entry. In a new and rapidly expanding industry, the opening of new markets and the high rate of technical progress usually characteristic of such situations make for uncertainty as to the most profitable policies. The entrance of new firms, if it takes place, may lead to further unsettlement of industry policies and under these circumstances, firms may grow without imposing losses on their rivals. In so far as any given number of firms find it possible to have a tight hold on a stable industry, they can hold their position more readily than the same firms in an industry that is open to rapid expansion. If such firms are not disposed to engage in competitive activity, they may, by their passivity, not only discourage the entry of rivals, but of new techniques which might, in turn, permit the industry to reduce costs and to expand. On the other hand, such passivity itself may well prove a substantial incentive to the entry of newcomers who might otherwise be deterred by the prospect of immediate, active stiff competition.

(6) *Character of Market Incentives to Competitive Moves*

Competition may be effective or ineffective, depending upon how the market is organized and behaves, and according to what incentives there are for independent competitive actions: the hope of gain for the individual seller, and the risk of loss. The strength of these incentives may depend on factors which are in themselves neutral and become important only as they influence incentives. The intervals between a competitive move and the expected response, for example, are not themselves *indicia* of effective competition or its absence. But they come under study in seeking to determine whether incentives are relatively strong or weak.

In general, and outside of such specialized markets as organized exchanges and others of similar character, effective competition may hinge on the condition that the initiator of a competitive action can expect a gain in volume of business at least for a time. That is, the customers' response to an inducement may be quicker than rivals' responses for at least long enough to provide a pay-out period for the competitive action. The incentive to innovation, to price changes, or to other directly competitive moves is an interval during which an innovator may reasonably expect to have an advantage because his moves cannot be met and neutralized promptly enough by his rivals.

Where these competitive moves are not promptly matched and offset, therefore, or where uncertainty exists as to the pattern of rival responses, an influence exists which, *other things being equal*, provides inducements for effective competitive rivalry. Where uncertainty prevails – perhaps because of the presence of a company which refuses to follow prevailing patterns – sellers may be more likely to conclude that they have a chance to make a gain from a competitive innovation, than if the system of market responses had been securely built up by past habits, agreements, or experience. The mere existence and quick dissemination of information on price changes is not of itself evidence either way. But co-operative efforts by an industry to eliminate uncertainty and promote instant knowledge for everybody of everybody else's price may be a device to curb price cutting. Thus, a conviction that rivals will respond immediately may discourage any independent competitive action.

One circumstance that favors a time interval for gain through innovation or price reductions or other competitive moves is the fact that the initiator of a competitive move may gain business at the expense of all his competitors, thus gaining more than any one of them loses, so that they do not have the same decisive need to retaliate.

While information on continued price rigidities may be some indication of the existence or absence of incentives to competitive moves, such information cannot of itself be determinative from an economic standpoint of either effective monopoly or effective competition. Monopolies may change prices in their own interests, and competitive industries may have periods of stable demand and supply conditions. Price changes, or the absence thereof, must therefore be considered in their market settings in order to evaluate their significance.

(7) *Product Differentiation and Product Homogeneity*

The definition of the word 'market', and that of workable competition itself, both turn on the actual and direct competition a seller confronts from the closely related products of others. An important factor in determining the boundaries of the market is the knowledge of buyers as to the alternatives open to them. If other conditions are equal, it would seem for this reason to follow that the more homogeneous the product of rival sellers, the more easily buyers could switch from the output of one competitor to that of others; and therefore the wider the market and the greater the degree of competition in it.

The effect of product differentiation depends on the market setting in which it is placed. Extreme production differentiation, by tending to insulate the demand for one product against that for rival products, may allow real positions of monopoly to develop. Relatively mild differentiation of products within a market otherwise effectively competitive, however, may be a factor favorable to the intensiveness of competition, including price competition and competition in quality. This will tend to be most forcibly the case if the product differentiation reflects product rivalry, that is, product improvement, rather than mere heterogeneity of closely similar products. For product differentiation, especially if it constitutes or embodies a genuine innovation, may be a means whereby the seller can take advantage of the time interval the market allows within which he can expect to gain from a competitive move. Particularly if the situation is such as to justify uncertainty as to the speed and completeness with which rivals will counter the initial move, such a move, in the form of product differentiation, may contribute to the competitiveness of market behavior. This would not be the case if the innovation is fortified by obstacles to imitation by rival producers, or obstacles to the sale of cheaper and simpler models. Thus the impact of product differentiation on the effectiveness of competition will, as in the case of all the other factors mentioned, have to be judged in each case in its market setting, and in relation to more central *indicia* of effective competition. It is not, as such, evidence either way.

The fact that product homogeneity is the rule in a given market may be a significant element in determining the kind of market structure needed for effective competition. Product homogeneity may increase the zone of competition. Where the primary factors in the market situation indicate little question as to the effectiveness of competition, clearly this result will follow. The active and effective competition on organized exchanges and like markets depends upon product homogeneity within grades. But, in other markets, special inquiry may be required to determine whether product homogeneity tends to reduce any one seller's chance to gain through a competitive move. Where, in such markets, there is substantial product homogeneity, an open reduction of price is almost certain to be met instantly although, if not so met, a gain in volume as a result of the move is assured.

(8) *Meeting or Matching the Prices of Rivals*

The above analysis of the varying effects which product homogeneity and differentiation may have on competition in the economic sense in different market settings has a bearing also on the question of meeting or matching the prices of competitors. It is of the essence of effective competition that competitors should try to meet, or offer an equivalent for, any superior inducement which one of them offers. Meeting a rival's inducements is the means whereby competition diffuses the gains of productive efficiency. To forbid a seller to meet his rival's price would involve a *reductio ad absurdum*, so long as the market structure itself is untouched. For example, in the case of homogeneous products, if A only part-way meets B's price, it does A no good – he still cannot sell his goods – and if A more than meets B's price, then B cannot sell his goods, or not until he in turn has more than met A's price. Under these circumstances, in the absence of a change in demand, there is no place where competitive price can level off, and no adjustment permitting a number of competitors to remain in the market in question, unless a seller is permitted to meet his competitor's price. This is the error in holding that a firm is not competing unless it is exceeding its rival's prices.

However, effective competition also involves freedom to undercut rivals' prices. Thus an inflexible requirement that any existing price may be met, but not undercut, would mean that when demand falls off, or when there is a reduction in cost, the decline in price which would follow under effective competition might be aborted, because it would be to no one's interest to make the first move, since it would be matched forthwith. In many such situations, it would be to everyone's interest not to cut prices.

Effective competition is therefore compatible either with meeting (or matching) the prices of rivals, or with undercutting them. Furthermore, prices uniform as among the respective sellers may under the pressure of falling demand give way to a period of undercutting, after which price again settles down to uniformity at a lower level. Hence these are not two mutually exclusive patterns, and price uniformity as of any given short period is not significant, even when the costs of various sellers are widely different from one another. But a rigid uniformity over periods of changing supply and demand, or a persistent failure by firms to increase or decrease prices when their independent self-interest would seem to dictate such a move, is not usually compatible with workable competition. This is a problem altogether distinct and apart from the legal question of whether a complex and rigid system of price-setting and price-changing can only be explained by an agreement or conspiracy. The legal problem transcends although it includes the economic. But any rule, public or private, which forbade the meeting of prices, or one which forbade the undercutting of prices, would be a rule against workable competition.

A climate more stimulating to effective competition might be introduced into such a market in several possible ways, including: new entry, if large profits were being made; price discrimination; variations in the product or in the other terms of the bargain; a change in the structure of the market, by an increase in the number of sellers; or utilization of other competitive devices such as product, service and customer relations improvement and more effective selling. This should not be interpreted as a general recommendation of a policy of discrimination, but is meant merely to point out some of the available alternatives in situations of this kind. Perhaps something could be accomplished by not preventing – and certainly by forbidding private groups the power to prevent – a reasonable variety and variability in pricing practices.

(9) *Excess Capacity*

'Excess capacity' is a term difficult to define satisfactorily, and even more difficult to identify. The term is commonly used to describe capacity unused during a general depression, as well as 'excesses' of capacity which may be generated by investment booms in competitive industries. Both these senses should be distinguished from the excess of capacity confronted by a declining industry. In a period of generally good business, for a growing or stable business, the existence of unused capacity, which could be utilized at or near prevailing costs, may help to demonstrate the presence of either effective monopoly or effective competition in connexion with other facts. If the companies in an industry tend generally to pursue policies of making more money by charging high prices and restricting production, the industry may have chronic excess capacity as a result. The practice of a company purchasing and dismantling unused capacity in this sense – that is, capacity which could be utilized at normal costs – has always and rightly been considered strong evidence of attempt to monopolize. On the other hand, a moderate and varying amount of excess capacity naturally tends to develop from time to time as a result of expansion or in response to the rise and fall of demand in a competitive industry, or incident to competitive efforts of producers to increase their share of the market. And its presence is favorable to the effectiveness of competition, if other criteria of competition are present. It permits producers to handle added business at no great increase in unit cost of production, or even at a decrease in average unit costs, depending upon cost conditions at the time. And, as business approaches conditions in which efficient capacity is fully utilized at high profit, a failure on the part of the industry to expand in response to high levels of demand and profit might suggest the possibility of some restrictive arrangement to prevent the normal response of a competitive market.

(10) *Price Discrimination*

Some types of price discrimination may stimulate effective competition; others may be evidence of effective monopoly, in the economic sense. Before proceeding to examine the differences among the various types of price discrimination, a word of preliminary warning is in order.

Price discrimination as seen by an economist not only is not necessarily the same as 'price discrimination' in the sense followed or applied in decisions under the *Robinson-Patman Act*, but it may be entirely antithetical. Furthermore, even when a price structure happens to be discriminatory in both senses, this may be evidence of either effectively monopolistic or effectively competitive forces, depending on its setting. Finally, even when price discrimination in an economic sense (whether or not in the sense proscribed under the *Robinson-Patman Act*) is evidence of departures from conditions of effective competition, it does not necessarily result in or denote violation of law.

Price discrimination, in the economic sense, occurs whenever and to the extent that there are price differences for the same product or service sold by a single seller, and not accounted for by cost differences or by changes in the level of demand; or when two or more buyers of the same goods and services are charged the same price despite differences in the cost of serving them. In order to know when there is or is not price discrimination, in the economic sense, between two or more buyers, it is necessary to know not only the price but also the total costs applicable to each class of transaction under comparison.

From the economic point of view, no particular definition of 'price' is required; 'price' is simply what the buyer has paid the seller as consideration for the goods and related services he has sought and purchased; nor is any close definition of the 'goods' or 'products' required except that there be some substantial elements of comparability. 'Cost', for analysis of situations contemplated in this section of our Report, means average cost. The idea that the cost of serving a given buyer is less than that of serving other buyers, for no other reason than that this buyer's additional purchases spread the overhead, imputes arbitrarily to a particular buyer the savings of larger volume. And such cost differences as are relevant are those consistently characteristic of the categories of business being compared, not transitory or incidental differences. The actual lower costs of serving one or more buyers can arise from a great variety of circumstances. The product sold to some buyers may be physically somewhat different, in lacking certain appliances or finishing touches or quality. There may be differences in the services which go along with the goods to form the complete package for which consideration is given – such services as delivery, packaging, storage, credit extension, risk of default, handling, clerical attention, sales force attention, and many others. There may for these or other reasons be savings on large quantities sold, or on large volume over some time period (entirely apart from the savings arising from spreading the overhead); but large quantities or volumes, without more, are not necessarily more economical. These are all matters of factual detail.

Because many costs, particularly distribution costs, involve large elements of overhead, it may be difficult or impossible to estimate cost differentials with great precision. This is not to say, however, that the task should not be done, nor that cost differentials should be deemed not to exist, in the absence of precise estimates.

Occasional statements in the economic literature that price discrimination is proof of the existence of monopoly elements have been widely misunderstood and, as misunderstood, repeated by non-economists. Under pure competition (and *a fortiori* under perfect competition) no price discrimination could exist. Every seller would sell at the going price and would have no power to charge more and no need to take less. But any attempt to infer from this that price discrimination, in the economic sense, is 'inherently monopolistic' or presumptively anti-competitive, is implicit acceptance of pure or perfect competition as a workable goal of public policy. We have already shown that the terms 'pure' and 'perfect' mean merely precise or complete in the theoretical sense, not ideal or desirable. We therefore repudiate pure and perfect competition as direct goals of anti-trust policy. We do, however, recognize that under workable competition there should exist substantial pressure driving the price of any given product or service toward uniformity, and toward its cost of production, so that there is a potent incentive for a business firm to maintain satisfactory profits over the long run by innovation in products or processes. The constant efforts of businessmen are and ought to be to get into new and higher-margin markets; and the constant effect of competition is to narrow margins in some markets as compared with others, for the leveling force is not felt with equal speed everywhere at the same time. Some amount of discrimination in the economic sense is therefore an inevitable part of the business scene. It remains to examine the circumstances under which it may be considered evidence of workable competition or of workable monopoly.

A single monopolist firm, or a group of firms exerting monopoly power in concert, would find it most profitable to divide up their customers and exact from each one the maximum that he could be made to pay. Such a scheme of discrimination would require that customers paying lower prices be prevented from reselling to those paying higher prices. The monopolist would need to control the product to point of final use, possibly by contract. If resale were practical, then competition among the customers would cause all the product to move through the lower-priced buyers, discrimination thus tending to disappear.

Price discrimination may also take the form of predatory price cutting in selected areas or on selected products in order to eliminate competitors or to force them to follow a price or other policy. The essence of this conduct is its temporary nature; for it only exists in order that prices may eventually be raised once rivals are removed or coerced. Such predatory price discrimination must, however, be carefully distinguished from vigorous competition, where prices are not cut for such temporary purposes, but in order to permit more efficient firms to earn higher profits at low prices than at high prices, or for some other equally competitive reason.

A milder form of what might be regarded as price discrimination in the economic sense, although not in the *Robinson–Patman Act* sense, may be practiced by a seller who keeps his prices very low or barely remunerative on products facing competition, while maintaining higher prices and profit margins on other products free from competition or facing less competition. In *United States* v. *United Shoe Machinery Corp.*, for example, the court considered this type of price discrimination as evidence of monopoly power, but it is significant that it did not attempt to extirpate such discrimination by its decree. Explaining its reasons therefore the court stated: 'Some price discrimination, if not too rigid, is inevitable. Some may be justified as resting on patent monopolies. Some price discrimination is economically desirable, if it promotes competition in a market whose several multi-product firms compete.'

Price discrimination, in the economic sense, may be practiced by a monopolist or by a group of sellers acting in concert, because they wish to build up or protect the position of certain customers, and weaken that of others. But price discrimination may serve to promote competition, and it may be relevant evidence that competition exists and is effective. While price discrimination of the type described above is therefore relevant to a determination of whether significant degrees of market power inhere in any individual company or group of companies acting in concert, further exploration is required to determine whether effective competition exists.

It is equally clear that in some cases differences in price not related to difference in cost may promote competition. Thus price discrimination may serve to disrupt or preclude any collusive or otherwise inter-dependent pricing. The very success of a concerted effort by a group of firms to raise prices above the competitive level by restricting output to less than the competitive level would make it attractive for some or all of the firms to offer better terms to some buyers. There is a tendency for such special bargains to be given more and more widely, as buyers try to play sellers off one against the other; and if the tendency is strong enough to make the special prices become the 'regular' prices in the course of time, the discrimination has served to make the market more competitive.

These examples illustrate the diverse ways in which price discrimination in the economic sense appears in our market system. Where price discrimination is sustained, persistent and stable, it may throw light either on collusion in price-formation, or on the presence of market imperfections so fundamental as to constitute evidence of effective monopoly power. For, when price discriminations are sustained and substantial, they may have far-reaching effects at several levels of competition, and lead to significant departures from standards of workable competition. Price discrimination may be a means of making existing markets less effectively competitive. [. . .]

6 A. Hunter

The Measurement of Monopoly Power

Excerpt from A. Hunter, *Competition and the Law*, Allen & Unwin, London, 1966, chapter 3.

The idea of devising a measure of monopoly power, with reference both to its general incidence and to particular situations, has been and probably always will remain an attractive prospect for economists who wish to probe in this field. Many devices have been tried. Measures directly derived from theoretical models have been proposed such as Lerner's divergence between price and marginal cost; Kalecki's estimated degree of monopoly for the whole economy; Triffin's conceptual arraying of the cross-elasticities of demand of particular companies into groups; and Rothschild's comparison of the slope of a firm's demand curve with the slope of the industry demand curve. Another group of measures are based on statistical series. For example Blair's index of divergence between plant concentration and company concentration. Profit rates of various sorts have been proposed – frequently adjusted on the basis of some theoretical concept or for replacement values – and have received considerable attention. And measurements of the relative price-inflexibility of products and industries have been explored in an effort to estimate the strength of monopolistic or oligopolistic control of markets.

The results of investigations using such measures rarely are satisfactory. First, in a conceptual sense they attempt, invariably, to measure some single aspect of monopolistic behaviour – usually that of control over output and price. This is an unsuitable measure for general analysis since high prices or profits are not necessarily the main or even the most important outcome of monopolistic power especially where restrictive agreements are concerned. Second, few of the proposed measures offer a practicable index in the sense that the data they can employ are readily available in reliable statistical series[1].

Nevertheless, some attempts at measurement have yielded important and significant bodies of information and evidence bearing on the incidence and operations of monopoly, oligopoly and, to a much lesser degree, restrictive practices. In particular, there is one set of measures which is generally accepted in this field as providing useful indicators. These measure industrial concentration. The acceptability and relative success of industrial concentration indexes is due partly to the availability and reliability of the data employed. But to a large extent it also can be accounted for in terms of a more realistic approach. Rather than being based on micro-economic theories of competition the concentration measure starts from what is basically an analysis of the actual structural characteristics of industry. However, success is no more than relative; while the explanatory value of concentration measures is high in terms of industrial structure, its connexions with theoretical concepts are of decidedly low value.

We should be clear on what is being measured. For example, the 'concentration of economic power' is a term frequently used in connexion with industry concentration measures. It makes, as Adelman remarks, a 'resounding phrase'. But it is highly emotive in content and frequently misleading in practice (1). In a superficial fashion it unites two ideas, large size and monopoly power, together in one significant-sounding term – but without being too explicit about the relationship. Analytically-speaking there is, of course, no necessary connexion between the two since monopoly and oligopoly are phenomena which depend on size relative to particular markets and not on any absolute dimension. Big business is not necessarily monopolistic either in structure or intent; nor is small-scale enterprise without monopoly features.

There are three distinct but imperfectly related approaches to the measurement of concentration. The first, using various data

1. F. Machlup, *The Political Economy of Monopoly*, Johns Hopkins Press, 1952, chapter 12, brings together all of these various measures in a single useful discussion of the conceptual and measurement problems involved. See also J. P. Miller in *Business Concentration and Price Policy*, a report of the National Bureau for Economic Research, Princeton University Press, 1955.

from the population of business enterprises (1), measures *changes in concentration for the economy as a whole* (2). Essentially, this procedure makes a comparison of the size structure of all enterprises at different points in time to discover any increase or decrease in the inequality of distribution. A simple tabulation of size distribution of companies at various dates based on stock exchange valuations or the net output data of production censuses provides one possibility. Then a more precise generalization of the degree of concentration can be expressed by a Lorenz curve relating the percentage number of companies of the economy (arranged in order of size) to their per cent possession of total assets. And a Gini coefficient of the inequality of distribution can be taken for different points over time.

But, although instructive, this general picture of concentration (for all enterprises in the economy) is not sufficiently direct. A more useful measure, for the purposes of analysing the significance of big business, concentrates on the percentage share of total assets or employment of all enterprises above a certain size. For example, those with more than 5,000 employees of £100 million assets. A favourite bench-mark is the share of the largest 100 manufacturing or 200 non-financial types of company (1). Most such studies, although not immediately suitable for the study of monopolistic or oligopolistic situations, help us understand the general structure of that part of the economy. They are important in relation to policy matters on, for example, ownership and control questions, the organization of the business economy for purposes of technological development, the diffusion or centralization of the decision-making units of the private sector, the distribution of income, etc.

Second, there is the measurement of *merger movements* which play a significant role in determining industrial concentration. Merger waves occur at certain critical periods in the development of most economies. Their incidence, which can be measured given adequate data and observation, is not always well understood but seems to be related to concentration measures in a particular way: at any given point in time the *absolute* size of companies is mainly the result of their internal growth supported only by the general development of the economy and without substantial assistance from mergers. But merger waves do intervene on occasion to establish the large dominant firms in certain industries and thus determine, for long periods of time, the *relative* size of enterprises for both industry and economy (4).

The third set of measures are the so-called *concentration ratios*. These measure market concentration rather than the concentration of industry in general. Thus, if the net output (or some other criterion of size such as sales or asset values) of the largest three or four enterprises of an industry is divided by the total sales of the industry, the degree of concentration can be expressed as a percentage. This percentage is the concentration ratio of the industry; and an index of concentration can be constructed for all available industries or sub-industries by arranging them in descending order of concentration. Naturally, this third measure of concentration, by which it is hoped to secure some estimate of the likelihood or otherwise of monopolistic practices, is of more direct interest to this study than the other types. But we shall, first of all, give the more general measures of concentration some brief inspection.

Trends in Concentration and Mergers

The most impressive and detailed studies in changes in concentration for the economy as a whole are for the U.S.A. Since that country is also the home of unfettered free enterprise and *a priori* is most likely to demonstrate the more extreme results of uncontrolled concentration development, it is worth our while to give a brief glance at some of these studies.

The most significant early work was the well-known study *The Modern Corporation and Private Property* written by A. A. Berle and G. C. Means in 1932. They found, for the years 1909–29, that 'there exists a centripetal attraction which draws wealth together into aggregations of constantly increasing size'. They saw no limit to development in concentration and predicted that, by 1950, 70 per cent of all corporate activity would be carried on by the 200 largest corporations. A most arresting conclusion and one which precipitated a debate which still continues.

In retrospect, from examination of the Berle and Means study, it appears that for the period 1909–24 their estimates may not have been too reliable owing to the inflation of gross asset values by Stock Exchange evaluations during this period. The extent of this 'water absorption' was great enough to confuse all subsequent investigations. On the other hand the 1924–9 period of their study is not seriously questioned. Also, a later study performed by Means for the National Resources Committee, *The Structure of the American Economy*, vol. 1 (1939), was soundly based. It showed an increase from 48 per cent to 55 per cent for the share held by the 200 largest non-financial companies over the period 1929–33. Even so, to some extent the increase represented a statistical rather than an actual phenomenon: in a period of rapidly falling prices the value of durable assets of large companies became inflated relative to other companies. But partly the increase was a genuine feature of any severe depression period – the ability of large established companies to survive and continue to earn profits.

However, analysis of what can reasonably be termed a more typical depression-free period from 1931–47, by Adelman, shows a different picture (1). In 1931 the largest 139 manufacturing companies (public utilities, financial corporations and legal monopolies excluded) held 49·6 per cent of all manufacturing assets; in 1947 they held 45·0 per cent. A drop of the order of 10 per cent of what they had originally held. Probably this particular computation also contained elements which overstated the movement downwards. But it seemed clear that over a period when big business appeared to flourish and, according to the Federal Trade Commission, concentration had been rapidly increasing, there had in fact been at least a slight decrease. More especially, the massive increase to a 70 per cent share of assets for the largest 200 companies predicted by Berle and Means simply did not materialize. The results of this experience can also be projected backwards to cast some doubt on the already dubious 1909–24 analysis by Berle and Means.

Finally, the position as between 1901 and 1947 was charted by means of a somewhat different technique (1). It appears that, whereas in 1901 about one-third of value-added production in manufacture was produced by companies with concentration ratios of 50 per cent or better, in 1947 the corresponding proportion was about one quarter. Market concentration ratios conceal, as we shall see, certain aspects of vertical integration and consequently understate. But when this result is added to the evidence for other periods calculated differently there seems little doubt that, for the U.S.A.

economy as a whole, concentration has not increased since the nineteenth century. It may even have diminished slightly (1). A most interesting if surprising result.

Merger movements are intimately connected with changes or apparent changes in concentration. And since American opinion is unusually sensitive to the dangers of concentration of economic power, much detailed work goes into their analysis. Three merger waves have been experienced in the U.S.A. Mergers were frequent during the 1870s and 1880s in steel, chemicals, petroleum, canned meat, cigarettes and tobacco. A merger wave culminated these developments during 1879–1903. During this five years there occurred the most remarkable set of mergers ever seen and it transformed industries characterized by small and medium-sized firms into industry groups dominated by one or a few large enterprises. It was a movement producing traditional-type monopolies rather than the nowadays more commonplace oligopolies. (Hence the initiation of the 'trust busting' legislation of the *Sherman Act* during this period.) And it was so great in magnitude, relative to the then population of manufacturing companies, that 'it laid the foundation for the industrial structure that has characterized most of American industry in the twentieth century'. Even by 1955 thirty-one of the largest 100 manufacturing companies of the U.S.A. could date their most important merger to the period before 1905 (5).

The second substantial merger movement took place during 1924–9. It reflected the emergence of, technologically speaking, new industries such as automobiles, aluminium and electrical engineering. But also it was partly an attempt to restore the concentration achieved at the turn of the century which had become somewhat diluted by the emergence of new firms, new products or varieties and by dissolution decrees under the anti-trust laws. (The fate, it seems, of most merger movements.)

Finally a third merger movement occurred after World War II. This turned out to be a much smaller affair both in absolute size of merger activity and relative to the now much larger population of business enterprises. Despite this demonstrably lower rate of merger activity the Federal Trade Commission was led to publish a report stating that: 'If nothing is done to check the growth in concentration either the giant corporation will take over the country or the government will be impelled to step in and impose some form of direct regulation.' Subsequent studies made it evident that this statement was unnecessarily alarmist if not down-right misleading (1). Giants did not combine with giants as in previous merger episodes. Indeed the combination of small companies or medium-sized companies actually reduced market concentration somewhat by offsetting the predominance of the largest companies. And the growth of the economy had made the net effect of new mergers negligible.

Looking back on concentration as a whole in the U.S.A. it now appears fairly certain that concentration increased only slightly from 1905 to 1931 despite the 1924–9 merger movement. Subsequent to 1931 it is difficult to detect any increase at all either for the period 1931–47 or for the period 1939–47. Indeed, the most outstanding feature of the U.S.A. scene seems to be the 'surprising stability' of concentration (1) after the great merger movement of the end of the century had laid down the main pattern of industrial structure.

For Britain, satisfactory estimates showing the progress of concentration for the economy as a whole are much scarcer. The study by Hart and Prais, using a rather special technique, examined concentration trends during 1885–1950 over ten-yearly intervals. It would seem that up to 1939 concentration increased among surviving firms for each of the decades analysed; but that most of this increase was offset by the birth of new firms and industries. Consequently, the net increase in concentration in the economy as a whole for the whole period probably was quite small. For the years 1939–50, although the estimates here are less decisive, the same study suggests that the rapid growth of smaller companies was such as actually to lower the net concentration between these two dates (2). Evely and Little (3), using a quite different set of data and conceptual approach (comparisons of certain market concentration ratios), found themselves unable to say decisively whether industrial concentration had, in general, increased between 1935 and 1950. The negative findings seem to support the view that there was very little increase between the 1930s and 1950s; and there may possibly have been some small reduction. It is perhaps significant that these results parallel the broad trends in U.S.A. concentration over the same periods.

Merger movements played a role in the formation of concentration in Britain much as in the U.S.A. For example, there was an early merger wave almost simultaneous with the 1898–1904 wave in the U.S.A. (6). (The degree of coincidence here is striking although not so far particularly explicable. The two economies were experiencing at the relevant time different rates of growth; they were of different maturities in respect of the stage of their railway development and growth of internal and external markets; legal attitudes to large 'trusts' were quite different; and the company laws which permitted mergers and holding companies had arrived on the scene much earlier in Britain (5).) Industries which consolidated in Britain during the first merger wave included chemicals, explosives, whisky distilling, mineral extraction and iron and steel. There were also mergers in cement, wallpaper, textiles and tobacco which appeared to be undertaken to secure the advantages of a monopolized market (3). And the brewing industry was then undergoing one of its periodical phases of concentration by region and by brand. The official inquiry to the *Committee on Trusts*, reporting in 1918, reflected in its language concern for the situation comparable with that already expressed by official statements in the U.S.A. at the turn of the century. 'We are satisfied that trade associations and combines are rapidly increasing in the country and may within no great distant period exercise a paramount control over all branches of British trade.'

The second merger wave also was duplicated in Britain in the late 1920s and early 1930s. It too seems to have been much less substantial than the first episode. But again the conditions were unlike and, apparently, the motivations to merge were of a different character. Britain, after 1920, suffered a prolonged period of recession which severely affected the staple industries. Thus many of the important mergers of this period were attempts to 'rationalize' industry and overcome surplus capacity problems – for example in the match industry, industrial chains, iron founding, fertilizers and steel tubes. Imperial Chemical Industries, a considerable consolidation of chemical companies, occurred in 1926 partly on account of surplus capacity conditions. In addition, there appeared in the same period, by process of merger, such companies as Unilever (margarine) and Tate & Lyle (sugar) (3).

A third wave of mergers developed in Britain but this time

chronological coincidence did not hold. Whereas in the U.S.A. the third merger wave was mainly in the 1940s, the corresponding movement in Britain was delayed until the late 1950s and early 1960s.

A considered judgement of the effects of concentration trends and merger movements is not easy to give in our present state of knowledge. The documentation and plotting of trends in concentration is, to say the least, imperfect. Only the U.S.A. has anything approaching a continuous series of the relevant phenomena. The British data is deplorably poor. And few other countries have anything other than a cursory analysis of concentration patterns. Further, the level of theoretical explanation for these phenomena is low. Practically no body of analysis exists to explain current levels of concentration for the economy as a whole. Mainly the economist profession has been content to comment on a number of substantially untested relationships between concentration and economies of scale. (On the other hand some critical analysis has been directed towards testing the *necessity* of different levels of concentration notably by Bain (9).) Nor are the phenomena of mergers – their incidence, their role in concentration, the connexion to technology or their necessity for economic growth – satisfactorily accounted for.

The most that can be said is that, in a historical rather than analytical sense, certain facts (and mysteries) have been established. (i) The massive mergers of the turn of the century appear to have been unique in the degree to which they crystallized the industrial structures of the U.S.A. and Britain into a concentration pattern which persists to the present day. (ii) The ebb and flow of merger activity subsequent to the 1890s–1900s phase appears to have had little permanent effect on concentration. Despite the apparent magnitude of many mergers they appear, in the long run, always to have been offset by a sufficient addition to the total population of enterprises. Here and there particular industries, for technological reasons, have concentrated heavily but total concentration has not significantly increased as between 1900 and the 1950s. (iii) An increase in the heterogeneity of product groups together with an associated diversification of the manufacturing interests of enterprises is observable although not so far measured. Thus, whereas the merger movements of the 1900s typically resulted in the creation in Britain of a monopolized industry (salt, wall-paper, petroleum refining, whisky distilling, tobacco) subsequent mergers seemed more likely to create oligopolistic groupings, the members of which are frequently multi-product firms (electrical goods, motor vehicles, chemicals, pharmaceuticals, etc.).

In sum, while there can be little doubt that concentration trends and merger movements present problems and merit close observation, a glance at the long-term experience of Britain and the U.S.A. is reassuring. There seems to be little reason to retain what was for a time a commonly-held view – that increases in concentration in the modern industrial economy are in some sense 'inevitable'.

Market Concentration

The reasons for measuring and subsequently analysing market concentration ratios are clear enough. The number of firms in an industry is one of the main factors determining the overall 'degree of monopoly'. Fewness of firms means, in theoretical terms, a greater incidence of companies with demand curves which are of a relatively low elasticity; more frequent instances of a wide divergence between price and marginal cost; and the general development of conditions in which the interdependence of market policies becomes recognized by companies as being the realistic basis for price determination decisions. In short, oligopolistic and monopolistic situations and the growth of collusive or collaborative practices are more likely to occur where a small number of the larger firms of an industry accounts for the majority of the output of that industry.

To provide a measure or coefficient of this fewness factor seems a useful idea. Concentration ratios attempt to do so – but not by counting the absolute fewness of firms. Instead, for a given small number of the largest firms, the share of the industry's output they account for is expressed as a percentage of the total output of the industry. The number of firms chosen for calculating the ratio usually depends on some fortuitous element – normally the census of production arrangements of the country concerned. In Britain the share of the three largest enterprises of a census industry or sub-industry is the basis for calculation (except where a larger number must be taken in order to avoid disclosing commercial matters of a particular undertaking among the largest firms) (3). In the U.S.A. production censuses the corresponding basis is the four largest firms.

The statistical indicators of market concentration are various. To measure concentration the productive *capacity* of the firms and industry may be chosen but is not normally employed on account of unused, obsolete or excess capacity. *Value of assets* is another indicator but presents problems this time in connexion with methods of accounting and the hazards of market valuation of assets. The *employment* figures of firms and industry is a highly convenient statistic and may be thought relatively unambiguous. But, since large firms can be expected to be capital-intensive and small firms labour-intensive in their productive methods, it can be misleading. However, it may be the only indicator available for measuring the share of activity contributed by small firms in some industries. *Gross output* values (total sales or value of shipments from factory door) is also a convenient measure readily available for most industries. But there is a danger. Since some industries are broadly defined in the census two or more stages of production may be included in the total calculation. There is therefore double counting and the possibility of an overstatement of the extent of concentration for the final product. It depends on the degree of vertical integration in the particular industry. Therefore, on the whole, the most valuable indicator is that of *net output* (value added by manufacture) (3). Certain problems connected with mis-reporting of inter-establishment transfers of production and poor collation of statistics can still occur. But, given adequate census facilities, it has the great advantage that there is no double counting and it is permissible to aggregate the net output of various groupings of industry if this is required. It is also the clearest indicator of the relative importance of different industries in terms of real value.

Certain specialist concentration studies, such as that by Evely and Little, make available several indicators simultaneously and employ them as seems appropriate for various types of problem. For our purposes, however, the breakdown given by the production censuses – for gross output, net output and employment – will suffice to convey the essential ideas.

Table I provides an example of concentration ratios tabulated by net output and employment. Two census years, 1951 and 1958, are

covered and all 125 manufacturing and mining industries, as classified in the 1958 census, are displayed. They are arrayed in the order
of their net output concentration ratios for 1958. Looking at
this Table a certain broad perspective of size structure and concentration in British industry can readily be seen. The relatively high
concentrations to be found in large-scale process industries such as
man-made fibres, explosives, soaps and detergents, cement and
sugar, come out readily. Certain engineering and metal industries
such as steel tubes, telegraph and telephone apparatus, cans and
metal boxes, wire and cable, ordnance and small arms, etc., also
are high. At the other extreme, as one might expect, industries
using traditional methods and organized on a small scale have low-
concentration indices – pottery, tools and implements, stone and
slate quarries, general publishing and printing and the various
clothing trades. The timber, furniture and construction industries
are also low on the index of concentration ratios.

At first glance this would appear to be a satisfactory and reasonably accurate display of the different degrees of concentration of

Table 1

Concentration Ratios in British Industry 1951 and 1958

	Three largest enterprises					
Industry	Net Output	Employ-ment	Net Output	Employ-ment	Net Output	Employ-ment
	1951	1951	1958	1958	1958	1958
	%	%	%	%	£m	'000
Man-made fibres	82	72	89	81	43	29
Mineral-oil refining	35	84	88	85	31	17
Locomotive and track equipment	—	—	60–82	63–85	34	52
Tobacco	74	70	81	77	78	38
Sugar	82	84	79	82	15	17
Explosives and fireworks	46–91	47–93	75	74	28	28
Dyestuffs	67–89	67–89	74	75	22	16
Margarine	64–85	58–77	71	72	7	4
Cement	67–89	66–87	70	71	23	11
Soap, detergents, etc.	71	63	69	58	29	13
Steel tubes	60–79	58–77	66	65	58	43
Salt and non-metalliferous mining	—	—	66	62	10	7

Table 1 – *contd*

| Industry | Three largest enterprises | | | | | |
	Net Output 1951 %	Employ- ment 1951 %	Net Output 1958 %	Employ- ment 1958 %	Net Output 1958 £m	Employ- ment 1958 '000
Watches and clocks	62	60	65	68	5	7
Asbestos	60	53	62	62	13	12
Railway carriages and wagons	—	—	62	67	37	51
Abrasives	53	56	61	55	6	4
Ordnance and small arms	—	—	60	60	31	35
Metalliferous mines and quarries	41	50	59	52	5	4
Telegraph and telephone apparatus	74	72	58	59	36	46
Spirit distilling and compounding	61	67	50–60	50–60	37	12
Cans and metal boxes	46–61	45–60	45–60	41–56	20	23
Insulated wire and cable	48	50	57	59	28	27
Motor cycle and cycle	—	—	57	58	16	21
Veg/animal oils and fats	—	—	55	48	15	8
Fertilizers and pesticides	58	56	54	52	23	14
Synthetic plastics and resins	51	53	54	50	26	15
Linoleum and leathercloth	52	54	53	60	9	9
Coke ovens and manufactured fuel	63	63	52	53	23	15
Polishes	33	41	50	46	5	3
Glass	51	46	50	43	43	35
Cutlery	45–60	25–33	49	40	9	4
Motor vehicles	—	—	47	37	194	127
Agr. machinery (not tractors)	40	32	46	40	10	7
Electric appliances (domestic)	45	49	45	39	22	18
Electric machinery	46	48	43	40	115	104
Cocoa, chocolate and sugar confectionery	38	34	42	36	40	36
Gelatine, adhesives, etc.	41	39	42	42	2	2
Jute	38	38	42	41	4	7
Industrial engines	—	—	42	43	21	23
Aircraft production and repair	47	46	42	41	118	111
Lubricating oils and greases	32	34	43	29	13	4
Coal-tar products	34	36	41	41	4	3
Office machinery	34	39	40	36	12	11
Biscuits	31	34	39	39	19	24
Textile machinery	36	36	38	37	20	22
Miscellaneous manufactures	—	—	38	28	13	9

Table 1 – *contd*

Industry	Three largest enterprises					
	Net Output	Employ-ment	Net Output	Employ-ment	Net Output	Employ-ment
	1951 %	1951 %	1958 %	1958 %	1958 £m	1958 '000
Grain milling	33	31	35	37	29	15
Fruit and vegetable products	—	—	34	29	22	20
Chemicals (general)	36–48	36–49	33	33	83	44
Rope, net and twine	36	24	33	31	3	4
Soft drinks, ciders etc.	18	19	33	19	18	8
Rubber	33	36	32	32	37	39
Hand-truck, perambulators, etc.	29	23	32	30	2	2
Paper and board	19	21	32	33	42	32
Toys and sports goods	—	—	31	31	8	10
Animal and poultry food	45	36	30	19	18	7
Iron and steel (general)	—	—	30	25	111	67
Miscell. electrical goods	—	—	30	30	29	32
Shipbuilding and marine engineering	—	—	30	33	84	110
Bolts, nuts, rivets, etc.	25	28	29	32	14	17
Carpets	24	26	29	29	10	11
Milk products	21	21	28	27	12	8
Stationers' goods	26	22	27	22	4	3
Quarrying and contractors' plant	—	—	27	24	10	11
Newspaper and periodicals	24	25	26	26	48	36
Cardboard box, cartons, etc.	17	18	25	21	12	12
Toilet preparations	41	35	25	26	6	3
Scientific instruments	21	16	24	17	28	20
Pharmaceutical preparations	19	23	23	27	19	14
Paint and printers' ink	—	—	23	19	15	9
Wire and wire manufactures	23	22	23	22	12	11
Starch and miscell. foods	—	—	22	23	7	5
Men and boys' outerwear	—	—	22	23	14	29
Bricks and refractory products	18	17	22	19	14	13
Bedding etc.	17	16	22	17	2	2
Jewellery, precious metals, etc.	—	—	22	18	8	8
Bread and flour confectionery	17	15	22	20	28	31
Mechanical handling	21	23	22	22	11	10
Cotton/rayon spinning and doubling	—	—	22	21	22	42
Bacon, meat and fish products	—	—	21	22	11	13
Brushes and brooms	18	13	21	18	3	3

Table 1 – *contd*

| Industry | Three largest enterprises | | | | | |
	Net Output 1951 %	Employment 1951 %	Net Output 1958 %	Employment 1958 %	Net Output 1958 £m	Employment 1958 '000
Paper and board products	—	—	21	19	15	13
Non-ferrous metals	20	27	21	26	36	39
Textile furnishing	24	22	20	21	13	19
Miscell. building materials	22	18	19	15	18	14
Radio and electronic apparatus	—	—	19	22	29	38
Tools and implements	12	11	19	16	5	5
Gloves	10	13	19	17	1	2
Machine tools	15	13	18	17	12	10
Iron castings	16	13	18	16	19	18
Chalk, clay, sand and gravel	20–26	24–29	18	20	7	4
Industrial plant and steelwork	—	—	16	17	26	23
Brewing and malting	11	13	15	16	23	12
Narrow fabrics	16	15	15	15	2	3
Miscell. textile industries	—	—	15	15	1	1
Canvas goods, sacks, etc.	8	10	15	11	2	2
Pottery	10	10	15	13	7	11
Shop and office fittings	15	17	13	12	3	3
Hats, caps and millinery	12	13	13	12	1	2
Corsets and miscell. dress	—	—	12	15	3	6
Engineers' small tools, etc.	—	—	12	12	7	7
Lace	8	12	11	15	1	2
Cotton/rayon weaving	—	—	11	8	9	10
Stone and slate quarries	—	—	10	14	3	4
General mechanical engineering	9	11	10	12	19	23
Fur	13	14	10	11	1	1
Footwear	8	8	10	12	8	13
Plastics fabrication	—	—	10	11	3	4
Leather tanning and dressing	7	11	10	10	3	4
Weatherproof outerwear	14	13	10	11	2	4
Women's/girls' outerwear	—	—	10	10	4	6
Hosiery and knitted goods	12	8	9	8	9	11
Leather goods	9	10	9	9	1	2
Miscellaneous machinery	—	—	8	9	27	28
Woollen and worsted	8	8	8	9	11	16
Overalls, shirts, etc.	—	—	8	8	2	5
Furniture and upholstery	9	7	8	14	7	13
General printing and publishing	8	7	8	7	17	16
Household textiles	—	—	7	7	1	2
Miscell. metal goods	—	—	7	6	18	18

Table 1 – *contd*

Industry	Three largest enterprises					
	Net Output	Employment	Net Output	Employment	Net Output	Employment
	1951	1951	1958	1958	1958	1958
	%	%	%	%	£m	'000
Wooden containers and baskets	5	6	7	5	1	1
Miscell. wood/cork products	—	—	6	5	1	2
Timber	3	4	4	5	3	4
Construction	—	—	4	3	46	43
Dress/lingerie, etc.	—	—	3	4	2	4

Note: Concentration ratios are here calculated on the percentage of total *net output* and *employment* for the three largest enterprises in each industry classification. An enterprise is one or more firms under common ownership as defined in the Companies Act 1948: that is a single company or a company together with these subsidiary companies in which it possesses a greater than 50 per cent shareholding or voting power. All of the 130 separate census industries (of the 1958 census) are shown except five – coal mining, gas, electricity, water supply and textile converting. But, as between 1951 and 1958, some reclassification of census industries took place and therefore the 1951 columns, in some cases, cannot show an exact counterpart of the 1958 entry. In addition some industries have no exact ratio for the largest three enterprises: data is supplied for more than three companies in order to conserve the confidential character of information given to the census by certain large companies. But reasonably conservative estimates are made in such cases; or a range of values are provided.

Sources: Board of Trade (10) and R. Evely and I. M. D. Little (3).

British industry. But closer examination reveals that the arrangement of this list is deficient in a number of respects. Many items are so widely classified as almost to be meaningless (fruit and vegetable products, miscellaneous electrical goods, tools and implements, electrical machinery, dress and lingerie, etc.). Other items appear fairly specific (footwear, agricultural machinery, rubber, electrical machinery, coal-tar products, general chemicals) but include, in practice, a wide range of products catering for various markets and sometimes originating in industries which differ technologically. For only a small number of items can it be said that the concentration index of Table 1 is specific and meaningful in that a fairly homogenous product emanating from one easily-identified industry is indicated (tobacco, man-made fibres, carpets, cement, biscuits). Then, even when apparently satisfactory classifications are employed, difficulties still arise. The ratio does not directly reflect the character of competition or the likelihood of collusion within the industry. Firms are not distributed symmetrically in size or importance, for example; and there may be competition *between* industries.

In short, because we are attempting to connect a theoretical construction (the degree of monopoly or extent of competition) with the raw materials of industrial life through the medium of official statistics, we encounter many difficulties of dissection and definition. Two groups of problems dominate. One we may term the census problems – arranging the data to best advantage for the purposes of measuring concentration. The other we may term the conceptual problems. However, it should be kept in mind that distinguishing these two groups is largely a conventional and even arbitrary exercise.

The census group of problems arises from a fundamental conflict in the character of the data which can never completely be overcome. Whereas concentration ratios are constructed in order to assist the analysis of the demand or substitutability relationships which condition monopoly situations, the census data in practice are derived mainly from the side of supply. No hidden labour-theory-of-value dogma is at work here. The facts are more prosaic. Figures are collected from industry in connexion with employment, types of skill, location of production, value of assets, value of production and many other matters. And the task of arranging the data of industry in some reasonable and convenient order throws up certain types of classification. The size structure of industry and the derivation of concentration ratios are almost incidental by-products of this activity.

The primary source of statistics is an establishment – the plant, mine or factory from which returns are made regardless of ownership. In classifying together particular groupings of establishment the statistician is influenced by certain fairly obvious factors. The type of goods produced by the factory is certainly one. And, indeed, the first principle of classification is to allocate an establishment to an industry where its goods coincide with 'the principal products' of that industry. But, in deciding what are the principal products to be placed together in order to constitute an industry, the census authorities must initially have regard for the technological facts of life. Similarity of treatment of a particular raw material may be sufficient to bring together a group of firms into one industry although they produce a variety of commodities. (Paper and board firms produce newsprint, cartons, wallpaper, paper bags, writing paper, etc.) The dependence of an industry on a particular type of skill, as in engineering, may be a unifying factor. A significant similarity in the technical processes of design and assembly may bring together quite distinct products. (Motor cars, agricultural tractors, commercial vehicles, motor cycles and cycles are in one census industry.) Some plants, for inescapable technological reasons, produce a variety of commodities or raw materials from one basic process. (As well as coke, coke ovens produce town gas, toluene, benzol, etc. And oil refining must, to be commercially viable, produce not only motor spirit, aviation spirit, kerosene, diesel oil, ship's oil fuel but also sulphuric acid and the raw material of plastics production and fertilizers.)

Thus, although the main principle on which the census authorities allocate establishments to industries – according to 'principal products' – ensures that an industry frequently produces a group of similar, substitutable commodities which may be expected to be in competition with one another, this is not always so. The various products of the machine tool industry – lathes, drills, presses, milling machines, etc. – most emphatically are not substitutable for one another. Cars, tractors and fork-lift trucks are not substitutable. Then, paradoxically, closely competing substitutes sometimes do not come from the same industry. Tin cans, glass jars and plastic containers, a closely competing group, originate in distinctly different industries. Also, paper wrapping and packaging competes with tinfoil, polyethylene or cellulose sheet and other alternative materials.

In short, the majority of census industries encompass establishments which produce an assortment of products most of which can be said to be characteristic of that industry but some of which properly would belong elsewhere were it not for the exigencies of census classification.

Some of this internally heterogeneous character of the census industries can be reduced by distinguishing sub-industries for separate treatment. For example, engineering industries can usefully be classified under prime movers (stationary), office machinery, ball and roller bearings, mining machinery, mechanical handling equipment, transmission chains, mechanical engineering (repairing), etc. Electrical engineering can subdivide into electric lamps, equipment for motor vehicles and aircraft, domestic appliances, wire and cable, radio apparatus, valve and cathode ray tubes, etc. However, there are problems here also. The broader industrial classifications, such as in Table 1, undoubtedly conceal concentration in many important sub-industries. For example, the motor vehicles classification obscures the concentration picture in commercial vehicles or cars and taxis. The bricks and refractory products classification camouflages what happens in building bricks; and electrical machinery gives no indication of the degree of concentration in the production of large generating sets. The wider the definitions the more the specialist firm in a particular sub-industry escapes attention from the concentration-index. On the other hand, if too narrow a definition is taken there is a different danger. The specialist product may then give a concentration ratio which overstates because it ignores near-substitutes in other classifications which do offer significant competition.

Finally, there is the problem of applying the substitutability criterion to practicable census definitions of industries and sub-industries. Even where satisfactory product groupings can be found it is unlikely that they will each emanate from industries which are also homogeneous in respect of technology, raw materials, capital interests, labour skills, etc. In short, the ideal census industry in which all products and enterprises have, between them, high cross elasticities of supply and demand is likely to occur only now and again. But, as Evely and Little express the matter, 'there is no escaping from this dilemma. The data relates to census trades and it is in terms of census trades that the analysis must proceed'.

In practice census authorities are surprisingly successful in their manipulations of industry data to secure homogeneity and comprehensiveness in terms of 'principal products' (3). For academic purposes further refinement is possible. Certain criteria can be devised to select those industries which do, in fact, conform fairly closely to the substitutability tests; and to reject those which do not. For example, the proportion of the gross output of an industry which consists of its principal products can be discovered. This is termed the *degree of specialization* of the industry or sub-industry. Then, the extent to which the establishments of an industry can account for the total national output can be found. This is referred to as the *degree of exclusiveness*. Where both of these criteria show a value of 100 per cent the census definition is highly accurate and the concentration ratio must correspond to the combined market share of the principal products of the industry held by the three largest producers. An unlikely event. But any classification which can show degrees of specialization and exclusiveness of 67 per cent or greater is satisfactory for most purposes. Evely and Little, using this approach, and rejecting industries with insufficient data to make tests, compile a viable group of 220 classifications out of a

Table 2

Selected Concentration Ratios: Sub-industries, 1951 Census

| Industry | Three largest enterprises | |
	Net output %	Employment %
Transmission chains	100	100
Razors (non electric)	99	94
Cotton thread	91	94
Asbestos cement goods	92	92
Motor cycles	87	86
Wallpaper	86	86
Valves and TV tubes	82	85
Prime movers – internal combustion	80	77
Rubber tyres and tubes	73	75
Ball and roller bearings	70	75
Fertilizers	75	73
Tinplate	72	71
Boilers and boilerhouse plant	62	67
Notepaper pads and envelopes	68	66
Ice cream	76	65
Bicycles and tricycles	69	64
Steel sheets	65	59
Iron ore and ironstone	55	58
Electric lamps	53	54
Magazines and periodicals	53	54
Commercial vehicles	51	49

Table 2 – *contd*

| Industry | Three largest enterprises | |
	Net output %	Employment %
Glass containers	45	47
Tea blending	45	43
Sanitary earthenware	47	38
Roofing tiles of clay	39	34
Cotton yarn – finishing	36	34
Mining machinery	32	33
Building bricks	32	30
Newspapers	32	30
Radio and gramophone apparatus	27	30
Marine engineering	27	27
Iron and steel melting	25	24
Knives	21	22
Constructional engineering	17	16
Iron engineering castings	17	15
Sugar confectionery	12	15
Pre-cast concrete goods	14	12
Brass manufacture	10	8
New building, construction	8	8
Retail tailoring and dressmaking	6	6
Laundry work	6	6
Woven cotton cloth	4	5
Motor vehicle and cycles (repairing)	4	4

Source: R. Evely and I. M. D. Little (3) pp. 52–60.

possible maximum of 397 industry and sub-industry classifications for the 1951 census of production. A few of these are reproduced, with their concentration ratios, in Table 2. On the whole, this technique tends to bring out concentration ratios for sub-industries significantly higher than those for the more heterogeneous industry groupings of Table 1; for example, in transmission chains, motor cycles, rubber tyres and tubes, ball and roller bearings and steel sheets. Others are lower than for the corresponding industry in Table 1; for example, iron and steel (melting), pre-cast concrete goods, sugar confectionery, knives and brass manufacture.

The distribution of high, medium and low concentration trades for 1951, as the result of this fairly sophisticated dissection of 220

Table 3

Distribution of 220 Industries by Concentration Category, 1951

Concentration Category	Industries No.	%	Employment '000	%
High (67% or over)	50	23	636	10
Medium (34–66%)	69	31	1,545	24
Low (33% or less)	101	46	4,188	66
	220	100	6,369	100

Source: R. Evely and I. M. D. Little (3) p. 51.

industry groupings can be seen in Table 3. There are fifty high concentration industries. They constitute more than one-fifth of the total sample: but account for only 10 per cent of total employment. There are sixty-nine medium-concentration industries, almost one-third of the population, with about one-quarter of the employment. The largest group is the low concentration trades, with 46 per cent of all trades included; and accounting for 66 per cent of the employment.

Then we come to the conceptual problems involved in the use of concentration ratios. Probably the most serious deficiency in this sense is the failure to take into account competition *between* census industries. The concentration ratio equates fewness in the market with monopoly power in a simple arithmetical fashion. But, as we have extensively commented, the classification of a census industry is necessarily somewhat arbitrary. For any collection of principal products defining an industry there may be a particular set of elasticities of substitution between them. Change the collection and there is likely to be a different set. More important, it is difficult to arrange for each of the census industries adopted, that, while its principal products make a fairly homogeneous collection, there are no products in other census industries which also are strongly related through a high elasticity of substitution and therefore are effective competitors. (Ball and roller bearings, typewriters and industrial gases have few substitutes and therefore little competition from other classifications. On the other hand, steel sheet competes with asbestos products, aluminium and plastics materials, glass bottles with tin containers, electric cookers and heaters with their gas equivalents, etc.) Putting the matter generally, no matter how fine the dissection of census data or how ingenious the allocation of principal products to industries there is no way easily to arrange always to have low elasticities of substitution between product groups. Thus, an industry with a very high concentration index may have effectively a low degree of monopoly on account of competing products in other census industries (for example, asbestos cement goods and margarine). Vice versa, some lower concentration ratios do not rule out the possibility of a well-protected oligopolistic position (for example, jute, textile machinery, building bricks and sanitary earthenware).

A related point concerns the distribution of enterprises within a census industry. There may exist substantial differences in size between the individual shares of the three largest firms. Such phenomena can have a significant bearing on monopolistic or behaviour and price leadership among them. Further, the remainder of the industry may be comprised predominantly of either a small group of medium-sized firms or of a large body of small firms. Obviously, these alternatives also have some relevance to market behaviour. All such variations in size structure are concealed by a single concentration ratio.

It is becoming clear that a numerical coefficient is not the best measure of that complex pattern of relationships we term 'competitiveness' or 'degree of monopoly'. But even if it were there is still a body of minor objections bearing on the apparent arithmetical exactness of the concentration ratio. Various factors in the industrial organization and circumstances of a particular industry can cause the index to overstate. A different set can cause understatement (3).

The likely sources of overstatement of concentration are few but are undeniably significant for certain industries. The existence of substantial exports and imports can distort the ratio. Some large producers may be primarily exporters; and therefore their contribution to the concentration ratio (which refers to domestic production) may be exaggerated. A more significant effect could be the impact of imports on a highly concentrated industry. Imports of quite small volume, regardless of whether originating from a small group or a scattered set of foreign producers, would substantially reduce the real market power of large domestic producers. Another possibility of overstatement lies in the existence of countervailing power. If, among industrial users or the distributive trades, there are strong buyers, the monopolistic power of the large producers of a given industry may be seriously diminished. Monopolies Commission reports show this is far from being a negligible possibility. Especially as between industries purchasing one another's semi-fabricated products and components, the incidence of countervailing power situations, and the resultant bilateral oligopoly or monopoly, is surprisingly high. But it occurs in an unsystematic fashion; it cannot be relied upon to appear; and is therefore best left for *ad hoc* consideration (11).

On the whole there is more reason to expect understatement of concentration ratios. For example, take the definition of a subsidiary as used by census authorities. To qualify as the fully-controlled subsidiary of a parent enterprise there must be a greater than 50 per cent holding of shares or voting power by the parent. Such a minimum is in accord with company law and clearly gives *de jure* control. But, as is well-known, *de facto* control of a stable and permanent character frequently requires less than a 50 per cent holding – often very much less. Consequently, the true extent of the control of large enterprises is likely to be underestimated in many industries.

Vertical integration offers the same problem in a rather different guise. An integrated enterprise often cannot be accommodated within a single census classification; it is likely to appear in several. Thus, a paper company can have timber and pulp interests, be a manufacturer of paper and board, of fine papers, of cartons, packaging paper, newsprint and possibly also have interests in newspaper publishing. Each of these has a separate census classification for good reasons. However, the power of a large integrated concern to affect prices and competition, not simply at any one given level of production but at several levels, is as a result understated by the concentration ratio; the large concern may be a supplier of raw materials to its competitors at one level; and a buyer of their finished or semi-finished products at another.

The large multi-product firm offers a problem which is similar in that some of its market power is concealed by diversification into

115

different census industries. Bigness gives a better financial standing, access to superior sites, to raw materials at larger discounts, better qualified management and some of the intangible influence and power of a price leader in the various industries covered by its activities. The concentration ratio cannot account for the special standing of the large multi-product firms.

There is also the problem of the size of the market to which the concentration ratio refers. Not all markets are national although the concentration data is computed on this basis. Some markets are fragmented into regional or local areas usually on account of the high transport costs of the products concerned. For example, the bricks, cement, publishing, brewing and oil-refining industries. Within these areas it is likely that the degree of monopoly power possessed by the local companies is greater than can be demonstrated by the national concentration ratio. Properly to analyse the likely market behaviour of such industries it would be preferable to treat each self-contained region separately. For an economy as concentrated as the British economy this is necessary only in a few cases. But for such a geographically dispersed economy as the U.S.A. it is a more serious problem. Kaysen and Turner, for example, have made a fairly sophisticated reclassification of industries taking into account not only their concentration ratios, but the width of their regional or local markets (12).

Finally the connexion between concentration and collusion requires a mention. Whether high concentration assists the formation of collusive practices, thus extending the incidence of monopoly power in a different form, is an open question. *A priori*, a high concentration ratio for the largest three-four firms of an industry suggests that collusive practices will probably occur either in the form of tacit understandings on prices, outputs, market shares, etc.; or in restrictive agreements operated through a trade association. It seems equally reasonable to suppose that, the larger the number of enterprises in an industry and the lower the degree of concentration, the more difficult it becomes to secure stable lasting agreements of any kind. In practice, however, there are examples of concentrated industries which obviously are very competitive, although not necessarily through price. (Motor vehicles, soap and detergents, office machinery, biscuits and margarine.) And, on the other hand, there are many low-concentration industries with a fairly wide membership which, as Monopolies Commission reports and Restrictive Practices Court cases show, operate price agreements which are remarkably well-organized and well-observed (bread, book publishing, copper semi-manufactures, sand and gravel, timber imports, etc.). It is difficult to perceive any systematic connexion between concentration and collusion. Fortuitous historical and organizational elements in the formation of restrictive agreements are much more common. All that can safely be said is this: where restrictive practices have become established in an industry and there is also a high concentration ratio (electric lamps, pneumatic tyres, metal windows, bolts, nuts and rivets, brewing) then the large firms of that industry, through their influence on the smaller members of the trade association, are likely to exert a power of control which is not properly reflected by the concentration ratio.

Concentration Measures and Monopoly

It seems evident that concentration measures take one only a short distance towards the full analysis of monopoly and restrictive practices. This stricture applies especially to measures of concentration for the whole economy. Essentially they are concerned with the general size distribution of companies rather than the impact of bigness on particular commodities or markets. Thus they provide practically no concrete evidence of actual monopolistic or oligopolistic situations; and nothing at all about the incidence of collusive practices. Analysis of the trends in concentration can however be informative, interesting and may on occasion help confirm the relevance of policies touching on the control of companies legislation on shareholding, on ownership, etc. They may even have a bearing on *general* ideas about competition and monopoly. But, essentially, the contribution of such analyses consists in providing a statistical and historical background to the problems of monopoly power.

Market concentration measures by contrast bring us much closer to actual situations. In the first place, they permit us to make at least some reasonable assessment of *the likelihood* of monopolistic and oligopolistic situations in industry – an important pre-requisite for evaluating the necessity or otherwise of

Table 4

Concentration in Australia, Britain and U.S.A.[1]

Industry	U.S.A. 1947 Largest 4 % Value of shipments	Australia[2] 1949–50 Largest 4	Largest 3	U.K.[3] 1950 Largest 3 % Employment	%Net output
Refined zinc	53	100 (400)	100 (300)	68	82
Pig iron	67	100 (400)	100 (300)	45	47
Ball and roller bearings	61	100 (400)	100 (300)	75	70
Linoleum	80	100 (400)	100 (300)	75	76
Industrial gases	83	100 (400)	100 (300)	N.A.	N.A.
Sheet glass	88	100 (400)	100 (300)	46	51
Writing papers	N.A.	100 (400)	100 (300)	83	80
Steel making and rolling	45	100 (200)	100 (150)	24	25
Steel sheet	N.A.	100 (200)	100 (150)	59	65
Sugar refining	70	100 (200)	100 (150)	N.A.	N.A.
Matches	83	100 (133)	100	85	86
Alkalis and chlorine	70	100 (133)	100	N.A.	N.A.
Electric lamps	92	100 (133)	100	55	56
Radio valves and TV tubes	73	100 (133)	100	85	82
Glass containers	63	100 (133)	100	47	45
Plastic materials	44	100	95	53	51
Tyres and tubes	77	100	(90+)	75	73
Carpets	52	100	(75+)	28	26
Floor and wall tiles	51	100	(80+)	32	37
Paper and paper board	16	97	93	21	19
Asbestos and cement products	57	95	93	92	92
Petroleum refining	37	93	77	84	35
Cigarettes & tobacco	90	(94+)	(90+)	70	74
Cotton spinning	N.A.	84	74	27	25
Tin containers	78	(75+)	(70+)	60	61
Cars and taxis	N.A.	69	54	69	80
Paint and varnish	27	68	59	19	20
Newspapers	21	64	55	30	32
Cement	30	56	46	87	89

1. For a full account of the sources and construction of this table see the original article, A. Hunter 'Restrictive practices and monopolies in Australia' (13) p. 281. Only industries comparable as between the U.S.A.

Census of Manufactures and the British Census of production were selected; with the further qualification that each had a clear counterpart, on a trade or product basis, in Australian sources. Although necessary, this procedure excluded many interesting comparisons which may only have been slightly inaccurate, such as general chemicals, electrical machinery, wire manufacture, motor vehicles and spares, etc.

2. Australian figures are mainly net output or gross output values. In a few cases employment or capacity figures were used.

3. Neither the British nor U.S.A. index is suitable for measurement of Australian concentration ratios since many industries are, effectively, occupied by one, two or three large firms. Hence the conventional concentration ratios considerably understate the degree of concentration in the upper half of the table. To increase the value of the comparison, the Australian index has been increased *pro rata* for these industries. (For example where one firm occupies the whole market the ratio is inflated to read 400 per cent, for two firms 200 per cent and for three firms 133 per cent on the basis of the U.S.A. index. On the U.K. index, the ratio for a one-firm dominated industry is 300; and two firms rate a 150 per cent reading. These figures are placed in brackets for the top fifteen industries of the table.) Given an industrial structure with frequent readings of this very high order a more satisfactory method of constructing a concentration index is to state the ratios inversely. That is, arrange it by the *number of firms* which occupy a given share of the market, say 80 per cent. G. Rosenbluth, for example, adapts this method for Canadian manufacturing industry.

legislation. It is of course possible to take the position that, in principle, no increases in monopolization will be permitted; or that all monopoly-oligopoly situations will be subject to judicial or semi-judicial inquiry from time to time. But before being committed to the value-judgements implicit in such legislation it is useful and always desirable to be exposed to some relevant factual data such as concentration ratios.

It may even be helpful to consider the comparable ratios for other countries. However, given the varying circumstances and outlook of different societies we should not expect too decisive a result from such comparisons. For example, consider Table 4. It sets out a comparison of the market ratios of twenty-nine selected industries and sub-industries in each of three countries, Australia, Britain and the U.S.A. (13). Concentration in this group of mainly high-concentration industries is clearly much higher in Australia than in Britain; and higher in Britain than in the U.S.A. Paradoxically it is the U.S.A. which has seen fit to operate the most comprehensive and severe anti-trust laws; Britain has only a mild degree of control over such industries and Australia, at the relevant dates, had no legislation whatsoever.

It could be argued that concentration ratios are low in the U.S.A. precisely because of its legislation. But most observers are agreed (5) that anti-trust laws have very little impact on the development of concentration. The most important explanation is a simple arithmetical one turning on the sharply differing size of the three economies. For a given similarity of technology the degree of concentration is inversely related to the size of the economy. This elementary point helps suggest some of the hazards of deriving value judgements purely from numerical data. Australia, on the concentration criterion, is more in need of legislative control than either of the other two countries but, until recently, has managed to get along without it. Observation suggests that this is so because competition and monopoly are regarded differently in a small economy. A small society can learn to live with high concentrations of economic power. Given sufficient determination it may even, precisely because in a small economy monopoly positions are obvious and vulnerable, learn both to live with it and control it. But in practice the lesson rarely penetrates.

To conclude, the most useful application of market concentration measures is in bringing rough quantitative criteria to bear on particular industries. But there are severe limitations on their use in this respect. The difficulty of reconciling census classifications of industry with the main economic entities – products, industries and markets – has received extensive comment already. Even where a strong correspondence of industry and product can be found there are yet further fundamental deficiencies; concentration ratios cannot dissect within industries the internal patterns of restriction – price leadership and restrictive practices for example; nor can it account for differing degrees of competitiveness between industries. In a word, the notion that a single numerical coefficient of concentration can successfully distil the essence of competitive and monopolistic relationships is absurd.

What then is the essential contribution of market concentration ratios? Where there is legislation designed to take legal action or inquire into monopoly-oligopoly situations or mergers, the concentration indices have some value. They can provide a rough but reasonably systematic sorting and appraisal of the relevant industries before litigation or inquiry. They are, providing their rather numerous qualifications are kept in mind, suitable jumping-off points for preliminary analysis.

References

1. M. A. ADELMAN, 'The measurement of industrial concentration', *Review of Economics and Statistics*, vol. 34, 1951.
2. P. E. HART, and S. J. PRAIS, *Journal of the Royal Statistical Society*, Series A, vol. 119, part 2, 1956.
3. R. EVELY, and I. M. D. LITTLE, *Concentration in British Industry*, Cambridge, 1960.
4. J. F. WESTON, *The Role of Mergers in the Growth of Large Firms*, University of California Press, 1953.
5. R. L. NELSON, *Merger Movements in American Industry 1895–6*, Princeton University Press, 1959.
6. H. W. MACROSTY, *The Trust Movement in British Industry*, Longmans, 1907.
7. G. C. ALLEN, *The Structure of Industry in Britain*, Longmans, 1961.
8. Central Statistical Office and Board of Trade, *Economic Trends*, April issues nos. 102 and 114, H.M.S.O., 1962 and 1963.
9. J. S. BAIN, *Barriers to New Competition*, Harvard University Press, 1956.
10. Board of Trade, *Reports of the Census of Production 1958*, Parts 133–5, H.M.S.O., 1962–3.
11. A. HUNTER, 'Notes on countervailing power', *Economic Journal*, vol. 69, November 1959.
12. C. KAYSEN, and D. F. TURNER, *Anti-Trust Policy*, Harvard University Press, 1959.
13. A. HUNTER, 'Restrictive practices and monopolies in Australia', *Economic Record*, vol. 37, March 1961; and reprinted in H. W. Arndt and M. W. Corden (editors), *The Australian Economy*, Cheshire, 1963.

7   J. K. Galbraith

The Theory of Countervailing Power[1]

Excerpts from chapters 9 and 10 of J. K. Galbraith, *American Capitalism*, revised edition, Hamish Hamilton, London, 1957.

The Theory

[. . .]

As with social efficiency, and its neglect of technical dynamics, the paradox of the unexercised power of the large corporation begins with an important oversight in the underlying economic theory. In the competitive model – the economy of many sellers each with a small share of the total market – the restraint on the private exercise of economic power was provided by other firms on the same side of the market. It was the eagerness of competitors to sell, not the complaints of buyers, that saved the latter from spoliation. It was assumed, no doubt accurately, that the nineteenth-century textile manufacturer who overcharged for his product would promptly lose his market to another manufacturer who did not. If all manufacturers found themselves in a position where they could exploit a strong demand, and mark up their prices accordingly, there would soon be an inflow of new competitors. The resulting increase in supply would bring prices and profits back to normal.

As with the seller who was tempted to use his economic power against the customer, so with the buyer who was tempted to use it against his labor or suppliers. The man who paid less than the prevailing wage would lose his labor force to those who paid the worker his full (marginal) contribution to the earnings of the firm. In all cases the incentive to socially desirable behavior was provided by the competitor. It was to the same side of the market –

---

1. While Galbraith succeeded in introducing an interesting new idea into the armoury of controls over monopoly not all economists agreed with him that the theory of countervailing power fitted into the structure of orthodox welfare theory (see Stigler (1) and Hunter (2)). [ed.]

the restraint of sellers by other sellers and of buyers by other buyers, in other words to competition – that economists came to look for the self-regulatory mechanism of the economy.

They also came to look to competition exclusively and in formal theory still do. The notion that there might be another regulatory mechanism in the economy has been almost completely excluded from economic thought. Thus, with the widespread disappearance of competition in its classical form and its replacement by the small group of firms if not in overt, at least in conventional or tacit collusion, it was easy to suppose that since competition had disappeared, all effective restraint on private power had disappeared. Indeed this conclusion was all but inevitable if no search was made for other restraints and so complete was the preoccupation with competition that none was made.

In fact, new restraints on private power did appear to replace competition. They were nurtured by the same process of concentration which impaired or destroyed competition. But they appeared not on the same side of the market but on the opposite side, not with competitors but with customers or suppliers. It will be convenient to have a name for this counterpart of competition and I shall call it *countervailing power*.

To begin with a broad and somewhat too dogmatically stated proposition, private economic power is held in check by the countervailing power of those who are subject to it. The first begets the second, The long trend toward concentration of industrial enterprise in the hands of a relatively few firms has brought into existence not only strong sellers, as economists have supposed, but also strong buyers as they have failed to see. The two develop together, not in precise step but in such manner that there can be no doubt that the one is in response to the other.

The fact that a seller enjoys a measure of monopoly power, and is reaping a measure of monopoly return as a result, means that there is an inducement to those firms from whom he buys or those to whom he sells to develop the power with which they can defend themselves against exploitation. It means also that there is a reward to them, in the form of a share of the gains of their opponents' market power, if they are able to do so. In this way the existence of market power creates an incentive to the organization of another position of power that neutralizes it.

The contention I am here making is a formidable one. It comes to this: Competition which, at least since the time of Adam Smith, has been viewed as the autonomous regulator of economic activity and as the only available regulatory mechanism apart from the state, has, in fact, been superseded. Not entirely, to be sure. I should like to be explicit on this point. Competition still plays a role. There are still important markets where the power of the firm as (say) a seller is checked or circumscribed by those who provide a similar or a substitute product or service. This, in the broadest sense that can be meaningful, is the meaning of competition. The role of the buyer on the other side of such markets is essentially a passive one. It consists in looking for, perhaps asking for, and responding to the best bargain. The active restraint is provided by the competitor who offers, or threatens to offer, a better bargain. However, this is not the only or even the typical restraint on the exercise of economic power. In the typical modern market of few sellers, the active restraint is provided not by competitors but from the other side of the market by strong buyers. Given the convention against price competition, it is the role of the competitor that becomes passive in these markets.

It was always one of the basic pre-suppositions of competition that market power exercised in its absence would invite the competitors who would eliminate such exercise of power. The profits of a monopoly position inspired competitors to try for a share. In other words competition was regarded as a *self-generating* regulatory force. The doubt whether this was in fact so after a market had been pre-empted by a few large sellers, after entry of new firms had become difficult and after existing firms had accepted a convention against price competition, was what destroyed the faith in competition as a regulatory mechanism. Countervailing power is also a self-generating force and this is a matter of great importance. Something, although not very much, could be claimed for the regulatory role of the strong buyer in relation to the market power of sellers, did it happen that, as an accident of economic development, such strong buyers were frequently juxtaposed to strong sellers. However the tendency of power to be organized *in response to a given position of power is the vital characteristic of the phenomenon I am here identifying.* As noted, power on one side of a market creates both the need for, and the prospect of reward to, the exercise of countervailing power from the other side. This means that, as a common rule, we can rely on countervailing power to appear as a curb on economic power. There are also, it should be added, circumstances in which it does not appear or is effectively prevented from appearing. To these I shall return. For some reason, critics of the theory have seized with particular avidity on these exceptions to deny the existence of the phenomenon itself. It is plain that by a similar line of argument one could deny the existence of competition by finding one monopoly.

In the market of small numbers or oligopoly, the practical barriers to entry and the convention against price competition have eliminated the self-generating capacity of competition. The self-generating tendency of countervailing power, by contrast, is readily assimilated to the common sense of the situation and its existence, once we have learned to look for it, is readily subject to empirical observation.

Market power can be exercised by strong buyers against weak sellers as well as by strong sellers against weak buyers. In the competitive model, competition acted as a restraint on both kinds of exercise of power. This is also the case with countervailing power. In turning to its practical manifestations, it will be convenient, in fact, to begin with a case where it is exercised by weak sellers against strong buyers.

The operation of countervailing power is to be seen with the greatest clarity in the labor market where it is also most fully developed. Because of his comparative immobility, the individual worker has long been highly vulnerable to private economic power. The customer of any particular steel mill, at the turn of the century, could always take himself elsewhere if he felt he was being overcharged. Or he could exercise his sovereign privilege of not buying steel at all. The worker had no comparable freedom if he felt he was being underpaid. Normally he could not move and he had to have work. Not often has the power of one man over another been used more callously than in the American labor market after the rise of the large corporation. As late as the early twenties, the steel industry worked a twelve-hour day and seventy-two-hour week with an incredible twenty-four-hour stint every fortnight when the shift changed.

No such power is exercised today and for the reason that its earlier exercise stimulated the counteraction that brought it to an end. In the ultimate sense it was the power of the steel industry, not the organizing abilities of John L. Lewis and Philip Murray, that brought the United Steel Workers into being. The economic power that the worker faced in the sale of his labor – the competition of many sellers dealing with few buyers – made it necessary that he organize for his own protection. There were rewards to the power of the steel companies in which, when he had successfully developed countervailing power, he could share. [. . .]

Elsewhere in industries which approach the competition of the model one typically finds weaker or less comprehensive unions. The textile industry, boot and shoe manufacture, lumbering and other forest industries in most parts of the country, and smaller wholesale and retail enterprises, are all cases in point. I do not, of course, advance the theory of countervailing power as a monolithic explanation of trade-union organization. No such complex social phenomenon is likely to have any single, simple explanation. American trade unions developed in the face of the implacable hostility, not alone of employers, but often of the community as well. In this environment organization of the skilled crafts was much easier than the average, which undoubtedly explains the earlier appearance of durable unions here. In the modern bituminous coal-mining and more clearly in the clothing industry, unions have another explanation. They have emerged as a supplement to the weak market position of the operators and manufacturers. They have assumed price- and market-regulating functions that are the normal functions of managements, and on which the latter, because of the competitive character of the industry, have been forced to default. Nevertheless, as an explanation of the incidence of trade-union strength in the American economy, the theory of countervailing power clearly fits the broad contours of experience. There is, I venture, no other so satisfactory explanation of the great dynamic of labor organization in the modern capitalist community and none which so sensibly integrates the union into the theory of that society.

The labor market serves admirably to illustrate the incentives to the development of countervailing power and it is of great importance in this market. However, its development, in response to positions of market power, is pervasive in the economy. As a regulatory device one of its most important manifestations is in the relation of the large retailer to the firms from which it buys. The way in which countervailing power operates in these markets is worth examining in some detail.

One of the seemingly harmless simplifications of formal economic theory has been the assumption that producers of consumers' goods sell their products directly to consumers. All business units are held, for this reason, to have broadly parallel interests. Each buys labor and materials, combines them and passes them along to the public at prices that, over some period of time, maximize returns. It is recognized that this is, indeed, a simplification; courses in marketing in the universities deal with what is excluded by this assumption. Yet it has long been supposed that the assumption does no appreciable violence to reality.

Did the real world correspond to the assumed one, the lot of the consumer would be an unhappy one. In fact goods pass to consumers by way of retailers and other intermediaries and this is a circumstance of first importance. Retailers are required by their situation to develop countervailing power on the consumer's behalf.

As I have previously observed, retailing remains one of the industries to which entry is characteristically free. It takes small capital and no very rare talent to set up as a seller of goods. Through history there have always been an ample supply of men with both and with access to something to sell. The small man can provide convenience and intimacy of service and can give an attention to detail, all of which allow him to co-exist with larger competitors.

The advantage of the larger competitor ordinarily lies in its lower prices. It lives constantly under the threat of an erosion of its business by the more rapid growth of rivals and by the appearance of new firms. This loss of volume, in turn, destroys the chance for the lower costs and lower prices on which the firm depends. This means that the larger retailer is extraordinarily sensitive to higher prices by its suppliers. It means also that it is

128

strongly rewarded if it can develop the market power which permits it to force lower prices.

The opportunity to exercise such power exists only when the suppliers are enjoying something that can be taken away: that is, when they are enjoying the fruits of market power from which they can be separated. Thus, as in the labor market, we find the mass retailer, from a position across the market, with both a protective and a profit incentive to develop countervailing power when the firm with which it is doing business is in possession of market power. Critics have suggested that these are possibly important but certainly disparate phenomena. This may be so, but only if all similarity between social phenomena be denied. In the present instance the market context is the same. The motivating incentives are identical. The fact that it has characteristics in common has been what has caused people to call competition competition when they encountered it, say, in agriculture and then again in the laundry business.

Countervailing power in the retail business is identified with the large and powerful retail enterprises. Its practical manifestation, over the last half-century, has been the rise of the food chains, the variety chains, the mail-order houses (now graduated into chain stores), the department-store chains, and the co-operative buying organizations of the surviving independent department and food stores.

This development was the countervailing response to previously established positions of power. The gains from invading these positions have been considerable and in some instances even spectacular. The rubber tire industry is a fairly commonplace example of oligopoly. Four large firms are dominant in the market. In the thirties, Sears, Roebuck & Co. was able, by exploiting its role as a large and indispensable customer, to procure tires from Goodyear Tire & Rubber Company at a price from twenty-nine to forty per cent lower than the going market. These it resold to thrifty motorists for from a fifth to a quarter less than the same tires carrying the regular Goodyear brand.

As a partial consequence of the failure of the government to recognize the role of countervailing power many hundreds of pages of court records have detailed the exercise of this power by the Great Atlantic & Pacific Tea Company. There is little doubt that this firm, at least in its uninhibited days, used the countervailing power it had developed with considerable artistry (6). In 1937, a survey by the company indicated that, for an investment of $175,000, it could supply itself with corn flakes. Assuming that it charged itself the price it was then paying to one of the three companies manufacturing this delicacy, it could earn a modest 68 per cent on the outlay. Armed with this information, and the threat to go into the business which its power could readily make effective, it had no difficulty in bringing down the price by approximately ten per cent. Such gains from the exercise of countervailing power, it will be clear, could only occur where there is an exercise of original market power with which to contend. The A & P could have reaped no comparable gains in buying staple products from the farmer. Committed as he is to the competition of the competitive model, the farmer has no gains to surrender. Provided, as he is, with the opportunity of selling all he produces at the impersonally determined market price, he has not the slightest incentive to make a special price to A & P at least beyond that which might in some circumstances be associated with the simple economies of bulk sale. [. . .]

The more commonplace but more important tactic in the exercise of countervailing power consists, merely, in keeping the seller in a state of uncertainty as to the intentions of a buyer who is indispensable to him. The larger of the retail buying organizations place orders around which the production schedules and occasionally the investment of even the largest manufacturers become organized. A shift in this custom imposes prompt and heavy loss. The threat or even the fear of this sanction is enough to cause the supplier to surrender some or all of the rewards of his market power. He must frequently, in addition, make a partial surrender to less potent buyers if he is not to be more than ever in the power of his large customers. It will be clear that in this operation there are rare opportunities for playing one supplier off against another.

A measure of the importance which large retailing organizations attach to the deployment of their countervailing power is the prestige they accord to their buyers. These men (and women) are the key employees of the modern large retail organization; they are highly paid and they are among the most intelligent and resourceful people to be found anywhere in business. In the everyday course of business, they may be considerably better known and command rather more respect than the salesmen from whom they buy. This is a not unimportant index of the power they wield.

There are producers of consumers' goods who have protected themselves from exercise of countervailing power. Some, like the automobile and the oil industry, have done so by integrating their distribution through to the consumer – a strategy which attests the importance of the use of countervailing power by retailers. Others have found it possible to maintain dominance over an organization of small and dependent and therefore fairly power-less dealers. It seems probable that in a few industries, tobacco manufacture for example, the members are ordinarily strong enough and have sufficient solidarity to withstand any pressure applied to them by the most powerful buyer. However, even the tobacco manufacturers, under conditions that were especially favorable to the exercise of countervailing power in the thirties, were forced to make liberal price concessions, in the form of advertising allowances, to the A & P and possibly also to other large customers. When the comprehensive representation of large retailers in the various fields of consumers' goods distribution is considered, it is reasonable to conclude – the reader is warned that this is an important generalization – that most positions of market power in the production of consumers' goods are covered by positions of countervailing power. As noted, there are exceptions and, as between markets, countervailing power is exercised with varying strength and effectiveness. The existence of exceptions does not impair the significance of the regulatory phenomenon here described. To its devotees the virtues of competition were great but few if any ever held its reign to be universal.

Countervailing power also manifests itself, although less visibly, in producers' goods markets. For many years the power of the automobile companies, as purchasers of steel, has sharply curbed the power of the steel mills as sellers. Detroit is the only city where the historic basing-point system was not used to price steel. Under the basing-point system, all producers regardless of location quoted the same price at any particular point of delivery. This obviously minimized the opportunity of a strong buyer to play one seller off against the other. The large firms in the automobile industry had developed the countervailing power which enabled them to do precisely this. They were not disposed to tolerate any limitations on their exercise of such power. In explaining the quotation of 'arbitrary prices' on Detroit steel, a leading student of the basing-point system some years ago recognized, implicitly but accurately, the role of countervailing power by observing that 'it is difficult to apply high cartel prices to particularly large and strong customers such as the automobile manufacturers in Detroit'.

The more normal operation of countervailing power in producers' goods markets has, as its point of departure, the relatively small number of customers which firms in these industries typically have. Where the cigarette or soap manufacturer numbers his retail outlets by the hundreds of thousands and his final consumers by the millions, the machinery or equipment manufacturer counts his customers by the hundreds or thousands and, very often, his important ones by the dozen. But here, as elsewhere, the market pays a premium to those who develop power as buyers that is equivalent to the market power of those from whom they buy [(3), (4) and (5) – ed.]. The reverse is true where weak sellers do business with strong buyers. [. . .]

The development of countervailing power requires a certain minimum opportunity and capacity for organization, corporate or otherwise. If the large retail buying organizations had not developed the countervailing power which they have used, by proxy, on behalf of the individual consumer, consumers would have been faced with the need to organize the equivalent of the retailer's power. This would have been a formidable task but it has been accomplished in Scandinavia where the consumer's co-operative, instead of the chain store, is the dominant instrument of countervailing power in consumers' goods markets. There has been a similar though less comprehensive development in England and Scotland. In the Scandinavian countries the co-operatives have long been regarded explicitly as instruments for bringing power to bear on the cartels; that is, for exercise of countervailing power. This is readily conceded by many who have the greatest difficulty in seeing private mass buyers in the same role. But the fact that consumer co-operatives are not of any great importance in the United States is to be explained, not by any inherent incapacity of the American for such organization, but because the chain stores pre-empted the gains of countervailing power first. The counterpart of the Swedish Kooperative Forbundet or the British Co-operative Wholesale Societies has not appeared in the United States simply because it could not compete with the A & P and other large food chains. The meaning of this, which incidentally has been lost on devotees of the theology of co-operation, is that the chain stores are approximately as efficient in the exercise of countervailing power as a co-operative would be. In parts of the American economy where proprietary mass buyers have not made their appearance, notably in the purchase of farm supplies, individuals (who are also individualists) have shown as much capacity to organize as the Scandinavians and the British and have similarly obtained the protection and rewards of countervailing power. The Grange League Federation, the Eastern States Farmers Exchange and the Illinois Farm Supply Company, co-operatives with annual sales running to multi-million-dollar figures, are among the illustrations of the point.

However, it must not be assumed that it is easy for great numbers of individuals to coalesce and organize countervailing power. In less developed communities, Puerto Rico for example, one finds people fully exposed to the exactions of strategically situated importers, merchants and wholesalers and without the apparent capacity to develop countervailing power on their own behalf. Anyone, incidentally, who doubts the force of the countervailing power exercised by large retailer-buying organizations would do well to consider the revolution which the entry of the large chain stores would work in an economy like that of Puerto Rico and also how such an intrusion would be resented and perhaps resisted by importers and merchants now able to exercise their market power with impunity against the thousands of small, independent and inefficient retailers who are their present outlets.

In the light of the difficulty in organizing countervailing power, it is not surprising that the assistance of government has repeatedly been sought in this task. Without the phenomenon itself being fully recognized, the provision of state assistance to the development of countervailing power has become a major function of

133

government – perhaps *the* major domestic function of government. Much of the domestic legislation of the last twenty years, that of the New Deal episode in particular, only becomes fully comprehensible when it is viewed in this light. To this I shall return in the next section. [. . .]

Countervailing Power and the State

The role of countervailing power in the economy marks out two broad problems in policy for the government. In all but conditions of inflationary demand, countervailing power performs a valuable – indeed an indispensable – regulatory function in the modern economy. Accordingly it is incumbent upon government to give it freedom to develop and to determine how it may best do so. The government also faces the question of where and how it will affirmatively support the development of countervailing power. It will be convenient to look first at the negative role of the government in allowing the development of countervailing power and then to consider its affirmative role in promoting it.

At the outset a somewhat general distinction – one that is implicit in the discussion of the last chapter – must be made between countervailing and original power. When, anywhere in the course of producing, processing or distributing a particular product, one or a few firms first succeed in establishing a strong market position they may be considered to be the possessors of original market power. They are able, as the result of their power over the prices they pay or charge, to obtain more than normal margins and profits. These are at the expense of the weaker suppliers or customers. This is the monopoly position anciently feared by liberals and as anciently condemned by economists, and their instincts were sound. Countervailing power invades such positions of strength, whether they be held by suppliers or customers, and redresses the position of the weaker group.

The rule to be followed by government is, in principle, a clear one. There can be very good reason for attacking positions of original market power in the economy if these are not effectively offset by countervailing power. There is at least a theoretical justification for opposing all positions of market power. There is no justification for attacks on positions of countervailing power which leave positions of original market power untouched. On the contrary, damage both in equity and to the most efficient operation of the economy will be the normal consequence of doing so.

The problems of practical application of such a rule are mostly in the field of the anti-trust laws and they are a good deal more difficult than the simple articulation of the rule implies. However a general distinction between original and countervailing power is, in fact, now made in the anti-trust laws – it has been forced, against the accepted current of ideas concerning competition, by the practical reality of the phenomenon itself. [. . .]

A more precise and conscious use of the distinction between original and countervailing power would take account of the fact that some trade unions and some farm groups are clearly the possessors of original power. Thus workers in the building trades, although they are not highly organized or exceptionally powerful in any absolute sense, are strong in relation to the small-scale employers with whom they do business. They are clearly the possessors of original market power. The special nature of their power, as compared with that of the trade-union movement generally, explains the distress of men and women who have reacted sympathetically to the role of unions in general but who, in this uncomfortable case, have found themselves on the side of organizations that have plenary power to restrict output and enhance their own income. The obvious answer to the problem lies in the distinction between original and countervailing power. This, logically, would make restrictive practices of master plumbers or plasterers a proper object of interest by the Department of Justice while the absolutely (though not relatively) far more powerful unions in steel or automobiles who impose no similar restrictions on the supply of their labor would not be.

Similarly, there are undoubted cases of exercise of original power by groups of agricultural producers. The immunity granted by existing laws is not complete – the Secretary of Agriculture is authorized to enter a complaint if, as a result of the activities of the co-operative, prices are 'unduly enhanced', and a co-operative cannot merge its power with non-agricultural corporations. As a result there have been a scattering of prosecutions of farmers' organizations – of the former California Fruit Growers' Exchange (Sunkist oranges) and of a Chicago milkshed producers' organization which was charged with being in combination in restraint of trade with milk distributors, unions and even a college professor. But such cases have been infrequent.

However, the more serious consequences of the failure to perceive the role of countervailing power have been within the fabric of industry itself. The anti-trust laws have been indiscriminately invoked against firms that have succeeded in building countervailing power, while holders of original market power, against whom the countervailing power was developed, have gone unchallenged. Such action has placed the authority of law on the side of positions of monopoly power and against the interests of the public at large. The effects have been damaging to the economy and also to the prestige of the anti-trust laws.

As the last chapter has made clear, one of the most important instruments for exercise of countervailing power is the large retail organization. These by proxy are the public's main line of defense against the market power of those who produce or process consumers' goods. We have seen that they are an American counterpart of the consumer co-operatives which, in other countries, are viewed explicitly as an instrument for countering the power of the cartels. Yet the position of the large retail organizations has been not only a general, but also in some measure a unique object of government attack. Chain stores and other large buyers have been frequent recent objects of Sherman Act prosecution and are the special target of the Robinson–Patman Act which is especially designed to inhibit their exercise of countervailing power.

Under the provisions of the Robinson–Patman Act a chain store may receive the benefit of the demonstrably lower costs of filling the large orders which it places; it may not receive concessions that are the result of its superior bargaining power. The effect, since these concessions are important only when won from positions of original economic power, is to discriminate in favor of original power and against countervailing power.

The effects of failure to distinguish between original and countervailing power have been especially noteworthy in the several suits against the Great Atlantic and Pacific Tea Company. This company was prosecuted before the war for violation of the Robinson–Patman Act, was convicted of violation of the Sherman Act in a case brought in 1944 and finally decided in 1949, and was thereafter, for a period, again a defendant. In spite of its many legal misadventures, the company has not been charged with, or even seriously suspected of, exploiting the consumer. On the contrary, its crime has been too vigorous bargaining, which bargaining was, effectively, on the consumer's behalf. In the case brought in 1944 it was charged with seeking to increase its volume by reducing its margins and with bringing its bargaining power too vigorously to bear upon its suppliers in order to get price reductions. These suppliers – which included such powerful sellers as the large canning companies – had long been involved in a trial of strength with A & P over prices. They were left undisturbed. The government was in the highly equivocal position of prosecuting activities which have the effect of keeping down prices to the consumer. The positions of market power, which had given A & P its opportunity, were left untouched (6).

The litigation against A & P was strongly defended. Although the firm did rather less than ten per cent of the food-retailing business, had strong rivals, and was in an industry where, as observed in the last chapter, the entry of new firms is singularly easy, the danger was much stressed that it might achieve an effective monopoly of food-retailing. Nevertheless one can hardly doubt that these cases were a source of serious embarrassment to friends of the anti-trust laws. No explanation, however elaborate, could quite conceal the fact that the effect of anti-trust enforcement, in this case, was to the disadvantage of the public. Viewed in light of the present analysis the reason becomes evident. The prosecution, by inhibiting the exercise of countervailing power, provided protection to the very positions of market power that are anathema to the defender of the anti-trust laws.

No one should conclude, from the foregoing, that an exemption of countervailing power should now be written into the anti-trust laws. A considerable gap has always separated useful economic concepts from applicable legal ones. However, a number of conclusions, with immediate bearing on the anti-trust laws, do follow from this analysis. In the first place the mere possession and exercise of market power is not a useful criterion for anti-trust action. The further and very practical question must be asked: Against whom and for what purposes is the power being exercised? Unless this question is asked and the answer makes clear that the public is the victim, the anti-trust laws, by attacking countervailing power, can as well enhance as reduce monopoly power.

Secondly, it is clear that some damage can be done to the economy by such legislation as the Robinson–Patman Act. This legislation is the culmination of a long and confused legal and legislative struggle dating from 1914 over what economists have come to call price discrimination. The ostensible motive of the legislation is to protect competition. The seller is prevented from giving a lower price to one customer than to another where the lower price cannot be justified by the economies associated with the particular sale and where the effect is 'to injure, destroy, or prevent' competition either with the seller or between his customers. The practical effect, reinforced by recent court decisions, is to make any important price concessions to any large buyer of questionable legality.

Even those who are unwavering in their belief in competition have been inclined to doubt whether this legislation does much to protect competition. What is not doubtful at all is that the legislation strikes directly at the effective exercise of countervailing power. To achieve price discrimination – to use bargaining power to get a differentially lower price – is the very essence of the exercise of countervailing power. In trying, with questionable effect, to preserve one of the autonomous regulators of the economy the government is seriously impairing another.

Finally, the theory of countervailing power throws important light on the advantage of different numbers of firms in an industry and on the objectives of the anti-trust laws in relation thereto. One of the effects of the new ideas on market theory was to raise serious doubts whether an industry of small numbers was, in fact, socially preferable to a monopoly. Once firms had recognized their interdependence, it was believed that they would find a price, output and profit position not greatly different from that which would be achieved by a single firm. This made it doubtful whether it was worth while to prosecute a monopoly in order to create an oligopoly.

The examination of the relation of oligopoly to technical change and development will already have raised some questions about this conclusion. There is reason to suppose that an industry characterized by oligopoly will be more progressive than an industry controlled by one firm. Recognition of the role of countervailing power suggests a further clear advantage on the side of the oligopoly. One can hardly doubt that, in general, it will be much easier for countervailing power to break into a position of market strength maintained by an imperfect coalition of three, four or a dozen firms than into a position held by one firm. When there is more than one firm in a market there are opportunities for playing one off against another. Mistrust and uncertainty can be developed in the mind of one entrepreneur as to the intentions and good faith of others. These, in turn, can be translated into bargaining concessions. Such opportunities abruptly disappear when the number is reduced to one.

Thus the theory of countervailing power comes to the defense of the anti-trust laws at what has been a very vulnerable point. Efforts to prevent or to disperse single-firm control of an industry can be defended for the greater opening they provide for the exercise of countervailing power. Similar and equally good reasons exist for resisting mergers. Those who have always believed there was something uniquely evil about monopoly are at least partly redeemed by the theory of countervailing power. [. . .]

References
1. G. J. STIGLER, 'An economist plays with blocs' *American Economic Review Proceedings*, vol. 44, no. 2, May 1954.
2. A. HUNTER, 'Notes on countervailing power', *Economic Journal*, vol. 48, March 1958.
3. The Monopolies Commission, *Electrical and Allied Machinery and Plant*, H.M.S.O., February 1957.
4. The Monopolies Commission, *Electronic Valves and Tubes*, H.M.S.O., December 1956.
5. The Monopolies Commission, *Pneumatic Tyres*, H.M.S.O., December 1955.
6. M. A. ADELMAN, *A. & P: A Study in Price-Cost Behaviour and Public Policy*, Harvard University Press, 1954.

8 B. S. Yamey

Resale Price Maintenance: The Economic Issues

Excerpt from B. S. Yamey (ed.), *Resale Price Maintenance*, Weidenfeld and Nicolson, London, 1966, chapter 1.

Introduction

Resale price maintenance is a restrictive business practice: it restricts or eliminates price competition in the distributive trades affected. In the typical situation it raises retail prices and narrows consumers' choice; and by widening the gross margins of distributors without at the same time eliminating all forms of competitive behaviour, it attracts more labour and other resources into distribution. It is not surprising, therefore, that in the post-war period there has been growing public and official concern with r.p.m. in all Western countries which are experiencing strains on their national resources in conditions of full or over-full employment.

Further, since r.p.m. bears directly on retail prices, the practice provokes mounting criticism in periods of inflation, more particularly when, as is increasingly the vogue, governments attempt to introduce and implement general prices and incomes policies. It should be clear, however, that the relationship between r.p.m. and the process or the control of inflation is tenuous. The practice has little, if any, influence on *total* national money expenditure or on the availability of *total* national resources. It is relevant to the economy-wide issues of inflation mainly in so far as it affects the flexibility of particular prices. Moreover, the act of eliminating r.p.m. may create a situation of price reductions which may be favourable tactically for particular measures of policy to control or to contain inflation. But this in its nature can be no more than a once-for-all possibility. One cannot abolish r.p.m. every few years. The real importance of r.p.m., or of its prohibition or reduction, lies in its effects on the prices of particular goods and the deployment of resources between different economic activities. It is to be judged primarily in these terms, seen in the wider context of competition in industry and trade, and also in the yet wider context of the interests of consumers.

Distributors' Margins and Retail Prices

The proposition that r.p.m. raises retail prices and retailers' margins turns on the proposition that competing retailers do not have uniform costs per unit of sales.[1] Inter-firm differences in cost provide the basis for price competition; the independent pricing decisions of competing retailers and the responses of consumers lead to the elimination of the least efficient retailers, to the expansion (including the establishment) of more efficient firms, and to the availability of a range of competing offerings of different combinations of retail prices and services to meet the varied and varying preferences of consumers. Resale price maintenance obstructs the process of price competition. It therefore keeps distributive margins and resale prices higher than they would otherwise be and involves more resources in distribution.

The basic proposition is sometimes called in question. Thus it has been suggested or implied that the costs of retailing (or of distribution) are almost wholly fixed, and the elimination of r.p.m. would mean simply that the prices and gross margins of certain articles are reduced, while those of other articles are raised, with the average level of prices and gross margins left much the same as before. In other words, it seems that consumers as a body have to bear a given quantum of retailing costs whatever happens; the presence or absence of r.p.m. affects merely the distribution of the total costs among the various goods bought by them. If this were so, the case for the abolition or reduction of r.p.m. would be weakened, though even then it is not obvious that the distribution of the total costs with r.p.m. is in any sense better than that without r.p.m. But the thesis of the fixed quantum of distribution costs, or any analysis implying its validity, is untenable on several grounds.

The thesis of the fixed quantum seems to be derived from the

1. For convenience in exposition, the discussion proceeds in terms of 'retailers' rather than the more embracing and strictly more relevant 'distributors'. The argument applies, *mutatis mutandis*, also to 'wholesalers'.

proposition that the costs of running a particular shop are almost all in the nature of fixed overheads. This proposition is, however, seriously inadequate, if only because a large part of the gross profits of small-scale retailing consists of the earnings of the proprietors; and this element is not fixed. But even if, *arguendo*, the proposition be accepted that the running costs of any one shop are a fixed quantity, it would not follow that each shop has the same level of fixed costs. Location, density of shopping traffic, range and quality of services, scale of operation and efficiency are among the factors affecting the level of the (assumed) fixed costs, both absolutely and also relatively to turnover. The thesis would apply only if the abolition of r.p.m. and the restoration of retail price competition did not affect the number, distribution, size, and ownership of shops and the level of services provided in them. A prediction of such an outcome cannot be entertained seriously in the representative case. Retailer supporters of r.p.m. would certainly not subscribe to it: and several of the standard arguments for r.p.m. reject implicitly the thesis of the fixed quantum of retailing costs. The thesis would have relevance, indeed, only if retailing were different from all other forms of business activity, because it postulates both that the requirements of customers are uniform and also that the unit costs of suppliers are uniform, or sufficiently so as to rule out the possibilities of competitive substitution.

It is the disregard, in a system of r.p.m., of differences in consumer requirements and preferences and of differences in costs of retailing which points to the conclusion that r.p.m. keeps the retail prices of the goods in question higher than they would otherwise be. By stopping price competition in retailing, the practice impedes the replacement of high-cost by low-cost forms of retailing, and of less efficient by more efficient firms. The brake on price competition is especially severe on the development of new forms of retailing.

Although one can assert with some confidence that, typically, r.p.m. raises retail prices and retail gross margins above their competitive levels, it is more difficult to measure the extent of these effects. Thus it is difficult to predict with confidence by how much prices and margins would fall in a particular trade if r.p.m. were to be abolished in that trade. Examination of such matters as the shopping behaviour of consumers or the costs and profits of retailers engaged in the trade in question would be of little help in guiding the prediction, because they are conditioned by the practice of r.p.m. itself. Moreover, it is not easy to determine the effects of r.p.m. on prices and margins even after it has been terminated in a particular trade. The more immediate effect on prices can, of course, be observed; but then it is not always easy to distinguish the more lasting price reductions from the more spectacular price cuts executed by high-spirited and publicity-conscious retailers released from the irritations of r.p.m. As, however, the date of the end of r.p.m. recedes into the distance, the particular effects of r.p.m. and of its termination are increasingly difficult to gauge. Thus the relative costs of factors of production used in manufacturing and in distribution do not stand still; consumer preferences change; and the general price level rises or falls for reasons quite unconnected with r.p.m. or its absence.

Even where, miraculously, there are no disturbances of this kind, time-series of retailers' margins, in particular, may contain pitfalls for the incautious. These arise from the fact that different retailing enterprises engage to a greater or lesser extent in what can be called wholesaling activities. Thus, broadly, large-scale retailing enterprises tend to do all or most of their own wholesaling, buying direct from manufacturers, whilst the smallest-scale retailing enterprises use extensively the services of independent wholesalers; and there are endless gradations between the two poles. The gross margin of a retailing enterprise, which in reality is a vertically integrated wholesaling-retailing enterprise, refers to a span of economic activity which is wider than that of a more strictly retailing enterprise. Censuses of distribution do not ask vertically integrated distributors to split their over-all margin, the difference between final selling prices and initial buying prices, into separate 'retail' and 'wholesale' margins (and if they were required to do so, the split would be arbitrary). Hence a census average of gross margins in a trade is an average of individual margins which do not relate to the same span of activity. This would not matter if, over time, the relative proportions of different categories of retailer remained substantially unchanged and if retailers in a particular category did not change their degree of vertical integration with wholesaling. But these conditions are not likely to be satisfied, except within the limits of very short periods. Indeed, if the analysis of r.p.m. and its effects is correct, the abolition (or introduction) of r.p.m. would be likely to change the relative proportions of different categories of retailer and might also induce changes in the extent of vertical integration engaged in by some of them. In such a situation, a recorded change in *average* retail gross margins would be difficult if not impossible to interpret. Paradoxically, the average retail gross margin of a group of retailers may increase even where the average gross margin of each constituent category of retailers has fallen.

To escape from the complications introduced by the passage of time, it may seem more promising to make price comparisons between pairs of territories, only one of which has r.p.m. in a particular trade. Such comparisons are valid for the purpose of measuring the effects of r.p.m. only where the two territories are substantially the same in all relevant respects such as density of population, consumer preferences, costs of factors of production, intensity of manufacturers' advertising, and taxes on goods and transactions, and different only in respect of the presence and absence of r.p.m. There is therefore not much point in comparisons between, say, the United States and the United Kingdom. The United States itself, however, provides scope for more relevant comparisons, since some states allow r.p.m. and others do not. As Professor Hollander shows, several studies on this basis have been made; and he discusses their findings and limitations (1). [. . .]

Confidence in the proposition that r.p.m. has the typical effect of raising retail prices would be severely shaken if such studies, when carefully conducted in appropriate situations, found in favour of r.p.m. In fact, they have not done so. Confidence would be even more seriously shaken if consumers could be seen to be behaving in a way which contradicted the proposition. Such behaviour would be where consumers living in an area without r.p.m. in a particular trade bought the goods in question from a near-by area with r.p.m. (and otherwise reasonably comparable in relevant respects) either by making systematic shopping forays into that area or by mail-order buying from retailers operating from that area. There is no evidence of this kind. There is, on the contrary, evidence of inter-area trade in the opposite direction, as the proposition would lead one to expect. Professor Hollander refers to the importance of such trade in the United States; and Mr Boggis draws attention to analogous developments undermining r.p.m. in some countries within the European Economic Community (1).

The preceding discussion has been conducted explicitly in terms of the typical working of r.p.m. This qualification is necessary because special circumstances are conceivable in which r.p.m. may have little or no effect on prices, and yet more exceptional circumstances in which it may serve to keep retail prices (and margins) *lower* than they would be otherwise. The conceivable exceptions considered here fit into the general analysis; they depend on the presence of conditions in which price competition (or, indeed, any form of competition) among retailers for some reason or other is weak or non-existent regardless of whether or not there is r.p.m.

Competitive pressures may be low in a trade because of its peculiar structure: the 'shopping' mobility of consumers of the goods may be so low and their total demand so limited that the retailers in each locality are few in number, uncompetitive in behaviour, and protected from the competition of retailers in other localities. The abolition of r.p.m. in such situations may leave prices, margins and the structure of retailing virtually undisturbed. In this connexion the role of resale price *recommendations* (not enforced by the manufacturers) may be important. They may provide a framework of retail pricing to support and to strengthen the non-competitive tendencies and behaviour of the retailers. But this is not the inevitable effect of resale price recommendations. In other circumstances they may encourage and accentuate retail price competition. It is interesting that in Ireland the retailer in some cases is not allowed to advertise his own selling price together with that of the manufacturer's recommended price: the purpose of the prohibition is to mitigate competition. (See (1), the Canadian, the Danish and Swedish chapters also include discussions of price recommendations.)

The most exceptional and unusual situations are those in which the termination of r.p.m. may cause the retail prices of the goods in question to be higher than otherwise by causing retail margins (for a given span of distributive activity) to be higher than otherwise. Consider a situation in which each retailer has an effective monopoly of the sale of goods in his market area, and does not have to fear actual or potential competition. The resale prices he would set in his own interests might conceivably be higher than those which the manufacturer would wish to set in his own interests. The retailer's optimal resale prices would reduce sales below the level which would be optimal for the manufacturer. Should the manufacturer be able to prescribe fixed resale prices for his goods, he could force the retailer away from his optimal position towards his own optimal position, reduce the retailer's profits and increase his own. Here, r.p.m. would reduce retail prices. The manufacturer, it may be noted, could achieve the same object not by fixing his resale prices but by prescribing and enforcing *maximum* resale prices; and yet another method would be the stipulation of a minimum sales quota for each local monopolist stocking his goods, a device which, applied effectively, would indirectly allow the manufacturer to set an upper limit to the retailer's price.

The situation has been considered above in terms of local retail monopolies. The analysis is largely applicable also to local groups of retailers agreeing effectively to concert policy on pricing, as in the Swedish tobacco trade discussed by Professor af Trolle (1). It is unlikely, however, however, that such situations (and those discussed in the paragraph preceding the last) are common in a modern economy, though national differences in the density of population preclude broad generalizations. Many shoppers are mobile and have easy access to important market centres. Mail-order business also breaks down the power of local monopolies or monopoly groups. The important and persistent cases are likely to be those where entry into retailing or changes in the number of retailers handling a particular important brand of products are controlled restrictively, either as a by-product of official control over the use of sites for business purposes or in pursuance of a manufacturer's policy of marketing through selected exclusive dealers, each with a sales territory assigned to him. A possible example in which both influences are combined is noted briefly in the chapter on the United Kingdom (1).

Retail Price Competition and Manufacturers' Price Competition

The economics of r.p.m. are generally discussed in terms of its effects on competition in the distributive trades. The practice may, however, also affect price competition among manufacturers.

Although it is difficult to assess the significance of r.p.m. in this respect, it nevertheless seems improbable that r.p.m. is less important for its effects on competition in distribution than for its effects on competition in production.

The control of resale prices may affect price competition in manufacturing industry in various ways. The most direct way is where manufacturers who have a price agreement sell part of their output direct to consumers or users and part to resellers. For the agreement to be effective, the manufacturers have to fix both their price to the trade and their (higher) price to be charged on direct sales to users. Their reseller customers are, however, also their competitors in relation to sales to some or all final buyers. Insistence on r.p.m. ensures that the resellers, whatever their wishes may be, in effect become parties to the price agreement. If r.p.m. were not practised manufacturers would tend to become involved in price competition in sales to final consumers or users. This competition might, in turn, weaken or undermine the entire price agreement, and so provoke price competition among the manufacturers both in sales to resellers as well as in sales to final consumers or users. Whether such disruptive effects need be serious in the long run depends on the considerations discussed at the end of this section.

Resale price maintenance can serve the purposes of a group of manufacturers acting together in restraint of competition by being part of a bargain with associations of established dealers to induce the latter not to handle the competing products of excluded manufacturers. Collective policies of r.p.m. have often been part and parcel of agreements among manufacturers (2), as is illustrated in several of the studies (1).

Resale price maintenance may affect competition in manufacturing in a different way. By eliminating or restricting price competition in retailing, it may prevent or retard the growth of large firms in retailing, and thereby inhibit the building-up or strengthening of bargaining power which could be used to disrupt price agreements or non-collusive oligopolistic price structures in supplying industries. A weaker explanation sometimes encountered is that large distributors who possess bargaining power are under less pressure to use it when their own margins and selling prices are protected by r.p.m.; the removal of r.p.m. and the release of price competition in retailing force them to use their bargaining strength to the full. This explanation is weaker because it assumes that large distributors would not use their bargaining power unless they themselves were subject to competitive stress.

Retail price competition may provoke price competition in manufacturing in yet another way. Especially in industries in which there are only a small number of manufacturers, non-competitive price policies (whether the result of formal or informal price agreements or the result of individual restraint induced by the logic of an oligopolistic situation) may be subverted by price competition in the retail markets. This comes about when price competition among retailers has the effect of causing changes in the relative sales (market shares) of the brands of the members of the oligopoly group. Such changes occur whenever retail price-cutting is not spread evenly over all brands, but favours the sale of some brand(s) at the expense of the others. Changes in relatives sales, if they are material and also not ephemeral, are likely to weaken the restraint of the particular manufacturer(s) who is at a disadvantage; and to that extent concealed (or even open) reductions in trade prices are likely to be offered to selected (or all) retailers in attempts to recapture business. Should retail price-cutting shift from brand to brand, the resulting instability in market shares may well disrupt established non-competitive price policies and make it difficult to resurrect them. Furthermore, experience of increased instability in the market shares of the leading brands brought about by retail price competition may embolden each individual manufacturer to seek to increase his share (and not merely to maintain a given share) by concealed and possibly selective reductions in his trade price. Each of them may reckon that his competitors might desist from retaliation for some time because they might be more likely to ascribe an observed change in market shares to disturbances emanating independently in the retail market than to infer that he was attracting more business by cutting his price to retailers; and price competition would ensue from such (mutually frustrating) tactics. In general, the wider the 'normal' expected fluctuations in market shares, the less likely are price agreements or non-competitive price policies to be effective (3).

Resale price maintenance, by eliminating one external source of instability, to that extent tends to support price agreements or pricing arrangements in manufacturing industry. It is extremely difficult to judge the importance of this effect in general terms. To give much importance to it is to imply a high degree of 'instability' in price competition in retailing. Instability of this kind does not seem to be a prominent feature of retail price competition.

The Supply of Retail Services

That r.p.m. restrains price competition in retailing, and that it sometimes has the effect of restraining price competition in manufacturing industry, constitute two serious charges against the practice. In defence of the practice, on the other hand, a number and variety of claims in favour of r.p.m. have been developed over the decades, ranging from the claim that it (in specific cases or in general) is necessary to protect certain trading or manufacturing interests from price competition to the claim that price competition as such harms the interests of consumers as well as of the economy at large.

Professor af Trolle presents an analysis of a number of them in his chapter (1). No exhaustive catalogue or examination will be attempted here. The multiplicity and multiformity of the claims are not correlated with the cogency and weight of the case for r.p.m. It is more to the point to consider a group of claims which have analytical interest and have some bearing on a number of types of market situation which have been prominent in the devising and implementation of official policies towards r.p.m. These claims all relate to the supply of services by retailers to consumers. They are not as a rule applied by their advocates indiscriminately to all situations in which r.p.m. is or has been practised, but only to those situations in which particular retail services are more or less plausibly, considered to be important for consumers or for manufacturers of the goods in question.

The underlying idea is that, because r.p.m. ordinarily widens their gross margins and safeguards them against erosion, retailers are in a position to give more services to their customers together with the sale of the goods; and that, because competition (apart from price competition) is not prevented by r.p.m., retailers are obliged to give more services in order to win or retain customers.

Thus consumers have the benefit of competition in the form of more retail services; they pay for them in the prices of the goods they buy.

While this effect of r.p.m. in enlarging the provision of retail services seems indisputable, it is difficult to establish that it is in the consumers' interest, and less difficult to suggest that it is unlikely to be in their interests when the general implications of r.p.m. are kept in mind. First, in order to show that the effect is in the interests of consumers, it must be shown that in the absence of r.p.m. consumers would not be supplied with the same volume of services on the same or better terms if it is assumed (as the claim must assume) that the consumers in some collective sense want that volume of services and are prepared to meet its costs. Second, it is realistic to suppose that not all consumers want the same amount and kinds of retail services; some of them would be willing to do without certain services if they were free to choose from among several competing combinations of retail price and type and quality of retail service. With r.p.m., they cannot exercise such a choice and express their preferences. In this respect, r.p.m. involves the subsidization of some consumers by those others who in fact do not use their 'share' of the services for which they pay. Third, while it is reasonable to say that r.p.m. increases the total expenditure by retailers (and hence by consumers) on retail services, it does not follow that the practice is effective in increasing expenditure on any particular kind of retail service. In so far as a particular claim for r.p.m. is that it augments the supply of a certain kind of service desired by consumers, there is a gap in the reasoning. The retailer is not required by r.p.m. as such to use his additional margin to increase his expenditure in any particular way. Should a manufacturer wish to see the supply of a certain kind of retail service increased, he may well find it more effective to achieve this end by rewarding only those retailers who carry out his wishes. He can do this by confining the sale of his goods to retailers who do what he wants or by giving better terms to those retailers who meet his requirements. (He can also himself supply the 'retail' services to consumers, regardless of the retail outlet patronized.) These practices are independent of a policy of r.p.m.

The analysis sketched above can be applied to various categories of retail service. Services such as credit, delivery, installation and maintenance provide no support to the case for r.p.m. There is no difficulty in the way of retailers to make separate charges, by charging higher prices, for those of their customers who want the services. Services such as the availability of selections, demonstrations and stocks of goods and the provision of advice to customers are, however, in a different category. They cannot be charged for separately; and those who use the services need not buy the goods from the shops which incur the costs of providing them, but may patronize, instead, shops which avoid these costs and reduce their prices accordingly. Thus r.p.m., it seems, would stimulate the supply of such before-sales services, to the benefit of those consumers who want them and would be prepared to meet their costs (and to the disadvantage of those other consumers who do not want them). The difficulty remains, however, that r.p.m. by itself cannot ensure that pre-sales services will be increased: it is possible, and sometimes highly probable, that competing retailers will find it in their interests to use the additional margin of r.p.m. on other services such as more convenient and more expensive locations, more attractive decor and amenities and more credit.

Two more specialized claims for r.p.m., in which the subsidization effect of r.p.m. is recognized to be at the heart of the matter, require some discussion. The first claim is the tendency for r.p.m. to increase the number and the geographical dispersion of shops selling the goods or brands in question. In this way retail service to consumers is improved: they have more convenient access to more numerous sources of supplies. It may be thought that, in the absence of r.p.m., the number and dispersion of outlets would be adjusted more accurately to the varied and varying preferences of consumers, and that the optimal amount of shopping convenience would ensue, with each consumer in the position of being able to choose from among a variety of combinations of retail price and shopping convenience. At this point, however, the subsidization effect has to be introduced specifically into the analysis. It is conceivable that, without r.p.m., some localities may be denuded of shops selling the particular goods. If many of the consumers living in the locality find it profitable to buy their needs elsewhere, too few less mobile consumers may be left to support the stocking of the goods in that locality. Resale price maintenance would be in the interests of such groups of consumers if, given the uniformity of retail prices imposed by r.p.m., more of the consumers would prefer to buy locally and hence make profitable the stocking of the goods. The advantages gained by these groups would, however, be paid for by the rest of the consumers (4).

Although both claims involve the subsidization of some consumers at the expense of others, the second claim differs from the preceding one in that it refers to subsidization of the sale of some goods at the expense of others, not some places of sale at the expense of others. Thus it is sometimes said that while r.p.m. in certain trades raises the retailers' gross margins on some articles (the fast-moving popular articles), it enables the gross margins on other articles (the articles in less popular demand) to be lower than they would be otherwise. The retailer obtains a satisfactory average gross margin, even though the sale of the less popular articles is subsidized. Two comments are in point. The first comment is that it is not clear why the manufacturers of the goods in question should find it desirable or expedient to bring about this cross-subsidization. It is not clear, that is, why those manufacturers who are predominantly interested in the sale of the popular items should wish to burden them with higher retail margins and prices than they thought necessary for *their* effective distribution, simply in order to facilitate the reduction of the gross margins on less popular items, predominantly supplied by other manufacturers. It would appear, therefore, that the cross-subsidization can at best be expected to be found in those situations in which all or most of the manufacturers are as interested in the production of the slow-moving as they are in that of the fast-moving lines: specialists concentrating on the latter would have no reason to follow the pricing pattern voluntarily. Even where this condition were satisfied, it is not obvious that the implied cross-subsidization would be profitable for the manufacturers. The purposive adoption of pricing practices to achieve cross-subsidization would seem to require, further, that the manufacturers have some non-pecuniary interest in the production and sale of the slow-moving lines.

The second comment echoes a point made earlier, namely, that r.p.m. as such does not ensure that the additional margin allowed, *ex hypothesi*, to retailers on the sale of the fast-selling lines will be used by them to stock and sell the slow-selling lines, the sale of which, again *ex hypothesi*, has been made unprofitable for them. The implied over-generous rewarding of the resale of the fast-sellers would seem to encourage retailers to concentrate on their sale; and would achieve the unintended subsidization of retailers rather than the intended subsidization of slow-selling lines. It is of interest, in this connexion, to refer to the earlier temporary exemption of the book trade in Sweden from the prohibition of r.p.m. (1). The argument based on the cross-subsidization of slow-selling books by fast-selling books was accepted by the authorities; but, in addition to r.p.m. in the book trade, there were other trade regulations which required booksellers to take copies of all new books at their publishers' discretion and on consignment terms. Such regulations helped to ensure that whatever cross-subsidization was inherent in resale pricing was made more effective in achieving a desired purpose.

In the preceding discussion in this section various claims made for r.p.m. have been examined critically and their limitations explained. The criticism cannot, however, establish that there can be no special cases in practice, and that, where the special effects of r.p.m. are achieved, they cannot in some sense be in the interests of consumers collectively. Indeed, the possibility of special cases perhaps helps to explain why only one country, Canada, has yet seen fit to prohibit all r.p.m. without any exceptions or provisions for possible exceptions, although Sweden will soon have reached the same result by a different route. The more common post-war approach, exemplified in the policy measures considered in several of the succeeding chapters, is to provide, in some way or other, for exceptions from the general principle that r.p.m. is against the public interest. It must be a matter of judgement whether it is worth while to devise elaborate arrangements for the discovery and exemption of exceptional cases.

Loss Leaders

In an undated manuscript, published after his death, Alfred Marshall wrote that 'there must always be a good many movements of retail price which stand in no relation to changes in the wholesale trade [meaning, in the context, changes in the wholesale price], or are even in opposite directions'. Included in the examples given is that of the individual retailer who 'may move the price of a certain commodity apparently at random, when he or a neighbouring rival begins or ceases to make it a catch article'. Marshall concluded: 'But all cases of this kind put together cover a very small part of the transactions of life: and it would not have been worth while to call attention to them at all, were it not that they have furnished sensational material to writers who have argued that retail prices generally are arbitrary and scarcely at all subject to economic law' (5). Similarly, but in a different context, it would not have been worth while to consider here, however briefly, the practice of loss-leader selling were it not for the prominent place it frequently has assumed in public discussion and political debate on the subject of r.p.m. The attention paid to loss-leader selling in those discussions of r.p.m. has been wholly disproportionate to the intrinsic importance and quantitative extent of loss-leader selling (unless it is meaninglessly equated with all retail price competition).

The charges laid at the door of loss-leader selling – and constituting defences of r.p.m. – are directed against three types of effect it is said to have. First, it is said to jeopardize the goodwill of established brands, to disturb their steady supply and thereby raise costs, affect their ready availability or prejudice the maintenance of their quality. Second, it is said to be a device by which large-scale retail firms can drive their competitors out of business and so establish effective monopoly positions. Third, it is said that consumers, as shoppers, are confused and misled by loss-leader selling. Having listed the charges, it will not be necessary to go into an examination of them, either analytically or in terms of the available evidence. Professor Skeoch's chapter includes an extended discussion of the loss-leader question, and several of the other chapters also refer to it (1). Moreover, the tendency in public policy is to divorce the issue of r.p.m. from that of loss-leader selling. Thus where loss-leader selling is considered to be a problem requiring control in the public interest, it is being treated separately without involving the retention of r.p.m. This is both reasonable and sensible, because r.p.m. is at best a crude instrument with which to attempt to curb or to control loss-leader selling. It is more questionable whether it is necessary, in the interests of consumers or of the economy as a whole, to have any controls over loss-leader selling, since these controls may have unintended consequences to the detriment of the public.

The Stability of Resale Price Maintenance

It is sometimes said that r.p.m. is inherently unstable in the sense that it creates the conditions for its own eventual collapse or weakening. The long-run forces of competition will destroy or circumvent r.p.m. even where this is practised by manufacturers who are intent on retaining it and enforcing it. The thesis is that those distributors who do not need or want the higher margins given by r.p.m. will in due course disrupt the system by selling the goods at the lower margins and retail prices made possible by their own efficiency or low-cost methods of operation.

The historical evidence on the stability of r.p.m. is not easy to interpret. On the one hand there is the record of effective r.p.m. in several branches of trade in the United Kingdom and some other countries: r.p.m. has prevailed for half a century or more, with at most occasional temporary setbacks, despite changes in general economic conditions, in methods and organization of production, in the organization of distribution, in the share of price-maintained goods in the total trade, and in the methods of enforcement open to price-maintaining manufacturers. There is ample evidence, that is, of persistent and enduring r.p.m. There are, on the other hand, several instances of the collapse of r.p.m. The United States provides some major examples. But it is not simple in such cases to decide the relative contributions to the breakdown made by the long-run pressures of competition and by the peculiar difficulties of enforcement caused by the multiplicity of jurisdictions and differences in state policies which played into the hands of price-cutting retailers. Professor Hollander reviews this problem in his chapter (1). Differences in national policies towards r.p.m. in the member-countries of the European Economic Community may result in similar problems of enforcement, as Mr Boggis explains (1). In yet other examples it is not easy to decide whether the withdrawal of r.p.m. by certain manufacturers was due to a recognition of its imminent collapse under the stress of changing competitive conditions in the distributive trades, or whether it reflected little more than voluntary submission to changes in public opinion. The German experience of extensive breakdown of r.p.m. does, however, seem to be unambiguous, although the law and its administration made some contribution.

Assuming no such disturbance as a change in the law, r.p.m. in a particular trade may be expected to crumble or to decline in importance in certain circumstances, whatever the manufacturers may prefer. Thus where one or a few important retailers, who already had built up a large volume of trade in the price-maintained goods, decide to cut their prices, the manufacturers may find it expedient to give way. Historically, however, situations of this type do not seem to have been common. The threat to r.p.m. has not usually come from well-established large-scale retailing firms with a large stake in the distribution of the particular goods. More frequently, it seems, the threat has come from newly established firms wishing to try new methods of distribution or different price policies. (This is also true, though perhaps to a smaller extent, of the exploitation of the new opportunities opened up by an official prohibition of r.p.m., as is illustrated, for example, by Mr Kjølby in his chapter on Danish experience (1).) But threats from such a source are generally not serious. Newcomers to the retail trades tend to be operating on a small scale initially. Moreover, because of r.p.m., they cannot quickly build up a large volume of business in the goods while conforming to the resale price conditions, and then change their spots by becoming price-cutters. The most likely threat in this context possibly comes from large-scale retailers who are well-established in some branch of trade operating on a low-cost, low-price basis and who then turn their attention, making use of their goodwill, to the price-maintained lines of another branch of trade. But even they would be up against the difficulty of building up a large volume of sales in the new lines when they, in the process, cannot offer competitively attractive price reductions on them; and until they have achieved such sales, their power to challenge the manufacturers is limited.

Another set of circumstances in which r.p.m. may be expected to crumble is where low-cost retailers can gain access to competing goods which they can market as their own 'private' brands and which they can price as they like. A necessary condition is that entry into the industry manufacturing the goods is not difficult, whether it is entry by an independent manufacturer or by the distributor. Where entry is relatively easy, in fact r.p.m. has rarely been important, as in many food and textile products. Resale price maintenance has been strong where private branding is handicapped, if not rendered impossible, by the presence of significant economies of large-scale production, by the need for large-scale sales promotion for the success of a brand, or by institutional constraints such as the laws relating to patents and copyright. Moreover, in so far as r.p.m. inhibits the establishment and growth of large competitively aggressive retailing firms, it makes it more difficult for private brands to be developed in effective opposition to the national brands. The ease of entry into private branding is in part a matter of the scale of requirements.

It should be added that the development of private brands by one or several large distributors need not always undermine r.p.m. In some situations it may be the most profitable course for the private-branding distributor(s) not to price his private brands so competitively as to force the manufacturers of the national brands to jettison their r.p.m. or to reduce their prices. The private brander may find it expedient to act as if he were part of the oligopoly group. Alternatively, a large-scale distributor may find it profitable to refrain from having private brands – even where this would present no difficulties on the supply side – if the manufacturers of the national brands recognize that he presents a threat by granting him specially favourable terms on the purchase of their price-maintained brands.

The Diversity of Policies

Whatever the strength of the long-run forces of competition and economic change might be, it is apparent that governments which have been worried about r.p.m. in the post-war period have not been prepared to rely on those forces either to cause the breakdown of the practice or the moderation of its exercise. For one reason or another, to achieve one purpose or another, various governments have intervened with compulsory prohibition, curtailment or amendment of r.p.m. A variety of policies has ensued. The differences reflect a number of considerations, pressures and influences. There have been differences in the assessment of the economic effects of alternative policy measures; differences in the weights attached to various interest groups; differences in legal institutions and traditions; and differences in the approach to monopoly and restrictive arrangements generally. The seven chapters which follow have as one main theme the development of policy towards r.p.m. in a number of countries, and they illustrate a diversity of approach and method.

Despite the diversity of policies adopted and the differences in the economies in which they are applied, three conclusions emerge with some clarity. First, the termination of r.p.m. does not automatically and in every instance lead to price competition in distribution. Competitive pressures are sometimes low: there is little of them to be released. Further, it requires careful ancillary provisions in the law to ensure that something akin to r.p.m. does not operate after the practice itself has been formally discontinued. Moreover, where apprehensions about the depredations allegedly caused by loss-leader selling have given rise to measures to combat such activities, it is possible that 'genuine' price competition may be blunted in the process. Second, the termination or breakdown of r.p.m. has generally made it possible or easier for major changes to take place in the structure of retailing and wholesaling; it has facilitated or accelerated the kind of change which has been to the advantage of consumers. Third, subject to one or two documented exceptions consumers do not seem to have been hurt by the termination of r.p.m. along the lines predicted by supporters of the practice, and frequently they have derived substantial advantages from such a course.

References
1. L. A. Skeoch, S. C. Hollander, U. Af Trolle, H. Kjølby, F. O. Boggis and C. Brock, chapters 2–7 in B. S. Yamey (ed.), *Resale Price Maintenance*, Weidenfeld and Nicolson, London, 1966.
2. L. G. Telser, 'Why should manufacturers want fair trade', *Journal of Law and Economics*, vol. 3, 1960.
3. G. J. Stigler, 'A theory of oligopoly', *Journal of Political Economy* vol. 72, 1964.
4. J. R. Gould and L. E. Preston, 'Resale price maintenance and retail outlets', *Economics*, vol. 32, 1965.
5. A. Marshall, 'Retail prices' in A. C. Pigou (ed.), *Memorials of Alfred Marshall*, Macmillan, London, 1925.

Part Three   The Legal Framework

In making arrangements to control monopoly and competition
a government has, broadly speaking, three choices open to
it. First, it may do nothing in the statutory sense.
'Conspiracies' to monopolize or restrain trade may instead
be left to the jurisdiction of the ordinary law of the land;
and the initiative in seeking relief left with the private
individual or company. Second, a government may lean
towards the *control* of monopoly and restrictions of
competition. On the one hand, monopolies may be left free
to develop; but must be subject to surveillance and possibly
to direction. The British Monopolies Commission does this.
On the other hand, restrictions of competition may be brought
within some regularization arrangement. They become subject
to registration and cartelization; they have their rules, the
scope of their activities and their price levels approved;
and the contractual obligations between members made
specific. The German Cartel Decree of 1923 was of this sort.
Third, a government may prohibit completely, at least in
principle, all monopolization activities or restrictive
practices. This is the method of the U.S.A. In the following
readings Rostow shows the development of legal ideas in the
U.S.A. and Britain; the inherent difficulties involved in placing
economic judgements in the hands of a court are brought out
by Stevens and Yamey; and Neale provides an analysis of the,
still-developing, policy content of anti-trust law in the U.S.A.

9 E. V. Rostow

The Development of Law on Monopoly and Competition

Abridged version of E. V. Rostow, 'British and American experience with legislation against restraints of competition', *Modern Law Review*, vol. 23, no. 5, September, 1960.

The U.S.A.

[. . .]

After the middle of the nineteenth century, and more particularly in the last quarter of that century, the perennial problems of monopoly and restraint of trade began to present themselves in a new guise in all the industrialized countries. Such problems, raising basic issues of social justice and economic policy, have always been of concern to the law – occasionally, as in Tudor and Elizabethan times, of acute concern. About one hundred years ago, however, they changed in content and appearance. Both British and American courts began to face situations more difficult than price-rings among local brewers, coopers or salt merchants, and restrictive covenants in the sale of doctors' practices. Science was creating new industries, often on a large scale, and transforming the organization of old ones. To the familiar rhythm of the railway age, there was added the equally familiar rhythm of the modern factory system. Populations speeded up their movement from farm to city in the vast trek which everywhere defines the industrial revolution.

In the United States, the new industrial economy of the late nineteenth century took shape in a pattern which was somewhat different from that in Great Britain, France and Germany. American corporation law – the law governing the powers of joint stock companies – was state law, and not national law, for reasons characteristic of our federal system. At the time, it was weak law. And Gresham's most famous principle tended to make it weaker. It offered great freedom to the business leaders of the period in devising and carrying out schemes of amalgamation.

As Marshall remarked, the industrial temper in the United States was quite different from that in England.

> Here few of those who are very rich take a direct part in business, they generally seek safe investments for their capital; and, again, among those engaged in business the middle class predominates, and most of them are more careful to keep what they have than eager to increase it by risky courses. . . . In England . . . the dominant force is that of the average opinion of business men, and the dominant form of association is that of the joint-stock company. But in America the dominant force is the restless energy and the versatile enterprise of a comparatively few rich and able men who rejoice in that power of doing great things by great means that their wealth gives them, and who have but partial respect for those who always keep their violins under glass cases. The methods of a joint-stock company are not always much to their mind; they prefer combinations that are more mobile, more adventurous, and often more aggressive. For some purposes they have to put up with a joint-stock company; but then they strive to dominate it, not to be dominated by it. (1)

The American Titans hid neither their lights nor their violins. Advised by an imaginative bar, and financed by imaginative bankers, they established a series of giant holding companies, which had few exact counterparts in Britain, and were in turn different from the Continental cartels. Towards the end of the century, companies of this kind, or somewhat looser groupings of a few great combinations, had acquired positions of monopoly or near-monopoly in many basic industries – in steel, oil, sugar refining, anthracite coal, explosives, tobacco, meat packing, the manufacture of farm machinery and shoe machinery, and certain other important trades. Local railways were put together into regional systems, and programmes were developed to eliminate competition among them. One man of towering ambition, E. H. Harriman, even tried to combine all the railway networks of the country into one.

In the United States, as in other countries, protest against the burdens and injustices of industrialization and urban life gained in strength as the movement itself accelerated its momentum. Discontent was aggravated by the prolonged depression of the late nineteenth century, punctuated in the United States by occasional financial crises and panics, and by endemic and damaging bank

E. V. Rostow

failures. It was also a period of falling wheat prices, intensifying the protest of the farming regions. The adjustment of the economy and of the society to the vagaries of the trade cycle and to the pace of its rapid secular growth was both facilitated and complicated by the immense flood of immigrants who poured into the country at this time, largely into the industrial cities and towns. Trade unions were formed, and farmers' organizations of real power emerged, to seek redress against the railroads which transported their products, and against the groups dominating the markets in which they sold, and from which they bought. Vehement and effective popular books, newspapers, pamphlets and cartoons strongly coloured public opinion, in the mood of what was then called 'muck-raking'. And in that pre-television age, itinerant lecturers travelled up and down the land, denouncing the 'malefactors of great wealth', in President Theodore Roosevelt's phrase, and the abuses they were inflicting on the American people. The Business Heroes of the time – or Robber Barons, if you prefer – provided a dramatic focus for the sense of protest. The grandiose scale of their activities, and their manifest power, helped to revive ancient fears of exploitation, and gave strength to the outcry against monopoly.

The atmosphere was starkly described by Mr Justice Harlan of the Supreme Court of the United States in 1911:

All who recall the condition of the country in 1890 will remember that there was everywhere, among the people generally, a deep feeling of unrest. The nation had been rid of human slavery, fortunately as all now feel, but the conviction was universal that the country was in real danger from another kind of slavery sought to be fastened on the American people; namely, the slavery that would result from aggregations of capital in the hands of a few individuals and corporations controlling . . . the entire business of the country, including the production and sale of the necessaries of life. Such a danger was thought to be then imminent, and all felt that it must be met firmly and by such statutory regulations as would adequately protect the people against oppression and wrong. (2)

It was a time of violent strikes, of occasional riots, and of widespread bitterness. Words like Haymarket and Homestead, Pullman, the Molly McGuires and Pinkerton ring in American ears with a force akin to the echoes here of Peterloo and Chartism.

These sombre emotions were discharged, or at least somewhat reduced in intensity, by their release through political action, as well as by the return of prosperity, which relieved some of the economic misery of the eighties and nineties.

The political expression of these grievances was accomplished through the forms of American politics, which, in the examples of Jefferson, Jackson and Lincoln, had already established effective modes for dealing with social discontent. The American movement of social protest never became Marxist, although there were strong Socialists among its early leaders. Nor did it result, as was the case in Great Britain and other countries, in the formation of a political party based on the trade unions and the farmers' societies, or more broadly, on the organized support of the working classes. The historic pattern of the American party system proved to be too strong to be radically altered at this time by the thrust and counterthrust of industrialism and reform. The party system in the United States takes its shape from the electoral provisions of the Constitution. They make it necessary to elect a President through cumulative majorities, state by state. That need requires our national parties to be coalitions of state and regional parties, not truly national parties at all. Party alignments were then, as they probably are still, too strongly influenced by the passions of the Civil War and the Reconstruction period after it to be fundamentally affected by the new wave of popular feeling. The great cities of the North, with their large immigrant populations, were becoming largely Democratic in their party allegiance, along with the whole of the South. At that time, the South was agrarian and often, though by no means always, quite conservative in economic and social policy, save on the special question of the tariff. While the Republican Party after the Civil War was closely linked to the emergent business class, it included great farm areas in the West, which had been staunchly Unionist during the Civil War. And business groups were not at all united in their views on big business and monopoly. The smaller independent business man and banker, and many large business men as well, were quite as opposed, then and now, to economic dominance by a tiny group of Titans as were the leaders of farm groups and trade unions. The Republican Party was therefore a coalition, too, and, even after its catastrophic split in 1912, it was rich in progressive and even radical leaders, who appealed in many areas to the spirit of reform.

The nature of the party system determined the way in which the movement of protest found its fulfilment. The pressure of the movement was diffuse, and both parties responded to it, in a long cycle of legislative action which has continued to this day.

The first major response of the law to these demands was the enactment of two federal statutes, the Inter-State-Commerce Act of 1887, and the Sherman Act of 1890. Neither was passed by a party vote, and both parties have vied since in claiming credit for their passage, and their subsequent development. These statutes have become centres of far-reaching systems, whose influence has been felt in many parts of the economy and the public law.

The Inter-State Commerce Act accepted the railroads as natural monopolies, and established an administrative agency, the Inter-state Commerce Commission, to undertake their regulation on a continuing basis. At first the powers of the Commission were far from adequate. Gradually, however, as experience accumulated, the statutes were amended, and the Commission's understanding of its problems grew. That the laws and practices through which our transportation industries are now controlled require radical reform, in the light of totally changed conditions, is no reproach to the legislators of seventy years ago, who established the mechanism, and set it on its course.

In the Sherman Act, Congress chose the opposite approach. It did not view monopoly and restraint of trade as inevitable outside the field of public utilities. Nor did it choose the path, which has often seemed congenial to Marxists, of rather encouraging the growth of monopolies, as a stage in capitalist development which could hasten the day when their capitalist integuments would fall away, so that they could readily be nationalized as instruments of the public good. Rather, Congress looked to the competitive market as the principal regulator of price and output, and of wages, interests and profits. The Congressmen and Presidents of the day were confident that a competitive economy would assure a wide dispersal of power and of economic opportunity; they thought it would preserve the most appropriate economic foundation for a political and social order which, as Tocqueville saw, has always considered equality the first of its social ambitions. The policy of competition was even to be applied, to a significant extent, in the railroad industry itself, and later in other industries partially supervised by administrative bodies.

The Sherman Act contains only two brief substantive provisions. It condemns as criminal every contract, combination in the form of trust or otherwise, or conspiracy in restraint of trade or commerce among the several states, or with foreign nations. And equally, it condemns monopolizations, or attempts or conspiracies to monopolize any part of that trade or commerce. It embraces the entire constitutional area of Congress's power to regulate commerce, and declares for that realm two simple, and seemingly absolute, rules of business behaviour. There follow several novel procedural provisions, which give the Act a potentiality for influence far greater than that of the common law. The federal government is empowered to enforce the Act in criminal proceedings, or, what is more important, through suits in equity. And private persons, injured in their persons or property by violations of the Act, are authorized to sue, and to recover three times their actual damages, and costs, including a reasonable attorney's fee. This provision reincarnates an old English device, and multiplies the number of enforcement opportunities under the Act. There was a fourth enforcement procedure provided in the Act, that of libel, or condemnation of property held under any contract or other arrangement which violated the Act. It was an ingenious idea, but has not proved to be useful.

On the face of it, the immediate background of the Act, and the policy choices made by Congress in drafting it, offer several striking contrasts to the background and structure of the British legislation of 1948 and 1956. Why did Congress place its principal reliance on the ordinary federal courts, and why did it pass such sweeping legislation, absolute in form, and more complete in its prohibitions than comparable legislation in this and other countries?

Congress might have used an administrative agency, like the Interstate Commerce Commission it had just established, or specialized courts, like the Restrictive Practices Court here, or our own Tax Court, and Court of Customs and Patent Appeals. Experiments of that kind were in fact tried from time to time in the United States. We had a specialized anti-trust court, called the

Commerce Court, for a few years, and we still have the Federal Trade Commission, established in 1914 as a reform measure to improve anti-trust enforcement. But the main enforcement agency for the anti-trust laws was and remains that of the ordinary federal courts. Their inherent strength in the American scheme of things has made them more satisfactory and more acceptable than any rival institution, over the long run.

The reason for this decision, I think, is the special authority of the judiciary within our public law, and public life. The extraordinary importance of the American judiciary derives in large part from its power to declare statutes and acts of the executive unconstitutional. The power is a discreet one. It is exercised in a common-law matrix, and can only be asserted when a constitutional problem arises inescapably in the course of public or private litigation. Often resisted, it has thus far always prevailed. And it has become a valued, indeed an almost sacred, part of the political system. It is accepted by the public as a way of keeping political organs within the boundaries of their constitutional power, and of protecting minorities against the risk of majoritarian tyranny. The influence of this function colours the attitude of the American judges to their work, and of the public to the judges. In consequence, our judges approach their tasks with a good deal of the freedom and vigour which characterized the common law of an earlier day. It was thus entirely natural, in the American setting, to turn the policy problems implicit in the Sherman Act over to the judges, who already had quite comparable responsibilities on their desks.

If the task of enforcement was to be carried out primarily by judges, why wasn't the idea of a specialized and expert court accepted? Part of the reason for this choice, I think, was the magnitude of the problem presented. If the Sherman Act was enforceable at all, it would be beyond the reach of a single court, however expert. Then too, it was felt that offences which occurred in different parts of the country should be passed upon by local judges and local juries. And finally, there was an almost instinctive preference for a course which would require large parts of the bar, the judiciary and the public to confront these trying problems, and to be educated in their meaning by participating in their solution. *Per contra*, there is an advantage in having technical problems

167

finally resolved not by experts alone, but by the common sense of the ordinary judicial outlook.

The answer to the second question – why so sweeping a delegation of powers? – should be made in terms both of the situation to which the law was addressed and of the political system which enacted it. Congress was seeking to take a bold and massive step, commensurate with the visible growth of monopolies in the country, and the high state of public feeling on the subject. Legislative records in those days were not so revealing as they are today, with the modern development of congressional committees. But enough is available to confirm that Congress wanted to move energetically in altering the pattern of economic organization. It was not notably precise in defining its goals, nor did it see clearly how far it could succeed in busting the trusts. But it wanted radical action, and sought to take it, through a statute whose words sounded comfortingly familiar to a group of common-law lawyers, but were in fact untried. The absolute declaration of illegality in the Act was thought by some to be at least a respectable version of the common law, and in the United States perhaps the dominant one, the rule, that is, that all general restraints of competition, as distinguished from partial ancillary restraints, are void without regard to their extrinsic reasonableness.

There is another theme in the debates of the time. Congress wanted to give the courts discretion in interpreting the law, but not too much discretion. The Congressmen were seeking to confine the power they gave the courts, as well as to define it. They intended to confer what is sometimes called a 'judicial' rather than a 'legislative' discretion, a narrower rather than a wider range of choice for deciding cases in terms of the judges' own ideas of social and economic policy. By the logic of American public life, the courts were their natural choice among possible agencies of enforcements. But Congressmen are men of affairs, and realists. They know that judges tend to be older men, naturally conservative in spirit, who often reflect the ideas of the previous generation. By giving them a firm rule to administer, the Congress hoped to keep them from straying too far from the policy it had rather vaguely in mind.

For the first thirty years or so after 1890, the Supreme Court decided almost all the important cases which reached it in favour of the government. These decisions began to constitute a noticeable economic influence, first in the railroad industry, and then in other industries, as judgements multiplied, and were translated by counsel into the realm of advice, and later of managerial policy.

Even more important than the immediate economic consequences of the Act, in this formative period, was the debate the judges conducted as to its essential meaning. Did the statute do no more than declare the common law rules against monopoly and restraint of trade for the federal realm of interstate and foreign commerce, where common law rules were deemed in this instance not to exist without legislation? Or did it assert a policy as distinctive as its modes of enforcement? Did the word 'every' in section one mean 'every', though the Heavens fall, or some term of less universal implications? The inquiry focused on the chameleon word 'reasonable', which the common-law judges had used in several senses in defining public policy towards the enforceability of contracts in restraint of trade.

The controversy within the Supreme Court was resolved in 1911, in two decisions which have remained, for all their ambiguity, as the basic starting point of American anti-trust law ever since (3). Those cases, and most notably the *Standard Oil* case, announced what was called 'the rule of reason' in construing the statute. The formula was bitterly contested at the time, as a retrograde step which weakened the law. But the 'rule of reason', as it was announced, and as it has developed in the course of almost fifty active years, differs strikingly from the 'rule of reason' which was applied as a matter of common-law doctrine by some American courts, and by the British courts, and which is embodied in effect in the 1948, and especially in the 1956 British statute.

The American rule of reason is presented in the first place as an independent legislative policy, not a codification of pre-existing common law (4). This was a distinction of importance, which freed the Act of a stifling potential incubus. The early cases had revealed that there were almost as many versions of the common law as there were judges. Any alternative solution would have sent our judges back to the year books, and loaded the Act with a burden of history which might well have sunk it without a trace. This risk was heightened by the presence on the Supreme Court of Mr Justice Holmes, a considerable legal historian, and an acknowledged authority on the common law, who thought the Sherman Act was 'humbug', and in several early cases presented a theory of the older doctrine that would have proved inadequate to the work before the courts.

In the *Standard Oil* case, the Supreme Court acknowledged that the Sherman Act used words which took at least their 'rudimentary meaning' from their common law background. It then presented a version of that common law meaning which few of the judges or professors would have recognized. The common law, and the statute, the court said, were concerned with one question, and one question only: does the restraint, viewed in its market setting, constitute a quantitatively significant limitation on competition? If it does, it is illegal as an 'undue', and therefore an 'unreasonable' restraint of trade. If the practice before the court is price-fixing, or market division, or boycott, or other conduct which could be considered clearly anti-competitive in purpose, in nature, or in actual or necessary effect, then it is 'conclusively' presumed to be illegal – that is, it is illegal *per se*, even though the defendants lack monopoly power, or anything close to it, and sometimes even if they hold relatively weak positions in the markets where they do business. Once the court has found an undue limitation of competition in this sense, its discretion under the 'rule of reason' is exhausted. It can go no further in considering whether the prices fixed are reasonable or not; whether special circumstances in the industry, such as high fixed costs, secular decline, excess capacity, or the like, justify even a limited degree of cooperation among sellers, as in the public interest. In short, the Act did not forbid bad trusts, and condone good ones. It applied to all, by equating the public interest strictly with the elimination of substantial restraints on competition.

The consequence of the *Standard Oil* case, over the long run, was an essentially economic definition of the offences established by the Sherman Act, condemning all monopolizations, and those restraints of trade, or partial monopolies, which significantly affected competition in the markets where the defendants carried on business, or, under the more limited tests of the Clayton Act, those restraints which were found to be probable potential clogs on competition in such markets.

This gloss on the rule of reason was not to emerge clearly for thirty years or more, in the normal ebb and flow of the judicial process. I warn you that some of my respected colleagues would not accept the view I have presented, even now. None the less, I believe that it corresponds to the reasoning and the language of the 1911 cases, and, even more important, that it fits the pattern and doctrine of the latter decisions which derive from them.

The American anti-trust statutes went through several cycles of development and interpretation. And they were significantly amended by Congress, most notably in 1914, when the Clayton Act and the Federal Trade Commission Act were passed; during the Depression of the thirties, when they were virtually suspended in favour of compulsory cartelization under the N.R.A.; and in 1950, when the provision of the Clayton Act against mergers was revived from a condition of judicial euthanasia.

This is not the occasion to attempt even a summary sketch of contemporary anti-trust doctrine, nor an appraisal of its impact on the economy of the United States. I should contend that we have at last achieved a coherent anti-trust theory. In terms of that theory, the various offences of the Sherman Act and the Clayton Act are distinguished largely as embodying different degrees or quantities of monopoly power; and many restrictive practices are treated summarily as illegal, without lengthy trials, on the ground that they are obviously anti-competitive in character or in necessary effect, or that they impose on rivals disadvantages not based on superior efficiency. The ideas of the anti-trust laws have spread widely throughout our public law. They play a part in many of the statutes which establish administrative regulation for the transportation and communications industries, and for banking. Their weight is strongly felt in our law of patents, trade marks and copyrights, and in other branches of law as well – the policy adopted for disposing of surplus plant owned by the government at the end of the war, for example (5).

The economic consequences of this effort, extending over seventy years now, are harder to evaluate, and impossible to reduce to statistics. The monopolies of the turn of the century have all disappeared, often in response to direct action under the anti-trust laws. Several studies of the degree of concentration in the American economy show a rough balance between the forces making for monopoly, and those making for more competition. Studies of specific industries permit one to see the anti-trust influence in action, along with the influence of changing technology, the development of substitutes, and declining costs of transportation, as a factor making for more competition in markets (6). It is apparent to any observer that the law has denied to American industry some of the easy and efficient forms of open collusion in price making, such as most of those now being examined by the Restrictive Practices Court here, and that it has forced business men interested in collusion to retreat to less obvious, and often less workable, procedures of co-operation. I believe that the laws have had a considerable effect, if not always a uniform one, on the evolution of the American economy, on its structure, its price behaviour, and its atmosphere, and have helped especially to minimize barriers to entry that might otherwise have been insuperable.

The politics of American anti-trust are also worth noticing. The anti-trust laws are defended by sensitive and well-informed members of Congress. The state of public opinion, and the balance between our parties, are such as to require from a Republican Administration an anti-trust enforcement programme quite as zealous and far-reaching as the anti-trust programme of its rival. Even if it wished to do so, the Republican Party could not safely relax or amend the law without risking the accusation of favouring big business against small – a rallying cry any sensible politician would much rather not have to confront.

Britain

The British legislation of 1948, 1953 and 1956 is the product of a political environment conspicuously different from the one I have sought to describe in the previous section. And it came out of an economic setting which reveals significant differences as well.

If we go back to the eighties and nineties of the last century, when the American anti-trust tradition took shape, several formative differences between the relevant circumstances in the two countries appear.

In the first place nothing like the exuberant and dramatic American merger movement occurred in the United Kingdom. A few big combines were formed, it is true, but there was no general explosion of monopoly or near-monopoly in railroads, banking, steel, coal, textiles, shipbuilding, engineering, or other key industries. Interestingly enough, where one such company was established – the Imperial Tobacco Company – it seems to have been created defensively, in response to a violent intrusion into the British market by the American Tobacco Company (7). And several of the monopolies which emerged later functioned in new industries, such as the chemical industry, or in the older model of the great colonial trading companies. Practices of collusion probably existed, as did certain trade tactics generally regarded as coercive or unfair – blacklisting, harassment, the use of bogus independents, ordeal by patent litigation, and the like. Donald Dewey concludes that such tactics 'were never so ruthlessly and blatantly employed in Britain' as in the United States, 'although they may have been more widespread than was generally believed' (8). What documentation there is confirms that both industrial cooperation and local price fixing were far from rare in the British economy, in part by reason of the persistent survival of habits rooted in the customs of the eighteenth century and earlier times. But, as is so often the case, the facts in this instance may be of less importance than what people thought them to be. Public opinion in Britain was not agitated, as American opinion was, by the spectre of an octopus of monopoly.

Secondly, British industry, evolving from its earlier forms of corporate organization without a dramatic break in continuity, was far more exposed to international competition, and far less protected by tariffs, than its American counterpart. The industrial sector of the American economy, conducted behind the protective wall of a high tariff, was then mainly oriented to a vast and growing domestic market. The importance of this factor in British thought about the monopoly problem is evident in the judgement of Lord Parker of Waddington in the *Adelaide Steamship Company* case. He was commenting on the concept of monopoly as a limiting factor always establishing unreasonableness at common law, and as an element in the Australian Industries Preservation Act. 'Monopolies,' he said, 'in the popular sense of the word are more likely to arise, and, if they do arise, are more likely to lead to prices being unreasonably enhanced in countries where a protective tariff prevails than in countries where there is no such tariff.'

Thirdly, the prolonged depression of the late nineteenth century was probably somewhat shorter and less acute in the United Kingdom than in the United States. Depression, obviously, is a great exacerbator of social tension. And in the United States much of the animus heightened by that experience was directed at the target of big business, and big business men.

From the point of view of public opinion, the immediate context of political action, two differences between the countries seem worth special notice. The mood of social protest was of course quite as vehement in the United Kingdom as in the United States. But it was concerned with a somewhat different combination of issues and aims.

First of all, like most modern British political philosophy, British opinion was not nearly so preoccupied as American political thinking always is with the problem of power. Many elements of American experience, from the federal structure of the nation to the pattern of the Constitution, make American politics extremely sensitive to the risks of concentrated power. It was historically natural that American opinion reacted strongly and emotionally to the threat of economic dominance by a small group of rich men, most of whom lived in New York. And it was equally natural that the threat of economic concentration seemed less real, and less ominous, in Britain. The British social order is historically different from the American, far more unified, and seemingly less egalitarian, in all its symbols of prestige. The system of Cabinet Government represents a unification of political power, in fact and in form. And it hardly seems shocking to British opinion that the reins of authority be held in large part by small groups, centered in London, trained in the same schools, and moving in the same society. The thought of what is now called an Establishment carries one set of connotations in Britain, a modern democracy which has used and preserved the forms of older social systems, is governed from one capital, and has an immense capacity to canalize new social forces into familiar channels, but carries quite another in the United States, a larger country, with many scattered centres of influence, governed neither from New York nor Washington, and obsessed with dreams of equality, and with fears of anything resembling the ancient oligarchy against which it once revolted.

In the second place, the British literature of social protest towards the end of the last century was different in positive content from that of the United States. Its dominant voices proposed notably different approaches to the miseries and injustices of the day. The Webbs and Bernard Shaw, the other Fabians, the cooperators, and the Toynbees were never interested in busting trusts. Socialism, not competition, was the favoured radical answer to concentrated economic power. There was therefore notably little political interest in the kind of reform undertaken in the United States. The new Labour Party was on another track. Its members tended to regard the Sherman Act as either a sham, or as a superficial and foredoomed attempt to interfere with the laws of history. Indeed the Labour Party has only recently come to the view that legislation to prevent restraints of competition is worth much effort, or has much promise. The Liberal Party was absorbed in a variety of other problems of great public interest. And the Conservative Party had not yet seen its advantage, in the spirit of Tory Democracy, in seeking by legislation to encourage more competition, more enterprise, and freer entry into the markets of the economy.

The economists were as much against monopoly in Britain as in the United States. But for all their influence, they never considered the monopoly problem a major issue of policy for the United Kingdom, comparable in importance to monetary policy or free trade.

Thus it happened that in the great wave of progressive political action in Britain before the first war, legislation to curb monopoly played no significant part, even as a proposal which failed of adoption after a useful battle.

This temper of relative disinterest in the problem of monopoly is reflected in the occasional opinions of the British courts in passing on restrictive practices in the law of contract, tort, conspiracy and property. There are not many such cases – very few, compared with the volume of litigation on the subject in an active commercial state like New York. Several factors may account for the contrast. The costs of litigation are reputed to be higher here than in the United States, and the British business man may be a less litigious creature than his American cousin. There may be a greater reluctance on the part of British business men to spoil commercial relations by litigation. Sir David Cairns has suggested that agreements among competitors, while frequent, were generally assumed to be invalid, and were therefore enforced privately, and not put to the test in court (9).

The British judgements are fairly consistent in expressing a point of view towards the problem of restrictive trade practices which only a minority of American courts supported before 1890. I must confess, on reading over this line of cases, that I found the differences between their holdings and those of the American courts to be rather less conspicuous than the differences in language and reasoning. The differences in articulating the rules, however, are clear enough.

The key issue in the battle over the meaning of the common law tradition can be seen perhaps most clearly in Judge Taft's classic opinion in the *Addyston Pipe* case. That judgement was one of the most influential documents in the American debate which culminated in the *Standard Oil* decision of 1911, although the Supreme Court's opinion did not fully accept Judge Taft's view.

Judge Taft faced a contract among manufacturers of cast-iron pipe, largely sold to municipalities and utilities on public bidding. The partners, providing two-thirds of the supply in a large area of the country, agreed to meet secretly in advance of the contracts being let, and to bid among themselves for the work. The highest bidder in the ring became the lowest bidder at the sale, the others sometimes putting in higher bids for the sake of appearances. The winner then shared his profits with his collaborators. The plan was defended on the usual grounds of preventing price wars, cut-throat competition, economic suicide, and the like.

The first question the court faced was whether the Sherman Act went beyond the common law, or adopted common law tests. Judge Taft thought the Act was independent of the common law, but prudently put his opinion on the ground that the defendants' conduct violated the common law in any event, and therefore came within the defendants' theory of the statute. He distinguished two lines of cases in the common law, defining the public policy limitations on freedom of contract. The first view, which he supported, would confine the power to make contracts in restraint of trade to those situations where the restraint was ancillary to some other transaction – the sale of good will, for example, the dissolution of a partnership, an employment contract involving knowledge of the employees' trade secrets. Such restraints, he said, were permissible, but only to the minimum extent that they were 'reasonably' necessary to permit the principal object of the transaction to be effectuated, and 'reasonably' confined as to time and space, by the nature of that transaction. In his opinion, all non-ancillary restraints of competition, such as agreements among competitors as to the prices they charged, the markets they served, the supply they could offer, were invalid at common law, without more. 'It is true,' he said, 'that there are some cases in which the courts, mistaking, as we conceive, the proper limits of the relaxation of the rules for determining the unreasonableness of restraints of trade, have set sail on a sea of doubt, and have assumed the power to say, in respect to contracts which have no other purpose and no other consideration on either side than the mutual restraint of the parties, how much restraint of competition is in the public interest, and how much is not.

'The manifest danger in the administration of justice according to so shifting, vague, and indeterminate a standard would seem to be a strong reason against adopting it.' (10).

Be that as it may, the prevailing rule in the British courts, it is often said, did give precisely this gloss to the element of 'reasonableness' which the judges could take into account in determining the enforceability of contracts which had no purpose other than the limitation of competition. While most of the modern British cases actually deal with the reasonableness of partial, ancillary restraints, such as those involved in the sale of a business, the liquidation of partnerships, the termination of employments, and the like, there were several dicta, and a few decisions, which support the view commonly asserted. The courts seemed to take this position, in partial contrast to that of Judge Taft. The question of the reasonableness of the restriction on grounds of public policy is one of law, not of fact. The judges have been historically jealous of such contracts. Although older views were modified during the nineteenth century, such contracts will not be approved unless the judges are convinced they are reasonable, in reference to the interests of both the contracting parties and the public. Without more, restraints are contrary to public policy, and void, although special circumstances may be proved to justify them. 'The onus of proving such special circumstances must, of course, rest on the party alleging them. When once they are proved, it is a question of law for the decision of the judge whether they do or do not justify the restraint. There is no question of onus one way or another'.[1] Where a trade or an industry has passed or is likely to pass into the hands or under the control of a single individual or group of individuals, or where a restraint of trade is likely to produce this result, the restraint may on grounds of public policy be unenforceable, as a monopoly illegal at common law and under the Statute of Elizabeth, however reasonable in the interest of the parties. Whether an effective attempt to secure such a monopoly is really being made is almost always a question of fact; in cases of lesser restraint, where the risk of monopoly in this sense does not arise, the judges may approve as enforceable even a general restraint deemed reasonable in the interest of the parties, and not otherwise injurious to the public. In such cases, however, where the reasonableness of a restraint between the parties is in issue, the parties must be seeking to protect some interest other than their advantage in avoiding competition: 'the covenantee is not entitled to be protected against competition *per se*', and finally, the concept of criminal conspiracy is not co-terminous with that of the unenforceability of contracts; 'no contract was ever an offence at common law merely because it was in restraint of trade. The parties to such a contract even if unenforceable, were always at liberty to act on it in the manner agreed'.[2]

From these cases there emerges, although not sharply in terms of holdings, the position that, in the absence of monopoly, the British

---

1. *Herbert Morris, Ltd* v. *Saxelby* [1916] 1 A.C. 688, 707 (judgement of Lord Parker of Waddington). See also, *Mason* v. *Provident Clothing and Supply Co., Ltd* [1913] A.C. 724, 733. ('The respondents have to shew that the restriction they have sought to impose goes no further than was reasonable for the protection of their Business.') These views, derived from Lord Macnaghten's judgement in *Nordenfelt* v. *The Maxim Nordenfelt Guns and Ammunition Co., Ltd* (1894) A.C. 535, 565, seem to provide a basis, or at least a background for the presumption of illegality in the Restrictive Practices Act, and for the distribution of burdens of proof it establishes.

2. *Attorney-General of the Commonwealth of Australia* v. *Adelaide Steamship Co., Ltd* [1913] A.C. 781, 797 (words of Lord Parker of Waddington). See, however, the judgement of Lord Dunedin in *Sorrell* v. *Smith* [1925] A.C. 700, 716–29, especially at 725.

The summary in the preceding paragraph draws on language used in several of the leading cases, particularly *Adelaide Steamship Co., Mason, Morris, Northwestern Salt,* and *McEllistrim*.

courts could and should consider whether general, non-ancillary contracts in restraint of competition among competitors should be upheld as reasonable, or condemned as unreasonable, in the light of the prices charged, the circumstances of the trade, and other factors of private and of public interest. In the *North Western Salt Co., Ltd* case, for example, which turned in the end on a question of pleading, Lord Parker of Waddington remarked, 'The competition between salt producers within the area covered by the agreement . . ., either *inter se* or with salt producers outside this area may have been so drastic that some combination limiting output and regulating competition within the area so as to secure reasonable prices may have been necessary, not only in the interests of the salt producers themselves, but in the interest of the public generally, for it cannot be to the public advantage that the trade of a large area should be ruined by cut-throat competition.'

This line of thought does define a difference between the common law in Britain and in the United States, and between the British law and the law of the Sherman Act. The approach of the British courts helps to fix the approach taken in the British statutes of 1948 and 1956.

What would seem more important than this difference in the content of the word 'reasonable' was the difference between the two systems in modes of enforcement. After 1890, the American courts faced a wide range of cases, largely selected by the Government for their public importance, and exploring every aspect of the economic problem of monopoly.[3] The British courts dealt with only a trickle of cases, brought by the happenstance of private litigation, and largely concentrated on the fringes of the problem. They were hardly cases which might have led the British judges to consider whether they really meant what they occasionally said about the possible reasonableness of non-ancillary restrictive arrangements among competitors.

The first of the Committee Reports which led to the 1948 legislation was filed in 1919. It proceeded from the investigation of profit levels during the First World War. The Committee on Trusts commented that trade associations and combines 'are rapidly increasing in this country, and may within no distant period exercise a paramount control over all branches of British

3. See Reading 12 for a selection of important U.S.A. cases [ed.]

trade'. Academic study of the problem, following Marshall's lead, developed slowly but steadily, with the work of Sargent Florence, Macgregor, Plant, Macrosty, Allen, and the Robinsons. They prepared the way for the present wealth of monographic investigations, which now constitute a considerable part of the literature of British economics. And a series of Committees and Commissions continued to examine various aspects of the problem, especially the vexed matter of resale price maintenance. Neither the twenties nor the thirties proved to be time for action on this front. Britain's painful and depressing ordeal of the twenties was dominated by other issues, and by the attitudes which had crystallized earlier. During the thirties, the setting of the problem of industrial organization in Britain changed. Free trade was abandoned; co-operation among domestic competitors continued to increase, unrestrained by countervailing effort; and there was more and more British participation in European cartels. And what might be called the Keynesian period in the orientation of economic policy began, with far-reaching consequences in this as in other areas. The British White Paper on Employment Policy in 1944 suggested two aspects of the monopoly problem which have played a considerable role, I should guess, in the development of Britain's vigorous and confident post-war economic policy: the potentialities of more competition in keeping prices down during periods of near inflation; and the advantages of competition over monopoly in permitting the economy to adjust quickly to programmes of stabilization and growth based on the use of fiscal and monetary policy.

Confronting the prospect of post-war inflation, the 1944 White Paper urged caution and moderation in wage and price policy. One could hardly admonish trade unions not to press for higher wages without contemplating the forces which may lead to rises in the price of goods. Beyond its precatory words to labour and to business, the White Paper commented on the apparently cumulative growth of monopolistic arrangements and influences in the British economy, and promised that the Government would look into the question further, and consider the possibility of public action against monopoly and restraints on competition.

The second theme of the White Paper – the superior cyclical resilience of a more competitive economy – was barely hinted at in the document, and was certainly not developed. The relationships between market structure and the course of the trade cycle have been a neglected problem in economic theory. But the suggestion of the White Paper is certainly not implausible, both from the point of view of the flexibility of the economy in responding to moves of fiscal and monetary action, and, perhaps more important, as a factor in the complex sociological process of innovation and productivity.

The inflationary bias of post-war full employment, the increasing urgency of British concern with productivity in the struggle for export markets, and, more recently, the articles, books and discussion stirred up by the Reports of the Monopolies Commission and judgements of the Restrictive Practices Court, have tended to bring the monopoly question for the first time into the forefront of consciousness in British thinking about economic policy. Developments in political thought about economic problems served to reinforce this professional and governmental interest, and to give it a wider popular base. As the Labour Party's programme of nationalization began to meet increasing political and intellectual resistance, it was natural for some members of that Party to become more and more attracted to anti-monopoly legislation as an alternative. This swing of the pendulum in public opinion was heightened by the unpopularity of direct controls as a means for dealing with the price consequences of excess purchasing power. Although the theory was wrong – under the pressure of excess purchasing power, prices seem to rise more in competitive than in monopolistic markets – it was widely believed that competitive market freedom, reinforced by the influence of legislation, could help to limit the price impact of excessive spending. Both in Britain and on the Continent, one of the recurring themes in discussing programmes for broader trading areas is the importance of international competition in keeping prices down. Then again, other countries, and the European Economic Community, were experimenting with anti-monopoly legislation, and visiting Americans never fail to preach its virtues. This trend in post-war thought, and law, was emphasized by the prolonged and thus far ineffective efforts to secure an international treaty against restrictive business practices, first through the Havana Charter, and later through a special United Nations Committee.

Against this background, the British Monopolies and Restrictive Practices (Inquiry and Control) Act of 1948 was passed, to be amended slightly in 1953, and substantially changed in content and procedure by the Restrictive Trade Practices Act of 1956, following on the important Report of the Monopolies Commission on Collective Discrimination, in 1955. The 1948 Act, in retrospect, seems to have been primarily an attempt to explore the realities of the problem in depth – a research effort, intended to accumulate information on the basis of which policy might later and more rationally design a suitable law. In that perspective, the 1956 Act appears as a first, but probably not the final response of the British Parliament to a problem whose contours are only beginning to be revealed. [. . .]

References
1. A. MARSHALL, 'Some aspects of competition' in A. C. Pigou (ed.), *Memorials of Alfred Marshall*, Macmillan, London, 1925.
2. *Standard Oil Co.* v. *United States*, 221 U.S. I, 83–4 (1911).
3. H. THORELLI, *The Federal Anti-Trust Policy*, John Hopkins, 1955.
4. A. O. WILBERFORCE, A. CAMPBELL and N. P. M. ELLES, *The Law Of Restrictive Trade Practices and Monopolies*, Sweet and Maxwell, London, 1957.
5. E. V. ROSTOW, *Planning for Freedom: The Public Law of American Capitalism*, Yale University Press, 1959.
6. S. N. WHITNEY, *Anti-Trust Policies, American Experience in Twenty Industries*, Twentieth Century Press, 1958.
7. W. H. NICHOLLS, *Price Policies in the Cigarette Industry*, Vanderbilt, 1951.
8. D. DEWEY, *Monopoly in Economics and Law*, Rand McNally, 1959.
9. D. CAIRNS, 'Monopolies and restrictive practices' in M. Ginsberg, (ed.), *Law and Opinion in England in the Twentieth Century*, University of California Press, 1959.
10. *United States* v. *Addyston Pipe and Steel Co.*, 85 Fed. 271, 283–4 (1898).

10   R. B. Stevens and B. S. Yamey

The Justiciability of Restrictive Practices

Excerpt from R. B. Stevens and B. S. Yamey, *The Restrictive Practices Court*, Weidenfeld and Nicolson, London, 1965, chapter 3.

I

By far the most important and controversial change made by the 1956 Act was the handing to the judiciary of the burden of the investigation of restrictive practices. It was both important and controversial in view of two peculiar but related aspects presented by the English judicial scene. The first is the urge, almost the obsession, for certainty in the law – 'the paramount importance of certainty' as Viscount Simonds, Lord Chancellor from 1951 to 1954, called it (1). This has resulted in the majority of English judges denying, in the words of an American commentator, any 'responsibility for remolding judge-made law in order to improve it, to keep it abreast of current conditions, and to make it better serve the needs of living people' (2). As another Lord Chancellor, Viscount Jowett, expressed it: 'The problem is not to consider what social and political conditions of today require; that is to confuse the task of the lawyer with the task of the legislator.' The other attitude which, at least in its intensity, is peculiarly English, is the habit of the English judges who 'purport to limit themselves to precedents and logic; they purport to have no concern for the policies on which the law necessarily rests'. As Mr Justice Gorman put it in a recent decision: 'it is essential not to confuse the reasons for a rule coming into force with the rule itself'. The result has been that while it has remained legitimate for judges to make determinations on what are regarded as 'legal' issues, to suggest that judges should decide 'policy' issues has come to be regarded, in the words of a senior Lord of Appeal, as a denial of 'the essential meaning of accepted parliamentary supremacy in twentieth-century democratic England' (3).

It is not suggested that these attitudes are shared equally by all the judges. Some members of the bench, such as Lord Denning, are keenly aware of the judicial power of creativity (4). Others, like Lord Radcliffe, are aware of the actual nature of the judicial process, but claim that there are 'excellent reasons' why the judges must not depart from their present formula (5). What is certain is that the overwhelming articulated view of the judiciary has reflected the two approaches discussed in the previous paragraph. Such approaches to the judicial function are, in many ways, a natural outcome of the social and political structure of modern Britain. Parliamentary sovereignty requires a subservience on the part of the judiciary which does not exist in countries which allow judicial review of legislation. Moreover, the English intellectual tradition finds little difficulty in distinguishing between decisions applying legal principles and those requiring the formulation of policy, just as a clear division is assumed to exist between law and fact. There are valuable aspects of such assumptions. The judiciary has not been affected by the democratization which has gone on in England during the last one hundred years, and the judges are still drawn from the same narrow section of the community they were drawn from a hundred years ago.[1] Politically, therefore, it is convenient, perhaps even necessary, that they should appear to have no power to make policy, and ideally should not even seem to implement policy. It has become commonplace for social

---

1. This position caused concern to some writers in the 1920s: T. Scrutton, 'The work of the commercial courts', *Cambridge Law Journal*, vol. 1, 1921, p. 6; M. Ginsberg, 'Interchange between social classes', *Economic Journal*, vol. 39, 1929, pp. 554, 562; H. Laski, 'The techniques of judicial appointment', in *Studies in Law and Politics*, 1932, p. 162.

But there is no reason to think the position has substantially changed. In 1961, of the 61 Supreme Court (Court of Appeal and High Court) Judges, at least 54 had been to Public Schools, and 50 to Oxford or Cambridge. In the same year a practising barrister was able to write: 'What manner of men are the English judges? Largely what you would expect: gifted and talented members of the upper classes. England has its normal quota of success stories from rags to riches; its millionaires who started as office boys, its tycoons who sold newspapers on street corners. But no one other than a gentleman, in the class sense of the word, has ever graced the high court bench. Working class origins are not recommended for anyone with judical ambitions.' F. Bresler, 'English law and lawyers', *Texas Quarterly*, vol. 3, 1961, pp. 197–8.

commentators to assume that judges should no longer be entrusted with policy decisions. Accepted political convention now requires that the judiciary should be left with a minimum of contact with issues of public law where aspects of policy are most obvious; and the true function of the judges is assumed to be limited to those areas of private law where the policies appear to have been settled by centuries, or at least by decades, of judicial interpretation (7).

It is in keeping with this tradition that the judges have been withdrawn, or have retreated, from those areas of the law where decisions require an overt policy choice. The best-known example of this general retreat is in trade union affairs. After a series of decisions culminating in the *Taff Vale* case in 1901, the legislature intervened to protect the unions against the judiciary, and after some further unsatisfactory judicial interventions, the courts largely accepted this verdict. Moreover, this process was repeated in other areas of public law. There was an increasing reluctance to interfere in any way with the operation of central government departments, and a willingness to assume that administrative procedure under social legislation excluded any possibility of intervention by the courts. The legislature also intervened from time to time to remove from the judiciary work which was thought to involve the application of sensitive social policies. Politicians on the Left, in particular, have insisted that the role of the judges, at least in matters of public law, must be confined as narrowly as possible. In this way the articulation of a dichotomy between decisions requiring the application of law and those requiring the determination of policy enabled the judiciary to weather the major political and social changes of this century.

II

As part of the general retreat from public law and issues of policy, the judges gradually extricated themselves from questions involving monopolies and restrictive practices, or any decision which might appear to involve the judiciary in the control of sectors of the economy. They insisted that the courts could not handle decisions such as these, since they involved developing policies. The earliest and best-known statement was that of Lord Justice Fry that 'to draw a line between fair and unfair competition, between what is reasonable and unreasonable, passes the power of the court'. Such a view was reiterated as the courts continued to give up their responsibility for protecting the public interest.

At common law, litigation may involve control of competition in two situations: in an action for conspiracy, and in contract actions where one of the parties alleges a restraint of trade. It was relatively easy for the courts to distinguish away their earlier decisions in conspiracy cases. This was mainly accomplished in the celebrated case of *Mogul Steamship Co.* v. *McGregor, Gow & Co.* decided in 1891. There the efforts by a former member of a shipping price ring to expand his share of the market had been met by a concerted system of discriminatory practices intended to drive him out of the business. He claimed damages, but met with judicial hostility at each stage of the action; the defendants being held only to be exercising their 'lawful' rights. From this time onward, the tort of conspiracy has only been allowed where the defendants have not had as their 'real and preponderant purpose' the 'advancing of their own lawful business interests', an exception so wide that it has insured that there has been no successful conspiracy action involving business men in recent decades.

In the area of contractual restraint of trade, however, it was not so easy for the judges to escape from the problems of competition. The courts had traditionally concerned themselves with pleas of 'restraint of trade' in cases concerning contracts of service and sales of businesses. But in 1894 in *Nordenfelt* v. *Maxim Nordenfelt Guns & Ammunition Co.* the view was expressed that the true test should be one of reasonableness. In propounding this test Lord MacNaughten said that the restraint should not only be reasonable between the parties, but also should be reasonable with reference to the interests of the public. This second requirement might have given the judges an opportunity to retain an active role in shaping the competitive nature of the economy. In fact, they behaved in much the same way as they had towards the tort of conspiracy; and, by equating the public interest with reasonableness between the parties to the contract, they excluded the judges from any serious concern with the economic impact of such contracts. Any further involvement in what was regarded as a policy issue – namely the control of competition – was avoided.

Yet in insisting that the courts were institutionally incapable of handling restrictive practices, the judges found themselves exposing their own views about policy – particularly the value of competition. In refusing to develop an effective tort of conspiracy and in equating the public interest with the interests of the parties where contracts were said to be in restraint of trade, the judges at the turn of the century made it clear that they had little use for the preservation of competition. In the *Mogul* case, for instance, Lord Chancellor Halsbury, while presiding in the House of Lords, declared that courts should not interfere with business activities:

All commercial men with capital are acquainted with the ordinary expedient of sowing one year a crop of apparently unfruitful prices, in order by driving competition away to reap a fuller harvest of profit in the future. . . . All are free to trade upon what terms they will.

His economic predispositions were shared by the other law lords. Freedom of trade meant freedom to contract rather than freedom of contract. In examining an oppressive tying clause imposed by a virtual monopolist, the Judicial Committee of the Privy Council held [*United Shoe Machinery of Canada* v. *Brunet*, 1909]:

By virtue of the privilege which the law secures to all traders, namely, that they shall be left free to conduct their own trade in the manner which they deem best for their own interests, so long as that manner is not in itself illegal, the respondents are at liberty to hire or not to hire the appellant's machines, as they choose, irrespective altogether of the injury their refusal to deal may inflict on others. The same privilege entitles the appellants to dispose of the products they manufacture on any terms not in themselves illegal, or not to dispose of their products at all, as they may deem best in their own interest, irrespective of the like consequences. This privilege is, indeed, the very essence of that freedom of trade in the name and in the interest of which the respondents claim to escape from the obligations of their contracts.

It was clear that the public interest was not synonymous with competition. In another Privy Council case, Lord Parker announced [*A. G. of Australia* v. *Adelaide S.S. Co.*, 1913]:

It was proved that the prices prevailing when negotiations for this agreement commenced were disastrously low owing to the 'cut-throat' competition which had prevailed for some years. . . . It can never, in their Lordship's opinion, be of real benefit to the consumers of coal that colliery proprietors should carry on their business at a loss, or that any

187

profit they make should depend on the miners' wages being reduced to a minimum. Where these conditions prevail, the less remunerative collieries will be closed down, there will be great loss of capital, miners will be thrown out of employment, less coal will be produced, and prices will consequently rise until it become possible to reopen the closed collieries or open other seams. The consumers of coal will lose in the long run if the colliery proprietors do not make fair profits or the miners do not receive fair wages. There is in this respect a solidarity of interest between all members of the public.

An almost identical view on the value of competition was expressed the following year by the Liberal Lord Chancellor, Haldane, presiding in an English appeal, in the House of Lords [*N.W. Salt Co.* v. *Electrolytic Alkali Co.*, 1914]:

Unquestionably the combination in question was one the purpose of which was to regulate supply and keep up prices. But an ill-regulated supply and unremunerative prices may, in point of fact, be disadvantageous to the public. Such a state of things may, if it is not controlled, drive manufacturers out of business, or lower wages, and so cause unemployment and labour disturbance.

A judiciary with such views was unlikely to prove an effective bulwark against the growing anti-competitive tendencies in the business community. They upheld as in the public interest a price ring among hop producers when one of the members tried to cut prices, a market-sharing agreement in the salt industry, bid rigging at auctions, and even a tying arrangement whereby a bus company was forced to buy its requirements of petrol in perpetuity from the vendor of a piece of land. The maintenance of monopolies by the leasing of machines was supported to the extent of an injunction indirectly compelling the use of the leased machines. One court held that letters written by a monopoly inducing its customers not to trade with a potential competitor were original literary works within the meaning of the copyright laws, and enjoined efforts to publicize them (8). Where resale price maintenance was concerned the public interest was assumed to require the judges to go to inordinate lengths to make certain the system was enforced.

The judges then had made it clear that they felt themselves ill-equipped to decide such obvious policy issues as were involved in evaluating restrictive practices in industry. In so doing they had also exposed their scepticism about the value of competition. The 1956 Act, in deciding to hand the issue back to the judges, was therefore an act of faith. Would the judges now take a more sympathetic view towards the value of competition; or could the Act force them to be more sympathetic? More important still, had the judges at the turn of the century been right in their diagnosis that courts were not equipped to handle such problems?

III

Whether some particular procedure is correctly described as administrative, judicial or quasi-judicial is a question which has generated considerable dispute in England. With that aspect of justiciability the debates on the 1956 Act were not concerned: beyond all doubt the procedure which was invoked was judicial. The aspect of justiciability which was in issue was whether the problem to be solved was one which was apt for a judicial solution – in the sense of the submission of the problem to what was essentially a new division of the High Court. The Labour Party insisted strongly that it was not. Its real political objection may well have been its belief that the Bill was a sham, and its true hostility to the use of the judges may have been because they were suspected of economic illiberalism; but the battle was fought out entirely on this aspect of justiciability. Could the issues in the Bill be made sufficiently clear to be submitted to a court?; in other words, could the policies involved be made subject to legal standards? This was the basic problem with which Parliament was faced.

The Labour Party was in favour of implementing the recommendations of the majority made in the Monopolies Commission Report on Collective Discrimination, and declaring certain restrictive practices to be illegal, and in this it received some support from the press. An outright prohibition, it was insisted, would provide an ideal legal standard which might easily be applied to the facts of any particular case. The Labour Party, therefore, opposed the establishment of the Restrictive Practices Court. Labour members purported to be incensed because they alleged that, from party political speeches, it was clear that the Government had committed itself to a judicial solution and then sought – unsuccessfully in their view – to make the issues involved justiciable. The chief spokesman for the Opposition was Sir Lynn Ungoed-Thomas, a former Labour Solicitor-General, and now a High Court judge. He had fundamental objections to the use of a court for deciding such issues [549 House of Commons debates, col. 2029, April 12th 1956]:

The function of a court is not that which is mentioned in the Bill; it is entirely different, namely, to interpret and administer law, and not to make it. The Bill hands over to this court governmental and parliamentary power. All judgments are founded upon law or upon facts, but in this case the decision which really matters will be a decision founded neither upon law nor upon fact. It will be a political and economic decision.

The Government spokesmen, while willing to admit that the new court involved certain innovations, were at pains to show that there was nothing extraordinary in the function it was expected to perform or basically different from those traditionally performed by the courts. It was pointed out that the courts had, on many occasions, to determine what amounted to the public interest, particularly in cases involving contracts alleged to be in restraint of trade. The courts were also said to be involved with economic issues when they were granting or revoking patents; and much prominence was accorded to the Railways and Canals Commission in which laymen had sat with judges to determine whether certain contracts of carriage were 'just and reasonable'. These instances were summed up by Mr Walker-Smith, as junior to Mr Thorneycroft. He insisted that the process proposed was in no way alien to the traditional judicial process [549 House of Commons debates, col. 2042, March 6th 1956]:

It is just not true to say that Parliament alone is concerned with economic and social matters and that the Court has no part in them. The courts deal with many social and economic matters under the guidance of principles laid down by Parliament. There are many examples in the spheres of landlord and tenant and of public health. The distinction is not between the kind of subject dealt with. The true distinction is between the level at which that subject is dealt with. Parliament is not in a position to examine, control, or to judge the individual levels of economic activity. It is a doctrine which has proved true in many fields.

It was on these main themes that the government based its case: that the courts had handled such questions before, were fully competent to handle questions of reasonableness, and that the issue had been made justiciable by reducing it to an individual level (9).

The Opposition would have none of this. Of the argument that judges often had to decide questions of reasonableness, and this was essentially all they were required to do in this new court, Sir Lynn Ungoed-Thomas replied [551 House of Commons debates, col. 404, April 12th 1956]:

It has been said that the courts are accustomed to deciding whether a thing is reasonable or not; of course they are. Whenever they assess damages they assess what is a reasonable amount. That argument begs the question, which is the ambit within which reasonableness has to be exercised. If it is within a justiciable issue, then the courts of law exercise reasonableness, but no one will suggest that because there is an exercise of reasonableness in Budget decisions therefore Budget decisions are things which ought to be submitted to a court of law.

Nor would the former Solicitor-General concede that justiciability had anything to do with the fact that problems were dealt with individually. Justiciability

depends not upon reasonableness or unreasonableness, or upon whether or not it is an individual case, but essentially upon the nature of the issue that has to be considered by the body that we set up. We know that the function of the court of law is to apply the general rules of law to the facts of a particular case. The rules and the definition are there and the Court interprets the definition as part of its function in applying it to the facts of the case. The law, therefore, applies equally to everybody. It is an essential part of the rule of law that we have in this country that there is a general rule which courts of law apply indiscriminately to the facts of the particular case.

He concluded his argument by declaring [551 House of Commons debates, col. 404, April 12th 1956]:

This is not really a matter suitable for justiciable decision according to the rules and the ordinary way in which we conduct matters in the courts of law in this country at all. It is a matter of a decision to be made from the greatest accumulation of knowledge and experience which is available, and the greatest accumulation of knowledge and experience available in this country is only available, in the last resort, to the Minister. It is essentially a governmental decision.

Moreover, it was argued that it was unfair to force judges into deciding cases where their predispositions would be likely to become obvious [549 House of Commons debates, col. 2053, March 6th 1956]:

We do not, by submitting what are essentially political matters to the decision of a court turn them into legal matters. We cannot convert a political matter into a legal matter merely by asking the opinion of a judge about it. It is, in fact, the height of folly to drag the judges into these matters. It is not pleasant when we have cases, such as the famous trade union cases, which impinge upon politics. They are not welcome cases, but they are quite inevitable on occasion, and what we are doing here is to drag the judges into the vast field of political and economic matters.

It would be wrong, however, to assume that opposition to the use of the judiciary for this new task was confined to the Parliamentary Labour Party. The *Economist*, while welcoming the Bill, was extremely chary of the idea of using the judges. It feared not only their economic illiberalism, but also their method of reasoning: 'the idea that a decision should change if the climate of opinion changes, even though other things remain the same, is not an idea that will be easily digestible by trained legal minds.' As the Bill progressed, *The Times* cast considerable doubt on the wisdom of using the judges. It took the view that the judiciary might be compromised:

Close thought must be given to the probable effect on the judiciary itself. Will judges who have been watched in the new tribunals weighing these highly controversial questions of expediency, however closely their terms of reference are limited, carry back to the Queen's Bench or Chancery quite the same unassailable reputation for detachment from political considerations that they have hitherto enjoyed?

More important, however, *The Times* agreed with the Labour Party that parts, at least, of the Bill were not justiciable. This remained the core of the dispute.

IV

The clash on the concept of justiciability lay between the argument on the one hand that the nature of the problem involved determined the question, and on the other that the level at which a problem was approached was crucial. That this clash, on what was essentially a matter of jurisprudence, should divide on party lines is by no means surprising. Traditionally in England it is the Right which favours judicial creativity, and the Left which advocates judicial restraint. Nor is it surprising that many of the arguments advanced during the debates were dealing with ideas which have been little canvassed in England (10). The social, political and intellectual climate has made the issue of justiciability seem relatively unimportant.

There is an element of truth in the views advanced by both parties. Some issues may appear to be unsuitable for decision by the courts because they require a decision involving such a wide exercise of discretion that even with the invocation of legal principles the judges would be forced into overt policy making. But some development of policy is inherent and justifiable in the ordinary judicial process in the common law, provided it is made subservient to the criteria or standards which are embodied in rules of law which in turn are made as objective as possible. Some element of policy making and the exercise of some discretion cannot be equated with non-justiciability. Even in the operation of the simplest of legal situations the judge may find himself consciously or unconsciously examining the policy of or the underlying reason for a rule or statute in order to determine whether it should be applied to the facts before him. Just as a judge may find himself interpreting and so developing the law, so he may find himself interpreting and so developing policy. Hence, to insist that every question, by its very nature, is justiciable or not because of the existence or non-existence of an element of policy, merely clouds the issue. There is a wide spectrum of issues in most political societies ranging from the political, where opposed policies are publicly advanced and attacked, to issues which, after centuries of tending by the judiciary, have reached a state where the relevant legal doctrine is sufficiently settled for it to be thought unnecessary to re-examine its underlying policies (11). But the judicial function need not be so limited. What is crucial for justiciability is the ability to contain the policy either by or within traditional and accepted principles and standards.

That issues are either more or less justiciable, rather than inherently justiciable or not by reason of some pre-ordained order, has been obscured in England by the refusal of the judges to articulate their decisions in any but strictly legal terms and by the constantly articulated view that for judges to consider policy issues would violate the separation of powers and hence be un-democratic. There is a coy reluctance to discuss judge-made law or to admit that judges may have to mould policy when exercising discretion, or help to shape policies embodied in legal principles. As has been seen, to admit the existence of such functions is regarded as tantamount to a denial of certainty in the common law, and hence of predictability and the rule of the law itself. It is scarcely surprising that Labour spokesmen should have aligned themselves with this tradition and have insisted that any element of policy making left to the judges made the Act unworkable.

The Walker-Smith view must, however, more nearly represent actuality. The inductive nature of the judicial process in the common law and the element of 'open texture' in a language mean that in every decision the judge, frequently only in a very narrow sense, is involved in 'making' law and *a fortiori* exercising dis-cretion in making or following some particular policy. Even in deciding whether a certain fact situation falls within some prin-ciple or not, or whether some situation comes within concepts such as negligence or reasonableness, the judge will be engaged in such a process. Any Act of Parliament which fails to be inter-preted by the courts involves some discretion and some power to extend or restrict the principle it embodies. The test of jus-ticiability is not whether the statute involves applying a policy, nor whether the judges have some discretion in applying the statute. If neither of these were involved in the ordinary judicial process there would, for instance, be rather less need of appeal judges whose work is concerned to a large extent with develop-ing the law in one direction or another by choosing between one policy or another embodied in competing legal principles. The issue of justiciability is simpler than this. It resolves itself into a question of the ability of the legislature so to embody into a principle the policies which it intends to be effectuated by the Act, that the courts are left with sufficiently clearly defined stan-dards to operate the judicial process efficiently by keeping dis-cretion within narrow limits. This by no means implies that the judges have a purely mechanistic function within the judicial process; but justiciability does involve the primacy of principles and standards over all the other factors which go into judicial decision-making. When writers talk of the essence of a justiciable issue being in the application of pre-existing legal principles to determine existing rights, they are restating this concept from a more traditional standpoint, yet one that is basically the same.

The practical end of either restatement is similar. Courts of law examining factual situations provide an imperfect method of formulating fundamental policies. English judges allow themselves access only to information provided in the form of a legal argument by counsel. As evaluators of that evidence they are probably unsurpassed. But if required to make a policy choice which is not clearly circumscribed by doctrine they appear to have no peculiar skills in selecting from among alternative policies which might be pursued, nor in integrating any policy they might choose with general government policy and planning. The tradition of the British Constitution is that such basic policies are better shaped and implemented by legislators and civil servants. Courts are, however, ideal places to effectuate generalized policies in individual cases. But they can only do this where major governmental policies have been translated into legal principles from which the courts can apply standards. The better the standard available the more effective the judicial solution. Even the most perfect of statutes will not exclude judicial discretion in the development of policy entirely; and the judges will always be concerned to some degree with the underlying policies of the doctrines or statutes they are applying. But the more firmly the legislature is able to settle the basic policy, both by crystallizing the principles involved and by restricting the discretion left to the judges, the more likely is it that the judicial process will prove an apt means of handling the problem.

V

Only if the matters in issue are so politically controversial that an attempt to solve them by the judicial process would be impracticable can it be said meaningfully that something is non-justiciable. The area of restrictive practices seems not to be in such a category. It is therefore suggested that there was nothing inherently wrong in thinking of a court as a means of handling restrictive practices. The Labour Party's insistence on a clear and permanent distinction between legal and policy issues was un- justified. The question at issue is whether the Restrictive Practices Court was provided with the tools to operate in a judicial manner. It is only in this sense that policy is all important. This requirement was spelled out in the *Report of the Royal Commission on the Press*, which, after having recommended a court of law along the lines of the Restrictive Practices Court to investigate press mergers and decide where the public interest lay, made the following reser- vations:

The adoption of this system, however, imposes one firm necessity. A court of law cannot be asked to adjudicate at large upon broad issues of public advantage without being brought too much into the political arena, and the criteria of public interest to be applied would have to be stated by Parliament with sufficient precision to create justiciable issues which were capable of decision according to evidence.

Since the clearer the policy the greater likelihood there is that an effective judicial solution can be developed, the most satis- factory scheme from a lawyer's point of view might have been the total banning of certain restrictive practices. The view of the majority in the Collective Discrimination Report reflected the same attitude: 'A general prohibition would give industry clear and unequivocal guidance as to the Government's policy, and would avoid the uncertainty and waste involved in detailed in- quiries in each individual case.' The Government rejected any such clear-cut policy involving a general acceptance of the virtues of competition and the outright banning of certain anti-competitive practices. Whatever its drawbacks, such a solution would have provided a clear standard, so leaving the issue of justiciability in no doubt at all. The task of the courts would then have been limited solely to the ascertainment of whether the alleged practice in fact existed.

In place of this, the Court's future was dependent on the vital section – section twenty-one. Did this present 'unequivocal guidance' to the businessman, and were the criteria stated 'with sufficient precision to create justiciable issues'? As appears from a detailed examination of the economics of section twenty-one, if it has not already emerged from a discussion of the political background of the Act, no one clear underlying policy emerges. The Act is a step towards the promotion of competition, but it is very far from accepting competition as invariably desirable. Moreover while it does not assert the primacy of the advantages of competition, at the same time it does not assert the primacy of any other single policy objective such as, for example, the promotion of the interests of consumers or the maintenance of full employment.

Gateway (b), requiring the Court to determine whether the 'purchasers, consumers and users' of goods would be deprived of 'specific and substantial benefits' if the agreement went and to measure this against a presumption that the agreement was contrary to the public interest, illustrates most vividly the absence of any one clear policy. The speeches in Parliament were not helpful in seeking to elucidate the meaning of 'public interest' and 'benefit' to the 'public'. The memory of the decisions in the early part of this century in which the judges had generally upheld restrictive agreements as being in the public interest was enough to convince some M.P.s that the judges would use the concept of the public interest to undermine the purported thrust of the 1956 Act. An attempt to insert a definition of the public interest to guide the judges was defeated. It was asserted by some that the public interest could not be reduced to a justiciable standard; by others that even if it were possible it certainly had not been achieved by the draftsmen of this section. The absence of a definition of the public interest meant that 'that fundamental consideration that law must be general and impartial is missing'.

The true place of public interest in law is as the foundation and reason for a general rule, which the law then applies. It is not for a judge to conceive what, in all the circumstances, he considers the public interest to be. That is not law; it is the negation of law.

Thus the judges were left 'with an immense field of discretion in a major matter of policy'. The same point was put in a different way by another lawyer M.P. who insisted that where the 'factual domain of public interest' was involved the 'matter should be put in the hands of an instrument which is popularly nearer to the public than is a court of law'.

In this sense, then, the formulation of policy was clearly left to the new Court. In every statute some discretion must be left to the judges by way of interpretation. A judiciary which is capable of giving a meaning to 'cruelty' in divorce and 'natural justice' in administrative law, or distinguishing between 'capital' and 'income' in revenue cases, could scarcely cavil at being given some power to infuse a meaning into the words with which Parliament presented it in 1956. But the Act went beyond any traditional delegation of interstitial legislation to the judges. No doubt 'injury' in gateway (a) and 'preponderant part of the trade' in gateway (d) fell within the customary ambit of judicial operations. The Court might have no difficulty, if it is called upon to decide the question in evaluating whether a restriction was made 'with a view to preventing or restricting competition'. But leaving the Court to work out a scheme for determining what amounts to 'specific and substantial benefits' to purchasers fell far short of a traditional legal standard. Indeed, the tone of all the gateways was more that of a directive issued by a minister as a guideline for disposing of administrative applications, than the type of standard which the English judges have traditionally expected the legislature to spell out for them.

It was true that some of the gateways embodied more clearly specified policies than did gateway (b). But they also had to be subjected ultimately to the vague policy represented by the balancing process required by the tailpiece. If the Opposition refused to believe that gateway (b) was any more than the delegation of a political question to the judiciary without any serious standards by which the judges might guide their decisions, the tailpiece provided an even more dramatic source of scepticism. Mr Thorneycroft endeavoured to explain how the Court could be expected to operate the tailpiece [552 House of Commons debates, col. 714, May 5th 1956]:

Weighing is the right word because this a question of balance which, I admit frankly, is not easy. But, however difficult the task may be, it is right that I should set out what we want to happen here. Therefore, the Court must weigh the various advantages or benefits or avoidance of evils that have been shown in paragraphs (a) to (g) and then weigh them against any detriment to the public. It is not exactly a measuring operation. It is not enough to show that they could not avoid the damage to the public because of the necessity to do the specific thing. That is not enough. They must weigh the balance of advantage, which they have already shown, against any detriment to the public which may flow.

Sir Lynn Ungoed-Thomas claimed that of all things the balancing provision [551 House of Commons debates, col. 406, April 12th 1956]:

is essentially a political decision. That is not a decision for a court of law at all – to decide whether, on balance, something or other is or is not contrary to public interest. . . . This is the place and the Government is the body to do it – to take decisions as to whether something is contrary to public interest. It is essentially a decision on the balance of advantage to the public as a whole and that, of course, is a political decision. We are not here applying a general rule that is laid down. We are not here dealing with a case in which a court is merely inquiring whether or not the case is within a general rule. . . . We have an entirely different function.

The absence of a clear policy underlying the Act, the insufficiently precise criteria provided by the gateways and the invitation in the tailpiece to balance conflicting policy objectives, meant that the judicial process was being invoked to deal with issues which it was institutionally ill-equipped to handle. Parliament, moreover, not only forced the Court to develop the policies which the legislature had failed to settle; it also required the Court to develop them by adopting processes which were alien to the English judicial tradition. Under gateway (b), for instance, the Court has to consider whether the public will be denied a benefit 'likely to be enjoyed by them' as the result of the abandonment of the registered agreement. Such an invitation to predict future business behaviour and economic conditions is required under all the gateways. In both the export and unemployment gateways, for instance, the Court has to consider not only current economic conditions, but also those 'reasonably foreseen'. Ordinary courts do, of course, predict future events. They decide whether or not the man arrested with housebreaking implements would have committed a burglary; and they predict how much money a plaintiff would have earned (and the amount of income tax which would have been deducted) if the negligent driver had not maimed him.

Where there is an anticipatory breach of contract, they have to predict what the profits would have been had the agreement been carried out. But these predictions are carried out within the framework of clearly established present and past facts, with a limited number of variables and within areas familiar to the judges.

Where section twenty-one deviates most seriously from the norm is in requiring the judges to decide which of two or more economic hypotheses is the appropriate one on which to base specific economic predictions. In such circumstances the duty of the judges appears to be different both in kind and spirit from the traditional task of judges as evaluators of evidence. An ability to predict the future behaviour of the British economy or any particular industry is eminently desirable. Yet this skill has often eluded the British Treasury and the Board of Trade in the years since 1945, despite their possession of a far greater fund of data and expertise than could ever be made available to the courts. The point was neatly expressed by a perceptive Conservative M.P. during the debate [A. Maude, 552 House of Commons debates, col. 667, May 3rd 1956]:

During his Budget speech, the Chancellor of the Exchequer talked about the difficulties of economic forecasting, and said that experts were always looking up trains in last year's Bradshaw. But to think of them looking up trains in next year's Bradshaw before a judge who has not even a copy of it is even more terrifying.

It is not easy to see that there is anything in the analyses required under section 21 to make the issues peculiarly appropriate for the judicial process.

References
1. C. GRUNFELD, 'Reform in the law of contract', *Modern Law Review*, vol. 24, 1961.
2. K. C. DAVIS, 'The future of judge-made public law in England; a problem of practical jurisprudence', *Columbia Law Review*, vol. 61, 1961.
3. F. R. EVERSHED, 'The judicial process in twentieth century England', *Columbia Law Review*, vol. 61, 1961.
4. A. T. DENNING, *From Precedent to Precedent*, Clarendon Press, 1959.
5. C. J. RADCLIFFE, *The Law and Its Compass*, Faber & Faber, 1960.
6. A. SAMPSON, *Anatomy of Britain*, Hodder & Stoughton, 1962.
7. D. LLOYD, *Public Policy*, Athlone Press, 1953.

8. MONOPOLIES AND RESTRICTIVE PRACTICES COMMISSION, *Report on the Supply of Certain Industrial and Medical Gases*, 1956.

9. P. HUTBER, *Wanted – A Monopoly Policy*, Fabian Society, no. 219, 1960.

10. G. MARSHALL, 'Justiciability' in H. G. Guest (ed.) *Oxford Essays in Jurisprudence*, Oxford University Press, 1961.

11. *Report of the Committee on Administrative Tribunals and Enquiries*, Cmd 218, 1957.

11 A. D. Neale

The Policy Content of Anti-Trust[1]

Excerpts from chapters 1–6 of A. D. Neale, *The Anti-Trust Laws of the U.S.A.: A Study of Competition Enforced by Law*, Cambridge University Press, 1960.

Section 1 of the Sherman Act and restrictive trade-agreements

Danger lies in restraint of trade because the result of suppressing or limiting competition may be to build up a position of power in a market. People in a position of power in a market can make the terms of bargains more favourable to themselves and less favourable to others than they would otherwise be. There are two obvious ways of achieving market power. One way is for the sellers (or buyers) to band together and exert their joint power by agreement instead of competing one against the other. The other way is for a single firm to achieve off its own bat a dominant position in the market, in other words to monopolize it. Section 1 of the Sherman Act deals with restraint of trade arising from agreement or combination; section 2 deals with monopolization. This description of anti-trust case-law begins with the law under section 1 concerning agreements between competitors.

There are also two main ways of exerting power in a market. The first is to use it to influence prices directly; in the case of sellers, to raise prices above the level that would otherwise be reached or, as it may sometimes be regarded, to prevent their falling below a level that those concerned think fair. The second is to use it to exclude competitors from the market, thus consolidating or extending the original degree of market power. Power over prices and power to exclude competitors have always been regarded as the earmarks of monopoly and restraint of trade. The use of market power to exclude competitors is in a sense secondary, since its aim is to consolidate a strategic position; ultimately the

1. This reading should be considered in conjunction with the cases set out in Reading 12 [ed.].

object of market strategy is to gain some control over price. (Control does not necessarily mean exploitation, of course, for the stability of price- and profit-levels is often regarded in practice as more important than short-term maximizing of gains.) Certainly the law has always attached predominant importance to restraints of trade which directly influence prices, even to the extent of dealing with other forms of restriction, such as output restriction, largely in terms of their effect on price. It will be apt, therefore, to start with those agreements between competitors which seek directly to affect prices.

Price-agreements: the *per se* rule against price-fixing

Agreements between independent firms to fix a common price for their products violate section 1 of the Sherman Act. This was made clear in some of the earliest cases. For example, in *United States* v. *Addyston Pipe and Steel Company*, decided by the Sixth Circuit Court of Appeals in 1898, part of the charge was that six manufacturers of cast-iron pipe made an agreement whereby in many southern and western States the prices of pipe for all six were fixed by a central agency. Evidence showed that these prices were set just low enough to keep eastern manufacturers out of the area and that the public were deprived of the lower prices that might have resulted if the local factories had competed among themselves. It was said in defence of the agreement that the fixed prices were reasonable, and many affidavits from buyers to this effect were produced. The defendants, however, lost the case. The Court said about the level of the prices: 'We do not think the issue an important one, because, as already stated, we do not think that in common law there is any question of reasonableness open to the courts with reference to such a contract. Its tendency was certainly to give defendants the power to charge unreasonable prices had they chosen to do so.' These words clearly foreshadow the opinion of Mr (later Chief) Justice Stone in the *Trenton Potteries* case in which it was established that price-fixing was illegal *per se*.

United States v. *Trenton Potteries Company* (1927) is the leading case on price-fixing. Prices of vitreous pottery for bathrooms and lavatories were fixed by the Sanitary Potters' Association, whose members were responsible for over 80 per cent of the national output. The defence was that the prices fixed were reasonable and worked no injury to the public. Mr Justice Stone's rebuttal of this defence is a classic statement of anti-trust doctrine:

That only those restraints upon interstate commerce which are unreasonable are prohibited by the Sherman Law was the rule laid down by the opinions of this court in the Standard Oil and Tobacco cases. But it does not follow that agreements to fix or maintain prices are reasonable restraints and therefore permitted by the statute, merely because the prices themselves are reasonable. . . . Whether this type of restraint is reasonable or not must be judged, in part at least, in the light of its effect on competition, for whatever difference of opinion there may be among economists as to the social and economic desirability of an unrestrained competitive system, it cannot be doubted that the Sherman Law and the judicial decisions interpreting it are based upon the assumption that the public interest is best protected from the evils of monopoly and price-control by the maintenance of competition.

The aim and result of every price-fixing agreement, if effective, is the elimination of one form of competition. The power to fix prices, whether reasonably exercised or not, involves power to control the market and to fix arbitrary and unreasonable prices. The reasonable price fixed today may through economic and business changes become the unreasonable price of tomorrow. Once established, it may be maintained unchanged because of the absence of competition. . . . Agreements which create such potential power may well be held in themselves unreasonable or unlawful restraints, without the necessity of minute inquiry whether a particular price is reasonable or unreasonable . . .

In other words, price-fixing is illegal *per se*: no evidence of the reasonableness of the prices fixed need be heard by courts or submitted to juries. The emphasis in Stone's argument is laid on the effect of price-fixing on competition: by eliminating price-competition the members of the association obtained a position of power in the market which might be used arbitrarily. Deliberately to seek such power is an offence regardless of whether its exploitation in any particular period can be proved.

This argument derives from early anti-trust authority. Chief Justice White in 1911 had pointed to the deliberate drive for market power of the oil and tobacco trusts as the earmark of their offences and contrasted it with what he called 'normal methods of industrial development'. A price-fixing combination would not appear as a 'normal method' simply because of an assertion that the prices were reasonable. White would probably have taken Stone's point that the reasonable price fixed today may become the unreasonable price of tomorrow; and the courts at all times would in any case have disclaimed any competence to judge whether a particular price was reasonable. [. . .]

Price-filing and 'open competition' cases

Price-fixing agreements throw up few borderline questions of law. By definition they are never merely incidental to competition nor ancillary to legitimate transactions. Moreover, differences of degree hardly ever have to be considered, since agreements that might escape under a *de minimis* rule are not in practice made. There is nothing, in short, for the modern rule of reason to bite on. This, indeed, is what is meant by saying that price-fixing is illegal '*per se*'.

Anti-trust cases against price-fixing, however, sometimes involve difficult borderline questions of fact. Nearly all these questions turn on the point whether in fact any agreement exists. It will be remembered that the offence under section 1 of the Sherman Act is not simply the absence of vigorous price-competition. The offence that has to be proved is the existence of an agreement – a contract or conspiracy – relating to prices. Whether or not there is an agreement is a question of fact and in some circumstances it may be a very difficult fact to elicit. Difficulties arise in particular when industries engage in activities which are in themselves legitimate but which may also be used to disguise or facilitate collusion.

A trade association may, for example, collect and circulate statistics relating to the current production, stocks, sales and prices of member firms. Sometimes it is agreed that member firms will file all price-changes with the association so that all competitors may know what they are up against; it may even be agreed that price-changes will not be put into effect until there has been time for all members to be notified. Similarly, bids for competitive tenders may be filed with a central agency. Trade associations may also promote uniform methods of cost accounting and collect and circulate figures of current labour and material costs together with average or 'standard' figures for overhead costs in the industry.

On the one hand, it must clearly be legitimate for businessmen to seek to be well informed about market conditions. Knowledge of relevant data can hardly be thought incompatible with freedom of decision; and the economic theory of competition does not require decisions to be made in the dark. Some trade association services have obvious educative value; cost-accounting methods in small businesses, for example, are often primitive, and outside help in this field may well be desirable in the interests of efficiency.

On the other hand, it is clear that these activities may be used to facilitate collusion between firms. At trade association meetings a general understanding may develop that production should be cut back when stocks reach a given proportion of current sales and the circulation of the relevant figures may be the means of giving effect to this understanding. When price-changes or bids for contracts are filed with a central body, especially when it is agreed to leave a waiting period before making the change or bids, the opportunity exists for pressure to be put on the firm that would reduce prices or make a particularly low bid to think again. Advice about cost accounting may amount to prescribing formulas that ensure uniform prices or at least set a minimum price.

In sum, these activities may make it a great deal easier for firms in an industry collusively to avoid price-competition without going to the extent of making express agreements about particular prices. When elaborate interchanges of information are found going together with uniformity and inflexibility of prices, it is not surprising that the law-enforcing agencies, acting on the belief that price-competition ought to occur, become suspicious of concealed collusion. A number of anti-trust cases reflect situations of this kind, and the problem for the courts is to decide whether there is in fact an agreement or conspiracy to limit price-competition.

American Column and Lumber Company v. *United States* (Supreme Court, 1921) concerned an association of hardwood manufacturers who adopted what was known as an 'open competition' plan. This plan was avowedly based on the proposition that 'knowledge regarding prices actually made is all that is necessary to keep prices at reasonably stable and normal levels'. Participation in the plan was optional, but in practice 90 per cent of member firms, accounting for about one-third of the national output of hardwood, took part in it. The participants were required to let the secretary of the association have daily reports of all their sales and deliveries, with copies of invoices, and monthly reports of production and stocks. Each member had also to file a price-list every month, and the association employed inspectors to check up on the grades of timber offered by the members, so that the price-lists should be comparable. The secretary of the association in turn sent out periodical reports to the members, showing what sales had been made at what prices and summarizing the various price-lists. Meanwhile there were periodic meetings of members in different areas at which prices and output policies were discussed. There was evidence to show that at these meetings members were encouraged to adjust their price and output policies to the general aim of keeping the industry profitable and given expert advice designed to avoid weak selling through over-production. Many quotations from letters and speeches at meetings were produced to illustrate the forcefulness of the warnings against too much output.

The Supreme Court condemned these arrangements. Although no specific agreement to restrict output or fix prices was proved, the Court found that:

The fundamental purpose of the plan was to procure 'harmonious' individual action among a large number of naturally competing dealers with respect to the volume of production and prices, without having any specific agreements with respect to them, and to rely for maintenance of concerted action in both respects, not upon fines and forfeitures as in earlier days, but upon what experience has shown to be the more potent and dependable restraints of business honour and social penalties – cautiously reinforced by many and elaborate reports, which would promptly expose to his associates any disposition in any member to deviate from the tacit understanding that all were to act together.

The Court concluded that the conduct of the defendants was not that of competitors but: 'clearly that of men united in an agreement, express or implied, to act together and pursue a common purpose under a common guide'. This was not a new form of competition, as the trade claimed, but an old form of combination in restraint of trade.

Nevertheless, the issue was a close one; Mr Justice Brandeis, for example, dissented from the majority view on the grounds that there was no coercion and that the information gathered by the association was not kept secret from the public. He argued that the Sherman Act did not require that business rivals should compete blindly and without the aid of relevant trade information. He found no evidence of uniformity of prices; and if prices had sometimes been higher than they otherwise would have been because well-informed sellers avoided weak selling, that in itself was no offence. The expert warnings against over-production were meant to curb the greed of the sellers rather than to exploit the consumers. Finally, he feared that if the industry were not allowed to 'rationalize competition' it would go in for consolidation by mergers, with real monopoly as the outcome.

A similar result was reached in *United States* v. *American Linseed Oil Company* (Supreme Court, 1923). This case involved much the same sort of scheme. It appears that there was particularly strong evidence of pressure on the participants to keep in line. Attendance at monthly meetings was mandatory, and 'at the regular meetings the conditions in the industry were discussed and members were "put on the carpet" and subjected to searching inquiry as to their transactions'. The Supreme Court found that the manifest purpose of the arrangements was to evade the Sherman Act. 'We are not called upon to say just when or how far competitors may reveal to each other the details of their affairs. In the absence of a purpose to monopolize, or the compulsions that result from contract or agreement, the individual certainly may exercise great freedom; but concerted action through combination presents a wholly different problem, and is forbidden when the necessary tendency is to destroy the kind of competition to which the public has long looked for protection.' [. . .]

The detection of collusion in pricing; pricing in conditions of oligopoly

What comes out of this line of price-filing and 'open competition' cases? Many of the decisions are close and it is tempting to regard the different results from rather similar sets of facts as reflecting inconsistency and vacillation among the courts. And indeed there may be an element of luck in some of these cases – a flash of well-timed ingenuity by a particular advocate, a failure of penetration by a particular judge. But it would be unwise to give too much weight to this factor. Brief summaries of the facts, even a full record of the court proceedings, are in no way equivalent to the actual hearings at which the court can observe the demeanour of witnesses and find an inference strengthened or weakened by subtleties of inflexion or evasion.

The job of detecting collusive price-fixing amid legitimate interchanges of information about business conditions and intentions seems to be done on the whole with realism and good sense. The cases show, first, that collusive price-fixing, like any other violation of law, may be established by circumstantial evidence: direct evidence of an express agreement is not needed. If this were otherwise, evasion would obviously be too easy.

There are in practice two main lines of argument by which a circumstantial proof of collusive price-fixing may be built up; sometimes both lines may be used in the same case. One starts from the existence of an agreement – any trade association activity reflects an agreement of some kind – and seeks to show that the agreement, even though not expressly concerned with price-fixing, necessarily involves a significant restriction of price-competition. In the *Sugar* case, for example, there was an express agreement among the refiners that each would adhere without deviation to the prices he announced. Although each was free to vary the announced price as he wished, it was held that this agreement necessarily restrained an important type of price-competition.

The alternative line of argument starts from the absence of price-competition and seeks to show that this state of affairs could not be maintained without collusion. This type of argument was successful in the *Lumber* case when the Court inferred agreement from the behaviour of the parties. For this second line of argument various types of evidence are important. Uniformity of prices among ostensible competitors is only the starting-point. It is usually important to show that uniformity is maintained when diversity would be expected. It impresses the courts more, for example, when prices are shown to go up simultaneously than when a price-reduction is promptly met. It may be shown too that price-changes become markedly less frequent after an 'open competition' scheme is introduced than before or that prices become much less responsive to changes in raw-material costs. (Both these tests were used in the *Sugar* case.) The question whether deviations from list prices are rare or frequent will be of interest. Even more important will be evidence of any action taken by an industry when deviations do occur. Are they ignored or endured in the same way as changes in the weather? Or do they, on the other hand, become a matter of industry-wide concern – the subject of meetings, exhortations, even organized sanctions?

It is often argued on the defence side that uniformity of prices is an unfair test of collusion, since in any market the prices of different sellers are made uniform by normal competitive pressures. But in practice uniformity at a particular moment is never relied upon, and when all the evidence of price-behaviour over a period is aggregated, the matter of drawing an inference of collusion is seldom so complex or arbitrary as skilled defence counsel may make it appear. It is the kind of thing about which reasonable men with no axe to grind would often be able to agree.

As the *Maple flooring* case and the recent *Tag* case show, moreover, the burden rests on the prosecution to build up such a case that the inference of collusion becomes virtually inescapable. Collusion means in this context a real 'meeting of the minds' in a common endeavour to suppress or limit price-competition; moreover, it is implied that the plan or understanding can be relied upon with reasonable confidence by the participants. The individual firm, in other words, must be under some fairly effective inhibition as regards 'breaking the price-line' when the temptation to do so is apparently strong.

Conversely, when the members of a trade group are genuinely left free in their pricing decisions and do in practice exercise their own discretion, collusion cannot be inferred and no anti-trust offence can be established. And this is so even when interchanges of information have some dampening effect on price-competition. As Mr Justice Brandeis put it in his dissent in the *Lumber* case: 'But there is nothing in the Sherman Law to indicate that Congress intended to condemn cooperative action in the exchange of information, merely because prophecy resulting from comment on the data collected may lead, for a period, to higher market prices.' If all that happens is that the firms in an industry, having become better informed as a result of exchanges of information, act 'oligopolistically' – that is to say, avoid price-reductions on the theory that these would be immediately met and would result only in reducing the revenue of all firms in the industry – the necessary element of collusion or conspiracy is lacking.

To distinguish between informed oligopoly and collusion as the cause of damped-down price-competition is the most difficult task that the courts have to face in this field, given that they must give due weight to normal legal safeguards in favour of accused persons and yet avoid being deceived by merely specious arguments. It would not be claimed that they never make a mistake in this task. Indeed, the distinction is not always hard and fast; one can imagine situations in which it would be genuinely difficult even for the businessman himself to say whether he was acting from individual prudence or under the suasion of a common understanding. Inevitably the courts are criticized from both sides.

Many people in industry in the United States would hold that the courts are at times too readily persuaded of collusion and that they give too little weight to the good reasons which prudent and well-informed businessmen often have – independently of any agreement – for not upsetting the going price. It may perhaps be that the courts are not always so rigorous in their handling of circumstantial evidence in price-fixing cases as they would be in matters of major crime. It is a very human tendency in law to make the evidence fit the crime no less than the punishment; evidence good enough to secure a conviction for a minor motoring offence would often be found wanting in a murder trial. To this extent the complaint may have some substance. But there is little evidence that injustice to defendants is other than extremely rare, and the *Flooring* and *Tag* cases show that the prosecution case must be solidly based.

On the other hand, fears are sometimes expressed by anti-trust supporters that it is too easy to get away with tacit collusion in avoiding price-competition, and it is possible that among very small groups this is sometimes successful. But again it can hardly be frequent. In many trades, price schedules are so complicated – with different grades of product, functional and quantity discounts, freight charges and so forth – that competitive variation is bound to break out at one point or another unless the mere desire of individual sellers for price-stability is reinforced by some actively collusive arrangements. Certainly the risks involved in deliberately exploiting the borderline between collusion and oligopoly in order to evade the law are formidable. If collusion really occurs, attempts to suppress evidence of it in an industry of any size are not likely to succeed. Some at least of the participants will surely keep damaging material on files to be presented to the court in due course by government counsel. Moreover, any firm which has to be subjected to any degree of pressure to abide by an understanding about price-competition is a potential prosecution witness.[2] It must be noted, too, that if an attempt at evasion is made and fails, the court may use its equity powers to prevent even innocent interchanges of information from being carried on in the future.

Thus the safest rule for the businessman is to assume that the courts will most of the time get at the truth. If he really has entered into a common understanding with his competitors, the courts will probably find it out and the reckoning will be unpleasant. If he is acting independently, even though he is well informed in an oligopoly situation and takes account of the probable reactions of his competitors, the courts will not simply invent collusion where there is no evidence to support it. And it must be stressed once more that cases which are exactly poised on the borderline are extremely infrequent as compared with those that are straightforward. Given that the law requires a line to be drawn between collusion and oligopoly in situations where price-competition appears to lack vigour, it seems likely that the courts get the right answer as often as can be expected of any human institution.

The wider question remains of whether this borderline makes sense in the context of the policy of maintaining competition. Is the legal immunity of non-collusive oligopoly a serious loophole

2. To the extent that successful anti-trust enforcement in the past has conditioned businessmen (and their advisers) to keep files clear of damaging material, to keep tabs on potential witnesses and so forth, the authorities have necessarily been forced to rely more and more on circumstantial evidence. Thus anti-trust supporters might contend that the efforts of the authorities to get somewhat indirect evidence of collusion accepted by the courts are, to some extent, a reaction to sophisticated business efforts to avoid straightforward types of agreement and the provision of clear-cut evidence.

in anti-trust? Does the dampening effect on price-fluctuations, which occurs when well-informed sellers recognize the interdependence of their decisions, frustrate the general policy? Does 'pure' oligopoly occur very often in practice? These are essentially questions of assessment and appraisal, and, as such, must be deferred to below. Certainly some zealots in anti-trust faith see these points as weaknesses in the system and as a problem to be tackled. This view has led to attempts to stretch the legal meaning of 'conspiracy', and some cases illustrating such attempts and their treatment in the courts will be described below.

Price-leadership

This section may suitably end with a brief note on 'price-leadership' situations. Price-leadership raises no new point of principle. In a trade where the sellers are kept fully and promptly informed about the price-decisions of their rivals, it may happen, as has been seen, that price-fluctuations will be damped down because of prudent individual calculation and without collusion. In a price-leadership situation this result occurs not because of the mutual canniness of more-or-less equal competitors but because one seller has a predominant position which others, if they are prudent, will not see fit to challenge. If a small local manufacturer of, say, paint wishes to keep his position in the market, he may well think it wise to accept the going price of the large mass-producer. He may know that if he should start a challenge by competing in price and begin to extend his market, he could easily be swamped by the powerful competitor. Where competitors are very unequal in power and resources, uniformity of prices may well occur without any collusion. Price-leadership is a special case of oligopoly.

It is clear that where the evidence in a case establishes no more than the existence of a price-leadership situation, neither the leader nor the followers will be found to have violated the anti-trust laws. It may be, of course, that the dominance of the price-leader will be found on other grounds to result from monopolization, and a case under section 2 of the Sherman Act may then be brought. Alternatively, it may prove on investigation that as a result of collusion there has been a conscious allocation of initiative in price-matters to a particular firm. A spurious 'price-leadership' situation would be a possible device for evading the law, and solid evidence of an understanding between firms to abide by the price-decisions of an appointed leader would be enough to establish a case of illegal conspiracy under section 1 of the Act. But evidence based solely on uniformity of prices would, as before, be insufficient to sustain the case. As it was put in a frequently quoted sentence from the opinion of the Supreme Court in *United States* v. *International Harvester Company* (1927): 'The fact that competitors may see proper, in the exercise of their own judgement, to follow the prices of another manufacturer does not establish any suppression of competition nor show any sinister domination.'

Once again the question may be raised whether the legal immunity of genuine price-leadership situations seriously frustrates the policy of maintaining competition. As in the case of oligopoly generally, the answer will depend in part on the frequency with which genuine price-leadership situations occur and on the extent to which they are likely to be stable and lasting. These too are questions which must be raised in the context of assessing the success and value of the anti-trust policy. [. . .]

Agreements other than price-agreements

Not all restraint of trade is directed to influencing the level of prices. While the ultimate aim of market strategy is to obtain favourable terms in bargaining, the immediate objective of many restrictive agreements is to build up or maintain or enhance a position of power in the market. Power in the market is, of course, a necessary condition of effective action even for those whose purpose in limiting competition is defensive and directed to stabilizing a situation in which competition is believed to be excessive. Whether the intention is defensive or exploitative, the classic prescription for improving a bargaining position is to exclude competitors from the market and confine the available trade so far as possible to a manageable number of participants. This section will deal first with those agreements between competitors which seek in various ways to regulate entry into the market or to keep out of the market those outside a favoured group.

The amount of competition in a market may also be reduced by agreements between competitors to keep out of each other's way.

When a market is divisible, whether geographically by areas, functionally by classes of customers, technically by types of product or in other ways, some suppliers may agree to confine themselves to a particular selling area or class of customers or technical field in return for undertakings from others not to compete in that part of the market. These market-sharing agreements have the same aim as exclusionary agreements, that is, to improve the bargaining position of the participants by reducing the amount of competition; the difference is that market-sharing agreements seek this result from a voluntary division of effort among the participants, whereas in exclusionary agreements all the participants band together to resist encroachments from outsiders.

A link between these exclusionary and market-sharing agreements and direct price-fixing agreements is provided by agreements to limit output of a commodity or the amount of it coming into the market. There is an obvious sense in which restrictions of output or sales come into the class of restraints of trade designed to enhance bargaining power. Such restrictions reduce the amount of competition in the market by removing a part of the supply. The effect of restrictions of output or sales on prices is, however, very direct. For this reason, and because the law has always looked to effects on price-levels as the surest criterion of illegal restraint of trade, it has usually been found best in anti-trust enforcement to attack output restrictions as a form of price-manipulation. The *Socony-Vacuum* case, for example, is always quoted as a leading case in the field of price-fixing, though it rests on the planned removal of 'surplus' quantities of petrol from the market. The result is that anti-trust case-law contains hardly any case in which output restriction as such is the central issue. There can, however, be little doubt that collusive arrangements to limit the amount of a product reaching the market are illegal *per se* under Section 1 of the Sherman Act and would be so found even in the unlikely event that a case arose in which no evidence of concomitant effects on prices could be produced.

It can, of course, happen that direct restrictions of price-competition, restrictions of output, arrangements to divide a market and arrangements to exclude new competitors are all found together in one set of trade-agreements. The separate elements are here abstracted and dealt with seriatim for ease of exposition and not because they do not in practice commonly co-exist.

Collective exclusive-dealing agreements; the *Standard Sanitary* case

The most comprehensive aim of exclusionary agreements is to pre-empt a market completely for the participating group and keep outsiders away. Some of the most impressive examples of agreements with this aim are to be found in situations where the exclusionary device is control over patents. Other cases show how powerful individual firms or small groups in an industry have sometimes succeeded in excluding or greatly hindering competitors by pre-empting sources of supply of vital materials or by tying essential channels of distribution exclusively to themselves. Where large groups are concerned, it is usually necessary for agreements to be made between associations of traders at different market-levels if outside firms are to be effectively impeded. An association of wholesalers, for example, even though their total share of a trade is very large, can do little by themselves to exclude new entrants; but if they can make an agreement with an equally dominant group of manufacturers whereby no non-participating wholesaler will be supplied, the exclusionary effect may be strong. The manufacturers will probably require on their side of the bargain that the wholesalers do not distribute the goods of any manufacturer outside the participating group, and in this way the competition of non-participating manufacturers will also be hindered. The power and advantage of agreements of this kind often arise from their reciprocity. They are known as *collective exclusive-dealing agreements* and they violate section 1 of the Sherman Act just as much as price-fixing agreements.

From an early stage in the enforcement of the Sherman Act there have been cases involving large groups or associations which have sought in this way to pre-empt or foreclose markets. As early as 1903, in *Montague and Company* v. *Lowry* (Supreme Court), an agreement whereby a group of wholesalers undertook to obtain supplies of tiles only from a particular group of manufacturers and the manufacturers agreed in turn to distribute their goods only through the group of wholesalers was found repugnant to the Sherman Act. Another early case may be mentioned here, even though it involved patents, as setting the tone for this line of decisions. This was *Standard Sanitary Manufacturing Company* v. *United States* in 1912, in which again associations of manufacturers and dealers made agreements by which the dealings of each group were to be confined to the other. These agreements were also condemned by the Supreme Court: 'The agreements in the case at bar combined the manufacturers and jobbers of enamelled ware very much to the same purpose and results as the association of manufacturers and dealers in tiles combined them in *Montague and Company* v. *Lowry* . . . which combination was condemned by this Court as offending the Sherman Law. The added element of the patent in this case at bar cannot confer immunity from a like condemnation.'

It may be taken as an established rule of anti-trust that all agreements between trade associations or groups at different levels of the market – for example, between manufacturers and wholesalers, wholesalers and retailers, jobbers and contractors – whereby the flow of supplies (or orders) from one of the groups is confined to members of the other, are illegal *per se*. Nor is it a question only of the flow of supplies; agreements whereby only firms within the participating associations can obtain certain favourable terms of trade, such as special discounts and rebates, fall under the same ban. In the most general terms the rule is that any collective arrangements under which supplies (or orders to supply) or preferential terms and conditions of sale (or of purchase) are confined to an exclusive group of firms, whether this group is defined by a formula or enumerated in a list and whether or not it is co-extensive with the membership of a particular trade association, are restraints of trade within the prohibition of section 1 of the Sherman Act.

Thus, while it may be unobjectionable for an individual supplier of, say, building materials to grant 'functional discounts' of different amounts to different types of distributor and user, it is never permitted for these arrangements to be formalized into trade-association agreements, under which the persons entitled to receive a particular level of discount are determined collectively. All the 'classification' agreements which are so commonly found in building materials and other industries in many parts of the world are in this way offensive to the Sherman Act.

Since collective exclusive-dealing agreements are regarded as illegal *per se*, the courts will not accept, any more than with price-fixing agreements, defence arguments resting on alleged social or economic advantages of limiting competition. Nor does the share of the output of a product that is controlled by the participating groups have to reach some given percentage, so long as a significant effect on competition is produced or intended. In practice no agreement is likely to escape the law on the ground that its effect on competition is negligible, since exclusive-dealing agreements are not easy to organize or negotiate, and businessmen are unlikely to go to the trouble of making agreements that have no effect.

Collusion and oligopoly: the law of conspiracy in anti-trust

It was shown above that all price-fixing agreements between competitors, including agreements designed to 'manipulate' price-levels by keeping surplus supplies off the market, are illegal *per se* under the Sherman Act, so long as they have or are meant to have a significant effect on competition. Most cases reaching the courts are in practice straightforward, so that the *Trenton Potteries* case, for example, is an adequate model for settling them. But sometimes, as was seen, difficult borderline questions of fact arise. If businessmen are fully informed of all the factors in the market situation, may it not happen that they independently and quite rationally refrain from cutting each other's throats, so that an absence of price-competition is explained without postulating agreement or conspiracy? How is this situation, which is beyond the reach of the law,[3] to be distinguished from that which arises from illegal agreement? The 'open competition' and basing-point cases illustrating this point showed, however, that it is very difficult, at least for large groups of competitors, to avoid price-competition without to some extent 'organizing' the requisite mutual restraint; in practice, collusion is often present and, if present, is usually detected. But it still seemed possible that among small groups of competitors an absence of price-competition

3. 'The defendants cannot be ordered to compete, but they properly can be forbidden to give directions or to make arrangements not to compete.' Mr Justice Holmes in *Swift and Company* v. *United States* (1905).

might escape legal penalty, either because it arose from a genuinely 'oligopolistic' mutual restraint or because, if there were a common understanding among the group, it might be successfully concealed.

Much the same point was reached previously in respect to agreements between competitors to exclude outsiders from the market or to divide the market and avoid competition among themselves. Once again the majority of cases are in practice straightforward and easily decided by reference to such precedents as the *Addyston Pipe* case or that of the *Fashion Originators Guild*. Once again there come a point at which borderline questions of fact have to be determined. If the major companies in the motion-picture industry all decline to have their films shown in a particular cinema, is this the result of a set of independent decisions reached on genuine commercial grounds, or is it the result of an illegal agreement designed to hamper the small exhibitor and favour the powerful cinema chain or the subsidiary exhibiting interests of the major companies themselves? Is there a danger that the second situation may successfully ape the first, so that the wicked flourish like the green bay tree?

All these borderline questions point to the existence of a margin of possible inefficiency in anti-trust, a chance for 'getting away with' restrictive behaviour. It is understandable that convinced champions of the anti-trust policy would like to eliminate this margin. Their efforts to this end raise two quite separate issues. The first is simply that of the efficiency of the courts in getting at the truth. Are the courts readily deceived by efforts to conceal collusion? Do many illegal conspiracies in practice go undetected and unpunished? It is, of course, entirely proper that law-enforcing authorities should seek to eliminate sheer error in dispensing justice. But, as is suggested in the previous chapters, it does not seem likely that errors are frequent. In any event, error is a factor that may cut both ways, and it is a respectable tradition in law that those on trial should receive the benefit of the doubt, lest the innocent suffer.

The second and much more important issue is that of the legal definition of conspiracy. Some of those who seek the maximum effectiveness of anti-trust are concerned not only to eliminate error but also to break free from restrictive definitions of such terms as 'conspiracy' or 'agreement' when these appear to place uncompetitive situations beyond the reach of the law. Anti-trust, they argue, is intended to maintain a state of lively competitiveness in American commerce; situations in which competition is lacking or stagnant are therefore a matter for reproach; all such situations require remedy, and the law should be so written as to make this possible. At the extreme the view is held that 'oligopolistic' behaviour, which has the effect of limiting competition, ought to be regarded as a form of collusion and that powerful firms following parallel courses of action with restrictive effect should be deemed conspirators. Some commentators go so far as to claim that the law already requires these conclusions, not merely that it ought to require them.

In recent years views of this type have attained a good deal of influence, certainly in the selection and presentation of cases by the enforcement agencies and to some degree in the judgements handed down by the courts. In this section the discussion of restrictive agreements between competitors will be concluded by an examination of some cases in which the limits of the legal meaning of 'conspiracy' have been probed and, as some think, stretched.

As a starting-point we may take two propositions about the law of conspiracy under anti-trust that would not be seriously disputed. First, as has been seen already, an agreement or conspiracy in restraint of trade may be proved by circumstantial evidence. No express agreement, let alone an agreement in writing, between the parties has to be produced in court for a case to succeed, so long as a chain of evidence can be built up for which the only plausible explanation is a common understanding or plan. Even those who feel most strongly about improper extensions of legal doctrine in anti-trust would accept that this is settled law and could hardly be otherwise. Secondly, it is clear on the other hand that anti-trust knows no doctrine of 'constructive conspiracy'; that is to say, the existence of a restrictive agreement cannot be proved simply by showing that the effects usually associated with such an agreement have occurred. It is not enough to show that prices have been uniform and unchanged or that no new entrants have appeared in an industry for ten years and invite the court to jump directly to a conclusion of conspiracy. The most ardent trust-buster would in turn accept this as settled law. Within the limits of what may count as circumstantial evidence without being mere construction, there is, however, plenty of room for subtle minds to manoeuvre.

The underlying issue is what, at the minimum, constitutes that 'meeting of the minds' which must be directly or circumstantially established; what degree of mutual knowledge and confidence among businessmen amounts to a common understanding and hence, if there is a restrictive effect on competition, to an illegal conspiracy within the meaning of the Sherman Act? The precise location of this legal boundary is of the highest importance for assessing the impact of anti-trust on American business. Many industries in the United States are 'oligopolistic' in the sense that three or four big firms are responsible for the great bulk of the output. These firms exist of necessity in a state of lively mutual awareness. If – to take an extreme hypothesis – this type of mutual awareness were in itself enough to constitute illegal conspiracy, when coupled with restrictive effects on competition, a huge sector of American business would be in legal jeopardy.

The cases chosen to illustrate this section deal particularly with situations in which a number of firms act in the same way, and the questions are raised whether their parallel courses result from collusion or from some other cause and how the correct explanation can be established. It should be mentioned here, however, that these questions at the margin of the law of conspiracy are not the only ones that the general problem of the impact of anti-trust on oligopoly raises. It is also possible to approach the legality of concentrated industries through the law of monopolization, and the questions raised by this alternative approach will be considered below. [. . .]

'Conscious parallelism of action'; the *Triangle Conduit* case

The phrase 'conscious parallelism of action' had actually been invented in 1948 in a statement issued by the Federal Trade Commission in connexion with a price-fixing case involving a multiple basing-point system of delivered-prices. As a footnote to the previous section it is worth while to review this further application of the concept of parallelism.

It has been noted above that, even though the Federal Trade Commission in the post-war years won a number of cases against

221

price-fixing agreements that were carried on by means of delivered-price systems, it was feared that these might prove Pyrrhic victories, since these systems, once established, might persist without leaving much trace of fresh collusion. Some sanction against the individual firm seemed to be required if tacit collusion was to be effectively prevented.

This situation is not uncommon in the administration of anti-trust. The usual way of meeting it is for the Commission or the Court in their order or decree to impose on the participants in an illegal scheme a series of injunctions against all activities – even activities not in themselves illegal – that might enable the restrictive effects of the conspiracy to be carried on. In the delivered-pricing cases, however, the Commission's lawyers sought a more direct sanction against the individual firm. In a number of cases the firms concerned were not charged only with taking part in a conspiracy, but there was a second charge alleging that, apart from the conspiracy, they were individually guilty of illegal discrimination.

In one important case, however, the Commission's second charge did not rely on the Robinson–Patman Act but was brought under section 5 of the Federal Trade Commission Act. This was *Triangle Conduit and Cable Company* v. *Federal Trade Commission* (Seventh Circuit Court of Appeals, 1948), in which it was charged that the members of the Rigid Steel Conduit Association, quite apart from the conspiracy, individually violated section 5 'through their concurrent use of a formula method of making delivered-price quotations with the knowledge that each did likewise, with the result that price-competition between and among them was unreasonably restrained'.

This charge was clearly directed against consciously parallel business action on the part of competitors. Such a charge might be used in any situation in which, without any sign of a common understanding, firms were found to be following the pricing decisions of a powerful leader or refraining from making price-changes because of their expectations about the reactions of their rivals in an oligopolistic market. The word 'knowledge' in this charge refers simply to knowledge of fact – that is, the fact that other suppliers were for the time being using a particular formula; it is not implied that each firm knew of a mutual obligation to use the formula.

222

Since this charge was brought under section 5 of the Federal Trade Commission Act, it did not directly involve the law of conspiracy, for 'unfair methods of competition' under this section may be the methods of individual firms. This, however, would give little comfort to the business world, for if it became an offence under section 5 for individual firms to act on lines consciously parallel with those of their rivals, a strict definition of 'conspiracy' under the Sherman Act would no longer avail them; they would be out of the Sherman Act frying-pan into the Federal Trade Commission Act fire. There was, therefore, great anxiety in business circles when the Commission's decision on this charge went against the members of Rigid Steel Conduit Association and was upheld on appeal by the Seventh Circuit Court of Appeals.

The Court of Appeals found authority in the Supreme Court's opinion in the *Cement* case for the view that: 'Individual conduct . . . which falls short of being a Sherman Act violation may as a matter of law constitute an "unfair method of competition" prohibited by the Trade Commission Act. A major purpose of that Act . . . was to enable the Commission to restrain practices as "unfair" which although not yet having grown into Sherman Act dimensions, would most likely do so if left unrestrained. The Commission and the courts were to determine what conduct, even though it might then be short of a Sherman Act violation, was an "unfair method of competition".'

The Court went on to describe the conduct of members of the association in using the basing-point system in the following terms: 'Each knows that by using it he will be able to quote identical delivered-prices and thus present a condition of matched prices under which purchasers are isolated and deprived of choice among sellers so far as price-advantage is concerned. . . . Each seller consciously intends not to attempt the exclusion of any competition from his natural freight-advantage territory by reducing his price, and in effect invites the others to share the available business at matched prices in his natural market in return for a reciprocal invitation. . . . We cannot say that the Commission was wrong in concluding that the individual use of the basing-point method as here used does constitute an unfair method of competition.'

Shortly after this the Federal Trade Commission sought to

explain their view of the law in a public statement of policy. In a paragraph describing the situation in the *Rigid Steel Conduit* case the statement ran:

It would have been possible to describe this state of facts as a price-conspiracy on the principle that, when a number of enterprises follow a parallel course of action in the knowledge and contemplation of the fact that all are acting alike, they have in effect, formed an agreement. Instead of phrasing its charge in this way, the Commission chose to rely on the obvious fact that the economic effect of identical prices achieved through conscious parallel action is the same as that of similar prices achieved through overt collusion, and, for this reason, the Commission treated the conscious parallelism of action as violation of the Federal Trade Commission Act. Should the Supreme Court sustain the Commission's view, the effect will be to simplify proof in basing-point cases, but to expose to proceedings under the Federal Trade Commission Act only courses of action which might be regarded as collusive or destructive of price-competition.

Like *Milgram* v. *Loew's*, this case and the ensuing statement represent a high point of influence of those among the enforcers of anti-trust who would have the law bite on uncompetitive situations without being restricted by rigid legal concepts. (Note how courses of action that are 'destructive of price-competition' are regarded in this statement as actionable *per se* and not only when they are also collusive.) It must be noted that the *Rigid Steel Conduit* case has not subsequently been overruled by the Supreme Court. Nevertheless, it is pretty clear that its influence has waned. It must be remembered that a conspiracy had been properly established in the *Rigid Steel Conduit* case and that the second charge was essentially directed to preventing its revival. So far as the case has authority, it probably means only that the Commission, after a conspiracy has been proved, may bring a charge under section 5 of the Federal Trade Commission Act as an alternative means of preventing individual firms from tacitly carrying on in a manner consistent with the continuance of the conspiracy. It does not appear that the Commission is prepared to follow the logic of their second charge to the extent of prosecuting cases in which individual sellers simply follow the lead of more-powerful competitors where no agreement or conspiracy is ever established. This impression is borne out by evidence given on behalf of the

Commission to Congressional committees and certainly, in the years that have passed since the decision, no attempt has been made to press its logic to this point. [. . .]

Section 2 of the Sherman Act; monopoly and monopolizing; the legal meaning of 'intent'; the significance of the remedies to be achieved

The previous sections have dealt with restraints of trade proceeding out of agreement or combination between competitors: the position of power in the market which is achieved by combination is typically used to influence the level of prices or to exclude competitors from the market. Sometimes a position of power in the market is achieved by a single firm which thereby becomes capable of producing the same economic effects as a combination. Section 2 of the Sherman Act is designed to bring this type of situation within the scope of anti-trust. 'Every person who shall monopolize or attempt to monopolize, or combine or conspire with any person or persons to monopolize any part of the trade or commerce among the several States, or with foreign nations, shall be deemed guilty of a misdemeanour. . . .' In this and the two subsequent chapters the case-law under section 2 will be examined.

There are a number of important differences between the considerations that the courts must have in mind in section 2 cases and those which have been shown to apply to section 1. Perhaps the most important is the broader scope for the rule of reason under section 2; monopoly as such is not and cannot be illegal *per se*. The reason for this is obvious. The first firm to bring a new product on to the market is inevitably a monopolist for a time, but it would be ludicrous to charge it with a criminal offence against the system of free competition. A town of 25,000 people may be unable to support more than one newspaper; here again it would be absurd to regard the publisher's monopoly as criminal. Then, too, it is always possible in a competitive system that a firm, by its sheer efficiency, will – for a time at least – win the competition; in terms of business folklore it may simply have 'made a better mousetrap' and attracted all or nearly all the demand for mousetraps. This must surely be counted a success of the competitive system, not an assault upon it.

This point is recognized in the wording of section 2 itself – by the use of the active verb 'monopolize'; the Act does not prohibit 'monopoly'. To monopolize is not simply to possess a monopoly: the word implies some positive drive, apart from sheer competitive skills, to seize and exert power in the market. The same point has been expressed in recent case-law in the form that a monopoly which is 'merely thrust upon' an enterprise is not illegal. The job of the courts under section 2 of the Sherman Act is to isolate and define the elements of positive drive that constitute monopolizing.

The next point that the courts have to watch is the application (and the limitations) of the apparently straightforward analogy between monopolizing and forming a restrictive agreement or combination. It is tempting to suppose that one might derive the law under section 2 simply by translating the various legal rules about restrictive agreements into rules of conduct for the single dominant firm. Since, for example, it is illegal for a combination to raise prices or make exclusive dealing or boycott arrangements, so 'monopolizing' might be said to occur when a dominant firm raises prices or excludes competitors. A lot of the time these translations turn out near enough right, but the analogy always needs careful handling and at times breaks down.

Several instances of the faulty use of this analogy will appear below. Meanwhile the difficulty may be conveniently illustrated by reference to price-fixing. Every agreement between competitors to fix prices is illegal *per se* and it is of no consequence under section 1 of the Sherman Act whether or not the prices fixed are reasonable. The offence is the agreement not to compete in price. If one tries to apply this rule to a single dominant firm – that is, a firm enjoying by itself as much power in the market as is created by an agreement between competitors – the analogy breaks down. Such a firm must sell at some price, and the price it 'fixes' will not be a price arrived at by competition. Going by the analogy, one should conclude that a monopolist is inescapably guilty of illegal price-fixing. But this cannot be right: such a rule would catch the involuntary monopolist and make monopoly illegal *per se*.

The reason why the analogy leads to a false conclusion on this point is that it ignores the vital element of the intent or purpose lying behind the achievement of market power. The purpose of those who achieve market power by combining or agreeing together scarcely needs stating and in consequence can largely be ignored in the case-law under section 1. Unless the parties intend to limit competition, there is no point in their meeting and negotiating and finally agreeing: and, in any case, their restrictive purpose is normally made manifest in the content of their agreement. It may be an agreement to avoid price-competition or to divide the market or to impede new entrants: but an agreement for no purpose would be meaningless.

All this is different in the case of a single firm which achieves a position of market power. The achievement does not necessarily reflect a purpose on the part of the firm to seize and exert power; the power may have been 'thrust upon' it by economic necessity or it may simply have accrued to it by virtue of a normal exercise of competitive skills. Moreover, there is no equivalent in the case of a single firm to the content of a restrictive agreement; once such a firm enjoys a position of power in the market, the question whether its power will be exploited to enhance prices or exclude competitors is not to be answered by reference to the heads of an agreement – since no agreement exists – but only by examining the intent or purpose of those who control its policies. Thus the principal task of the courts under section 2 of the Sherman Act in seeking to isolate the element of positive drive which constitutes monopolizing is to identify the intent of the firm.

Since the nature of a firm's intent or purpose plays so large a part in the law of monopolization, it is necessary to digress briefly at this point in order to consider what is normal legal doctrine on the subject of criminal 'intent'. The traditional analysis has it that there are two elements in a crime – the wicked deed (*actus reus*) and the guilty mind (*mens rea*); *mens rea*, which is in effect criminal intent, is held to be indispensable to the notion of most types of crime. This analysis, which springs from an ancient logic, might suggest that, having detected a murder, the enforcer of law must then search for some additional 'substance' in the mind of the murderer before a conviction of crime can be obtained. But this is misleading.

In legal practice the search for the criminal intent is normally cut short by applying the rule that a man is to be held responsible for the natural consequences of his acts. 'He who wills the means wills the end.' Thus the commission of the act is in most cases sufficient

227

witness to the intent. The need to show '*mens rea*' has in practice a mainly negative significance; it enables an accused person to plead in his defence that because of some special factor such as infancy, insanity or duress, he was not responsible for his act and thus lacking in criminal intent.

In anti-trust law these same principles apply. A firm's intent may be made manifest by its particular acts or by its general course of action. When a firm in a position of power has exploited the public by charging excessive prices or has driven small competitors out of business, there is no need to look further for its intent to monopolize. Even without particular, identifiable acts of exploit-ation or predation, a firm's general course of policy and behaviour may be such as to give rise to an inference of monopolistic intent. This was established as early as 1905 in *Swift and Company* v. *United States* when Mr Justice Holmes pointed out that a general allegation of intent and purpose to monopolize might 'colour and apply to' all the specific charges and that the court had to look at the plan or policy as a whole. 'It is suggested that the several acts charged are lawful. . . . But they are bound together as the parts of a single plan. The plan may make the parts unlawful.'

Thus in cases of monopolization, as in criminal law generally, the prosecutor is not expected to prove a specific criminal intent as something distinct from the behaviour of the accused firm. The only exception to this rule arises when the charge is one of 'attempt-ing to monopolize'. This charge presupposes that the firm con-cerned has not yet achieved a position of power in the market but is trying to build up such a position. Being without power to exploit or exclude, such a firm must be shown to have a specific intent to achieve these results. This rule too was clearly stated by Mr Justice Holmes in the *Swift* case.[4]

Finally, by way of preamble, a further big difference must be noted in the problems facing the courts in section 2 cases as com-pared with those arising under section 1. This difference relates to

4. 'Where acts are not sufficient in themselves to produce a result which the law seeks to prevent – for instance, the monopoly – but require further acts in addition to the mere forces of nature to bring that result to pass, an intent to bring it to pass is necessary in order to produce a dangerous pro-bability that it will happen. . . . But when that intent and the consequent dangerous probability exist, this statute . . . directs itself against that dangerous probability as well as against the completed result.'

the matter of remedies. A successful prosecution of a restrictive agreement simply puts a stop to the agreement. If the case is a criminal one, fines are imposed and the parties presumably will not risk repeating the offence. In a civil case the equity powers of the court may be used to decree detailed injunctions against specific practices of the parties. Either way, the firms concerned still exist and have only to modify their conduct.

In a case of monopolization, on the other hand, the exaction of a criminal penalty may have no significant effect on the situation. The maximum fine permitted by law may impose no financial burden whatever on a rich monopoly; and, in any case, no deterrent against repeating the offence will have any meaning when the offence is monopolizing. For if an industry has been successfully monopolized, there is no need to repeat the offence. Consequently, it is normal for the anti-trust authorities when bringing charges under section 2 to rely on a civil action (either alone or in conjunction with a criminal suit) and to try to persuade the court of equity to decree the dissolution or break-up of the monopoly concern. The court is then faced with the responsibility not of merely telling businessmen to stop a given practice but of actually ordering them to dismember the existing structure of their industry. Such action may have far-reaching, indeed unforeseeable economic repercussions stretching beyond the business concerned to the well-being of the nation as a whole. It is small wonder, then, that the courts may be inclined to tread warily in this field.

To sum up, the legal task of the courts under section 2 of the Sherman Act is to apply the rule of reason to a diagnosis of the intent of firms which achieve a monopoly position. In carrying out this task they are subject to the stringent discipline that is imposed by the knowledge that weighty economic consequences are involved in their decisions. [. . .]

Part Four The Law as Formulator of Economic Policy

Legislators cannot anticipate all the complexities of advantage and detriment which may surround a monopoly or restriction of competition. Consequently, courts, or quasi-legal tribunals, become the *formulators* of law in this area, not merely the interpreters. In the U.S.A. code the *Trenton Potteries* case contains the classic judicial rejection of the concept of a 'reasonable' price-fix. While that of *Socony Mobil* definitively reports that any attempt to influence price-levels, regardless of market strength, is illegal. Justifications for exclusive dealing are disallowed in the *Standard Stations* case; and tying devices are judged to be dangerous extensions of market power in that of *American Can*. On the monopolization issues the U.S.A. code is less dogmatic. Mere size is no offence records the *U.S. Steel* case. In the 'cellophane' case the concept of economic performance or workable competition is employed to free *E. I. duPont de Nemours* from a charge of monopolization. But, by contrast, in *American Tobacco* the parallel pricing of four large companies is found to be a conspiracy to monopolize. In Britain, judges are more pragmatic. *Yarn Spinners* (and other cases) appeared to introduce a severity of test comparable with those of the U.S.A. But later cases – *Cement*, *Metal Windows* and *Net Books* for example – showed that agreements to restrict competition, if they succeeded in holding down prices, in advancing technology or providing the consumer with a service he seriously desires or needs, can be permitted to survive. The practice of resale price maintenance, judging by the *Chocolate Confectionery* and other references, is on the retreat. To turn to another statutory agency, the Monopolies Commission cannot make law. But, by means of intensive investigation and reports, it exercises a considerable indirect surveillance; and it influences governments.

12 The U.S.A. Jurisdiction

Notable Anti-Trust Judgements[1]

United States v. Trenton Potteries Co. et al.
Supreme Court of the U.S.A., book 71 (273), no. 392 (1926)

Mr Justice Stone delivered the opinion of the Court:

Respondents, twenty individuals and twenty-three corporations, were convicted in the District Court of violating the Sherman Anti-Trust Law. . . . The indictment was on two counts. The first charged a combination to fix and maintain uniform prices for the sale of sanitary pottery, in restraint of interstate commerce; the second, a combination to restrain interstate commerce by limiting sales of pottery to a special group known to respondents as 'legitimate jobbers'. On appeal, the Circuit Court of Appeals reversed the conviction on both counts on the ground that there were errors in the conduct of the trial. [. . .]

Respondents, engaged in the manufacture or distribution of 82 per cent of the vitreous pottery fixtures produced in the United States for use in bathrooms and lavatories, were members of a trade organization known as the Sanitary Potter's Association. [. . .]

There is no contention here that the verdict was not supported by sufficient evidence that respondents, controlling some 82 per cent of the business of manufacturing and distributing in the United States vitreous pottery, combined to fix prices and to limit sales in interstate commerce to jobbers.

The issues raised here by the Government's specification of errors relate only to the decision of the Circuit Court of Appeals upon its review of certain rulings of the District Court made in the course of its trial. It is urged that the Court below erred in holding in effect: (1) that the trial court should have submitted to the jury the question whether the price agreement complained of consti-

1. These judgements should be read in conjunction with the policy considerations outlined in Readings 9 and 11.

tuted an unreasonable restraint of trade; (2) that . . . the trial court charged, in submitting the case to the jury that, if it found the agreements or combination complained of, it might return a verdict of guilty without regard to the reasonableness of the prices fixed, or the good intentions of the combining units, whether prices were actually lowered or raised or whether sales were restricted to the special jobbers, since both agreements of themselves were unreasonable restraints. [. . .]

The court below held specifically that the trial court erred and held in effect that the charge as given on this branch of the case was erroneous [because of the] mistaken view of the trial judge. [. . .]

The question therefore to be considered here is whether the trial judge correctly withdrew from the jury the consideration of the reasonableness of the particular restraints charged.

That only restraints upon inter-state commerce which are unreasonable are prohibited by the Sherman Law was the rule laid down by the opinions of this Court in the Standard Oil and Tobacco Cases. But it does not follow that agreements to fix or maintain prices are reasonable restraints and therefore permitted by the statute, merely because the prices themselves are reasonable. Reasonableness is not a concept of definite and unchanging content. Its meaning necessarily varies in the different fields of the law, because it is used as a convenient summary of the dominant considerations which control in the application of legal doctrines. Our view of what is a reasonable restraint of commerce is controlled by the recognized purpose of the Sherman Law itself. Whether this type of restraint is reasonable or not must be judged in part at least, in the light of its effect on competition, for whatever difference of opinion there may be among economists as to the social and economic desirability of an unrestrained competitive system, it cannot be doubted that the Sherman Law and the judicial decisions interpreting it are based upon the assumption that the public interest is best protected from the evils of monopoly and price control by the maintenance of competition. [. . .]

The aim and result of every price-fixing agreement, if effective, is the elimination of one form of competition. The power to fix prices, whether reasonably exercised or not, involves power to control the market and to fix arbitrary and unreasonable prices. The reasonable price fixed today may through economic and business changes become the unreasonable price of tomorrow. Once established, it may be maintained unchanged because of the absence of competition secured by the agreement for a price reasonable when fixed. Agreements which create such potential power may well be held to be in themselves unreasonable or unlawful restraints, without the necessity of minute inquiry whether a particular price is reasonable or unreasonable as fixed and without placing on the Government in enforcing the Sherman Law the burden of ascertaining from day to day whether it has become unreasonable through the mere variation of economic conditions. Moreover, in the absence of express legislation requiring it, we should hesitate to adopt a construction making the difference between legal and illegal conduct in the field of business relations depend upon so uncertain a test as whether prices are reasonable – a determination which can be satisfactorily made only after a complete survey of our economic organization and a choice between rival philosophies. . . . Thus viewed the Sherman Law is not only a prohibition against the infliction of a particular type of injury – it 'is a limitation of rights, . . . which may [otherwise] be pushed to evil consequences and therefore [should be] restrained'.

The charge of the trial court, viewed as a whole, fairly submitted to the jury the question whether a price-fixing agreement as described in the first count was entered into by the respondents. Whether the prices actually agreed upon were reasonable or unreasonable was immaterial in the circumstances charged in the indictment and necessarily found by the verdict. The requested charge . . . while true as abstract proposition [was] inapplicable to the case in hand and rightly refused. [. . .]

United States v. Socony – Vacuum Oil Company
Supreme Court of the U.S.A., book 84 (310), no. 150 (1939)

Mr Justice Douglas delivered the opinion of the Court:

Respondents were convicted by a jury . . . under an indictment charging violations of section 1 of the Sherman Anti-Trust Act. . . . The Circuit Court of Appeals reversed and remanded for a new trial. . . . The case is here on a petition and cross-petition for certiorari, both of which are granted because of the public importance of the issues raised. [. . .]

The indictment was returned in December 1936 in the United States District Court for the Western District of Wisconsin. It charges that certain major oil companies, selling gasoline in the mid-Western area, [. . .] (1) 'combined and conspired together for the purpose of artificially raising and fixing the tank car prices of gasoline' in the 'spot markets' in East Texas and mid-Continent fields; (2) 'have artificially raised and fixed said spot market tank car prices of gasoline and have maintained said prices at artificially high and non-competitive levels, and at levels agreed upon among them and have thereby intentionally increased and fixed the tank car prices of gasoline contracted to be sold and sold in interstate commerce as aforesaid in the mid-Western area'; (3) 'have arbitrarily', by reason of the provisions of the prevailing form of jobber contracts which made the price to the jobber dependent on the average spot market price, 'exacted large sums of money from thousands of jobbers with whom they have had such contracts in said mid-Western area'; and (4) 'in turn have intentionally raised the general level of retail prices prevailing in said mid-Western area'.

The manner and means of effectuating such conspiracy are alleged in substance as follows: Defendants, from February 1935 to December 1936 'have knowingly and unlawfully engaged and participated in two concerted gasoline buying programs' for the purchase 'from independent refiners in spot transactions of large quantities of gasoline in the East Texas and mid-Continent fields at uniform, high, and at times progressively increased prices'. The East Texas buying program is alleged to have embraced purchases of gasoline in spot transactions from most of the independent refiners in the East Texas field, who were members of the East Texas Refiners' Marketing Association, formed in February 1935 with the knowledge and approval of some of the defendants 'for the purpose of selling and facilitating the sale of gasoline to defendant major oil companies'. It is alleged that arrangements were made and carried out for allotting orders for gasoline received from defendants among the members of that association; and that such purchases amounted to more than 50 per cent of all gasoline produced by those independent refiners. The mid-Continent buying program is alleged to have included 'large and increased purchases of gasoline' by defendants from independent refiners located in the mid-Continent fields pursuant to allotments among themselves. Those purchases, it is charged, were made from independent refiners who were assigned to certain of the defendants at monthly meetings of a group representing defendants. It is alleged that the purchases in this buying program amounted to nearly 50 per cent of all gasoline sold by those independents. As respects both the East Texas and the mid-Continent buying programs, it is alleged that the purchases of gasoline were in excess of the amounts which defendants would have purchased but for those programs; that at the instance of certain defendants these independent refiners curtailed their production of gasoline. [. . .]

The methods of marketing and selling gasoline in the mid-Western area are set forth in the indictment in some detail. Since we hereafter develop the facts concerning them, it will suffice at this point to summarize them briefly. Each defendant major oil company owns, operates or leases retail service stations in this area. It supplies those stations, as well as independent retail stations, with gasoline from its bulk storage plants. All but one sell large quantities of gasoline to jobbers in tank car lots under term contracts. In this area these jobbers exceed 4,000 in number and distribute about 50 per cent of all gasoline distributed to retail service stations therein, the bulk of the jobbers' purchases being made from the defendant companies. The price to the jobbers under those contracts with defendant companies is made dependent on the spot market price, pursuant to a formula hereinafter discussed. And the spot market tank car prices of gasoline directly and substantially influence the retail prices in the area. In sum, it is alleged that defendants by raising and fixing the tank car prices of gasoline in these spot markets could and did increase the tank car prices and the retail prices of gasoline sold in the mid-Western area. The vulnerability of these spot markets to that type of manipulation or stabilization is emphasized by the allegation that spot market prices published in the journals were the result of spot sales made chiefly by independent refiners of a relatively small amount of the gasoline sold in that area – virtually all gasoline sold in tank car quantities in spot market transactions in the mid-Western area being sold by independent refiners, such sales amounting to less than 5 per cent of all gasoline marketed therein.

So much for the indictment . . . [the background to this conspiracy – overproduction of oil 1926–30 – is given in the record of the court].

The first meeting of the Tank Car Committee was held 5 February 1935, and the second on 11 February 1935. At these meetings the alleged conspiracy was formed, the substance of which, so far as it pertained to the mid-Continent phase, was as follows.

It was estimated that there would be between 600 and 700 tank cars of distress gasoline produced in the mid-Continent oil field every month by about 17 independent refiners. These refiners, not having regular outlets for the gasoline, would be unable to dispose of it except at distress prices. Accordingly, it was proposed and decided that certain major companies (including the corporate respondents) would purchase gasoline from these refiners. The Committee would assemble each month information as to the quantity and location of this distress gasoline. Each of the major companies was to select one (or more) of the independent refiners having distress gasoline as its 'dancing partner', and would assume responsibility for purchasing its distress supply. In this matter buying power would be co-ordinated, purchases would be effectively placed, and the results would be much superior to the previous haphazard purchasing. There were to be no formal contractual commitments to purchase this gasoline, either between the major companies or between the majors and the independents. Rather it was an informal gentleman's agreement or understanding whereby each undertook to perform his share of the joint undertaking. Purchases were to be made at the 'fair going market price'. . . . Before the month was out all companies alleged to have participated in the program (except one or two) made purchases; 757 tank cars were bought from all but three of the independent refiners who were named in the indictment as sellers. [. . .]

On 27 May 1935, this Court held [in another proceedings] . . . that the code-making authority conferred by the National Industrial Recovery Act was an unconstitutional delegation of legislative power. Shortly thereafter the Tank Car Stabilization Committee held a meeting to discuss their future action. It was decided that the buying program should continue. Accordingly that Committee continued to meet. [. . .]

In the meetings when the mid-Continent buying program was

being formulated it was recognized that it would be necessary or desirable to take the East Texas surplus gasoline off the market so that it would not be a 'disturbing influence in the standard of Indiana territory'. The reason was that weakness in East Texas spot market prices might make East Texas gasoline competitive with mid-Continent gasoline in the mid-Western area and thus affect mid-Continent spot market prices. . . . Early in 1935 the East Texas Refiners' Marketing Association was formed to dispose of the surplus gasoline manufactured by the East Texas refiners. [. . .]

As a result of these buying programs it was hoped and intended that both the tank car and the retail markets would improve. The conclusion is irresistible that defendants' purpose was not merely to raise the price of gasoline in their sales to jobbers and consumers in the mid-Western area. Their agreement or plan embraced not only buying on the spot markets but also, at least by clear implication, an understanding to maintain such improvements in mid-Western prices as would result from those purchases of distress gasoline. The latter obviously would be achieved by selling at the increased prices, not by price cutting. Any other understanding would have been wholly inconsistent with and contrary to the philosophy of the broad stabilization efforts which were under way. In essence the raising and maintenance of the spot market prices were but the means adopted for raising and maintaining prices to jobbers and consumers. The broad sweep of the agreement was indicated . . . before a group of the industry on 13 March 1935. . . . Certainly there was enough evidence to support a finding by the jury that such were the scope and purpose of the plan. [. . .]

[Markets, prices, jobbers operations and their effect on the buying programmes are described.]

Respondents do not contend that the buying programs were not a factor in the price rise and in the stabilization of the spot markets during 1935 and 1936. But they do contend that they were relatively minor ones, because of the presence of other economic forces. [. . .]

In *United States* v. *Trenton Potteries Co.* . . . , this Court sustained a conviction under the Sherman Act where the jury was charged that an agreement on the part of the members of a combination, controlling a substantial part of an industry, upon the prices which the members are to charge for their commodity is in itself an unreasonable restraint of trade without regard to the reasonableness of the prices or the good intentions of the combining units. . . . This Court pointed out that the so-called 'rule of reason' announced in *Standard Oil Co.* v. *United States* and in *United States* v. *American Tobacco Co.* had not affected this view of the illegality of price-fixing agreements. [. . .]

But respondents claim that other decisions of this Court afford them adequate defenses to the indictment. Among those on which they place reliance are *Appalachian Coals, Inc.* v. *United States,* [etc.] . . . But we do not think that line of cases is apposite . . . [the] only essential thing in common between the instant case and the *Appalachian Coals* case is the presence in each of so-called demoralizing or injurious practices. The methods of dealing with them were quite divergent. In the instant cases there were buying programs of distress gasoline which had as their direct purpose and aim the raising and maintenance of spot market prices and of prices to jobbers and consumers in the mid-Western area, by the elimination of distress gasoline as a market factor. The increase in the spot market prices was to be accomplished by a well organized buying program on that market: regular ascertainment of the amounts of surplus gasoline; assignment of sellers among the buyers; regular purchases at prices which would place and keep a floor under the market. Unlike the plan in the instant case, the plan in the *Appalachian Coals* case was not designed to operate *vis-à-vis* the general consuming market and to fix the prices on that market. Furthermore, the effect, if any, of that plan on prices was not only wholly incidental but also highly conjectural. For the plan had not then been put into operation. Hence this Court expressly reserved jurisdiction in the District Court to take further proceedings if, *inter alia*, in 'actual operation' the plan proved to be 'an undue restraint upon interstate commerce'. And as we have seen it would *per se* constitute such a restraint if price-fixing were involved. [. . .]

Thus for over forty years this Court has consistently and without deviation adhered to the principle that price-fixing agreements are unlawful *per se* under the Sherman Act and that no showing of so-called competitive abuses or evils which those agreements were designed to eliminate or alleviate may be interposed as a defense. [. . .]

Therefore the sole remaining question on this phase of the case is the applicability of the rule of the Trenton Potteries case to these facts.

Respondents seek to distinguish the Trenton Potteries case from the instant one. They assert that . . . But we do not deem those distinctions material.

In the first place, there was abundant evidence that the combination had the purpose to raise prices. And likewise, there was ample evidence that the buying programs at least contributed to the price rise and the stability of the spot markets, and to increases in the price of gasoline sold in the mid-Western area during the indictment period. That other factors also may have contributed to that rise and stability of the markets is immaterial. . . . [The more relevant point is the existence of] . . . Proof that there was a conspiracy, that its purpose was to raise prices, and that it caused or contributed to a price rise is proof of the actual consummation or execution of a conspiracy under section 1 of the Sherman Act.

Secondly, the fact that sales on the spot markets were still governed by some competition is of no consequence. For it is indisputable that competition was restricted through the removal by respondents of a part of the supply which but for the buying programs would have been a factor in determining the going prices on those markets. . . . Competition was not eliminated from the markets; but it was clearly curtailed, since restriction of the supply of gasoline, the timing and placement of the purchases under the buying programs and the placing of a floor under the spot markets obviously reduced the play of the forces of supply and demand.

The elimination of so-called competitive evils is no legal justification for such buying programs. . . . If the so-called competitive abuses were to be appraised here, the reasonableness of prices would necessarily become an issue in every price-fixing case. In that event the Sherman Act would soon be emasculated; its philosophy would be supplanted by one which is wholly alien to a system of free competition; it would not be the charter of freedom which its framers intended.

The reasonableness of price has no constancy due to the dynamic quality of business facts underlying price structures. Those who fixed reasonable prices today would perpetuate unreasonable prices tomorrow. . . . Those who controlled the prices . . . would have it in their power to destroy or drastically impair the competitive system. But the thrust of the rule is deeper and reaches more than monopoly power. Any combination which tampers with price structures is engaged in an unlawful activity. Even though the members of the price-fixing group were in no position to control the market, to the extent that they raised, lowered, or stabilized prices they would be directly interfering with the free play of market forces. The Act places all such schemes beyond the pale and protects that vital part of our economy against any degree of interference. Congress . . . has not permitted the age-old cry of ruinous competition and competitive evils to be a defense to price-fixing conspiracies. It has no more allowed genuine or fancied competitive abuses as a legal justification for such schemes than it has the good intentions of the members of the combination. If such a shift is to be made, it must be done by the Congress. Certainly Congress has not left us with any such choice. [. . .]

Under the Sherman Act a combination formed for the purpose and with the effect of raising, depressing, fixing, pegging, or stabilizing the price of a commodity in interstate or foreign commerce is illegal *per se*. . . . There may be effective influence over the market although the group in question does not control it.

Price-fixing agreements may have utility to members of the group though the power possessed or exerted falls far short of domination and control. Monopoly power . . . is not the only power which the Act strikes down, as we have said. Proof that a combination was formed for the purpose of fixing prices and that it caused them to be fixed or contributed to that result is proof of the completion of a price-fixing conspiracy under section 1 of the Act. The indictment in this case charged that this combination had that purpose and effect. And there was abundant evidence to support it. Hence the existence of power on the part of members of the combination to fix prices was but a conclusion from the finding that the buying programs caused or contributed to the rise and stability of prices. [. . .]

The judgement of the Circuit Court of Appeals is reversed and that of the District Court affirmed.

Triangle Conduit and Cable Company et al. v.
Federal Trade Commission

Federal Reporter, 2 series, vol. 168, p. 175 (1948)
Before Sparks, Kerner, and Minton, Circuit Judges.

Kerner, Circuit Judge:

Petitioners, fourteen corporate manufacturers of rigid steel conduit, and five representatives of these corporations ask us to
review and set aside a cease and desist order of the Federal Trade
Commission, upon a complaint on two counts, charging that petitioners collectively have violated section 5 of the Federal Trade
Commission Act . . ., which declares unlawful 'unfair methods of
competition in commerce'.

In substance the first count alleged the existence and continuance
of a conspiracy for the purpose and with the effect of substantially
restricting and suppressing actual and potential competition in the
distribution and sale of rigid steel conduit in commerce, effectuated by the adoption and use of a basing-point method of
quoting prices for rigid steel conduit. The second count did not
rest upon an agreement or combination. It charged that each
corporate petitioner and others violated section 5 of the Federal
Trade Commission Act 'through their concurrent use of a formula
method of making delivered price quotations with the knowledge
that each did likewise, with the result that price competition
between and among them was unreasonably restrained'. It alleged
that nearby customers were deprived of price advantages which
they would have naturally enjoyed by reason of their proximity to
points of production, and that such course of action created in said
conduit sellers a monopolistic control over price in the sale and
distribution of rigid steel conduit.

Petitioners answered the complaint. They denied any agreement
or combination. After extensive hearings before a trial examiner,
the Commission made its findings of fact and conclusions of law
therefrom. It found the charges to be fully substantiated by the
evidence. [. . .]

[A description of the industry and an account of its basing-point
practices enters the judgement here.]

The argument [of defendants] is that there is no direct evidence of any conspiracy; that if the Commission made such a finding, it is based upon a series of inferences; and that the general use of the basing-point method of pricing and the uniformity of prices does not justify an inference of conspiracy. We think there was direct proof of the conspiracy, but whether there was or not, in determining if such a finding is supported it is not necessary that there be direct proof of an agreement. Such an agreement may be shown by circumstantial evidence. [. . .]

In this case there was evidence showing collective action to eliminate the Evanston basing point, and collective activities in promoting the general use of the formula presently to be noted. The record clearly established the fact that conduit manufacturers controlling 93 per cent of the industry use a system under which they quote only delivered prices, which are determined in accordance with a formula consisting of a base price at Pittsburgh or Chicago plus rail freight, depending upon which basing-point controls at any particular destination or in any particular section of the United States; that as a result of using that formula the conduit producers were enabled to match their delivered price quotations, and purchasers everywhere were unable to find price advantages anywhere; and that purchasers at or near a place of production could not buy more cheaply from their nearby producer than from producers located at greater distances, and producers located at great distances from any given purchaser quoted as low a delivered price as that quoted by the nearest producer.

[An example affecting the tenders of the U.S. Navy Department is given.]

[. . .] Not only did petitioners match their bids when submitted under seal to agencies of public bodies, but each, with the knowledge of the others, did likewise – used the formula for the purpose of presenting to prospective private purchasers conditions of matched price quotations.

[. . .] Our study of this record and of applicable law has convinced us that the Commission was justified in drawing the inference that the petitioners acted in concert in a price-fixing conspiracy.

We now turn to consider petitioners' contention that the individual use of the basing-point method, with knowledge that other sellers use it, does not constitute an unfair method of competition. This contention embodies the theory of the second count of the complaint. [. . .]

[The cease and desist orders enjoined by the Federal Trade Commission against the individual companies are mentioned at this point.]

Briefly, the argument is that individual freight absorption is not illegal *per se*, and that the Commission's order is a denial of the right to meet competition. More specifically, petitioners say that conduit is a homogeneous product; that no buyer will pay more for the product of one seller than he will for that of another; that the buyer is not interested in the seller's cost of transportation or in any other factor of the seller's cost; that effective competition requires that traders have large freedom of action when conducting their own affairs; that in any particular market, the seller must adjust his own price to meet the market price or retire from that market altogether; that it has always been the custom of merchants to send their goods to distant markets to be sold at the prices there prevailing; that there is no lessening of competition or injury to competitors, when a seller absorbs freight traffic to meet lawful competition; and that it is for the court to decide as a matter of law what constitutes an unfair method of competition under section 5 of the Act. [. . .]

On the other hand, the Commission contends that unfair methods of competition include not only methods that involve deception, bad faith, and fraud, but methods that involve oppression or such as are against public policy because of their dangerous tendency unduly to hinder competition or create monopoly.

As already noted, each conduit seller knows that each of the other sellers is using the basing-point formula; each knows that by using it he will be able to quote identical delivered prices and thus present a condition of matched prices under which purchasers are isolated and deprived of choice among sellers so far as price advantage is concerned. Each seller must systematically increase or decrease his mill net price for customers at numerous destinations in order to match the delivered prices of his competitors. Each seller consciously intends not to attempt the exclusion of any competition from his natural freight advantage territory by reducing the price, and in effect invites the others to share the available business at matched prices in his natural market in return for a reciprocal invitation.

In this situation, and indeed all parties to these proceedings agree, the legal question presented is identical with the one the Supreme Court considered in the *Federal Trade Commission* v. *The Cement Institute* case. [. . .]

In the light of that opinion, we cannot say that the Commission was wrong in concluding that the individual use of the basing-point method as here used does constitute an unfair method of competition. [. . .]

The Commission's order is affirmed and an enforcement decree will be entered. It is so ordered.

Standard Oil of California and Standard Stations, Inc. v. **United States**
Supreme Court of the U.S.A., book 93 (137), no. 293 (1948)

Mr Justice Frankfurter delivered the opinion of the Court:

This is an appeal to review a decree enjoining the Standard Oil Company of California and its wholly-owned subsidiary, Standard Stations, Inc., from enforcing or entering exclusive supply contracts with any independent dealer in petroleum products and auto-mobile accessories. The use of such contracts was successfully assailed by the United States as violative of section 1 of the Sherman Act and section 3 of the Clayton Act.

The Standard Oil Company of California . . . owns petroleum-producing resources and refining plants in California and sells petroleum products in what has been termed in these proceedings the 'Western area'. . . . It sells through its own service stations, to the operators of independent service stations, and to industrial users. It is the largest seller of gasoline in the area. In 1946 its combined sales amounted to 23 per cent of the total taxable gallonage sold there in that year; sales by company-owned service stations constituted 6·8 per cent of the total, sales under exclusive dealing contracts with independent stations, 6·7 per cent of the total; the remainder were sales to industrial users. Retail service-station sales by Standard's six leading competitors absorbed 42·5 per cent of the total taxable gallonage; the remaining retail sales were divided between more than seventy small companies. It is undisputed that Standard's major competitors employ similar exclusive dealing arrangements. In 1948 only 1·6 per cent of retail outlets were what is known as 'split-pump' stations, that is, sold the gasoline of more than one supplier.

Exclusive supply contracts with Standard had been entered, as of 12 March 1947, by the operators of 5,937 independent stations, or 16 per cent of the retail gasoline outlets in the Western area, which purchased from Standard in 1947 $57,646,233 worth of gasoline and $8,200,089.21 worth of other products. Some outlets are covered by more than one contract so that in all about 8,000 exclusive supply contracts are here in issue. These are of several types, but a feature common to each is the dealer's undertaking to purchase from Standard all his requirements of one or more products. Two types, covering 2,777 outlets, bind the dealer to purchase of Standard all his requirements of gasoline and other petroleum products as well as tires, tubes and batteries. The remaining written agreements, 4,368 in number, bind the dealer to purchase of Standard all his requirements of petroleum products only. It was also found that independent dealers had entered 742 oral contracts by which they agreed to sell only Standard's gasoline. In some instances dealers who contracted to purchase from Standard all their requirements of tires, tubes and batteries had also orally agreed to purchase of Standard their requirements of other automobile accessories. [. . .]

Between 1936 and 1946 Standard's sales of gasoline through independent dealers remained at a practically constant proportion of the area's total sales; its sales of lubricating oil declined slightly during that period from 6·28 per cent to 5 per cent of the total. Its proportionate sales of tires and batteries for 1946 were slightly higher than they were in 1936, though somewhat lower than for some intervening years; they have never, as to either of these products, exceeded 2 per cent of the total sales in the Western area. [. . .]

The issue before us is whether the requirement of showing that the effect of the agreements 'may be to substantially lessen competition' may be met simply by proof that a substantial portion of commerce is affected or whether it must also be demonstrated that competitive activity has actually diminished or probably will diminish. [. . .]

It is . . . apparent that none of these [earlier cases in section 3 of the Clayton Act] controls the disposition of the present appeal, for Standard's share of the retail market for gasoline, even including sales through company-owned stations, is hardly large enough to conclude as a matter of law that it occupies a dominant position, nor did the trial court so find. The cases do indicate, however, that some sort of showing as to actual or probable economic consequences of the agreements, if only the inferences to be drawn from the fact of dominant power, is important, and to that extent they tend to support appellant's position.

Two of the three cases decided by this Court which have held section 3 inapplicable also lend support to the view that such a showing is necessary. These are, *Federal Trade Commission* v. *Sinclair Oil Co.* . . . and *Pick Mfg Co.* v. *General Motors Corp.* . . . [In] the third . . . the contract involved was one of agency and so is of no present relevance.

But then came *International Salt Co.* v. *United States.* . . . That decision, at least as to contracts tying the sale of a non-patented to a patented product, rejected the necessity of demonstrating economic consequences once it has been established that 'the volume of business affected' is not 'insignificant or unsubstantial' and that the effect of the contracts is to 'foreclose competitors from a substantial market'. . . . Upon that basis we affirmed a summary judgement granting an injunction against the leasing of machines for the utilization of salt products on the condition that the lessee use in them only salt supplied by defendant. . . . It is clear, therefore, that unless a distinction is to be drawn for purposes of the applicability of section 3 between requirements contracts and contracts tying the sale of a nonpatented to a patented product, the showing that Standard's requirements contracts affected a gross business of $58,000,000 comprising 6·7 per cent of the total in the area goes far toward supporting the inference that competition has been or probably will be substantially lessened.

In favor of confining the standard laid down by the International Salt case to tying agreements, important economic differences may be noted. Tying agreements serve hardly any purpose beyond the suppression of competition. The justification most often advanced in their defense – the protection of the good will of the manufacturer of the tying device – fails in the usual situation because specification of the type and quality of the product to be used in connexion with the tying device is protection enough. If the manufacturer's brand of the tied product is in fact superior to that of competitors, the buyer will presumably choose it anyway. The only situation, indeed, in which the protection of good will may necessitate the use of tying clauses is where specifications for a substitute would be so detailed that they could not practicably be supplied. In the usual case only the prospect of reducing competition would persuade a seller to adopt such a contract and only his control of the supply of the tying device, whether conferred by patent monopoly or otherwise obtained, could induce a buyer to enter one. . . . The existence of market control of the tying device, therefore, affords a strong foundation for the presumption that it has been or probably will be used to limit competition in the tied product also.

Requirements contracts, on the other hand, may well be of economic advantage to buyers as well as to sellers, and thus indirectly of advantage to the consuming public. In the case of the buyer, they may assure supply, afford protection against rises in price, enable long-term planning on the basis of known costs, and obviate the expense and risk of storage in the quantity necessary for a commodity having a fluctuating demand. From the seller's point of view, requirements contracts may make possible the substantial reduction of selling expenses, give protection against price fluctuations, and – of particular advantage to a newcomer to the field to whom it is important to know what capital expenditures are justified – offer the possibility of a predictable market. . . . They may be useful, moreover, to a seller trying to establish a foothold against the counterattacks of entrenched competitors. . . . Since these advantages of requirements contracts may often be sufficient to account for their use, the coverage by such contracts of a substantial amount of business affords a weaker basis for the inference that competition may be lessened than would similar coverage by tying clauses, especially where use of the latter is combined with market control of the tying device. A patent, moreover, although in fact there may be many competing substitutes for the patented article, is at least prima facie evidence of such control. And so we could not dispose of this case merely by citing *International Salt Co*. v. *United States*.

We may assume, as did the court below, that no improvement of Standard's competitive position has coincided with the period during which the requirements-contract system of distribution has been in effect. We may assume further that the duration of the contracts is not excessive and that Standard does not by itself dominate the market. But Standard was a major competitor when the present system was adopted, and it is possible that its position would have deteriorated but for the adoption of that system. When it is remembered that all other major suppliers have also been using requirements contracts, and when it is noted that the relative share of the business which fell to each has remained about the same during the period of their use, it would not be far fetched to infer that their effect has been to enable the established suppliers individually to maintain their own standing and at the same time collectively, even though not collusively, to prevent a late arrival from wresting away more than an insignificant portion of the market. If, indeed, this were a result of the system, it would seem unimportant that a short-run by-product of stability may have been greater efficiency and lower costs, for it is the theory of the anti-trust laws that the long-run advantage of the community depends upon the removal of restraints upon competition.

Moreover, to demand that bare inference be supported by evidence as to what would have happened but for the adoption of the practice that was in fact adopted or to require firm prediction of an increase in competition as a probable result of ordering the abandonment of the practice, would be a standard of proof if not virtually impossible to meet, at least most ill-suited for ascertainment by courts. [. . .]

Thus, even though the qualifying clause of section 3 is appended without distinction of terms equally to the prohibition of tying clauses and of requirements contracts, pertinent considerations support, certainly as a matter of economic reasoning, varying standards as to each for the proof necessary to fulfill the conditions of that clause. If this distinction were accepted, various tests of the economic usefulness or restrictive effect of requirements contracts would become relevant. Among them would be evidence that competition has flourished despite use of the contracts, and under this test much of the evidence tendered by appellant in this case would be important. . . . Likewise bearing on whether or not the contracts were being used to suppress competition, would be the conformity of the length of their term to the reasonable requirements of the field of commerce in which they were used. . . . Still another test would be the status of the defendant as a struggling newcomer or an established competitor. Perhaps most important, however, would be the defendant's degree of market control, for the greater the dominance of his position, the stronger the inference that an important factor in attaining and maintaining that position had been the use of requirements contracts to stifle competition rather than to serve legitimate economic needs.

Yet serious difficulties would attend the attempt to apply these tests. . . . Though it may be that such an alternative to the present system as buying out independent dealers and making them dependent employees of Standard Stations, Inc., would be a greater detriment to the public interest than perpetuation of the system, that is an issue, like the choice between greater efficiency and freer competition, that has not been submitted to our decision. We are faced, not with a broadly phrased expression of general policy, but merely a broadly phrased qualification of an otherwise narrowly directed statutory provision.

'In this connexion it is significant that the qualifying language [of the statute] was not added until after the House and Senate bills reached conference.'

We conclude, therefore, that the qualifying clause of section 3 is satisfied by proof that competition has been foreclosed in a substantial share of the line of commerce affected. It cannot be gainsaid that observance by a dealer of his requirements contract with Standard does effectively foreclose whatever opportunity there might be for competing suppliers to attract his patronage, and it is clear that the affected proportion of retail sales of petroleum products is substantial. In the view of the widespread adoption of such contracts by Standard's competitors and the availability of alternative ways of obtaining an assured market, evidence that competitive activity has not actually declined is inconclusive. Standard's use of the contracts creates just such a potential clog on competition as it was the purpose of section 3 to remove wherever, were it to become actual, it would impede a substantial amount of competitive activity.

Since the decree below is sustained by our interpretation of section 3 of the Clayton Act, we need not go on to consider whether it might also be sustained by section 1 of the Sherman Act. [. . .]

The judgement below is affirmed.

United States v. American Can Company

Federal Supplement vol. 87, p. 18

Harris, District Judge:

This action was instituted by the Government under the Sherman Act, sections 1 and 2 . . ., and the Clayton Act, section 3 . . ., seeking to enjoin the American Can Company from unlawful practices, allegedly in violation of both acts. The primary question for determination is whether defendant's requirements contracts and closing machine leases are illegal in the particulars specified.

The facts are not in serious dispute save with respect to a conspiracy charge against American Can Company and Continental Can Company, hereafter referred to as American and Continental. [. . .]

Plaintiff attacks defendants' contracts under which it sells its metal and fiber containers; plaintiff also challenges the legality of defendant's closing machine leases under which it lets its can closing machines which complete the metal and fiber containers. Plaintiff contends that the can contracts and closing machine leases constitute unreasonable restraints of trade and commerce and, in addition, that such contracts and leases, together with certain specified devices, means, methods which will be discussed below, constitute a violation of section 3 of the Clayton Act. Plaintiff further contends that defendant's contracts and closing machine leases constitute a mode of operation which gives rise to an attempt to monopolize trade and commerce in canning, in violation of sections 1 and 2 of the Sherman Act. [. . .]

The ultimate remedy sought by the Government is sweeping: it asks for elimination of requirements contracts and complete divestiture of the closing machine phase of the business. In connexion with the requirements contracts, American contends that, if the relief sought is granted, the user-customer will be relegated to an uncertain mode of supply and demand not based upon contracts giving rise to enforceable obligations. [. . .]

Incorporated in New Jersey in 1902, defendant has long been

foremost in the can manufacturing business of the United States. At its inception . . . defendant acquired sufficient plants to enable it to make 90 per cent of the cans used in the country.

At the time of the [company's] trial in 1913, American then consumed approximately one-third of the total tin plate used for domestic consumption in the can manufacturing business in the United States. It will be seen . . . that defendant has more than maintained its position in the industry. . . . On the basis of tin plate consumed, American's percentage of the whole was somewhat in excess of 40 per cent [in 1946].

Viewed from the standpoint of competitive sales as against total output of cans, American's percentage is even more impressive. Some canning concerns manufacture their own cans and are thus not in the buying market. Among the can manufacturers who sell on a competitive basis, the total received for cans in 1946 was $433,621,729. American's percentage of the total was 46·4 per cent.

What does the evidence disclose as to the business conducted by American's competitors? It shows that of not more than 125 manufacturers of cans, up to 25 make tin containers for their own use; of the competitive can companies only five manufacture what are known as packers' and general line cans. [. . .]

By graphical representation and statistical supporting data, the trial record is convincing, clear, and complete, that the defendant domination of the industry has grown over the intervening years; that Continental and American manufacture about 80 per cent of all cans made for sale; that there are six companies in the United States, making both packers' and general line cans, and they manufacture 93·6 per cent of all cans made for sale.

Viewed from the standpoint of growth American's portion continues to be impressive. [. . .]

From the above recital of facts, it is clear that from a national standpoint, defendant is the leader in the manufacture of cans, although it has competition in its business and is not in a position of complete monopoly. From a regional standpoint, the story of control is different. Thus, in such an area as Utah, defendant has the only plant which serves the needs of the packers in that state. A similar monopoly exists in Hawaii, while in Alaska defendant has 80 per cent of the can business. As might be expected American

is the dominant influence in specific sections of the United States.

Viewed from another standpoint – type of container manufactured – defendant far outdistances its competitors in several lines. For example in the sale of beer cans, coffee cans . . . American is the major manufacturer. . . .

The foregoing should suffice to indicate the dominant position of American in the industry.

With respect to closing machines

Since the canning industry progressed from the hole and cap cans, which were used at the turn of the century, to the sanitary or packers' cans which are closed by machines, American has moved into leadership in the manufacture and leasing of closing machines. Today it makes and leases to its customers substantially all of their closing machines. The leasing practice by American is followed by its competitors, with Continental also making its own closing machines for this purpose. The number of independent concerns engaged in the manufacture of closing machines is limited to two – Max Ams Company and the Angelus.

In terms of the closing machines leased to canners, American controls 54 per cent of all such machines, . . . Continental far outstancing other canning concerns with approximately 34 per cent of the total machines on lease. The independent can-closing machine makers are thus limited in their sales to a market of 12 per cent of the closing machine business.

It is the fixed and uniform policy of American to lease rather than sell its closing machines. The only exceptions to this policy arise in the few instances in which American sells machines abroad or sells a few single spindle semi-automatic machines in the Ozarks. Other canmaking concerns follow American's policy. Therefore, the two independent can-closing machine makers, Angelus and Max Ams, have a market limited to the small canmakers, for the ordinary canner will not purchase a can-closing machine as long as he can lease it from his can supplier. An important factor which induces canners to lease their machines has been the low rentals charged for such machines. The defendant admits that low rentals provide an effective 'sale tool'.

The present case is not directed toward American in its capacity

as manufacturer of closing machines. However, it should be noted that the practices of defendant in leasing at below cost figures have tended to restrict the market for closing machine manufacturers and have limited the number of concerns engaged in this business. The record disclosed that others would engage in the manufacture of closing machines if there were a free market in which sellers might compete on an equal basis with the canmakers who now lease their machines. [. . .]

With respect to the requirements contracts

The Government contends that defendant's contracts are the major tool by which it is able to exclude or limit competition in the canning business and, hence, is able to maintain its dominant position. American now has a standard form of contract which the plaintiff chooses to call 'total requirements contract'. [. . .]

Throughout its business life American has entered into requirements contracts of varied duration. These have ranged from three to twenty years. Recently, defendant prepared a standardized contract of uniform length for five years. For various reasons defendant believes that a contract of such duration best serves the interests of both canner and canmaker.

American offers an attractive discount on quantity purchases. The scale serves as an inducement for canners to purchase all of their needs from a single manufacturer. [. . .] In the 1946 contract requirements, contract customers enjoy a price differential in discounts which are not granted to open order customers. [. . .]

The defendant's degree of market control

The statistical data in this case is voluminous. So that we may appreciate the impact of 'bigness' as it relates to the canning industry, we must advert to the earlier [1916] remarks of Judge Rose in *United States* v. *American Can Company*. . . . The jurist said that American, although conceived in sin was leading a rather unblemished life and that the earlier transgression should be forgiven and forgotten as a result of its benign attitude. . . . [And] a decree of dissolution was not ordered. [. . .]

The defendants only listing makes clear an attempt was made both to restrain and monopolize the interstate trade in tin cans.

The closing machine leases executed by customers with the defendant are violative of section 3 of the Clayton Act

In the light of *Standard Oil Company* v. *United States* . . ., this phase of the case is reduced to comparative simplicity. In reaching the conclusion that the leasing practices must be proscribed, we must trace briefly the practices of American since the 'tying provision' was admittedly removed from the lease contracts covering closing machines.

In May 1917, in the course of an investigation of American by the Federal Trade Commission, the defendant agreed to eliminate from its forms of contract and lease . . . [objectionable clauses including] the offending 'tying clause.' [. . .]

The Government contends that the provision, although eliminated from the lease forms, has been kept alive and in effect as a result of the practices engaged in by American of a 'subtle and refined' character. The practices, in substance, are as follows.

Defendant leases closing machines only to customers who purchase their cans from it, and closing machine leases run for terms concurrent with the can contracts. Sales policies . . . bear out the Government's contentions that the 'tying provision' for all practical purposes has remained in the contract negotiations. The evidence introduced by the Government in this connexion abundantly supports [. . .]

That the closing machines represent a most valuable sales tool becomes increasingly manifest when it is considered that defendant has in excess of 9,000 machines on lease of an approximate value of 12 million dollars, many of which have been rented at nominal or low rental values in order to foreclose competition. The evidence herein discloses that American owns and controls more closing machines than the rest of the industry together, and demonstrates that defendant effectively ties the leasing of such machines to the sales of its cans. Defendant owns approximately 54 per cent of all closing machines available for lease to the industry.

It may be noted that the closing machines manufactured by American, with slight adjustment, may be used to close the cans of other can manufacturers; that there are no basic patent rights involved as was the case in the International Salt controversy. [. . .]

It is manifest to this Court from the record herein that abundant proof has been supplied by the Government, and the Court accordingly finds that the leasing practices of can closing machines violate the said Act for they affect injuriously a sizable part of inter-state commerce, that is, an appreciable segment of inter-state commerce.

The devices, means and methods used by defendant in accomplishing the monopoly

Much of the trial, which consumed approximately 117 days and embraced more than 7,000 pages of testimony, concerned the Government's charge that for years American has by various devices, means and methods, persuaded and induced canners to enter into the requirements contracts. Defendant describes this conduct in many instances as 'commercial massage'; the Government counsel refers to the same as 'commercial bribery' and other inelegant terms of comparable import.

Suffice it to say, that no useful purpose could be served by recounting herein the details of all the transactions spread over a period of years from 1930. They represent a saga of American business – so-called 'big business'. Taken alone, or disassociated from the general configuration or picture, many of the transactions would appear to be without probative value. However, as a composite they set a pattern of operations evidencing the extremes defendant saw fit to go in perpetuating the contractual relationship between defendant and the customer-user. The devices took many forms: defendant provided discounts in ancillary contracts; defendant paid large sums of money to obtain business of its customers; defendant furnished equipment, in addition to closing machines, at nominal rentals; defendant paid large claims when it appeared propitious and good policy; defendant purchased can-making equipment from its customers for inflated values in order to obtain can business.

The incidents, when examined realistically and not as mere abstractions, are deeper than the typical run-of-the-mill, day-to-day business transactions. They represent a studied, methodical and effective method of retaining and acquiring by refined, gentlemanly and suave means, plus an occasional 'commercial massage', the dominant position which American has had and maintained for at least a generation on and over the canning industry. A detailed analysis of this phase of the Government's case convinces that there is little room left in a competitive sense, for the independent small business man. As a competitive influence, he has slowly and sadly been relegated into the limbo of American enterprise.

The evidence establishes violations of sections 1 and 2 of the Sherman Act: the proof in this case compels the conclusion that the five year requirements contracts and closing machine leases unreasonably restrain trade in violation of the Sherman Act. The evidence discloses that competitors have been foreclosed from a substantial market by the contracts and leases. [. . .]

As demonstrative of the control and domination exercised by American in and over the industry we have referred to statistical information which stands uncontradicted.

With the premise established that American is in a dominant role and a position of pre-eminent power in the industry, we may then examine the record to determine whether: (a) competition has been foreclosed; (b) from any substantial market. [. . .]

Apart from the inevitable conclusion reached that the requirements contracts and closing machine leases, backgrounded by the configuration of the devices and practices, offend against the Sherman Act, sections 1 and 2 thereof, there is the problem of the user-consumer which must be approached not as a legal abstraction, but realistically. He should not be left without a source of supply. The canners are subject in many instances to the whims of nature over which they have no control. They are, therefore, required to have available a supply of tin containers, fluid in amount, and appropriate from the technological and marketing viewpoints.

In finding the five year requirements contract illegal, we are not thereby compelled to declare void any and all requirements contracts. We cannot ignore the testimony of countless witnesses who indicated the vital necessity of some sort of supply contract. [. . .]

Mindful that requirements contracts are not *per se* unlawful, and that one of the elements which should be considered is the length thereof, it is only fair to conclude after a careful review of the evidence, that a contract for a period of one year would permit competitive influences to operate at the expiration of said period of time, and the vice which is now present in the five year requirements contracts, would be removed. Under a contract limited to one year, the user-consumer would be guaranteed an assured supply and protected by a definite obligation on the part of American to meet the totality of needs of the canner, while he, in turn, would have a fixed obligation to purchase his seasonal needs from American.

The agreement to fix prices between American and Continental
[. . .]

It becomes unnecessary, under the issues as framed in this case, to make any finding with respect to a so-called conspiracy or to otherwise allude thereto. The conspiracy, or its absence, cannot serve as a premise in any logical reasoning leading to a conclusion with respect to the practices that are at issue. However, we do find that American and Continental, through their officers, agents, and servants, did directly agree to fix prices. This is manifest from the evidence, as well as the pattern of the price lists which appeared in the exhibits.

The remedies sought by the Government
[. . .]

The Court's conclusion being that there has been a violation of the Sherman Act as well as the Clayton Act, the final question is one of determining the equitable relief to be had. Counsel for both sides are entitled to be heard with respect to the same, and the ultimate order to be had herein. It may be that additional testimony . . . will be helpful in formulating the decree of the Court.

United States v. United States Steel Corporation
Supreme Court of the U.S.A., vol. 251, no. 417 (1919)

Mr Justice McKenna delivered the opinion of the Court:

Suit against the Steel Corporation and certain other companies which it directs and controls by reason of the ownership of their stock, it and they being charged as violators of the Sherman Anti-Trust Act.

It is prayed that it and they be dissolved because engaged in illegal restraint of trade and the exercise of monopoly.

Special charges of illegality and monopoly are made and special redresses and remedies are prayed, among others, that there be a prohibition of stock ownership and exercise of rights under such ownership, and that there shall be such orders and distribution of the stock and other properties as shall be in accordance with equity and good conscience. [. . .]

The Steel Corporation is a holding company only; the other companies are the operating ones, manufacturers in the iron and steel industry, twelve in number. There are, besides, other corporations and individuals more or less connected in the activities of the other defendants, that are alleged to be instruments or accomplices in their activities and offendings, and that these activities and offendings (speaking in general terms) extend from 1901 to 1911, when the bill was filed. [. . .]

The case was heard in the District Court by four judges. They agreed that the bill should be dismissed; they disagreed as to the reasons for it. . . . One opinion (written by Judge Buffington . . .) expressed the view that the Steel Corporation was not formed with the intention or purpose to monopolize or restrain trade, and did not have the motive or effect 'to prejudice the public interest by unduly restricting competition or unduly obstructing the course of trade'. The corporation, in the view of the opinion, was an evolution, a natural consummation of the tendencies of the industry on account of changing conditions. . . . [And] the concentration of powers (we are still representing the opinion) was only such as was deemed necessary, and immediately manifested itself in improved methods and products and in an increase of domestic and foreign trade. [. . .]

Not monopoly, therefore, was the purpose of the organization of the corporation, but concentration of efforts, with resultant economies and benefits.

All considerations deemed pertinent were expressed and their influence was attempted to be assigned and, while conceding that the Steel Corporation after its formation in times of financial disturbance, entered into informal agreements or understandings with its competitors to maintain prices, they terminated with their occasions, and, as they had ceased to exist, the court was not justified in dissolving the corporation.

The other opinion, by Judge Woolley and concurred in by

Judge Hunt . . ., was in some particulars, in antithesis to Judge Buffington's. The view was expressed that neither the Steel Corporation nor the preceding combinations, which were in a sense its antetypes, had the justification of industrial conditions, nor were they or it impelled by the necessity for integration, or compelled to unite in comprehensive enterprise because such had become a condition of success under the new order of things. On the contrary [it is demonstrable] that the organizers of the corporation and the preceding companies had illegal purpose from the very beginning, and the corporation became 'a combination of combinations by which, directly or indirectly, approximately 180 independent concerns were brought under one business control', which, measured by the amount of production, extended to 80 per cent or 90 per cent of the entire output of the country, and that its purpose was to secure great profits which were thought possible in the light of the history of its constituent combinations, and to accomplish permanently what those combinations had demonstrated could be accomplished temporarily, and thereby [did] monopolize and restrain trade.

The organizers, however (we are still representing the opinion), underestimated the opposing conditions and at the very beginning the corporation instead of relying upon its own power sought and obtained the assistance and the co-operation of its competitors (the independent companies). In other words, the view was expressed that the testimony did 'not show that the corporation in and of itself ever possessed or exerted sufficient power when acting alone to control prices of the products of the industry'. Its power was efficient only when in co-operation with its competitors, and hence it concerted with them in the expedients of pools, associations, trade meetings, and finally in a system of dinners, inaugurated in 1907 by the president of the Company, E. H. Gary, and called 'the Gary Dinners'. The dinners were congregations of producers and 'were nothing but trade meetings', successors of the other means of associated action and control through such action. They were instituted first in 'stress of panic', but their potency being demonstrated they were afterwards called to control prices 'in periods of industrial calm'. 'They were pools without penalties' and more efficient in stabilizing prices. But it was the further declaration that 'when joint action was either refused or withdrawn the corporation's prices were controlled by competition'.

The corporation, it was said, did not at any time abuse the power or ascendancy it possessed. It resorted to none of the brutalities or tyrannies that the cases illustrate of other combinations. . . . [Instead] it combined its power with that of its competitors. It did not have power in and of itself, and the control it exerted was only in and by association with its competitors. Its offense, therefore, such as it was, was not different from theirs and was distinguished from 'theirs only in the leadership it assumed in promulgating and perfecting the policy'. This leadership it gave up and had ceased to offend against the law before this suit was brought. It was hence concluded that it should be distinguished from its organizers and that their intent and unsuccessful attempt should not be attributed to it, that it 'in and of itself is not now and has never been a monopoly or a combination in restraint of trade', and a decree of dissolution should not be entered against it.

This summary of the opinions . . . [necessarily paraphrased] indicate that the evidence admits of different deductions as to the genesis of the corporation and the purpose of its organizers, but only of a single deduction as to the power it attained and could exercise. Both opinions were clear and confident that the power of the corporation never did and does not now reach to monopoly, and their review of the evidence, and our independent examination of it, enables us to elect between their respective estimates of it, and we concur in the main with that of Judges Woolley and Hunt. . . . In other words, our consideration should be of, not what the corporation had power to do or did, but what it has now power to do and is doing, and what judgement shall be now pronounced – whether its dissolution, as the Government prays, or the dismissal of the suit, as the corporation insists.

The alternatives are perplexing, involve conflicting considerations, which, regarded in isolation, have diverse tendencies. . . . Monopoly . . . was not achieved, and competitors had to be persuaded by pools, associations, trade meetings, and through the social form of dinners, all of them, it may be, violations of the law, but transient in their purpose and effect. They were scattered through the years from 1901 (the year of the formation of the corporation) until 1911, but, after instances of success and failure, were abandoned nine months before this suit was brought. There is no evidence that the abandonment was in prophecy of or dread of suit; and the illegal practices have not been resumed, nor is there any evidence of an intention to resume them. [. . .]

What, then, can now be urged against the corporation? Can comparisons in other regards be made with its competitors and by such comparisons guilty or innocent existence be assigned it? It is greater in size and productive power than any of its competitors, equal or nearly equal to them all, but its power over prices was not and is not commensurate with its power to produce.

It is true there is some testimony tending to show that the corporation had such power, but there was also testimony and a course of action tending strongly to the contrary. The conflict was by the judges of the District Court unanimously resolved against the existence of that power, and in doing so they gave effect to the greater weight of the evidence. It is certain that no such power was exerted. On the contrary, the only attempt at a fixation of prices was, as already said, through an appeal to and confederation with competitors, and the record shows besides that when competition occurred it was not in pretense, and the corporation, declined in productive powers – the competitors growing either against or in consequence of the competition. [. . .] The power of monopoly in the corporation under either illustration is an untenable accusation. . . . Against it competitors, dealers, and customers of the corporation testify in multitude that no adventitious interference was employed to fix or maintain prices, and that they were constant or varied according to natural conditions. Can this testimony be minimized or dismissed by inferring that, as intimated, it is an evidence of power, not of weakness, and power exerted, not only to suppress competition, but to compel testimony, is the necessary inference, shading into perjury, to deny its exertion? The situation is indeed singular, and we may wonder at it, wonder that the despotism of the corporation, so baneful to the world in the representation of the Government, did not produce protesting victims.

But there are other paradoxes. In one, competitors (the independents) are presented as oppressed by the superior power of the corporation; in the other, they are represented as ascending to opulence by imitating that power's prices, which they could not do, if at disadvantage from the other conditions of competition, and yet confederated action is not asserted. If it were, this suit would take on another cast. The competitors would cease to be the victims of the corporation, and would become its accomplices. . . . The suggestion that lurks in the Government's contention that the acceptance of the corporation's prices is the submission of impotence to irresistible power is, in view of the testimony of the competitors, untenable. They, as we have seen, deny restraint in any measure or illegal influence of any kind. The Government, therefore, is reduced to the assertion that the size of the corporation, the power it may have, not the exertion of the power, is an abhorrence to the law; or, as the Government says, 'the combination embodied in the corporation unduly restrains competition by its necessary effects . . ., and therefore is unlawful regardless of purpose'. . . . To assent to that, to what extremes should we be led? [. . .]

[. . .] The corporation is undoubtedly of impressive size, and it takes an effort of resolution not to be affected by it or to exaggerate its influence. But we must adhere to the law, and the law does not make mere size an offense, or the existence of unexerted power an offense. It, we repeat, requires overt acts, and trusts to its prohibition of them and its power to repress or punish them. It does not compel competition, nor require all that is possible. . . . But these are countervailing considerations. We have seen whatever there was of wrong intent could not be executed; whatever there was of evil effect was discontinued before this suit was brought, and this, we think determines the decree. We say this in full realization of the requirements of the law. It is clear in its denunciation of monopolies, and equally clear in its direction that the courts of the nation shall prevent and restrain them (its language is 'to prevent and restrain violations of' the act); but the command is necessarily submissive to the conditions which may exist and the usual powers of a court of equity to adapt its remedies to those conditions. In other words, it is not expected to enforce abstractions, and do injury thereby, it may be to the purpose of the law. . . . It is certainly a matter for consideration that there was no legal attack on the corporation until 1911, ten years after its formation and the commencement of its career. We do not, however, speak of the delay simply as to its time, or say that there is estoppel in it because of its time, but on account of what was done during that time – the many millions of dollars spent, the development made, and the enterprises undertaken; the investments by the public that have been invited and are not to be ignored. And what of the foreign trade that has been developed and exists? [. . .]

The Government, however, tentatively presents a proposition which has some tangibility. It submits that certain of the subsidiary companies are so mechanically equipped and so officially directed as to be released and remitted to independent action and individual interests and the competition to which such interests prompt, without any disturbance to business. . . . [The companies are enumerated.]

They are fully integrated, it is said – possess their own supplies, facilities of transportation, and distribution. They are subject to the Steel Corporation, is in effect the declaration, in nothing but its control of their prices. We may say parenthetically that they are defendants in the suit and charged as offenders, and we have the strange circumstance of violators of the law being urged to be used as expedients of the law.

But let us see what guide to a procedure of dissolution of the corporation and the dispersion as well of its subsidiary companies, for they are asserted to be illegal combinations, is prayed. And the fact must not be overlooked or underestimated. The prayer of the Government calls for, not only a disruption of present conditions, but the restoration of the conditions of twenty years ago.

In conclusion, we are unable to see that the public interest will be served by yielding to the contention of the Government respecting the dissolution of the company or the separation from it of some of its subsidiaries; and we do see in a contrary conclusion a risk of injury to the public interest, including a material disturbance of, and, it may be serious detriment to, the foreign trade. And in submission to the policy of the law and its fortifying prohibitions the public interest is of paramount regard.

We think, therefore, that the decree of the District Court should be affirmed.

So ordered.

American Tobacco Company v. United States
Supreme Court of the U.S.A., vol. 328, no. 781 (1945)

Mr Justice Burton delivered the opinion of the Court:

The petitioners are The American Tobacco Company, Liggett and Myers Tobacco Company, R. J. Reynolds Tobacco Company, American Suppliers, Inc., a subsidiary of American, and certain officials of the respective companies who were convicted by a jury, in the District Court of the United States for the Eastern District of Kentucky, of violating sections 1 and 2 of the Sherman Anti-Trust Act [pursuant to information].

Each petitioner was convicted on four counts: (1) conspiracy in restraint of trade, (2) monopolization, (3) attempt to monopolize, and (4) conspiracy to monopolize. Each count related to inter-state and foreign trade and commerce in tobacco. No sentence was imposed under the third count as the Court held that count was merged in the second. Each petitioner was fined $5,000 on each of the other counts, making $15,000 for each petitioner and a total of $255,000. [. . .]

The Circuit Court of Appeals for the Sixth Circuit . . . affirmed each conviction. . . . This opinion is limited to the convictions under section 2 of the Sherman Act.

The issue thus emphasized in the order allowing certiorari and primarily argued by the parties had not been previously decided by this Court. It is raised by the following instructions which were especially applicable to the second count but were related also to the other counts under section 2 of the Sherman Act. [The Court's instructions follow]:

Now, the term 'monopolize' as used in section 2 of the Sherman Act, as well as in the last three counts of the Information, means the joint acquisition or maintenance by the members of the conspiracy formed for that purpose, of the *power to control and dominate inter-state trade and commerce in a commodity to such an extent that they are able, as a group, to exclude actual or potential competitors from the field, accompanied with the intention and purpose to exercise such power.*

The phrase 'attempt to monopolize' means the employment of methods, means and practices which would, if successful, accomplish monopolization, and which, though falling short, nevertheless approach so close as to create a dangerous probability of it, which methods, means and practices so employed by the members of and pursuant to a combination or conspiracy formed for the purpose of such accomplishment.

It is in no respect a violation of the law that a number of individuals or corporations, each acting for himself or itself, may own or control a large part, or even all of a particular commodity, or all the business in a particular commodity.

An essential element of the illegal monopoly or monopolization charged *in this case is the existence of a combination or conspiracy to acquire and maintain the power to exclude competitors to a substantial extent.*

Thus you will see that *an indispensable ingredient of each of the offenses charged in the Information is a combination or conspiracy.* [Court's italics]

Simply stated the issue is: Do the facts called for in the trial court's definition of monopolization amount to a violation of section 2 of the Sherman Act?

[. . .] To support the verdicts it was not necessary to show power and intent to exclude *all* competitors, or to show a conspiracy to exclude *all* competitors. The requirements stated to the jury and contained in the statute were only that the offenders shall 'monopolize any part of the trade or commerce among the several States, or with foreign nations'. This particular conspiracy may well have derived special vitality, in the eyes of the jury, from the fact that its existence was established, not through the presentation of a formal written agreement, but through the evidence of widespread and effective conduct on the part of petitioners in relation to their existing or potential competitors.

[. . .] First of all, the monopoly found by the jury to exist in the present cases appears to have been completely separable from the old American Tobacco Trust which was dissolved in 1911. The conspiracy to monopolize and the monopolization charged here do not depend upon proof relating to the old tobacco trust but upon a dominance and control by petitioners in recent years over purchases of the raw material and over the sale of the finished product in the form of cigarettes. The fact, however, that the purchases of leaf tobacco and the sales of so many products of the tobacco industry have remained largely within the same general group of business organizations for over a generation, inevitably has contributed to the ease with which control over competition within the industry and the mobilization of power to resist new competition can be exercised. The verdicts indicate that practices of an informal and flexible nature were adopted and that the results were so uniformly beneficial to the petitioners in protecting their common interests as against those of competitors that, entirely from circumstantial evidence, the jury found that a combination or conspiracy existed among the petitioners from 1937 to 1940, with power and intent to exclude competitors to such a substantial extent as to violate the Sherman Act as interpreted by the trial court.

The position of the petitioners in the cigarette industry from 1931 to 1939 is clear. [Tables are supplied in the records of the Court.]

Although American, Liggett and Reynolds gradually dropped in their percentage of the national domestic cigarette production from 90·7 per cent in 1931 to 73·3 per cent, 71 per cent and 68 per cent, respectively, in 1937, 1938 and 1939, they have accounted at all times for more than 68 per cent, and usually for more than 75 per cent, of the national production. The balance of the cigarette production has come from six other companies. No one of these six ever has produced more than 10·6 per cent once reached by Brown and Williamson in 1939. . . . The second table shows that while the percentage of cigarettes produced by American, Liggett and Reynolds in the United States dropped gradually from 90·7 per cent to 68 per cent, their combined volume of production actually increased. [. . .]

The further dominance of American, Liggett and Reynolds within their special field of burley blend cigarettes, as compared with the so-called '10-cent cigarettes', is also apparent. In 1939, the 10-cent cigarettes constituted about $14\frac{1}{2}$ per cent of the total domestic cigarette production. Accordingly, the 68 per cent of the total cigarette production enjoyed by American, Liggett and Reynolds amounted to 80 per cent of that production within their special field of cigarettes. . . . In addition . . . they also produced over 63 per cent of the smoking tobacco and over 44 per cent of the chewing tobacco.

The foregoing demonstrates the basis of the claim of American,

Liggett and Reynolds to the title of the 'Big Three'. . . . Without adverse criticism of it, comparative size on this great scale inevitably increased the power of these three to dominate all phases of their industry. . . . An intent to use this power to maintain a monopoly was found by the jury in these cases.

The record further shows that . . . in . . . 1937, 1938 and 1939, American, Liggett and Reynolds expended a total of over $40,000,000 a year for advertising. Such advertising is not here criticized as a business expense. Such advertising may benefit indirectly the entire industry, including the competitors of the advertisers. Such tremendous advertising, however, is also a widely published warning that these companies possess and know how to use a powerful offensive and defensive weapon against new competition. New competition dare not enter such a field, unless it be well supported by comparable national advertising.[2] Large inventories of leaf tobacco, and large sums required for payment of federal taxes in advance of actual sales, further emphasize the effectiveness of a well-financed monopoly in this field against potential competitors if there merely exists an intent to exclude such competitors. Prevention of all potential competition is the natural program for maintaining a monopoly here, rather than any program of actual exclusion. 'Prevention' is cheaper and more effective than any amount of 'cure'.

The verdicts show that the jury found that petitioners conspired to fix prices and to exclude undesired competition against them in the purchase of the domestic types of flue-cured tobacco and of burley tobacco. These are raw materials essential to the production of cigarettes of the grade sold by the petitioners and also, to some extent, of the 10-cent grade of cigarettes which constitutes the only substantial competition to American, Liggett and Reynolds in the cigarette field of the domestic tobacco industry. [. . .]

The Government introduced evidence showing . . . that petitioners refused to purchase tobacco on these [auction] markets unless the other petitioners were also represented thereon. There were attempts made by others to open new tobacco markets but none of the petitioners would participate in them unless the other petitioners were present. Consequently, such markets were failures due to the absence of buyers. . . . In this way the new

2. See also *Household Detergents*, Reading 14 [ed.].

tobacco markets and their locations were determined by the unanimous consent of the petitioners and, in arriving at their determination, the petitioners consulted with each other as to whether or not a community deserved a market.

The Government presented evidence to support its claim that, before the markets opened, the petitioners placed limitations and restrictions on the prices which their buyers were permitted to pay for tobacco. None of the buyers exceeded these price ceilings. Grades of tobacco were formulated in such a way as to result in the absence of competition between the petitioners. There was manipulation of the price of lower grade tobaccos in order to restrict competition from manufacturers of the lower priced cigarettes. Methods used included the practice of petitioners of calling their respective buyers in, prior to the opening of the annual markets, and giving them instructions as to the prices to be paid for leaf tobacco in each of the markets. These instructions were in terms of top prices or price ranges. The price ceilings thus established for the buyers were the same for each of them. [. . .]

Where one or two of the petitioners secured their percentage of the crop of a certain market or were not interested in the purchase of certain offerings of tobacco, their buyers, nevertheless, would enter the bidding in order to force the other petitioners to bid up to the maximum price. The petitioners were not so much concerned with the prices they paid for the leaf tobacco as that each should pay the same price for the same grade and that none would secure any advantage in purchasing tobacco. . . . They were all to be on the same basis. [. . .]

At a time when the manufacturers of lower priced cigarettes were beginning to manufacture them in quantity, the petitioners commenced to make large purchases of the cheaper tobacco leaves used for the manufacture of such lower-priced cigarettes. No explanation was offered as to how or where this tobacco was used by petitioners. The composition of their respective brands of cigarettes calling for the use of more expensive tobaccos remained unchanged during this period of controversy and up to the end of the trial. The Government claimed that such purchases of cheaper tobacco evidenced a combination and a purpose among the petitioners to deprive the manufacturers of cheaper cigarettes of the tobacco necessary for their manufacture, as well as to raise the price of such tobacco to such a point that cigarettes made therefrom could not be sold at a sufficiently low price to compete with petitioners' more highly advertised brands.

The verdicts also show that the jury found that the petitioners conspired to fix prices and to exclude undesired competition in the distribution and sale of their principal products. The petitioners sold and distributed their products to jobbers and to selected dealers who bought at list prices, less discounts. ... The list prices charged and the discounts allowed by petitioners have been practically identical since 1923 and absolutely identical since 1928. Since the latter date, only seven changes have been made by the three companies and those have been identical in amount. The increases were first announced by Reynolds. American and Liggett thereupon increased their list prices in identical amounts.

The following record or price changes is circumstantial evidence of the existence of a conspiracy and of a power and intent to exclude competition from cheaper grade cigarettes. [The year 1931] ... was one of the worst years of financial and economic depression in the history of the country. On 23 June 1931, Reynolds, without previous notification or warning to the trade or public, raised the list price of Camel cigarettes, constituting its leading cigarette brand, from $6.40 to $6.85 a thousand. The same day, American increased the list price of Lucky Strike cigarettes, its leading brand, to the identical price of $6.85 a thousand. No economic justification for this raise was demonstrated. The president of Reynolds stated that it was 'to express our own courage for the future and our own confidence in our industry'. The president of American gave as his reason for the increase, 'the opportunity of making some money'. ... The officials of Liggett claimed that they thought the increase was a mistake ... but ... that unless they also raised their list price for Chesterfields, the other companies would have greater resources to spend in advertising and thus would put Chesterfield cigarettes at a competitive disadvantage. This general price increase soon resulted in higher retail prices and a loss in volume of sales. Yet in 1932, in the midst of the national depression with the sales of the petitioners' cigarettes falling off greatly in number, the petitioners still were making tremendous profits as a result of the price increase. Their net profits in that year amounted to more than $100,000,000. This was one of the three biggest years in their history.

However after the above described increase in list prices of the petitioners in 1931, the 10-cent brands made serious inroads upon the sales of the petitioners. These cheaper brands of cigarettes were sold at a list price of $4.75 a thousand and from 1931 to 1932 the sales of these cigarettes multiplied 30 times, rising from 0·28 per cent of the total cigarette sales of the country in June 1931, to 22·78 per cent in November 1932. In response to this threat of competition . . . the petitioners . . . cut the list price of their three leading brands . . . to $5.50 a thousand. The evidence tends to show that this cut was directed at the competition of the 10-cent cigarettes. . . . When the sale of the 10-cent brands had dropped from 22·78 per cent of the total cigarette sales in November 1932, to 6·43 per cent in May 1933, the petitioners, in January 1934, raised the list price of their leading brands from $5.50 back up to $6.10 a thousand. During the period that the list price of $5.50 a thousand was in effect, Camels and Lucky Strikes were being sold at a loss by Reynolds and American. Liggett at the same time was forced to curtail all of its normal business activities and to cut its advertising to the bone in order to sell at this price. [Subsequently increases brought the price to $6.25 in 1937 and $6.53 in 1940.]

It was on the basis of such evidence that the Circuit Court of Appeals found the verdicts of the jury were sustained by sufficient evidence on each count. The question squarely presented here by the order of this Court in allowing the writs of certiorari is whether actual exclusion of competitors is necessary to the crime of monopolization in these cases under section 2 of the Sherman Act. We agree with the lower courts that such actual exclusion of competitors is not necessary to that crime in these cases and that the instructions given to the jury, and hereinbefore quoted, correctly defined the crime. A correct interpretation of the statute and of the authorities makes it the crime of monopolizing, under section 2 of the Sherman Act, for parties, as in these cases, to combine or conspire to acquire or maintain the power to exclude competitors from any part of the trade or commerce among the several states or with foreign nations, provided they also have such a power that they are able, as a group, to exclude actual or potential competition from the field and provided that they have the *intent and purpose* to exercise that power. . . . [Italics supplied.]

It is not the form of the combination or the particular means used but the result to be achieved that the statute condemns. It is not of importance whether the means used to accomplish the unlawful objectives are in themselves lawful or unlawful. Acts done to give effect to the conspiracy may be in themselves wholly innocent acts. Yet, if they are part of the sum of the acts which are relied upon to effectuate the conspiracy which the statute forbids, they come within its prohibition. No formal agreement is necessary to constitute an unlawful conspiracy. Often crimes are a matter of inference deduced from the acts of the person accused and done in pursuance of a criminal purpose. Where the conspiracy is proved, as here, from the evidence of the action taken in concert by the parties to it, it is all the more convincing proof of an intent to exercise the power of exclusion acquired through that conspiracy. The essential combination or conspiracy in violation of the Sherman Act may be found in a course of dealing or other circumstances as well as in an exchange of words. . . . Where the circumstances are such as to warrant a jury in finding that the conspirators had a unity of purpose or a common design and understanding, or a meeting of minds in an unlawful arrangement, the conclusion that a conspiracy is established is justified. Neither proof of exertion of the power to exclude nor proof of actual exclusion of existing or potential competitors is essential to sustain a charge of monopolization under the Sherman Act. [. . .]

[A reference is made to Judge Learned Hand's decision in *United States* v. *Aluminum Company of America*, *Federal Reporter*, vol. 148, 2nd series, p. 416.]

In the present cases, the petitioners have been found to have conspired to establish a monopoly and also to have the power and intent to establish and maintain the monopoly. To hold that they do not come within the prohibition of the Sherman Act would destroy the force of that Act. Accordingly, the instructions of the trial court under section 2 of the Act are approved and the judgement of the Circuit Court of Appeals is affirmed.

United States v. E. I. duPont de Nemours and Company
Federal supplement, vol. 115, p. 41 (1951).

Leahy, Chief Judge, spoke:

This is a civil suit by the United States of America under section 4 of the Sherman Act, charging defendant with monopolizing, attempting to monopolize and combining and conspiring to monopolize trade and commerce . . . in cellophane caps and bands.

Defendant, E.I. duPont de Nemours and Company, is a Delaware corporation. It is successor to duPont Cellophane Company, Inc. Throughout the period covered by the complaint, it or its predecessors manufactured and sold, in interstate and foreign commerce, regenerated cellulose in the form of film (cellophane) and in the form of bands. Prior to the filing of the complaint in this case, it also manufactured and sold cellulosic caps.

DuPont entered the cellophane business in 1923. It collaborated, under written agreements with La Cellophane (a subsidiary of the Comptoir which is the largest French rayon producer), in establishing the first duPont cellophane company. In 1929 duPont Cellophane Company, Inc., was reincorporated as a wholly owned subsidiary of duPont. In 1936, duPont took over the operation of this business and dissolved duPont Cellophane Company, Inc. . . . [Other European producers were named as co-conspirators but not defendants.]

[The Court presented a discussion at this point on economic and legal views of monopoly and competition, stressing the differences between academic definitions and those contemplated by the Sherman Act.][3]

Certain issues of fact and law must control the decision in this case. When these controlling issues are isolated, it will be apparent there are fatal deficiencies in the Government's proof, and the record fails to establish those facts which are essential to support the charges in the complaint.

The history of duPont's cellophane business is a record of competitive achievement. DuPont was the first American company to manufacture this new wrapping material. To pioneer the cellophane business required foresight, and a willingness to take risks.

3. Reading 5 provides such a discussion in the U.S.A. context.

DuPont had little technical experience in this line of chemistry. The product had not been proven as a packaging material. It had had little acceptance in this country.

DuPont entered the business in the only manner that was practicable. It acquired the commercial process from the French. This process was obtained on the best terms duPont could negotiate. The two groups, American and French, had already been successful partners in rayon. No desire to limit competition was involved, for neither partner to the venture was engaged in business in competition with the other, and there is no indication anyone was interested.

DuPont saw the chance for profit and utility for cellophane if it could be introduced into the mass production packaging markets of the United States. It decided to bring a new competing material into the flexible packaging market, an established field of competitive business activity.

Cellophane was not at first acceptable in the trades to which it was offered. Manufacturing techniques were crude; quality unsatisfactory, and costs made price of cellophane prohibitive for many uses. There were distribution and merchandising problems to be met. Only by effective competition could duPont hope to gain recognition for its product in markets where other materials were entrenched. The business had to be built up by creative research.

DuPont's technological achievements were of high order. Through research it improved manufacturing efficiency, reduced costs, improved quality, developed new types of materials and lowered prices to obtain acceptance for its product, all in the face of competition. Research results were continuously put to use in its plants.

The product obtained from the French did not meet the needs of the American market. DuPont invented a new product, moistureproof cellophane, which proved to be the product upon which the cellophane business has been built. It obtained a product patent under which all its moistureproof cellophane was produced during the period of the monopoly charged in the complaint. It then exploited that patent, well within the purposes and intentions of the patent grant. Its production expanded; it made many types of moistureproof cellophane; it gave increasing service to its customers; it neither curtailed its initiative nor restricted the

275

capital which it was willing to devote to the enterprise. DuPont achieved through business methods an increasing success in its competition with other packaging materials.

As cellophane got recognition in the trade, others entered various phases of the business as converters, users, suppliers of raw materials, manufacturers of equipment, and the like. Cellophane creates competition. Throughout the flexible packaging markets this competition is felt. It stimulates efforts of other producers to manufacture more efficiently. It stimulates research. The consumption of flexible packaging materials including cellophane has grown at a rapid rate. Within these markets the competition is intense. New producers have entered. No one material or one supplier controls – certainly not duPont, which has neither the power to raise prices nor to exclude competitors.

After reviewing the development of this business, plaintiff has been unable to bring a single person who says he was injured or who claims to have been denied an opportunity to participate. Prices have consistently been lowered and reflect competitive pressures. Production has expanded. Benefits from research have been passed on to consumers. DuPont has not conducted its cellophane business in a restrictive way. There are no artificial controls which it can exercise in the markets. [. . .]

The charge here is duPont monopolizes cellophane. The charge involves two questions: 1. Does duPont possess monopoly powers? and 2. If so, has it achieved such powers by 'monopolizing' within the meaning of the Act and under *United States* v. *Aluminum Company of America*? Unless the first is decided against defendant, the second is not reached. First, then, to the question of existence of monopoly power. [. . .]

Cellophane is not a unique flexible packaging material in any functional or economic sense. In terms of uses for which cellophane is sold, and the qualities it brings to each use as a wrapping material, cellophane is interchangeable and *in fact* continually interchanged with many flexible packaging materials. [. . .]

[The voluminous record in this case required a summary treatment of the facts with respect to the technology, the research and the other companies involved in the development of cellophane. This account takes up thirty pages of the court record.]

When duPont commenced sale of cellophane, it was not of a quality which would enable it to compete for flexible packaging business. Cellophane was brittle, not available in the roll form essential for machine packaging operations, non-moistureproof. It was necessary for duPont to engage in research to overcome these deficiencies, and, as they were overcome to continue research looking toward a quality improvement so cellophane would remain competitive with other flexible packaging materials in meeting the requirements of buyers of flexible packaging materials.

DuPont did not engage in cellophane research with the intent of monopolizing the manufacture of cellophane. . . . The object of duPont was to reduce price to a level where cellophane could compete with other flexible packaging materials. Price of cellophane in relation to prices of other flexible packaging materials was such that only luxury items would use it as a wrap. It was necessary to develop volume, lower cost and improve quality and bring the price of cellophane down to a point where it would receive acceptance in the packaging markets. DuPont sought a low profit per unit of sale in effort to achieve lower prices which would develop volume sales and increase profits. [. . .]

The price of cellophane was reduced to expand the market for cellophane. DuPont did not reduce prices for cellophane with intent of monopolizing manufacture or with intent of suppressing competitors. . . . DuPont reduced cellophane prices to enable sales to be made for new uses.

DuPont never lowered cellophane prices below cost, and never dropped cellophane prices temporarily to gain a competitive advantage. . . . As duPont's manufacturing costs declined, 1924 to 1935, duPont reduced prices for cellophane. When costs of raw materials increased subsequent to 1935, it postponed reductions until 1938 and 1939. [. . .]

Cellophane is forced to meet competition of other flexible packaging materials. The competition between the materials is intense and duPont cannot exercise market control or monopoly powers . . . [over other industries].

[For 26 pages an account is given of the penetration of cellophane into various packaging markets – for bread, meat, candy, cereals, etc.]

During the period duPont entered the flexible packaging business, and since its introduction of moistureproof cellophane, sales of cellophane have increased. Total volume of flexible packaging materials used in the United States has also increased. DuPont's relative percentage of the packaging business has grown as a result of its research, price, sales and capacity policies, but duPont cellophane even in uses where it has competed has not attained the bulk of the business, due to competition of other flexible packaging materials. . . . [Some] Competition existed between duPont and Sylvania, and later Olin, for the sale of cellophane. Many customers have shifted back and forth between the producers, or divided their purchases between producers in changing proportions. [. . .]

Moistureproof cellophane was a duPont invention. No other party made any contribution to its development. DuPont got five basic patents upon its inventions of the product moistureproof cellophane and methods for its manufacture. [. . .]

Principal growth in the cellophane industry occurred after duPont's invention of moistureproof cellophane, which by 1940 accounted for over 80 per cent of all cellophane sales. . . . DuPont expanded cellophane capacity to meet reasonably foreseeable demand. In most cases sales achieved were in excess of the amount forecast at the time of plant expansion.

Capacity was not expanded with the purpose of stifling competition, creating excess capacity to overhand the market, or forestalling potential competitors. . . . Most of the increase in duPont's capacity to produce cellophane has resulted from improved efficiency of manufacturing with existing equipment rather than installation of new plant. Better efficiency resulted in increased output per unit. [. . .]

No proof was presented any person failed to manufacture cellophane as the result of any act done by duPont; there is no proof there has been any potential competitor who desired to manufacture cellophane and did not do so; and there is no proof duPont possesses power to exclude potential competitors who may desire to manufacture cellophane.

DuPont employed lawful business methods in attempting to keep apprised of competitive developments and did not attempt to stifle competitors. . . . [Further] no evidence was offered any potential competitor was excluded from manufacture of cellophane as a result of duPont's size or prestige. [. . .]

[Some twenty pages are given over to a discussion of distribution outlets, discount policies and use of patents by duPont.]

Sylvania began manufacture of moistureproof cellophane after issuance to duPont of its basic product patent. . . . DuPont established prices for its cellophane independently of Sylvania. There were no agreements as to what prices should be charged, one company would follow the prices of the other, or published prices would be observed. Proof does not support an inference of agreement between duPont and Sylvania as to prices. [. . .]

When duPont made a price reduction on its cellophane during the period 1930–47, Sylvania would obtain from its customers a copy of the new duPont price list, and thereafter, in order to remain competitive, would issue its own price list back-dated to an effective date the same as on the duPont list. Although effective date of the two lists was the same, the lists were not issued to the trade at the same time. [. . .]

DuPont acted in good faith in development of its cellophane business. It sought to act in ways that would not violate United States law. [. . .]

DuPont did not seek to attain success in the cellophane business with intent of suppressing or excluding competition. . . . In the conduct of its business, duPont took no step contrary to legal advice.

DuPont devoted manpower and expense to development of packaging machinery and did not attempt to assert any control over the use or sale of machinery to which its efforts had contributed, although the same machines handle competing cellophane and other flexible wrapping materials. DuPont encouraged end users to employ such machinery for packaging with unprinted cellophane, rather than protecting sales of duPont's converters. DuPont did not vertically integrate, either forward by engaging in conversion of cellophane, or backward by engaging in manufacture of wood pulp, the principal raw material. These actions are inconsistent with a monopolistic intent, but are consistent with a purpose to stimulate use of cellophane for volume packaging purposes. [. . .]

DuPont has been unable to achieve as much as 20 per cent of production of [all] flexible packaging materials.

The record establishes domestic buyers of cellophane do not lack alternative sources of supply, and duPont does not have power to restrain free competition at the distribution level of the industry. [. . .]

The record establishes duPont does not have power to exclude others who would engage in the manufacture and sale of cellophane.

No evidence was shown anyone desired to manufacture cellophane and was unable because of any act done by duPont.

No proof was shown duPont has economic power to prevent others from manufacturing cellophane.

No proof was shown duPont sought to exclude others from manufacturing cellophane.

No proof was shown duPont has power to subvert the use and to engross cellophane patents, trademarks, trade secrets, or 'know-how'. [. . .]

[After setting out summary conclusions on the facts the trial judge resumed.]

I recognized through trial the principal issue is whether duPont's position gives it market control, and hence monopoly power arbitrarily to raise prices and to exclude competitors. The complaint charges duPont 'has had for many years past virtually absolute control of the markets in the United States for cellophane' and such market control has resulted in monopoly powers that have 'become self-sustaining and self-perpetuating'. . . . Thus master factual questions are presented:

1. Does duPont have power, without regard to competitive forces, to raise price of cellophane either directly or by limiting production, deteriorating quality, or by any other means?

2. Does duPont have power alone to exclude competition in the production and sale of cellophane? [. . .]

Monopoly power can be distinguished from the normal freedom of business only in degree. Nothing except death is an absolute. Plaintiff cannot rest on a showing duPont makes cellophane and has some degree of control over its sales, production and prices.

Many sellers have some freedom over their price, production and general business conduct. Each must make his best guess of his future requirements; he must set price at which he will attempt to sell; and he may raise price if costs or other factors dictate. Such business decisions do not represent degree of control over prices or production which constitutes monopoly power. [. . .]

'Market control' or lack of 'market control' are ultimate facts. They are determined by fact-finding processes, and on the basis of knowledge and analysis of all competitive factors which bear on a seller's power to raise prices, or to exclude competition. Existence of monopoly powers is not made on the basis of assumptions as to competitive markets. If the price, quantity of production and sale, and the quality of a seller's product are determined by pressures exerted on him by buyers and sellers of another's product, the products and the sellers must, for purposes of any realistic analysis, be in the same 'market' and must be in competition with each other. [. . .]

Facts, in large part uncontested, demonstrate duPont cellophane is sold under such intense competitive conditions acquisition of market control or monopoly power is a practical impossibility. [. . .]

Power arbitrarily to raise prices is [a] principal *indicium* of monopoly power and market control. This is the test to be applied in adjudicating monopolization. Under market conditions which have prevailed, du Pont does not possess power to raise cellophane prices without regard for competitive pressures. The market would penalize any attempt to do so with lower sales and smaller profits. [. . .]

DuPont could not have developed volume of cellophane business without lowering its prices. It was only as duPont lowered price and narrowed relative spread between cellophane prices and the prices of these other materials that it was accepted for end uses where wax paper and glassine were established. Only by reduction of price has cellophane been able to achieve an appreciable volume of sales in competition with other packaging materials.

Evidence shows a degree of price sensitivity in the flexible packaging markets. This is reflected both statistically and in terms of concrete experience with specific accounts. Evidence discloses [that] quality improvements affected duPont's ability to sell. In instances where its quality was inferior it lost business.

The Government argues duPont's power to control prices is evidenced by its profits, and duPont was able to achieve pre-determined rates of return. Plaintiff's own proposed findings, however, disclose rates of return varied substantially from year to year. There is no evidence as to rate of return earned by any other manufacturer of flexible packaging materials, such as waxed paper or glassine. Evidence did show duPont's rates of return were some-what higher than Sylvania's, but this resulted from duPont's superior efficiency. Years of profit do not establish monopoly power over prices. [. . .]

After an examination of raw materials, technology and plant capacity to distribution, there is no evidence of power to exclude competition. [. . .]

For years courts have tussled with the task of reconciling the Sherman Act with lawful monopolies by patent grant. Many cases under the Act have drawn the line according to the larger aims of public policy – a vigorously competitive economy. Courts have recognized new processes and patents are perhaps the most desirable form of competition. The holder of a patent is, in accor-dance with the patent laws, permitted to exert monopoly control over what he has created.

Evidence does not disclose combining of competing or inde-pendent process patents or efforts to control unpatented products. We have here a case involving the grant to duPont on its own invention of a broad product patent, the validity of which is conceded by plaintiff, and a patent which evidence discloses was of such scope that no one without a grant of a license under it could have manufactured lawfully the product claimed. No case of this kind has ever been brought before. To declare, as plaintiff seeks, the award of this patent, with the rights implicit in its ownership, is to be ignored in applying the Sherman Act, is to ask the court to declare the Sherman Act repealed statutory provisions under which patents are granted. This I will not do. [. . .]

Defendant contends the offense of monopolization requires, in addition to proof of monopoly power or market control, proof such power or control was achieved in a manner prohibited by the statute. Plaintiff contends mere possession of the power, no matter how acquired, in itself establishes a violation. Once power has been obtained, plaintiff argues, it does not even have to be exercised. Mere possession of power, it is argued, is sufficient to constitute offense of monopolization.

It has been recognized under the Sherman Act 'monopoly in the concrete' is not prohibited under the section. . . . The Act, using the verb 'monopolize', prohibits conduct rather than status. It is directed against activities rather than results. This is not a matter of semantics. It is a matter of facts. That this is so is obvious from fact the statute carried criminal as well as civil sanctions. Thus decisions recognized the manner in which a monopoly position was obtained was a crucial consideration in determining whether or not a defendant has monopolized within the meaning of the Act.

The decisions state a defendant may lawfully obtain a monopoly position if that position is 'thrust upon it'. Thus the right to normal growth and to enjoy the results of technical achievement and successful competition has been preserved. [. . .]

The decisions on the contrary, demonstrate, if the challenged position is acquired, as it has been in this case, by superior technical skill and effective competitive activity, the resulting power from that position does not establish monopolization within the meaning of the statute. [. . .]

I am able, after critical examination of the record, to determine duPont's position is the result of research, business skill and competitive activity. Much of duPont's evidence was designed to show research, price and sales policies of that Company are responsible for its success and these policies were conceived and carried forward in a coordinated fashion with skill, gaining for duPont substantial recognition in the packaging industry.

DuPont was a pioneer. It was the first American company to manufacture cellophane. [. . .]

This record discloses from the outset duPont set on an intensive research program to improve the quality and characteristics of cellophane and to lower its cost. Starting with a single cellulose chemist in 1924, it built a substantial research organization. [. . .]

The facts destroy the charges here made. There has been no monopolization or conspiracy or combination or attempt to monopolize shown. The record reflects not the dead hand of monopoly but rapidly declining prices, expanding production, intense competition stimulated by creative research, the development of new products and uses and other benefits of a free economy. DuPont nor any other American company similarly situated should be punished for its success. Nothing warrants intervention of this court of equity. The complaint should be dismissed.[4]

4. The 'Cellophane' case runs to 182 pages altogether of statistics, evidence and legal argument in the Federal Supplement.

13 The British Jurisdiction

The Restrictive Practices Court[1]

Yarn Spinners' Agreement
Law Reports: Restrictive Practices, vol. 1 (January 1959).

Devlin J. read the judgement of the Court:

The respondent in this case is the Yarn Spinners' Association and the agreement which the court has to consider is one which binds the members of the association not to sell yarn containing 85 per cent or more of cotton at a price lower than that fixed under the rules of the association.

The spinning industry is concentrated in a small area about thirty-five by twenty-five miles in extent stretching from Wigan through Bolton to Oldham, mostly in Lancashire but partly in adjoining counties. The industry is now in the hands of about 225 concerns which employ something over 100,000 operatives. [. . .]

The twenty years from 1937 to 1957 have been a period of ups and downs. During the war, production was severely curtailed; one-third of the spinning capacity was closed down and production and employment fell to half the pre-war level. The Cotton Control was established and prices were fixed. At the end of the war, a technical committee was set up to investigate and report on prices which should be permitted in the cotton industry so long as it remained under Government control. A costings investigation was carried out, and in 1948 the committee made its recommendations about the method by which prices should be calculated. When in April, 1949, price control was removed, the association asked its members to treat the prices fixed under this report as minimum prices; and it was in this way that the minimum price scheme, which we have to consider, became inaugurated. [. . .]

1. The cases in this reading should be considered in conjunction with Reading 10.

In the early part of 1951 the industry reached its highest post-war peak of activity. The amount of yarn produced in this year was nearly 1,000 million pounds. But by the summer of 1951 a recession had begun to develop; and in 1952 the industry had the worst of its post-war years, with a production of under 700 million pounds. Thereafter trade gradually improved until there was another recession in 1955. This continued until the Suez crisis at the end of 1956 caused a revival of demand, which did not, however, last beyond the middle of 1957. The industry has since been and is now in a recession comparable with that of 1952. [. . .]

In theory, the minimum price is designed to tide the spinner over short periods of recession. Since there is no allowance in it for profit over and above interest on capital, one would suppose that the average spinner would not find it worth his while to remain in business for very long on the minimum price. But, . . . without investigating the accounts of each spinner individually, it is impossible to say whether the minimum price gives him a profit or not; and the fact is that for most of the time since 1952 the majority of spinners have been operating at the minimum price. Indeed, the minimum price has now very nearly become the fixed price.

We have heard much general argument and evidence about the object of the scheme and its merits and demerits and also about the principles which underlie minimum price schemes generally. We do not intend to pass judgement for or against minimum price schemes in principle, either in the cotton trade or in any other. We shall confine ourselves to this particular scheme. [. . .]

The scheme is designed to guard against cut-throat competition such as happened in and after the great slump of 1929–31 and the recurrence of which is feared by all sections of the cotton trade. The scheme is based on the theory that the spinning industry is one in which there occur from time to time short but violent recessions. In these periods, it is said, some spinners will, unless restrained by common agreement, seek to maintain their output by selling below cost. In the long term this would be suicidal, but some mills will do it and take any price they can get because without cash they would have to close down. Before 1939 they could have shut down temporarily; their workpeople would have gone into the pool of unemployed and would have come back when things were better. If a mill were to do that now, it would lose its labour – or at least its key labour, the young and the skilled – for ever. So the only alternative to closing down is for it to carry on for whatever price it can get in the hope that if it can weather the depression it will make big profits when demand revives.

This is what is meant by cut-throat competition and, it is claimed, it is bad for the industry. If one firm lowers its prices below cost, others will be tempted or compelled to follow suit; and in the battle for diminishing trade the weakest will go to the wall. It is argued that this will not in the long run be in the public interest. At the depth of the depression the public may benefit for a short while from cut prices; but if the cutting of throats has decimated the industry, it will be left unequal to normal demands when the recession is over; there will then be a period of shortages and the mills that have survived will take advantage of them to charge abnormally high prices so as to recoup themselves for their losses.

We have had to consider whether this is a correct diagnosis of the conditions in the spinning industry and, if so, whether this minimum price scheme is well designed to deal with it. The theory on which the scheme is based seems to presuppose that periods of recession when minimum prices are effective will be exceptional and that the industry will normally be operating above them. This hardly seems to have been the case since 1952. . . . [And] looking at the industry as a whole, it is difficult in the face of these figures to regard a recession – if what is meant by a recession is that the demand is not sufficient to push the price off the minimum – as exceptional.

In our judgement, this minimum price scheme is *not* what is sometimes called a 'stop-loss' scheme. It does not operate simply to prevent cut-throat competition and selling below cost when demand is exceptionally poor. By setting the operating cost margin at the middle of the lowest two-thirds, it may well have been thought that, unless the periods when the minimum price was effective were very brief, high-cost producers would inevitably be eliminated. But it has not happened in that way. One way or another the minimum price appears to insure a reasonable return all the time to the majority of spinners. The fact is that the calculation of the prices is so far divorced from actuality that the total effect of the formulae may have been extremely difficult to foresee.

It is a theoretical calculation, and in the words of the Weavers' Association, which is in a good position to judge, 'the actual financial results (practical rather than theoretical) achieved by most spinning firms – even including some with low machinery activity – appear to be disproportionately high'.

We are satisfied that there is now a substantial amount of excess capacity in the industry over and above the reserve capacity which it is prudent to keep in being to meet any sudden increase in demand. . . . We are satisfied that this excess capacity will not in the foreseeable future be eliminated unless the scheme goes. We are satisfied that the industry can and ought to be made smaller and more compact.

These are our general conclusions. But this case, like every other brought under the Act, falls to be determined in accordance with specific findings.

In category (b) we must be satisfied that the removal of the restriction would deny to the public, as purchasers, consumers or users of any goods specific and substantial benefits or advantages enjoyed or likely to be enjoyed by them as such. The association contends that by virtue of the scheme a number of benefits is enjoyed by the shopping public which purchases cotton goods. Alternatively, it contends that benefits are enjoyed by purchasers of yarn. [. . .]

[The court then went on to enumerate the benefits claimed for the minimum price agreement under category (b). These included: the preservation of manufacturing capacity and labour sufficient to meet fluctuation in demand which might otherwise inconvenience the public; sufficient income to permit modernization of the plant; the avoidance of 'price invasions' by one manufacturer or another; the accumulation of stocks of spun yarn during periods of low demand for disposal in busier times; the creation of competition in terms of quality and service; the prevention of mergers leading to monopoly or near monopoly; and price stabilization.]

[. . .] We have to balance these benefits against the detriment to the public generally that arises from the scheme.

But before we perform this balancing operation, we must consider whether we are satisfied that the circumstances described in category (e) have been proved to exist, since if we are, they too

288

must be put into the balance against the detriment to the public generally. The requirement in category (*e*) is that, having regard to the conditions actually obtaining or reasonably foreseen at the time of the application, the removal of the restriction would be likely to have a serious and persistent adverse effect on the general level of unemployment in an area, or in areas taken together, in which a substantial proportion of the trade or industry is situated.

Subject to . . . general observations about the value of the figures, we take as our basis the Ministry's figures relating to the eleven areas in October 1958. There were then in all industries 600,000 insured workers, of whom over 25,000 were unemployed, 11,000 wholly and 14,000 temporarily stopped. Thus, the general level of unemployment in these eleven areas then stood at 4·3 per cent. In the spinning and doubling industry in these areas there were 100,000 insured workers, of whom nearly 12,000 were unemployed, under 2,000 being wholly unemployed and 10,000 temporarily stopped. These round figures (they are not all absolutely up to date; in some cases it has had to be assumed that 1957 figures are substantially unaltered) are good enough as a working basis, since the factors which we have to apply are even more incalculable than the figures. How many mills will close down if the scheme goes? How many would have closed down anyway? What proportion of those who lose their jobs altogether are short-time workers already classed as unemployed? How many will get work elsewhere and how long will it take? We can make no specific finding on any of these points, and can only state in general terms the sort of considerations relating to them which have influenced us in determining whether or not the words of the sub-paragraph apply.

[The Court briefly discussed these considerations stressing the necessary imprecision of its deductions. Then Devlin J. went on to say.]

[. . .] We state the following assumptions in order to illustrate the sort of figures with which we have to deal. If we were to estimate that in the eleven areas the abrogation of the scheme would cause doublers to be thrown out of work in the same proportion as spinners; if we were to assume that 20 per cent of the spinners and doublers employed in the eleven areas were to be thrown out of work and further to assume that only half of them obtained employment elsewhere; and if we were to allow the considerations relating to registered persons, such as married women, and to short-time workers to cancel each other out, that is, if the association's case is not to be strengthened by including in the unemployment figures those who fall outside the statistics, but also is not to be weakened by the consideration that some of the increase in the figures of wholly unemployed may mean only a transfer from the temporarily stopped: there would be left a figure of 10,000 which would raise the general level of unemployment in the eleven areas from 4·3 per cent to 5·9 per cent. If similar assumptions were made in relation to the four areas, the general level of unemployment in them would be raised from 5·2 per cent to 7·8 per cent.

We have stated these as illustrative assumptions and not as findings because there is not sufficient certainty about any of these matters to enable us to compute the anticipated affect even in round figures. We are required to act without certainty and on the balance of probabilities, and to arrive at a general conclusion in the terms used in the Act. We find that the closing of mills consequent upon the abrogation of the scheme to be expected in the eleven areas as well as in the four will have a serious adverse effect on the general level of unemployment in those areas. We find, though with even greater doubt and hesitation, that that effect will be persistent.

We must now consider the detriments to the public relied on by the registrar as resulting from the scheme. They are pleaded in his answer under a number of heads. We think that all those that matter can be placed in three groups: first, the maintenance of a high price for yarn eventually reflected in the price of goods bought by the public; secondly, loss of or handicap to the export trade; thirdly, the waste of national resources caused by excess capacity. As to the first, we are satisfied that the price of yarn could be lower than it is. We agree that there will not be any appreciable lowering of the price of cotton goods unless the cost in the intermediate processes also comes down; but we think that a lowering of the price of yarn may well start reductions which could mount up in a way which would in the end be of appreciable – though not of great – benefit to the public. There is, therefore, a detriment here. As to the second head, we are satisfied that quite a considerable export business has been lost, not so much in yarn as in cloth, through the rigidity of the scheme and the inability of spinners (without special permission only reluctantly granted) to make even a small concession in price to help in securing export business. Exports of yarn and cloth do not form a large part of the country's export trade; but they are not insignificant, and we think that anything which appreciably hinders or diminishes the export trade must be regarded as a public detriment. As to the third head, Sir Andrew Clark has submitted that waste of national resources is too remote an effect of the scheme to be classed as a public detriment. We do not agree. Excess capacity in any industry means short-time working and idle plant. It is in the public interest that labour and capital should be employed as productively as possible, and we consider, therefore, that the excess capacity in the cotton industry is a public detriment.

Against these detriments we have found two sets of circumstances to be balanced. We give little weight to those that come under category (b); having regard to the detriments we have enumerated, we are quite clear that a restriction which secures benefits only to a small class of trade purchasers is unreasonable. The effect on the general level of unemployment is much graver. But whether it be in relation to the four or the eleven areas, the effect is localized; the price of its avoidance would have to be paid nationally. It would be paid not solely or primarily in the price of cotton goods or in the loss to export trade. Though both these are substantial, we have in mind chiefly the waste of national resources in the form of excess capacity. So long as the scheme lasts, concentration of the industry will be postponed; it will not be until the excess capacity has been got rid of that the industry can be made into a more compact entity, a reorganization which we believe will ultimately be beneficial not merely to the nation and the consuming public, but to the industry itself and those employed in it. We have decided that on balance it would be unreasonable to continue the restrictions in the scheme in order to avoid the degree of local unemployment which we fear. We find that the association has not made out a case under section 21 as a whole. [. . .]

Declaration accordingly.

Cement Makers' Agreement

Law Reports: Restrictive Practices, vol. 2 (March 1961).

Diplock J. read the judgement of the Court:

The federation's main contention is that the existence and method of operation of their common price agreement results in cement being sold and delivered at prices which, taking purchases throughout the country as a whole, are lower than they would be in the absence of the agreement. They claim that this brings the case within paragraph (*b*) of section 21 (1) of the Restrictive Trade Practices Act, 1956, since the removal of the 'restrictions' contained in the common price agreement would deny to the public as purchasers of cement the specific and substantial advantage of the lower prices for cement which they enjoy and are likely to continue to enjoy by virtue of the restrictions themselves or arrangements resulting therefrom.

It is no part of the federation's case that prices in some areas or to some particular classes of purchasers might not be lower if the agreement came to an end. What they claim is that, taking home trade in cement as a whole, the prices on balance would be substantially higher in the absence of the common price agreement.

We accept that, if the federation succeed in establishing the correctness of their main contention, they will have shown a substantial and specific benefit enjoyed by 'the public as purchasers'.

It has not been suggested on behalf of the registrar that the prices in fact fixed under the common price scheme have resulted in a profit to the industry as a whole which is unreasonable. Some individual makers, whose output is less than 10 per cent of the whole and who in the main supply local demands with low transport costs, have made consistently good profits, but the weighted average profits of the industry have shown no more than a modest return upon the capital employed.

Turning now . . . to a forecast of what is likely to happen in the future, the federation rely upon certain special features of the cement industry which are not really disputed. These are that: (*a*) taking one year with another the overall demand for cement will continue to expand at about the same rate as it has done in the past, namely, some $3\frac{1}{2}$ per cent to 4 per cent per annum; (*b*) the overall demand for cement would not be materially affected by rises or falls in the price level of the order of 5 per cent to 10 per cent; and (c) the industry is now working to full capacity and any increase in demand can only be met by the creation of new capacity.

They base their main contention, that the overall price of cement delivered in the United Kingdom would in the future be lower if the common price agreement continued than it would be if the agreement were abrogated, upon three broad propositions: (1) that in an expanding industry in the long term the price level under free competition will be at or around the level at which there is sufficient return on cement produced at new works (after providing sufficient depreciation) to attract the investment of capital in a new works; (2) that in the future supply will keep in step with demand except for short periods at particular times and places; and (3) that the minimum return which will attract investment in a new works is higher under free competition than under the common price agreement, because the risk is greater.

Each of these broad propositions was accepted as correct by the expert witnesses on both sides, and we also accept them. The next steps in the argument, however, are the crucial ones, namely, to satisfy the court that: (4) members of the federation would in fact exercise their power of fixing prices under the common price agreement at a level lower than that which would be required to attract investment of capital in new works under free competition; and (5) the difference in price level would be sufficient to constitute a 'substantial' benefit to the public as purchasers of cement.

Several of the expert witnesses gave their personal opinions of the return which a new entrant into the industry, thinking in terms of the industry in free competition, would expect on his equity capital before embarking on the costly venture of erecting new cement works. The individual estimates differed to some extent, but all, including that of the registrar's accountant, fell within the range of 15 per cent to 20 per cent, and we accept that the return required upon new capital invested in the cement industry under free competition would be in the range of 15 per cent to 20 per cent.

What effect would a return within this range have upon the price level of cement? The independent accountant has made two assessments, taking the cost of construction of new works at 1959 figures at the minimum of £15 per ton and working capital at £1 10s per ton, and adopting 'straight line' depreciation for fixed assets of 3⅓ per cent (a thirty years' average life). In the first assessment, he has assumed the costs of manufacture (excluding depreciation) to be the same as those of the lowest cost maker; in the second assessment he has taken them to be the same as those of the newest works in the industry.

To obtain a return of 15 per cent on capital invested would under the first assessment require a net realized selling price of 133s 1d or under the second assessment of 137s, while to obtain a return of 20 per cent these prices would have to rise to 149s 7d and 153s 6d respectively. The average net realized price for the industry in 1959 was 107s 1d, and the average net realized price obtained for cement from the newest works was 112s 8d. To obtain the postulated return of 15 per cent would, therefore, require either an increase in price or reduction in costs or a combination of the two of the order of 25s per ton, and to obtain a return of 20 per cent a similar increase in price or reduction in costs of the order of 40s per ton.

The evidence satisfies us that the members of the federation, following the advice of the independent costs committee, have been content in the past eight years to fix the price of cement at a level which shows a return of under 10 per cent on capital invested in new works, despite the fact that collectively they have had a monopoly of the trade in what has been almost continuously a sellers' market. We accept also that they have felt able to do this because of the added security of their investment afforded by the common price agreement, and that without that security they would have required and could have obtained a higher return of the order of 15 per cent. To obtain each additional 1 per cent return upon capital invested in new works at present-day costs of construction requires an addition of 3s 3·4d to the price of cement, and to increase the return from 10 per cent to 15 per cent requires an increase in price of 16s 6d per ton. The common price agreement, has, we think, been so operated as to keep down the overall price of cement to a level substantially lower than it would have been under free competition. If, therefore, we can be satisfied that if the common price agreement is allowed to continue in operation the federation are likely to fix the prices of cement in the same way and in accordance with the same principles as they have adopted in the past, the federation will have succeeded in establishing the existence of the circumstances specified in paragraph (*b*) of section 21 (1) of the Act of 1956.

Before deciding whether we can be so satisfied, we turn to consider the detriments to the public or to persons not parties to the agreement (being purchasers of goods sold by such parties) which it is alleged result or are likely to result from the operation of the common price agreement. [. . .]

[The judgement then, pp. 282–5, referred to and rejected the contentions that the delivered price agreement prevented adequate expansion of the industry through erection of new plants in the most suitable geographical areas; that it removed the natural advantage of the buyers located close to the cement works; and the element involved in the delivered price arrangements was detrimental to the public.]

We do not think that the alleged detriments outweigh the specific and substantial advantage of lower overall prices of cement upon which the federation rely under paragraph (*b*).

There remains, however, the difficult question as to whether we can be satisfied that the federation is likely to continue, under the common price agreement, to fix prices in the same way and in accordance with the same principles as they have adopted in the past, and to be content with a modest margin of profit on capital invested which reflects the security which the industry enjoys as the result of the fixed price arrangements.

As in *In re Black Bolt and Nut Association's Agreement* the restrictions contain no express provisions as to the basis on which prices are to be fixed. The chairman has given reasons, which in the case of this particular industry we think are cogent, for not seeking to write into the agreement a definite formula to be applied automatically. It would be difficult indeed to devise a formula to deal with such matters as changes in individual 'base prices' or 'distance zone' increments or to take account of such relevant factors in forecasting costs of production or delivery as the extent to which there is likely to be working to a particular percentage of capacity or the areas in which demand during a particular period is likely to arise. The chairman considers that it is better as has been done in the past to leave the actual decisions to be made by the makers, after receiving the advice of the independent costs committee given in the light of their past experience of the industry, their knowledge of its current costs and returns, and their appreciation of future trends.

We agree that in the special circumstances of this industry it would not be helpful to try to incorporate in the restrictions a price formula: but to leave the matter at large does involve relying upon the good judgement and moderation of those who will be concerned in the actual decisions upon price changes.

In the light of the evidence as to the way in which the common price agreement has in fact operated in the past, and of our confidence that the independent costs committee and the council of the federation, as at present constituted, will continue so to operate it in the future, and in the light of the assurances we have received, we are satisfied that the main price-fixing restriction is not contrary to the public interest.

Declaration accordingly.

Standard Metal Window Group's Agreement
Law Reports: Restrictive Practices, vol. 3 (July 1962).

Megaw J. read the judgement of the Court:

A large part of the evidence before us was concerned with the extent and effect of the group's exchange of costing and technical information. It was contended on behalf of the group that the effect has been, is, and if the agreement is allowed to continue, will be, to keep the costs of each manufacturing member of the group lower – substantially lower – than they would otherwise be; and that, in consequence, the prices of standard metal windows as a whole have been, and will be, lower for the ultimate purchasers and users than they would otherwise be; and also that the quality of standard metal windows as a whole, and the service of manufacturers to the purchasing public, are better than they would otherwise be. 'Otherwise', in this context, refers to the conditions which would have existed, and would now exist, in the absence of any agreement among the members of the group as to prices.

It is right that we should say at once, for reasons which we shall give in more detail later, that we accept on the evidence before us that the effect of the full and detailed exchange of information has been in a substantial degree to reduce or contain the costs of the manufacturing members of the group. It has also, in some degree, and notably in respect of the development of the rust-proofing of windows, assisted in the improvement of quality, and helped to bring about some advances in quality more quickly than would otherwise have been the case.

The mere fact that costs have been reduced would not, however, in itself establish that the agreement produces a benefit to the public. There remain the questions which in this case have caused us difficulty and have involved the most anxious consideration: whether and to what extent the collaboration would continue if the price arrangements were to be condemned; whether and to what extent the collaboration, if it continued in the future, would produce results comparable to those obtained in the past; and, the most difficult question of all, whether in all the circumstances any reduction, or keeping down, of costs which the manufacturers in the group might achieve, as a result of continuing collaboration dependent on the maintenance of the price arrangements, would have the consequence of keeping prices to the public of standard metal windows as a whole lower than they would otherwise have been.

[His Lordship referred to the history of the industry and to the group's method of price-fixing as set out above and continued:]

The restrictions are, for present purposes, sufficiently described as follow: (1) An agreed delivered price system, including agreed rebates for quantity orders. (2) A restriction against the granting of any discount, rebate, cash bonus or other consideration beyond those provided by the agreement. (3) An agreed allowance of 10 per cent on inter-trading between members. (4) As regards sales to merchants, an agreement to ensure that merchants observe resale price maintenance.

The benefits and advantages which the group contend are likely to be lost to the public as purchasers and users if the restrictions should be condemned may be summarized as follows: that as a result of the agreement, including the restrictions as necessary elements thereof, (1) prices of standard metal windows have been, are, and in foreseeable future conditions will be, in general lower than they would otherwise be; (2) the quality of those windows has been, is, and will be better, and the service provided by the manufacturers is and will be better; (3) the purchaser has had, has, and will have a wider choice of suppliers of those windows.

Various other suggested benefits have been mentioned in the course of the hearing, but, on analysis we think they are merely facets of those benefits which we have mentioned.

In the opinion of the court, after careful consideration of all the evidence and submissions, the suggested benefits or advantages mentioned under (2) and (3) have not been established as being specific and substantial advantages which would be lost to the public if the restrictions were no longer to apply. The group's case stands or falls by reference to (1). [Lower prices.]

The group's case as to lower prices by virtue of the restrictions has to be considered by stages. Before considering the several stages, we should make it clear that we are not going to attempt to review the voluminous evidence in detail. That would be a task of great length and would not, we think, serve any useful purpose.

The stages are: (i) Has the group prepared reasonably reliable and comparable costs? (ii) Has the group exchanged such costs and given valuable technical information one to another among its members? (iii) Has the result been to keep the costs of members lower than they would have been under any other system, including unrestricted competition among themselves? (iv) Have the prices been kept lower thereby? (v) To what extent, if at all, would the exchange of costs and technical information continue if the restrictions were to be condemned? (vi) Would the continuation of the present scheme be likely, in the foreseeable future, to keep prices of standard metal windows lower than they would otherwise be? (vii) Does the likelihood of such keeping down of prices as may be properly foreseen constitute a specific and substantial benefit or advantage to the public as purchasers or users?

We can deal with the first three of these stages together. The evidence that the costs as prepared by the group have been and are reasonably reliable and reasonably comparable as a result of the work of the costs determination committee was not only convincing, but was, in the end, virtually unchallenged. The full exchange of detailed costs, including time studies, between members, and the unrestricted interchange of information as to developments in technique, machinery, lay-out of plant, improvements in manufacturing processes and economy in the use of labour and material have been proved beyond doubt. While the ascertainment of members' costs is required for price-fixing purposes, it has another and most important use. That is, the comparison of members' costs with a view to ascertaining why one member's costs for a particular aspect of manufacture are higher than those of another. When the cause is discovered, close consideration is given, with the assistance of the production engineer in many cases, to the changes required to reduce the costs of the member whose costs are higher. In this context, accountancy and engineering or management skills go hand in hand. We do not set out any of the examples which have been proved in the evidence. They were numerous and, in their totality, convincing as to the effect of the cooperation in the reduction of manufacturing costs.

There are two features of the interchange of costs which deserve special mention. One is that the interchange is not merely of average costs, or of anonymous costs, or of costs under some code system to conceal the name of the member concerned. Each member is told what are the costs of each other member, in each aspect which is examined; and this is followed by visits and talks between members and their own cost accountants and technical experts with a view to deriving the full benefits of the experience and advances of their fellow-members. The other notable feature which, according to the evidence, may be unique, is that the members freely exchange full information as to the operational times for the various processes of manufacture. This, we think, is highly important in keeping down costs. The exchange of information bearing on costs, according to the evidence before us, is more detailed and comprehensive than in any other industry which is known to any of the witnesses, and those witnesses included the group's independent accountant, who has had many years' experience of the accountancy and costs of many different types of industry.

The evidence, mostly relating to the period before 1959, showed also, beyond dispute, that some significant reductions in costs have been achieved in particular processes, either generally among members, or in some instances by an individual member whose costs in some aspect had been unfavourably high in comparison with others. Moreover, the costs overall of the manufacture of standard metal windows by members had, at least since 1953, shown a markedly slower rate of increase, despite increases in the cost of labour and materials, than had the costs of the various individual items which go to make up the total cost.

Against this, it was very properly argued on behalf of the registrar that, whereas no doubt some reduction, or relative reduction of costs was attributable to the cooperation of members in exchange of costings and of technical information, no one could tell how far reductions would have been achieved without that cooperation, but with the stimulus of full competition between members. That is true. In many cases, no doubt, that argument would be very potent, especially bearing in mind the burden of proof which lies on respondents in these cases. In the present case, however, we are satisfied on the evidence which we have heard – and not merely because of the uncontradicted, and no doubt entirely responsible and honest, opinions expressed by the group's independent accountant and representatives of the members of the group – that substantially greater advances have been made in keeping down the costs of members of the group by reason of their cooperation than would have been achieved had they been in full price-competition with one another. One factor which cannot be ignored in this case is that there has been at all times keen price competition, affecting each member of the group; the price competition from wood windows and from manufacturers of standard metal windows outside, first, the association, and latterly, the group. Indeed, this competition has been more keen for members of the group since the group was formed than before, because they have had no price-fixing arrangement with Crittalls.

So far we have been considering the reduction of costs, not the reduction (or rather, in an inflationary era, the avoidance or containing of increases) of prices.

We now come to the fourth stage. Accepting, as we have found, that members' costs have been lower in the past than they would have been if there had been no agreement, can the same be said of prices? True it is, that the average profit margin has been relatively low. There has, therefore, been little room for absorbing higher costs by accepting lower profits.

We think that the principal factor in the past, in the fixing of prices by the group, may be said to have been the normal factor of what the market will stand, in the light of the existing competition among manufacturers of standard metal windows and of wood windows. There is no doubt that for some time past members of the group have been dissatisfied with the profit margins obtained. They would have liked to increase prices. They have not done so. Why not? Because of market conditions. The competition between makers of wood windows, makers of metal windows who are outside the group, and the manufacturing members of the group is keen and effective. None of the three sections can increase its prices as and when it pleases; prices have to be competitive. Perhaps this is another way of saying that prices cannot exceed what the market will bear; but what the market will stand is determined by several factors, one of which is the influence in terms of costs and prices of companies in the group. It is, in this context, that, in our view, cooperation between group members to reduce costs has been of benefit to purchasers of windows. Because, as we believe, the group scheme has kept costs lower than they would otherwise have been, members of the group have been and are more effective competitors in the market for windows, and prices have been and are probably lower as a result than would otherwise have been the case. In other words, without the greater efficiency, reflected in lower costs, which the group scheme promotes, member firms could not have offered the prices they have done and the tendency would have been for the prices of all windows (wood and metal) to be higher. Further, standard metal windows have thereby been more competitive with wood windows, and thus have retained a larger share of the total market for windows than they would otherwise have done: this has to be viewed against the background of the existence of a demand for standard metal windows.

The fifth stage raises this question: to what extent, if at all, would the exchange of costs and of technical information continue if the restrictions were to be condemned, so that there would no longer be price-fixing among the members of the group?

The evidence was unanimous that exchange of costs, especially of costs of members shown under their own names, and in anything like the present detail, and the cooperation as to operational times, would cease. So, to a large extent, would the exchange of infor-

301

mation as to technical advances. It was agreed, at least by some witnesses, that some cooperation might continue, though on much more general lines, such as collaboration in the association on general matters of assistance in the competition with wood windows. It was said that such an abandonment of close cooperation was inevitable as a matter of human nature, especially when the possibility would be in the minds of all members that each might be selling to undercut the others in price, and when the possibility existed, even though no member thought it probable, that a 'price war' might develop: a 'price war' in the sense that members would be driven to quote truly uneconomic prices – that showed no profit or even a loss – against one another.

On the evidence in this case, we do not think that a price war is likely to follow from the abandonment of fixed prices within the group; but we are satisfied that the extent of the cooperation would be very materially lessened, with a resulting reduction in the future savings of costs among members.

What, then, of the future so far as prices are concerned? This is the sixth stage in the group's case. Positive and direct evidence on this matter was given by the chairman and joint managing director of Henry Hope & Sons Ltd, giving evidence for the group, and by the chairman and managing director of Crittalls giving evidence for the registrar.

The former witness said that, if the agreement ceased to operate, his company would be disposed to raise all its prices by about 5 per cent above the present group prices, though it would keep, as it were up its sleeve, the idea of giving larger discounts to larger buyers. He thought that the market would stand an increase of price. He thought that Crittalls would be glad to follow suit. The latter, on the other hand, said that he thought that the result of the disappearance of the agreement would be to add, in effect, four more competitors (the five principal members of the group, as contrasted with the group as a single entity) to what is already an extremely competitive market. He would expect that this would produce at some stage fairly soon some diminution in price level. He would hope that this would not last too long nor go too far. So far as Crittalls was concerned, he did not think that, to start with, it would make any change in its prices. If Henry Hope & Sons Ltd were to increase its prices by 5 per cent, Crittalls would like to follow suit, but, having regard to the competitive factors, particularly from wood windows, he doubted very much whether Crittalls would do so.

The court has to assess, as best it can, what would be the position, so far as price levels are concerned, in the standard metal industry as a whole (*a*) if the agreement is destroyed, and (*b*) if the agreement survives. In making this assessment we have to bear in mind the competition with the wood window industry, which must always have an important influence on the price of standard metal windows, and, of course, vice versa. We have also to bear in mind the general structure of the metal window industry as it now is and as it is likely to be.

We are satisfied that prices of standard metal windows for the future are likely to be kept lower than they would otherwise be, to the extent that there is strong and effective competition within the standard metal window industry; and, further (for this is a matter which we are entitled to consider) the prices of windows as a whole – that is wood windows and standard metal windows – will tend to be kept lower to the extent that there is strong and effective competition on the part of standard metal windows with wood windows.

Hence, the crucial question in this case is: will competition within the standard metal window industry and hence within the window industry as a whole, be stronger and more effective (*a*) if the agreement is allowed to continue, or (*b*) if the agreement is brought to an end?

At first sight, the answer might appear to be that competition will be stronger and more effective if the members of the group join in the competition, competing against one another in price, as well as against those manufacturers, principally Crittalls, who are now outside the group. We have reached the conclusion, however, that, having regard to the special facts and circumstances of this case, that answer would be wrong. Crittalls has some 43 per cent of the market. It is in a very powerful position; its efficiency is undoubted and its costs are probably relatively low. When the association's agreement was ended, Crittalls' costs may have been something like 1 per cent below the costs of the lowest producer now in the group, though it is fair to say that the producer has since reduced its costs by at least that margin. Of course, Crittalls may also have reduced their costs. Against Crittalls' 43 per cent of the market, the six manufacturing members of the group among them have about 42 per cent of the market.

If the group were to be broken up, two consequences would follow. First, the individual members of the group would, by that very fact, be in a weaker position so far as sustained competition is concerned. Secondly, because of the conclusion which we have already expressed, the manufacturing costs of each member of the group would be likely to be higher than they would otherwise be through the absence of continued cooperation between the members. They would thus be weaker competitors in the long run, even if, in the short run, the competition might be more intense.

The answer, therefore, which we give to the question which we have posed is: competition within the standard metal window industry is likely to be stronger and more effective if the agreement is allowed to continue; and the stronger and more effective the competition within the industry, the more will the price of standard metal windows (and hence probably also of wood windows) be restrained through the force of the competition.

This probability is, in our judgement, on a fair assessment of this case as a whole, a specific and substantial benefit to the public as purchasers or users of windows; a benefit which is given by the agreement, including its restrictions, and the arrangements and operations resulting therefrom; and a benefit which is likely to be lost if the restrictions are condemned. This is our conclusion as to the seventh and final stage in the group's case.

Lest there should be any doubt about it, we should make it abundantly clear that our decision is founded upon the present structure of the standard metal window industry and the desirability of maintaining strong and effective competition in that industry. If, for any reason, there ceased to be full, free, and effective competition in price between the group and Crittalls and the other manufacturers – if, for example, there were to be any agreement or arrangement of any sort between the group and Crittalls as to prices to be charged or as to orders to be sought or not to be sought – the whole foundation of our decision in the present case would have gone.

In addition to all these matters, an undertaking was offered by counsel for the group on express instructions during his closing speech, That undertaking was that the group, if the restrictions are allowed to continue, will keep to 10 per cent as their target of profit on sales to be included in arriving at the prices in the pricing schedule. The court assumes that undertaking to mean that the percentages included for profit in arriving at the prices in the pricing schedules will be such that the prices are calculated, overall, to produce an average profit on sales of not more than 10 per cent on the assumption that the pre-determined activity is achieved and that all sales are made at the maximum rebate figure comprised in the rebate table. No doubt the group, in order to ensure that this undertaking is implemented, will wish to ask the independent chairman of the costs determination committee to check the calculations of profit involved in any new or revised pricing schedules. [. . .]

We come, finally, to the question of detriments arising out of the restrictions, which we are required by the concluding portion of section 21 (1) of the Act of 1956 to consider in order to arrive at a balance of public interest, as against the benefit which we have held to exist.

In this context, we should refer to the evidence given by a considerable number of witnesses on behalf of the registrar, most of whom were officials of local authorities with responsibilities as to the purchase of standard metal windows. All these witnesses in their proofs of evidence expressed, in one way or another, views which were either personal, or said to be held by the authorities concerned, adverse to any form of level tendering or price-fixing. In one instance the local authority required in its form of tender that the manufacturer tendering should certify that, *inter alia*, he was not a party to any agreement or arrangement to communicate the amount of his tender to any other person and that he had not adjusted the amount of his tender in accordance with any agreement or arrangement to do so made with any other person. We need scarcely say that, so long as the present agreement continues, no party to it could honestly give such a certificate.

In cross-examination, most, at least, of these witnesses agreed that, if it were the case that a price agreement resulted in prices being lower than they would otherwise be, their objections would not be valid. They all agreed that there was, at present, a strong degree of competition within the standard metal window industry.

For the reasons which we have given, in our judgement, the theoretical objection is, on the particular facts of this agreement in the present position of this industry, not justified. Beyond the statement of that specific conclusion, it would be improper and undesirable for us to go. There are, no doubt, many other factors affecting the views and attitudes of local authorities or other purchasers, which are not before us in this case, and which it is not our concern to seek to assess. [. . .]

Accordingly, subject to the undertaking and assurances which we have already mentioned, we hold that the restrictions in the agreement before us do not fall to be deemed to be contrary to the public interest under section 21 of the Act. We so declare.

Declaration accordingly.

Net Book Agreement
Law Reports: Restrictive Practices, vol. 1 (January 1959).

Buckley J. read the judgement of the Court:

The registrar's economist was at one stage inclined to suggest that the rates of discount given by publishers were arbitrary and insufficiently related to the risks and difficulty involved in stocking and selling particular books. We are satisfied that this is not so. The rates have been evolved by ordinary economic processes in the course of many years of business and broadly represent the margins which publishers find necessary to induce booksellers to stock and endeavour to sell their products. A book may be risky to stock and difficult to sell for a while and then become a runaway best seller; or it may be easy to sell for a while and then unexpectedly cease to attract purchasers. A book may be easy to sell in one district and difficult in another, and it may, we are told, even sell well in one shop and less well in another in the same town. It would, speaking generally, be quite impracticable for a publisher to vary his rate of discount according to the location or character of the bookseller's business or according to the state of public demand for the book at the time when a particular order is placed. The current rates of discount may, we think, be taken as approximating as nearly as is practical to the value to publisher's of the services which booksellers render to them in respect of the various categories of books to which those rates relate. They are not uniform or immutable: they represent the present point of equilibrium produced by the economic forces that affect them.

[His Lordship stated the facts relating to booksellers' profits, exports, libraries ... read the Net Book Agreement, 1957, and continued:] The following general observations on the agreement may first be made. No publisher is constrained by the agreement to make any book a net book: he is free to make his own decision in this respect in relation to every book he publishes, and is consequently free to determine in respect of every book he publishes whether the agreement shall or shall not apply to it. Secondly, the publisher is free to fix the net price of any net book published by him at any figure he chooses and could, if he wished, change that price from time to time (see the definition of 'net price' in standard condition (vi)). Thirdly, since the words 'except as we may otherwise direct' in standard condition (i) are understood by the parties to the agreement ... a publisher could at any time convert a net book into a non-net book and so take it out of the operation of the agreement. Fourthly, the agreement does not in any way restrict the freedom of the publisher himself to sell his product to anyone at any price: he is perfectly free to sell a net book to a member of the reading public or to a library or institution or to a middleman, that is, a wholesale or retail bookseller, whether in the United Kingdom or abroad, at the net price or at any discount he chooses.

The matters relied upon by the association in justification of the agreement occupy no less than 18 paragraphs and 12 pages of the statement of case, but it is unnecessary for us to set them out at length here, for Mr Bagnall for the association has made it clear that the abrogation of the agreement would, as it contends, result in (a) the prices of books overall becoming higher than they are, (b) the number of stockholding bookshops becoming less than it is and the services of those who survive becoming reduced, and (c) the number and variety of titles published becoming less than at present.

The association's case may be briefly stated as follows. It is beneficial to the public as purchasers and as users of books that publishers should publish adventurously and at low prices. To do so publishers must be assured that the books which they publish will have the best practicable chance at a reasonable cost to themselves of being brought to the attention of those members of the public who are likely to be retail buyers. Except for potential institutional buyers such as libraries, the best medium which has so far been devised for this purpose is the stockholding bookseller who offers to individual members of the reading public the opportunity of seeing and sampling a widely varied selection of newly published as well as back-list books, a skilled information service and a reliable special order service. The stockholding bookseller, moreover, shares the publishers' risks to the extent of his stock orders, and particularly by his [advance] subscription orders. Were it not for the benefits derived by publishers from the activities of the stockholding booksellers, and more particularly from their subscription orders and from their stocking and displaying books, publishers would be compelled to be more cautious in their selection of books to publish and in their printing orders. Works which are now marginal choices by publishers for publication would tend not to be published, and those books which were published would tend to be produced in smaller numbers and so at a greater cost per copy, so that the price to the public would be higher. If the agreement were condemned, it would become impossible for publishers to maintain the net prices of any of their books. In those circumstances price-cutting would become a feature of the book trade: the prices of some books would be cut at some retail outlets. Although not all books would become the subject of price-cutting and of many it might be unlikely that they ever would be so, nevertheless all books would become potential subjects of price-cutting. The consequence of such a state of affairs would be a reduction in the number of stockholding booksellers, a diminution of the stocks held by those remaining in business and a deterioration in the services rendered, a contraction of subscription orders and of orders for stock generally, and a demand by booksellers for higher rates of discount, which publishers would have to meet. This would result in less adventurous publishing and in retail buyers of books having to pay, generally, higher prices for their books.

As to institutional buyers and in particular public libraries, the association says that these would press for and probably obtain higher rates of discount from their suppliers than the 10 per cent allowed under the Library Agreement, but that as these higher discounts would come off higher list prices the libraries and those who use them would in the end be no better off than at present. It says, further, that the consequence of public libraries exacting these larger discounts would be either a deterioration in the services rendered by the suppliers or a demand by those suppliers for increased discounts from the publishers which would be a contributing factor towards yet higher list prices. The association also says that this pressure by public libraries for higher discounts would be beyond the capacity of stockholding booksellers to satisfy; that stockholding booksellers would lose the library business which they now have; and that this would be a strong contributing cause to many stockholding booksellers going out of business and to those who remained in business demanding greater discount margins from the publishers. Therefore, the association claim that by and large an end of retail price maintenance would confer no benefit on public libraries, but would in relation to library business accentuate or reinforce the ill-effects which for other reasons already indicated it would have on the general level of the prices of books.

Ignoring for the moment certain submissions on points of law which Mr Fisher made on the registrar's behalf, we proceed to state in a summary form the registrar's contentions on the merits of the case. The effect of the agreement, he says, is to protect stockholding booksellers from price competition to which they would be exposed if the publishers were to cease to maintain the retail prices of their net books. He concedes that an end of retail price maintenance would result from the abrogation of the agreement. There is, he contends, no adequate ground for differentiating between the production and marketing of books and the production and marketing of any other commodity: these are ordinary commercial processes governed by ordinary commercial principles. There is no *a priori* reason for supposing the present system of distributing books to be the best. A system which can only survive if given artificial protection against price competition cannot be regarded as satisfactory. Even with the protection of the agreement the trade of the stockholding booksellers is in a depressed state, and institutional buying, mainly by public libraries, is increasing in volume and importance. This institutional buying is of special value to the publishers precisely in those cases where the publishers' risk is great, for example, in the case of a first novel of which a small edition is printed, for libraries buy a high proportion of such an edition. The existence of the agreement is an obstacle in the way of innovation and improvement in the means of distributing books. It is disadvantageous to the public because it compels the retail seller in every case to retain the whole margin afforded to him by the publisher's discount, whether he needs it or not, and precludes him from passing any part of it on to the retail purchaser irrespective of whether he does or does not render the special services which it is claimed that stockholding booksellers perform free of charge. The agreement debars public libraries from negotiating better terms with library suppliers. Abrogation of the agreement would not put an end to the competitive advantage which the stockholding bookseller has over other booksellers by reason of the stock which he holds and the special facilities and services which he offers to the public. If publishers wished to keep stockholding booksellers in business notwithstanding the abrogation of the agreement, they could do so by readjustment of their discounts. There is, says the registrar, no reason to suppose that price-cutting would be otherwise than on a small scale and infrequent, and, in any case, it would affect only a small proportion of books. Even if the prices of books which were not the subjects of price-cutting were to rise because of price-cutting in relation to other books, the registrar submits that this would not be a detriment to the public as a whole but would merely mean that the purchasers of those books would no longer be subsidized by the purchasers of other books. The evidence, he says, does not establish that the prices paid for books by the public would on the whole be higher: some might be higher and some lower. [. . .]

Any view as to what will be likely to happen if the agreement comes to an end is bound to be speculative. Nobody now engaged in the publishing and bookselling trades has any experience of working in this country without the protection of some such agreement as the Net Book Agreement; hence any opinions they express must be largely theoretical. This has to be borne in mind in weighing the evidence tendered to us, and not the evidence of the association only: the witnesses called by the registrar had also to base their forecasts of the future on assumptions unsupported by experience or recent history.

What we have to consider is whether on the evidence which we have heard we think that the balance of probability is that certain results would follow the condemnation of the agreement. If we do think so, we must decide this case upon the footing that those results would follow. And it is the results which would ensue in the long run with which we are principally concerned, not those which might for a short time only follow the determination of the agreement.

To take prices first, the case for the association is that book prices would rise if the agreement were determined. This conclusion is reached by assembling a number of factors. There is the expectation that printing runs might be shorter and more expensive because without the agreement greater caution would be necessary; there is the view that list prices would have to be increased to meet the demand, likely to be irresistible, for larger discounts to booksellers; and there is the fact that if prices were increased, for any reason, authors' royalties would rise also and these would have to be covered by the new prices.

No doubt publishers would like to increase their prices, but in the keener competition engendered by the disappearance of the agreement, would they be able to do so and survive? That is the crucial question as regards prices. A publisher may feel he has a certain amount of latitude when fixing prices if he knows the retailer is bound to observe them. Might he not be more cautious if he feared that high prices might induce price-cutting?

The purpose of the agreement is to maintain retail prices: it was formulated and has been kept in being with the intention of preventing retailers from offering books for sale at less than net prices. Mr Fisher for the Registrar says that it is paradoxical to say that a consequence of ending such an agreement would be higher prices. But it must be borne in mind that the agreement is not a price-fixing agreement. Its object is not the maintenance of any particular prices or price level throughout the trade or any section of it. Net prices are fixed by publishers in conditions of free competition. The main object of the agreement is, in our view, to preserve retail price stability; it is not an instrument for fixing prices. We do not forget what this court said in *In re Yarn Spinners' Agreement* on the subject of price stabilization. In that case, however, the court was concerned with an agreement by which manufacturers bound themselves to observe minimum prices calculated on hypothetical average costs. The facts were, we think, materially different from those in the present case in which net prices are fixed in competitive conditions.

We are satisfied – and, indeed, it has been conceded by the registrar – that maintenance by publishers of the retail prices of net books could not long survive the end of the agreement. Although price maintenance would cease, publishers (as is also common ground) would for practical reasons still have to put prices upon their books. These marked prices we will call list prices, to distinguish them from maintainable net prices. Publishers would continue to sell to the trade at discounts off these list prices. Price maintenance having ceased, booksellers would be free to retail books at any price they chose. Although we think it probable that booksellers would sell most books at the publishers' list prices, particularly having regard to the long-established habit of the public to pay the price marked on a book, nevertheless we think that some competition in prices between retailers would certainly develop. We leave aside for the moment particular considerations relating to supplies to libraries. We do not think that serious price-cutting would be otherwise than occasional, but there would, we feel no doubt, be occasions when price-cutting would occur. Evidence which we have heard about conditions in Canada, where there is no retail price maintenance in respect of books, suggests the kind of thing that would be likely to occur here if retail price maintenance ceased. We had evidence from a witness who from 1946 till 1955 conducted a high-class stockholding book-seller's business in the English section of Montreal. His business there was considerably and adversely affected by price-cutting. From time to time at irregular and unpredictable intervals one or other of the department stores in Montreal, having a book depart-ment but not such as to rank as stockholding booksellers, would sell below list prices. The books affected would probably be either a standard series, such for example as Everyman's Library, or one or more current best sellers. The offer might be advertised either in the press or by means of a window display. Books which had been bought by the bookseller at a discount of 33⅓ per cent off list prices would commonly be offered in this way at 20 per cent to 25 per cent less than the list price. When this occurred the other booksellers in the town would reduce their own prices for the title or titles in question to the store's cut price or a little below it. Occasionally this process would eventually result in books being offered for sale below the price paid by the bookseller. Such price-cutting was a device to attract custom to the store. Books so dealt with were not surplus stocks, and the object of the operation was not to obtain an increased profit by higher sales resulting from the reduction in price. Something of this kind was liable to occur about twice a year. The process had a detrimental effect on the confidence of the public in the stability of book prices. It made booksellers much more cautious than they would otherwise have been in ordering for stock. [. . .]

The price reductions which resulted from price cutting did not, in the witness's opinion, in most cases increase the total sales of the book affected but merely shifted sales from one outlet to another. They occasioned, in his view, a contraction of the stocks of such stockholding booksellers as then existed in Canada and were responsible for the paucity of those booksellers.

We are satisfied that, if retail price maintenance ceased, the susceptibility of books to price competition – particularly those books which turn out to be comparatively easy to sell – would tend to reduce subscription orders and other orders for stock by stock-holding booksellers, who would become increasingly cautious about committing themselves to holding stock which in the event they might have to sell at little, if any, gross profit. [. . .]

Stockholding booksellers would be adversely affected in another way by an end of retail price maintenance for net books. We have already said that sales to public libraries form an important element in the business of at least some stockholding booksellers. At present they are protected against price competition from the specialist library suppliers by the terms of the Net Book Agreement, the Library Agreement and the Library Licence, which preclude the library suppliers from offering more than a 10 per cent discount. If the Net Book Agreement were abrogated library authorities would be free to negotiate such discounts as they could with their suppliers, and would certainly seek to do so. Indeed, even under existing circumstances, some library authorities press for better terms than the Library Agreement strictly permits. We had evidence from the county librarian of one of the largest county library authorities that to the knowledge of the principal officers concerned but (as we are surprised to hear) without reference to any committee to the county council one of the suppliers to his library had been induced to agree to supply books upon terms involving two recognized and material breaches of the conditions of the library's licence under the Library Agreement. Keen competition for library orders would certainly follow the cessation of price maintenance and stockholding booksellers, particularly smaller local bookshops, would be at a great disadvantage in competing with specialist library suppliers. Moreover, we think that there would be a tendency on the part of the library authorities to place increasingly large orders with library suppliers rather than to buy books through local booksellers. A number of public librarians gave evidence before us, most of whom said that in the event of the abrogation of the agreement they would expect their authorities to go to tender for their library supplies and services. [. . .]

[. . .] We accept the view put forward by the association that abrogation of the agreement would result in the loss by many stockholding booksellers of much, if not all, of their business with public libraries, which in some cases at present represents as much as about one-fifth of a bookseller's turnover.

The combined effect of price-cutting competition and the loss or reduction of library business would be that many stockholding booksellers would be driven out of business, and those so affected would not by any means necessarily be businesses which are inefficiently managed. Those who survived would hold less extensive and varied stock. Special order business, which is already a problem in the book trade, and in the case of the cheaper books is unprofitable to booksellers, would increase. Such library business as stockholding booksellers would retain would be likely to be business of the more difficult and less remunerative kind. Booksellers would inevitably press for larger discount margins from publishers to cover their increased costs and to allow them more room for manoeuvre in price competition. Publishers would find themselves compelled to offer increased discounts and list prices of books would rise accordingly. Moreover, the reduction in the number of stockholding bookshops and the contraction of the stocks of those which survive would, we think, result in a marked reduction in the number of subscription and stock orders received by publishers, even when allowance is made for increased orders from library suppliers resulting from their obtaining an increased share of library business. This would tend to produce a more cautious policy on the part of the publishers, resulting in smaller printing orders which would, for reasons already explained, tend to increase list prices further. The increase in list prices would exceed the amount required to cover merely the increase in book-sellers' discounts because of the increased cost of production per copy resulting from shorter printing runs and because of the increase in authors' royalties resulting from increased list prices. Royalty rates could not be easily adjusted because of the very large number of current contracts.

In those circumstances would books become dearer – not on the average but generally, if not universally?

To speak of the average price of books does not help in this connexion. An average of the prices of works on philosophy, history, science and theology and of novels is meaningless. A novel may sell for 15s and a book on philosophy for 50s. Arithmetically their average price is 32s 6d; but as the novel could not command that price and the philosophical work probably could not be produced for it, and since also the two books might well appeal to different people, the figure of 32s 6d is of no use whatever. So the question becomes: Would novels be dearer? Would works of scholarship be dearer? And so on throughout the whole range of published books.

The evidence of publishers who believe prices would be higher if the agreement came to an end rests largely, if not mainly, on calculations about the size of printing orders. In the absence of retail price maintenance, it is said, publishers would be reluctant to print as many copies at one time as they now do and a reduction in the number printed would necessarily increase the cost of producing each copy. It must be true that a smaller printing order would make each separate copy more expensive; it must also be true that beyond a certain price a particular book would not sell enough copies to repay the publisher's costs. These two forces exert pressure in opposite directions: in competitive conditions the publisher will succeed who is able to strike the right balance between the two pressures. The point of balance between freely

315

competitive forces pushing prices down and the cautious approach of publishers tending to put prices up would, no doubt, be different for different kinds of books.

We consider, however, that the upward thrust of the increased cost of production would be more urgent and effective than the reverse thrust of sales resistance. The public would pay higher prices for many, and probably most, books more readily than publishers would reduce their margins. The consequence would be a rise in the general level of list prices. This rise would not be uniform and, indeed, might not affect some books at all; but we consider that it would affect the large majority of books, and to a significant extent.

Library authorities and other large institutional purchasers would probably succeed in negotiating higher rates of discount than the 10 per cent permitted by the Library Agreement, but the new discounts would be off higher list prices. If, as we would expect, list prices were to increase, a proportionately much steeper rise in the rates of discounts would be necessary to produce the same retail prices. Thus if the list price of a book were to go up by no more than 10 per cent from, say, 10s to 11s, a library which had previously been able to buy such a book at a 10 per cent discount for 9s would require a discount of more than 18 per cent off the higher price if it were still to pay no more than 9s. If the list price of the book increased from 10s to 12s the new discount would have to be at 25 per cent. Even specialist library suppliers could not, we think, afford to give increased discounts of this magnitude without themselves obtaining increased discounts from publishers, which would contribute to the increase of list prices. Moreover, although the larger library authorities would probably be able to negotiate better than a 10 per cent discount, a possible consequence would be that smaller library authorities would have to be content with less than 10 per cent. The dislike of the Net Book and Library Agreements which was expressed by some (but not all) public librarians called as witnesses by the registrar was founded on a natural sense of frustration at being unable to make use of the strong bargaining position which their authorities as very large buyers of books would occupy if uncontrolled by such agreements. In our view however, these witnesses failed to appreciate the effect which an end of the Net Book Agreement would have on the general level of prices of books, and the effect of this upon the prices which library authorities would have to pay for books thereafter even with the benefit of freely negotiated discounts. We do not think that the net result of the abrogation of the agreement would be advantageous for any public libraries and certainly not those of smaller library authorities: on the contrary, we think that generally they would have to pay more for their books than under present circumstances, although in some cases not so much more as an ordinary member of the public would have to pay. [. . .]

The general contraction of the market for books in this country which would, we think, result from the reduction in the number of stockholding booksellers, and the general rise in the prices of books, would have a marked influence on publishers, not only when determining the size of their printing orders but also when deciding whether or not to publish marginal works. Self-interest would induce caution: it would, in our view, be unreasonable to suppose that in the new conditions publishers would be willing to publish as many books as they do now. Mr Fisher has impressed upon us by reference to various articles and reports of speeches contained in the documents submitted to the court that there are at present too many books published, although he could not induce any of the publisher witnesses to accept this view. Prolificacy has been recognized as an ineradicable characteristic of writers at least since the day of the author of Ecclesiastes and, no doubt, for much longer. The world might not be a worse place if some books went unpublished, but this court is not a censor of literary taste. It seems to us certain that, if the agreement ceased to operate, fewer books would be published, probably significantly fewer. The question we have to answer is, would the reduction in the number of new books be of such a character as to deprive the relevant public of specific and substantial advantages? There might be a fall in the number of titles classified by commercial libraries as light romance; there might also be a drop in the issue of romances which are not light in any sense of the word; but inevitably, we think, the effects would be most severe in the higher reaches of literature. The new author with something important to say, the scholar with new knowledge to communicate, the poet or the artist seeking to bring more beauty into the world, the philosopher desiring to increase understanding and illumine the minds of those who will read what he writes; these, we think, are the writers who would find it harder to get their work accepted for publication. In the more hazardous conditions that the termination of the agreement would create, many of them might not find publishers at all. We cannot doubt that this would deny to the reading public specific and substantial benefits. It is improbable that there are many 'mute inglorious Miltons' about nowadays, but there may be a few, and the likelihood of their muteness would be increased if publishers were constrained to be less adventurous.

It is, we think, probably true that the disappearance of the agreement would result in some fairly radical changes in the existing pattern of distribution in the book trade, and in this sense it may be true to say that the existence of the agreement inhibits experiments directed to finding new outlets for books; but it should not be thought that publishers are averse from trying to find and encourage new outlets for their products. On the contrary, they are active in these respects and there is nothing in the agreement to prevent this. Nor is there anything in the agreement to prevent innovation in methods of book production. As we have pointed out earlier, the publishing trade is a competitive one and individual publishers are consequently concerned to find and make use of more economical methods of production and more effective methods of distribution to win advantages over their competitors. No publisher would, of course, be likely to adopt a new outlet for his books of a kind or upon terms which he thought likely to damage his existing outlets, unless he considered that the advantage to be gained would outweigh the resulting disadvantages. There is, however, in our judgement. nothing in the agreement to fetter the free operation of competition amongst publishers in these respects. [. . .]

The association has satisfied us that abrogation of the agreement would produce . . . results . . . which can be summarily stated as (1) fewer and less-well-equipped stockholding bookshops, (2) more expensive books, (3) fewer published titles. In our judgement, each of these heads is sufficiently explicit, definable and distinct in character to justify the description 'specific', and the avoidance of any of these disadvantageous consequences can properly be termed a specific benefit or advantage. We are satisfied, moreover, that each of these consequences would arise in a sufficiently serious degree to make its avoidance a substantial advantage.[. . .]

On these grounds, we think that, subject to consideration of the balancing provision at the end of section 21, the association has succeeded in bringing itself within section 21 (1) (*b*).

The detriments to the public which the registrar says arise from the agreement are (1) that it reduces the incentive to publishers and booksellers to keep down costs, (2) that it deprives booksellers of opportunities to dispose of stock at their discretion and so increases their overheads and deprives the public of opportunities to buy more cheaply, (3) that by preventing price competition it keeps prices up, (4) that it prevents libraries and such-like purchasers from negotiating advantageous terms with their suppliers, (5) that by protecting margins it compels the public to pay more for books than would otherwise be the case.

Of these alleged detriments, (3) and (5) are in our view for reasons already given, generally speaking, the opposite of the truth. We have already dealt with (4). As to (1), we have already stated that the publishing trade is a competitive one and we think that publishers have a high degree of incentive to keep down costs. The profits earned by stockholding booksellers are modest and the margins upon which they trade are relatively small. They have a strong incentive for these reasons to keep their costs as low as possible. We do not think that the public suffers any detriment by reason of any such reduction of incentive as is suggested. As to (2), the agreement in standard condition (ii) offers booksellers a reasonable facility for disposing of stale stock but the evidence shows that it is only comparatively rarely used. The reason for this is that booksellers who want from time to time to dispose of slow-moving stock mostly prefer to use the National Book Sale. The National Book Sale in its present form is, as we appreciate, associated with retail price maintenance; but we doubt whether, if retail price maintenance were to cease, the public would obtain any better bargains than those they obtain through the National Book Sale, if indeed they would obtain as good ones. The unco-ordinated sale of stock at reduced prices would be one of the circumstances which we think, for reasons already explained, would contribute to the disinclination of stockholding booksellers to continue holding wide and varied stocks. Accordingly, we do not consider that it has been established that the public will suffer any detriment to be taken into account under the balancing provision. [. . .]

Declaration accordingly.

Newspaper Proprietors' and Retail Newsagents' Agreement
Law Reports: Restrictive Practices, vol. 2 (July 1961).

Diplock J. read the judgement of the Court:

With applications [to establish a retail newsagent business] coming in at the rate of 1,200 a year it is inherent in any control of this kind that decisions will be somewhat slap-dash and that injustices to individuals in the particular application of the general criteria will occur. If the necessity for control be once granted – and that is the question that we have to decide – it would not be right to suggest that the evidence leads us to any conclusion other than that the association has attempted with much expenditure of time to apply the control with an even hand, . . . Practices make it difficult to extract from the figures, which the association has furnished of numbers of applications and refusals, any very accurate picture of the extent to which the R.E.N.A. [Re-entrants and new applications] agreement has in fact restricted new entries into the retail newsagency trade. The only figures supplied relate to the last five years and to the London N.A.C. alone which apparently deals with about five-sixths of the total applications.

For the London committee during the last five years, the annual number of applications has averaged about 1,000, but these include an indeterminate number of re-applications probably of the order of 150 a year. New applications would appear to run at an average rate of about 850 a year, of which about 500 a year are granted, and the remainder refused. If all were granted, the number of new entries into the retail newsagency trade might be greater than it is at present by something of the order of between 350 and 450 a year including those dealt with by the Manchester committee or of the order of 1 per cent of the existing number of retail newsagents. We mention these figures because what seemed to us to be exaggerated fears were expressed and no doubt genuinely held by some witnesses in the retail newsagency trade as to the extent to which competition would increase if the R.E.N.A. restrictions were abolished.

Although there are a number of respects in which the method of administration of the R.E.N.A. scheme creates a sense of injustice, not always without reason, in the minds of unsuccessful applicants for permits, the evidence does not lead us to the conclusion that the public as a whole are not reasonably well served by the present methods of distribution of London daily newspapers. There appears to be throughout the country a reasonably efficient domiciliary delivery service at what is in most cases a modest delivery charge. [. . .]

But so far as the public is concerned this situation has existed for the last fifty years. There is no evidence that the delivery service was any worse before the federation was founded or that today any better service is provided to the public in the areas which have been developing since 1944 in which the R.E.N.A. scheme has effectively restricted the number of newsagents, than in those older areas in which the population is constant or falling which were already thickly supplied with retail newsagencies in 1944 and in which the R.E.N.A. scheme has probably had little effect upon their numbers. In general it would seem that the public needs in the distribution of London daily newspapers have been reasonably satisfied irrespective of whether the R.E.N.A. scheme, or its predecessors, has operated to restrict the number of selling outlets or not.

The test which we have to apply in the first instance is therefore: whether the association and federation have satisfied us that if the R.E.N.A. restrictions were abolished, the public, as purchasers of London daily newspapers, would be denied some specific and substantial benefit or advantage.

If the R.E.N.A. restrictions continue in operation, the distribution of London daily newspapers is, we think, likely to go on in much the same way as it has done since 1944. If the R.E.N.A. restrictions are removed, the association's and federation's forecasts of what would then happen are based upon two alternative, and at first sight contradictory, hypotheses. The first is that the abolition of the R.E.N.A. scheme would be followed by unrestricted entry into the retail newsagency trade of anyone desirous of selling London daily newspapers and free competition between retail newsagents; the second is that somehow or other the R.E.N.A. scheme would be replaced by restrictions upon entry into the retail newsagency trade more stringent and less advantageous to the public as purchasers of London daily newspapers than those currently imposed under the R.E.N.A. scheme.

This apparent contradiction, although it has inevitably presented forensic difficulties to the association and federation in the presentation of their case, is by no means fatal to their contentions. It is not illogical to argue, as they do, that one or other of two things must happen, and, that if either of them does happen, the public, as purchasers of London daily newspapers, will be deprived of advantages which they now enjoy and would have continued to enjoy if the R.E.N.A. scheme were not abolished.

We will, accordingly, consider first what the effect would be upon the public as purchasers of London daily newspapers if upon the abolition of the R.E.N.A. scheme, no restrictions, other than those due to ordinary economic forces operating under a competitive system, were imposed upon entry into the retail newsagency trade.

The federation's contention is that under such conditions the business of the individual retail newsagent would in general become so unprofitable that he would be unable or unwilling because of the inadequacy of the reward to continue delivery services to the extent that he now undertakes them, and that large numbers of the public would be deprived of the advantage of having their London daily newspapers delivered timeously at their residences; and that the retail newsagent, being unable to afford the risk of unsold copies, would fail to keep an adequate stock of newspapers and, in particular, of the less popular 'quality' newspapers for casual sales over the counter.

We are quite unable to accept this gloomy prophecy as to the results of exposing the retail newsagency trade to competitive conditions comparable to those which subsist without disaster either to the public or to the traders themselves in other branches of the retail trade.

The prophecy was based upon some calculations of the ultimate effect upon the annual net profits of six actual cases of retail newsagents of a decrease of 25 per cent in sales of all types of newspapers and periodicals and of all sales of other goods effected before 8.30 a.m. These calculations involve the assumptions: (1) that the total volume of sales of newspapers and periodicals throughout the country would remain constant notwithstanding any increase in selling points; (2) that the total number of retail newsagents would increase by $33\frac{1}{3}$ per cent; (3) that the sales of newspapers and periodicals by each existing newsagent would be reduced to the same ratio of his former sales as the total number of existing newsagents, that is 75 per cent; and (4) that all sales of other goods effected before 8.30 a.m. would be reduced in like ratio since they were made to customers who would not be attracted to the newsagent's shop if he did not sell newspapers and periodicals.

Each of these assumptions is, in our view, fallacious. No doubt sales of newspapers and periodicals go together, and it is reasonable to suppose that a person entering the retail news-agency trade in respect of London daily newspapers will desire to include among his wares other kinds of newspapers and periodicals; but we see no grounds for supposing that an increase in selling points would not lead to some increase in casual sales, although it may well be that in the case of London daily newspapers, of which about 70 per cent or more are now delivered to readers' residences, the increase would be small.

The assumption [2] that the total number of retail newsagents would increase by $33\frac{1}{3}$ per cent has no foundation in the evidence before us. Its origin appears to have been an observation in a report by an accountant called by the federation, who is also a newsagent, that if there were no economic factors operating under free competition to deter would-be entrants from embarking upon the retail newsagency trade, their numbers might increase by one-third or more. He drew attention, however, in his very helpful report, to various economic factors which would act as a deterrent to new entrants and expressed his own view both in his report and in his oral evidence that the increase in numbers of newsagents would be likely to be substantially less than $33\frac{1}{3}$ per cent. With this we agree. [. . .]

Very few newsagents indeed do not operate a delivery service to supplement their counter sales, although newsagents whose selling points were established before the R.E.N.A. scheme was inaugurated and who constitute probably 75 to 80 per cent of the total number of points in existence today are under no compulsion to do so. As the delivery boy also delivers periodicals and local papers at the same time as the London daily newspapers, such a service increases the newagent's sales of periodicals as well and, since deliveries are in response to firm orders, a delivery service ensures to the newsagent a steady trade free from the risk of loss on unsold copies. It would seem, indeed, that, except in the case of selling points in busy shopping centres, the provision of a delivery service by a retailer of London daily newspapers is necessary to make the newsagency pay. In a district which is already well served by newsagents' delivery services it is a slow and difficult task to attract satisfied customers away from their existing retailer and a would-be entrant to the trade in such a district would not be able to look forward to any rapid growth in this branch of his trade.

But even if a would-be entrant were undeterred by these considerations, he would have to find a wholesaler willing to supply him. We have already drawn attention to the rigid time schedule to which the wholesaler has to work, and to the added expense in which he is involved if he increases the number of dropping points, particularly if these are at any distance from existing dropping points. Furthermore, as the total circulation of London daily newspapers increases slowly, a wholesaler would have to consider whether the expansion of dropping points is likely to add to, or merely to diversify his total business. Operating on a gross profit margin of $10\frac{1}{2}$ per cent in the provinces and $14\frac{1}{4}$ per cent in London on the price of newspapers to retailers, viz. about 6d per quire of 26 copies in the provinces and about 8d per quire in the London area, it would not pay a wholesaler to increase his turnover by additional deliveries of small quantities of London daily newspapers at scattered delivery points, save at an additional delivery charge which would have to be met out of the gross profit margin of the retailer. An additional and potent factor is the necessity for the wholesaler to retain the goodwill of his existing customers. A wholesaler is unlikely to offend and risk losing the custom of an established retailer, unless he sees the prospect of larger sales to the newcomer, and this in itself, will tend to deter wholesalers from being eager to supply new selling points in close proximity to existing customers. Where, as in most parts of the country, there are competing wholesalers, the wholesaler who had no existing customers near the newcomer's premises would not be influenced by the same deterrent, but he is more affected by the additional expense of adding to his round a more distant dropping point. All these factors, which would operate under free competition, militate against the creation of new selling points except in areas where there is a shortage of existing newsagents, or where their inefficiency or inconvenient location indicates a substantial public demand for London daily newspapers for the newcomer to satisfy.

Turning now to the third assumption, it should hardly be necessary to point out that a new competitor in a retail trade does not either immediately or eventually take away the same proportion of the trade of each of his competitors. If the new entrant succeeds at all, and he may not, he does so because he provides a more efficient service to his customers if that expression be taken to include, as it should in the retail trade, geographical convenience of the selling point. If by providing a more efficient service he attracts customers from his competitors, this is merely the normal process whereby under competitive conditions less efficient tradesmen are eventually driven out of the trade and replaced by the more efficient to the advantage of the public as purchasers.

Finally, while no doubt sales of other goods, such as tobacco in particular, in the early morning are assisted by being combined with the sale of London daily newspapers, the assumption that up to as late as 8.30 a.m. they rise and fall in direct proportion to the sale of newspapers is a mere assumption unsupported by evidence.

We should not have thought it necessary to mention such elementary considerations, which are applicable in greater or less degree to competition in all forms of retail trade, were it not for the fact that many of the retail newsagents called as witnesses for the federation genuinely feared that the abolition of the R.E.N.A. scheme would be followed by a great influx of new entrants into the trade. Time and again reference was made to conditions thirty or forty years ago when, it was said, there was intensive competition from street newsvendors who bought and sold a few dozen newspapers to make 'beer money'. The great social and economic changes which have occurred since the 1920s make this comparison inapplicable. [. . .]

We are not, therefore, satisfied that if the R.E.N.A. restrictions were removed and entry into the trade in respect of London daily newspapers were left to the operation of the economic forces of free competition, the public, as purchasers of such newspapers, would be deprived of any specific or substantial benefit or advantage.

[. . .] The federation is a responsible body; its members are responsible and law-abiding citizens and the law, by which we do not doubt they will continue to abide, today includes the Restrictive Trade Practices Act, 1956. It is necessary, therefore, in considering the association's way of presenting its case in favour of the existing restrictions to consider the impact of the Act upon the sort of control of entry into the retail newsagency trade which the members of the association fear.

Mr Bagnall has suggested that it might be possible for the federation to devise restrictions which would fall outside the scope of Part 1 of the act, citing as an example an agreement which, while ostensibly dealing with the hours of work of workmen and so falling within the exclusion provided in section 7 (4) of the Act, would effectively prevent their employment in the distribution of London daily newspapers to traders who did not hold such permits or fulfil such other conditions as were specified in the agreement. Since this was only a hypothetical agreement, we are not called upon to express any concluded opinion upon it; it is sufficient to say that the likelihood of any such agreement's falling outside the scope of Part 1 of the Act seems to us so remote that we do not think that any practical importance should be attached to it. Furthermore, if an agreement in such a form were excluded from the provisions of Part 1 of the Act, it could be used to exclude from the provisions of the Act almost any restriction of any of the kinds specified in section 6. Even if we thought it probable – which we do not – that the Act, on its true construction, does enable persons to evade its provisions in the way in which Mr Bagnall has suggested, we should still have to look at the realities of the situation, and, in such an event, it is a not unreasonable assumption that Parliament would make the appropriate amendments to stop the gap so opened.

Declaration accordingly.

The registrar then applied for an injunction against the federation and its members.

Chocolate and Sugar Confectionery
(Reference under Resale Prices Act, 1964)[2]

1967 Weekly Law Reports, vol. 1, p. 117.

Megaw J. read the judgement of the Court:

The five respondents to this reference are Geo. Bassett & Co. Ltd, Cadbury Brothers Ltd, J. S. Fry & Sons Ltd (which is a subsidiary company of Cadbury), John Mackintosh & Sons Ltd, and Rowntree & Co. Ltd. They are suppliers who have registered claims for exemption under section 6 of the Resale Prices Act, 1964, in respect of certain goods. The definition of the goods in the notice of reference by which the Registrar initiated the proceedings is:

(1) Sugar confectionery, not containing cocoa; (2) Chocolate, chocolate goods and sugar confectionery containing cocoa in any proportion; (3) packs primarily of [the above-named] goods, but including another article capable of having an independent use; (4) chocolate coated biscuits or wafers in the form of bars or blocks individually wrapped.

The court has to decide, having heard and considered the evidence and arguments put forward by the registered suppliers and the registrar in a hearing lasting forty-three days, whether or not the goods in question shall be 'exempted goods for the purposes of [the] Act'. A decision that chocolate and sugar confectionery qualifies for exemption under the criteria laid down in section 5 (2) of the Act of 1964 would permit any supplier of those goods to continue hereafter, as has been done in the past by the registered suppliers and other manufacturers of confectionery, to *impose and enforce* resale price maintenance for its goods. [*Italics supplied.*]

Expressed simply, without going into detail or technicalities, that would mean that each of the registered suppliers, and any other supplier of confectionery, would be entitled to impose a legally enforceable condition, binding upon anyone who had notice of it, that the confectionery supplied should be sold by retail only at the particular prices specified by the manufacturer concerned. This contractual condition would be enforceable by injunction at the suit of a manufacturer, so that the authority of the courts would be available to ensure that no one retailing that manufacturer's con-

2. See Reading 8 for the economic analysis of resale price maintenance.

fectionery should sell below the price prescribed by the manufacturer. Each of the registered suppliers has said that, if the court orders that confectionery shall be 'exempted goods', it will enforce resale price maintenance for its confectionery products. What would be done by manufacturers other than the registered suppliers would be a matter for them. However, the registered suppliers, among them, account for such a substantial proportion of the confectionery trade in this country that it seems probable that, if each of them were to do what they say – and we accept that they would do so – there would continue to be, as there admittedly has been in the past, an effective system of maintained minimum resale prices in respect of the confectionery market.

On the other hand, the rejection by the court of the claim that confectionery should be 'exempted goods for the purposes of [the] Act' would render void any such contractual condition as we have mentioned above, and it would be unlawful for any such condition to be included in any future contract for the sale of confectionery. It would continue to be open to any supplier to prescribe *maximum* prices or to notify *recommended* prices. We again accept, on the evidence, that none of the registered suppliers would prescribe maximum prices, but that each of them would publish recommended prices. A recommended price, however, would be in no way binding or enforceable. Any retailer would be free to ignore it, and no sanction could be imposed upon him if he did ignore it. [*Italics supplied.*]

Section 5 (1) gives the court power to order that goods of any class shall be exempted goods for the purposes of the Act of 1964. Section 5 (2) is all important. It prescribes the criteria by which the court is to decide whether or not to grant exemption. It provides that an order directing that goods shall be exempted goods may be made (and it is not disputed that 'may' here means 'shall').

if it appears to the court that in default of a system of maintained minimum resale prices applicable to those goods – (*a*) the *quality* of the goods available for sale, or the *varieties* of the goods so available, would be substantially reduced to the detriment of the public as consumers or users of those goods; or (*b*) the *number of establishments* in which the goods are sold by retail would be substantially reduced to the detriment of the public as such consumers or users; or (*c*) the *prices* at which the goods are sold by retail would in general and in the long run be *increased* to the detriment of the public as such consumers or users; or (*d*) the goods would be sold by retail under conditions likely to cause *danger to health* in consequence of their misuse by the public as such consumers or users; or (*e*) any *necessary services* actually provided in connexion with or after the sale of the goods by retail would cease to be so provided or would be substantially reduced to the detriment of the public as such consumers or users, and in any such case the resulting detriment to the public as consumers or users of the goods in question would outweigh any detriment to them as such consumers or users (whether by the restriction of competition or otherwise) resulting from the maintenance of minimum resale prices in respect of the goods. (*Italics supplied.*)

The burden of establishing a case for exemption rests on the respondents. The standard of proof required on all issues is that of the balance of probability.

The *registered suppliers* do not rely upon paragraph (*d*) of subsection (2), but they do rely on each of the other paragraphs, and say that the abolition of resale price maintenance would produce a detriment to the public as consumers of confectionery under each of paragraphs (*a*), (*b*), (*c*) and (*e*). So far as paragraph (*a*) is concerned, they have not at the hearing asserted that there would be any substantial reduction of quality; their evidence and submissions under that paragraph have been confined to an assertion of a probable substantial reduction in the varieties of goods available. They assert also that there would be no detriment to the public arising from the retention of resale price maintenance, and, that, therefore, the concluding part of the subsection does not operate.

The *registrar* denies that the abrogation of resale price maintenance in this industry would produce the conditions described in paragraphs (*a*), (*b*), (*c*) or (*e*); he also contends that, if such conditions would arise in default of a system of resale price maintenance in respect of any of the paragraphs, the conditions thus produced would not be to the detriment of the public as consumers of confectionery; and, finally, the registrar, looking at the concluding part of the subsection, asserts that the continuation of resale price maintenance, resulting as he says it would in higher retail prices than would exist if resale price maintenance were abolished,

329

is a clear detriment to the public as consumers. It would, he contends, outweigh the sum of the detriments, if any, to the public which the registered suppliers might have established as being likely to arise, under paragraphs (a), (b) and (e), if resale price maintenance were abolished. This, it was made clear in the final speech of counsel for the registrar, was the only detriment on which he relied in this reference as being relevant under the concluding part of subsection (2).

Section 5 (4) defines 'necessary services', and then goes on to provide that 'consumers' and 'users' include persons consuming or using the goods for the purpose or in the course of trade or business or for public purposes.

We should make it clear that it has not been suggested that the court in reaching its decision in this reference can or should take into account any detriment or hardship or misfortune which might afflict any supplier of or dealer in confectionery as the result of the abolition of resale price maintenance, except in so far as such a consequence would in turn produce some detriment to retail purchasers of confectionery. It follows that, if it were clear on the evidence, for example, that some shopkeepers were likely to be driven out of business by the abolition of resale price maintenance on confectionery, or if it were clear that their level of income was likely to be reduced even to the point of producing in some instances, perhaps, personal hardship and financial loss, that would not be a matter which the court is permitted to take into account, except only to the extent that such hardship to the shopkeepers would in its turn result in detriment to retail purchasers of confectionery. The same applies to manufacturers and wholesalers. We can consider any adverse effects on them only if and in so far as those effects have a bearing on detriments to the retail purchaser.

How do the registered suppliers put their case under section 5 (2) of the Act of 1964? We cannot do better than to state it in the words used by their first and principal witness, Mr Robert Nelstrop Wadsworth, who is a managing director of Cadbury Brothers Ltd. He summarized his views clearly and succinctly in a supplemental proof of evidence. We shall quote that summary, which was confirmed and amplified by Mr Wadsworth in the witness-box, omitting merely certain references therein to paragraphs of his earlier proof in which he had dealt more fully with the various points. :

A (1) In the absence of resale price maintenance on confectionery some retailers will cut prices. Price cutting will not be confined to supermarkets, but they will start the cutting. Price cutting in these shops will be of two types: (1) regular cuts of a small number of leading lines, for example, $\frac{1}{2}$ lb Cadbury's dairy milk chocolate, and (2) special cuts lasting for not more than one to two weeks on a succession of leading lines including those in (1), some of which may be deep cuts. In general, supermarkets will sell other lines at manufacturers' recommended prices particularly because a substantial part of the trade is at round prices of 3d, 6d, and 1s. The overall effect on the price level of confectionery sold in supermarkets will, therefore, be less than the impression created by the price cuts made.

A (2) A trader who stocks a wide variety of products is in a better position to cut prices on a particular product than is a trader who specializes in that produce, because he can expect to draw people into his shop to buy other goods.

A (3) Overall demand for confectionery is static. Total demand is not significantly price or income elastic in our affluent society. Thus, any increase in sales by any one class of distributor will be at the expense of the sales of other distributors.

A (4) The outlets most seriously affected will be the large and medium sweet shops (particularly those near supermarkets), which offer a wide variety of confectionery and act as the shop 'window' for the industry. The trade of such sweet shops will also be adversely affected by the impression created by supermarket's price cuts. Widespread closure of such shops would: (1) result in a fall of total consumption because of the loss of many sales which are made on impulse or are otherwise dependent upon the existence of these shops, and (2) result in a fall in variety available because these are the distributors who stock the variety and upon whom manufacturers depend for its distribution.

A (5) Cadbury, and we believe other manufacturers, will not acquiesce in the disappearance of important outlets for confectionery and will seek to increase the percentage margin realized by sweet shops, so that their businesses remain viable on a smaller turnover. We consider that our trade will be harmed less by our increasing trade margins (or other display incentives) to the extent of, say, 2–3 per cent of consumer prices, than by the demise of outlets which this extra margin might help to save. I believe that in this affluent society the consumer would be prepared to pay and that the effect on the total demand would be relatively small.

A (6) It may be thought that this increased margin will only encourage the supermarket to cut to a greater extent and, therefore, fail in its purpose; but two points must be remembered: (1) retailer price cutting is relative, and the supermarket is anxious mainly to establish the impression of a differential between its prices and those of traders in general, and (2) competition at the retailer level is imperfect and many shops will be able to realize the increased margin.

A (7) The long term position which I envisage is, therefore, one in which: (1) a larger proportion of confectionery sales is sold through supermarkets. There will be a considerable expansion of special discounts and trade deals; I believe that in the final event the costs of these discounts are passed on to the consumer; (2) manufacturers' recommended prices will be higher than they would otherwise be. A narrow range of lines will be price cut, but in general confectionery will be sold at those higher recommended prices. On average prices will be higher than they would otherwise be; (3) there will be some reduction in the number of outlets and in the variety of confectionery available since the higher margins will not be sufficient to maintain all the present day outlets in business; (4) there will be a reduction in the sales and availability of seasonal lines.

A (8) I have considered what would be the position if manufacturers did not increase realizable margins, so that the court may be able to see the seriousness to the industry of those consequences. However, I do not believe that manufacturers will allow this situation to occur.

A (9) The Resale Prices Act (of 1964) provides for exceptions to the general abolition of resale price maintenance. We do not support resale price maintenance as a generality, and do not practise it for our grocery lines. However, we believe that confectionery is different from grocery products. I have given the reasons why I *forecast* that the consumer of confectionery would suffer detriment as a result of higher average consumer prices in the long run, fewer retail outlets, and a reduction in variety, all of which are 'gateways' provided for in the Act. I have had to forecast because no other method is available.

A (10) Facts are, of course, preferable to forecasts and I can only conclude by reminding the court that in the present situation with resale price maintenance: (1) The industry is competitive and efficient, and (2) that we undermine this satisfactory situation at our peril and to the detriment of the consumer.

Thus the registered suppliers' case, primarily and essentially and in each of its aspects, depends upon an assessment of the extent to which the abolition of resale price maintenance in this industry would be likely to result in the disappearance of outlets. [. . .]

We, therefore, propose to consider first, and express our conclusion upon, this topic. Mr Wadsworth, with the assistance of Mr David John Edward Brown, market research manager of Cadbury Brothers Ltd, put before the court an estimate of the effect of abolition of resale price maintenance upon the industry, with particular reference to the shifts which would be likely to occur in the amount of trade in confectionery as between different classes and types of retail outlets. They produced a table which showed the existing pattern, the pattern which they foresaw would be produced about the beginning of 1968, if resale price maintenance were to be abolished in July 1967, and the pattern which they thought would be found to exist in or about 1972 on the assumption that no 'rescue operation', to preserve sweet shops in being, had been undertaken meanwhile by the manufacturers.

The outlets which Mr Wadsworth thought would be most seriously affected, although others would also be affected, are those which he himself describes as 'the large and medium sweet shops (particularly those near supermarkets)'. These have also been described as 'the High Street confectioners' or 'the specialist confectioners in the High Street'. The description includes both independently owned shops and establishments which are part of a chain of such shops. Very few of these shops are 'specialist' in the sense that they sell nothing but confectionery. Almost all of them have some other activities: for example, usually they sell also tobacco and cigarettes; some of them sell newspapers and magazines; some of them sell toys and greetings cards, and so on. A phrase which has been much used throughout the case is 'C.T.N.' meaning 'confectioner, tobacconist, newspapers'. The proportions of turnover of individual C.T.N.s as between the various commodities, are of the widest possible range. There has been difficulty, throughout some of the evidence, in offering any accurate assessment of the extent to which the turnover or profit of any particular sub-classification of C.T.N.s, or, indeed, in some instances of individual C.T.N. shops, is related to sales of confectionery or of tobacco or of other commodities. [. . .]

Mr Brown produced an estimate of the numbers of the existing outlets selling confectionery, classified into various types, and of the percentage of the value of total sales which each type at present holds. This estimate can be accepted as being the best that can be made, and as reasonably accurate. It shows that the total number of outlets is of the order of 250,000. Supermarkets number 2,625 with $3\frac{1}{2}$ per cent of the sales; other self-service grocers are 17,400 with $5\frac{1}{2}$ per cent; counter-service grocers are somewhere between 100,000 and 110,000 with 13 per cent; other food retailers number 19,250, with 6 per cent; variety and department stores, 1,570, with 10 per cent; other non-food outlets, 8,080 with 2 per cent; and 'non-shop' outlets (that is, cinemas, etc.) say, 39,500, with 12 per cent. That leaves the sweet shops (substantially the C.T.N.s) with a total of 48 per cent, in value, of the sales.

We do not propose to refer in detail to the forecasts which Mr Wadsworth made as to the probable shift of trade between the various classes of outlet, following on the abolition of resale price maintenance in the confectionery industry. It is sufficient to say that they contemplate a very large movement of trade away from the sweet shops, and particularly from the large and medium sweet shops, which would be principally 'the High Street confectioners', to the supermarkets and the self-service grocers, and, in a lesser degree, to the department stores. [. . .]

[. . .] But on our assessment of all the evidence we cannot accept their conclusions, or their assumptions, whichever be the correct word. In particular, we find ourselves unable to accept, having due regard to the particular features of this industry, that there is likely to be anything like as substantial a switch of trade from the so-called 'specialist sweet shops' to the supermarkets and self-service grocers as is foreseen by Mr Wadsworth; nor do we think that there is a likelihood that there would be a fall in the total consumption of confectionery as a result of the abolition of resale price maintenance. If anything, we think that there would be some small increase.

It is agreed on all sides that, if resale price maintenance is abolished, the supermarkets will cut prices of confectionery, particularly of the leading brands. This is a necessary consequence of the general policy of supermarkets of conveying to the public the impression that commodities can be bought more cheaply in their shops than in those of their rivals, whether other super-markets or shops of other types. For a period, which might well extend until after next Christmas, cut-price confectionery would be news. Supermarkets would be likely to make a strong feature of it, as a means of drawing customers into their stores. Some prices would probably be drastically cut: possibly in some instances down to the trade price. But that period would pass. In passing it might, well have made some sweet shops more vulnerable; but it is not suggested that there would be any substantial closure of sweet shops during that period. What really matters for this purpose is the longer term prospects after the initial excitement has died down. [. . .]

The best forecast we can make, on the whole of the evidence before us, and taking into account the effect of the probable slight increase of trade margins which we are about to mention, is that by 1972 the fall in numbers of the High Street confectioners, as a consequence of the abolition of resale price maintenance, would be of the order of 10 per cent of their existing number. There might also be some reduction in the number of other sweet shops, but this would be much smaller in proportion to their present number and of little significance in relation to any issue which we have to consider. [. . .]

The manufacturers individually would come under some additional pressure, over and above that which no doubt is continually present, to increase trade margins, so as to compen-sate retailers for their sales of some lines of confectionery below the recommended prices in the new competitive conditions. It may well be that such pressure would come from supermarkets also. In the course of time, we think that there would probably be some slight increase in trade margins, and that increase, together with at least a part of the additional costs which the manufacturers would have to bear in arranging for 'promotions' of their goods by super-markets and others, would be added to the recommended prices. Of course, in the circumstances of no resale price main-tenance, an increase of recommended prices does not necessarily mean an increase of the price paid by the retail purchaser or in the margin realized by the retailer. Price competition between retailers, unknown in the confectionery trade for many years, may be expected to put some curb on attempts to raise prices.

We find ourselves unable to hold, on the evidence before us, that the abolition of resale price maintenance is likely to make any appreciable or predictable difference one way or the other to the prices at which confectionery would be sold by retail in general and in the long run. In the early days, there is no doubt much confectionery would be sold at lower prices than would have been the case if resale price maintenance continued; but the position would ultimately stabilize, and the general effect on retail prices overall would then, we think, be likely to be pretty evenly balanced. Of course, that does not mean that the prices will remain at their present level, with or without resale price maintenance. That is something which will depend on other factors altogether.

It follows from the conclusion which we have just expressed that the registered suppliers fail to make out their case under paragraph (c) of section 5 (2); and also that they are not faced with having to overcome the only countervailing general detriment alleged by the registrar as arising from the continuance of resale price maintenance.

It remains, therefore, to consider the registered suppliers' case under paragraphs (a), (b) and (e). Each of these, as we have said, essentially depends on our conclusion as to the disappearance of outlets.

We find ourselves quite unable to hold that the disappearance of outlets which we foresee as probable would be likely to result in a substantial reduction in the varieties of confectionery available, to the detriment of the public as consumers; or that the probable reduction of the numbers of establishments could properly, in the circumstances, be regarded as either substantial or detrimental to the public; or that there would be any substantial reduction to the detriment of the public of any 'necessary services', assuming, as solely for the purposes of this reference we are prepared to do, that the phrase 'necessary services', as defined in section 5 (4) of the Act, can be construed to include the keeping of good stocks of confectionery, the offering of good display to entice customers, and the undertaking of sales which involve the weighing out of confectionery from jars or boxes and the putting of it into bags for the customer.

The evidence which we have heard, taken as a whole, has led

us firmly to the conclusion that, so far as the public is concerned, such reduction as we foresee to be probable in the number and class and location of the existing confectionery outlets would not appreciably affect the convenience of the public at all. The outlets, which would remain, would be ample in all respect to meet the needs and convenience of the public, as they are now met.

Accordingly, the registered suppliers fail to make out their case under section 5 (2). The court will make an order declaring that it refuses to exempt the classes of goods referred to it for the purposes of the Act of 1964.

Order accordingly.

14 The British Monopolies Commission

Recommendations to a Government

Industrial Gases (December 1956)

Excerpts from Chapter 9 on 'Conclusions and Recommendations'

238. We are concerned with a number of 'monopoly' suppliers, of which [British Oxygen Company] is much the most important in relation to the gases in our reference. In the case of oxygen and dissolved acetylene, B.O.C.'s, monopoly is almost complete, and we deal first with these gases.

239. We have to consider whether the 'conditions' to which the Act applies operate or may be expected to operate against the public interest, and also whether any 'things done' by B.O.C. as a result of or for the purpose of preserving those conditions operate or may be expected to operate against the public interest. It is difficult in a case of this kind to draw a clear distinction between the effects of the conditions and the effects of 'things done' as a result of or in order to preserve the conditions. In the analysis which follows we consider these matters together, expressing our conclusions and making our recommendations on the various 'things done' as they arise and leaving our conclusion on the 'conditions' to the end.

240. There are possible dangers in the control by one supplier of so large a proportion of the market for two essential commodities such as oxygen and dissolved acetylene. It is in a position to determine within wide limits the profit which it wishes to make, and it can then fix its prices in relation to costs at a level which will normally ensure to it the return which it desires. Even if the powers which such a monopoly possesses are at a given time exercised with moderation, the risk will always remain that at some time in the future it may use its position to make excessive profits at the expense of the consumer. There is in addition the danger that the absence of competition may lead to lack of enterprise and inefficiency which in turn may give rise to unnecessarily high prices.

We recognize however, that in this industry there may be some substantial economies in operating as a monopoly whether on a national or a local basis. We understand that somewhat similar conditions prevail in some other countries, including France where there is something approaching a national monopoly, and Holland where there are a number of regional monopolies.

The Efficiency of B.O.C.

241. A point of great importance is whether because it is a monopoly B.O.C. is operated less efficiently than would be the case if there were more competition and whether, in consequence, the public suffers because resources are wasted, or because of deficiencies in the service rendered by B.O.C. [But we] . . . have had very few complaints from amongst B.O.C.'s many thousands of customers. [. . .]

243. Subject to what is said in the following paragraphs, we have no evidence to suggest that the efficiency, technical and otherwise, of B.O.C. falls below the standard which might reasonably be expected of a company of its standing and resources.

B.O.C.'s Technical Services

244. We have considered the technical services provided by B.O.C. to its customers. They are comprehensive, and we have had no complaint about them, but the cost of providing these services has to be covered in the selling price of oxygen and dissolved acetylene, and we have asked ourselves whether many consumers might not in fact be paying for services which they had little, if any, occasion to use. We think that in so far as the extent of the use made of the services by different classes of consumers can be ascertained, it should be reflected in the prices charged to each class. This point is covered by the recommendations which we make later (paragraphs 272 to 276) on the revision of B.O.C.'s price scales.

Research and Development

245. In view of its almost complete monopoly a heavy responsibility falls upon B.O.C. to ensure that the full requirements of industry,

of the hospitals and of the armed services will continue to be met and that in the field of research the United Kingdom will at least keep pace with other countries.

So far as development is concerned, B.O.C. has explained to us its plans over the next few years. These seem to be on a scale adequate to ensure that during, say, the next five years B.O.C. will be able in any reasonable expectation to supply in full the demands of the United Kingdom. B.O.C. now devoted $2\frac{1}{2}$ per cent of its income to research, but we cannot determine the proportion which is spent on the reference gases. It was only immediately after the war that a special research department was set up, and it will be seen from Chapter 4 that in its long history B.O.C. has *not* been responsible for the discovery of any of the successive important new processes for the production and distribution of oxygen. [*Italics supplied.*] Indeed almost all these were first developed abroad and B.O.C.'s part has been to acquire the necessary patent rights or licences and exploit them in this country. Our impression is that at least until recently most of the research work done by B.O.C. has related either to improvements in existing plant and machinery or to research into possible uses for the gases with a view to increasing sales. On such evidence as is available to us, it seems that rapid technical progress is still being made abroad, notably in the U.S.A. and Germany. In view of the monopoly position, it will depend entirely on B.O.C. whether this country keeps abreast of overseas manufacturers or whether we lag behind and remain dependent on them for improved methods of production and distribution. We do not find it possible, . . . to reach a definite conclusion as to whether the present research activities are adequate. We attach great importance, however, to a substantial effort by B.O.C. in the field of research.

Steps taken by B.O.C. to Develop and Preserve its Monopoly

246. We next consider:

(*a*) Whether B.O.C. has tried to obtain exclusive control over the provision of plant and equipment to other suppliers or to consumers who might wish to make their own gas.

(*b*) The steps taken by B.O.C. both to acquire other suppliers and to obtain plants worked by consumers.

(*c*) The use which B.O.C. has made of fighting companies.

(*d*) The making of agreements under which B.O.C. has the exclusive right to supply certain customers.

Control over Plant and Equipment

247. The steps by which B.O.C. has at various periods obtained control over the distribution of oxygen plant are described in paragraphs 39 and 40, and 115 to 123. As will have been seen from B.O.C.'s own explanation of these developments (see paragraphs 197 and 200), B.O.C. denies that it has ever been its policy to secure complete control in the oxygen field. According to B.O.C. there has for many years been little or no demand for customer plant for the production of oxygen, because it has been cheaper and more efficient to obtain the oxygen itself from B.O.C. It is claimed that this situation only began to change recently when the introduction of tonnage plants became possible and that it is for this reason that B.O.C. has not sold any oxygen-producing plant under the various agencies which it has acquired. B.O.C. has also stated that at the present time plant could be supplied in this country by any one of five companies:

The Butterley Company Ltd
Société L'Air Liquide (of France)
Air Products Inc. (of U.S.A.)
British Oxygen Linde Ltd
Messer G.m.b.H. (of Germany) (through Oxhycarbon Ltd)

Of these five, however, Oxhycarbon Ltd, which holds the Messer agency, is a wholly-owned subsidiary of B.O.C.; and British Oxygen Linde Ltd, which is half-owned by B.O.C., is in effect the agent for the German Linde plant. B.O.C. has told us in another connexion that it is very unlikely that either Linde of Germany or B.O.C. itself would quote in competition with each other or with their subsidiary. L'Air Liquide has told us that in the United Kingdom, owing to import duty and transport costs of roughly 30 per cent, it is only possible in 'very exceptional cases to compete with British manufacturers'. Butterley is the licensee in the United Kingdom for Air Products Inc, and for this purpose these two companies can be regarded as a single source of supply. The fact, therefore, appears to be that there is only one manufacturer of oxygen plant – Butterley – which is both independent of B.O.C. and able in practice to compete in the supply of plant. There is no evidence that B.O.C. exercises any control over the provision of plant for producing dissolved acetylene, or over the supply of customer generating plant for this gas. The capital cost of each is less than that of oxygen plant, and there are now no limitations on production due to patents.

248. The conclusion that we draw from the facts set out in Chapters 3 and 5 is that in the past B.O.C. has deliberately sought to control the provision of oxygen plant to others in order to maintain its monopoly in the supply of oxygen, and that it has had a considerable degree of success in doing so. On the evidence provided by statements of policy contained in B.O.C.'s Board minutes and internal memoranda (in particular the policy outlined in the memorandum dated 3 December 1953, which is quoted in paragraph 131 and of which we have seen no later modification), we are satisfied that B.O.C. is still pursuing this policy and that it is likely to continue to do so, although the extent to which it may be able to retain control may be reduced by two factors: the competition offered by Butterley, and the development of the new-style tonnage plants, which may make it more attractive to large users to produce oxygen for their own consumption. We consider that in so far as this policy is pursued with success this operates and may be expected to operate against the public interest since it may discourage or prevent the acquisition of oxygen plant by other producers, including consumers who might produce oxygen for their own use as well as producers who might supply others. The public may thus be deprived of the advantages of alternative sources of supply and such competition in service, technical development and price as this might produce. [. . .]

The Taking over of other Producers

250. We have also considered the evidence relating to the taking over of other suppliers of oxygen and dissolved acetylene and of the oxygen and dissolved acetylene plants of firms which formerly produced these gases for their own use. The evidence set out in paragraphs 31 to 37 and 41 to 44 leaves us in no doubt that it has

been B.O.C.'s consistent policy, wherever possible, to take over or to buy out other producers of oxygen and dissolved acetylene and that it has done this primarily, though not solely, in order to extend and preserve its own monopoly in the supply of these gases. There is, however, no evidence that B.O.C. is at present seeking to eliminate the small amount of competition that remains.

The Use of Fighting Companies

251. The evidence summarized in paragraph 52 shows that B.O.C. made use of Industrial Gases (Scotland) Ltd as a fighting company and that the activities of this company probably contributed towards the withdrawal of Saturn from the Glasgow area. B.O.C.'s ownership of this company and of two other companies, British Industrial Gases Ltd and Oxhycarbon Ltd, had still not been publicly acknowledged when the present inquiry started, and they continued to trade ostensibly in competition with B.O.C. It was only in 1955, in B.O.C.'s Report and Statement of Accounts for the year ended 31 December 1954 that their relationship to B.O.C. was disclosed, though we do not doubt that, as B.O.C. told us, it was known to some customers. We think that the use of Industrial Gases (Scotland) Ltd as a fighting company and the concealment of the ownership of all three were 'things done' by B.O.C. in order to preserve its 'monopoly'. It is in our view contrary to the public interest that a monopoly such as B.O.C. should take advantage of its position to eliminate competitors by making local and selective reductions in prices instead of extending to all consumers the benefits of any price reductions which may be possible. But since B.O.C.'s ownership of these companies has now been made public we need only recommend that, in meeting any competition which may arise in future, B.O.C. should refrain from making use of fighting companies.

Exclusivity Terms in Contracts

252. Certain terms of the standard contract which B.O.C. enters into with the majority of its larger customers make exclusive buying a condition of supply. These provisions are set out in paragraph 76. It will be seen that they applied only to 1,575 out of a total of 99,438 customers in 1954, and the main lines of the contract follow normal business practice. We have considered

whether the requirement of exclusive dealing is an unreasonable limitation upon the right of the consumer to buy where he pleases. The contract provides that the consumer must take from B.O.C. his total requirements of the named gases for which prices are stated (in the case of oxygen, whether in liquid or gaseous form), unless it is expressly agreed in writing to the contrary. It also lays down that B.O.C. will provide and maintain any necessary apparatus, on terms to be agreed, and that the consumer will use this apparatus only in conjunction with gas supplied by B.O.C. B.O.C. told us that it normally installed and maintained the apparatus free of charge and that it would not in practice enforce the requirement that a consumer must take his total supplies of gas from itself, but that it could not reasonably be expected to provide free apparatus and allow that apparatus to be used for the supply of gas by some other concern. We have come across one case in which the exclusivity clause in the contract has been expressly modified and a few where it seemed to be ignored, but it is clear that many customers do not question it. We do not object to the rule that any apparatus supplied free by B.O.C. must be used only in conjunction with gas supplied by B.O.C., but the requirement that the consumer must take from B.O.C. his total requirements of the named gases, including in some cases gas for which the apparatus is not used at all, seems to us to be too wide. Its purpose can only be to preserve B.O.C.'s monopoly position, and in our view it limits the customer's freedom of choice to an extent which is contrary to the public interest. A consumer ought not to be forced to use B.O.C. apparatus in order to obtain supplies of gas, and if he does choose to use B.O.C. apparatus for one gas he ought not, as a consequence, to be compelled to take from B.O.C. other gases or gas supplied in a form which permits it to be used without the apparatus. The principles to be applied should, we consider, be that B.O.C. should give the customer a free choice as to whether he buys and maintains the apparatus himself, whether he hires it from B.O.C. and maintains it himself, or whether he accepts B.O.C.'s offer to provide and maintain it free of charge. If he chooses to buy or hire the apparatus, B.O.C. should be prepared to sell or hire it to him at a reasonable price or rental and still to supply him on reasonable terms with any gas which he wishes to buy from B.O.C., while at the same time he remains free to buy from other sources if he so wishes. If the customer chooses free installation and maintenance by B.O.C. he may reasonably be required to take from B.O.C. such minimum quantity of gas as would justify the cost of installation and maintenance, and to use the B.O.C. apparatus only with B.O.C. gas, but he should not be compelled to take from B.O.C. his total requirements of gas if these exceed that minimum. We recommend that the exclusivity clause in B.O.C.'s contracts be amended accordingly. [. . .]

Price Policy: B.O.C.'s Profits

258. In considering the conduct of any monopoly, and particularly one as comprehensive as B.O.C., considerable importance attaches to the price policy which it follows. This raises a number of questions, the first of which is whether B.O.C. has taken advantage of its position to make profits which are unjustifiably high. It will have been seen from Chapter 6 that on the reference gases taken together, in 1952 and 1954, B.O.C. made a profit of 23 to 24 per cent on capital employed, the capital being calculated on an historical cost basis. In 1939 the rate for gases was 25 per cent, and B.O.C. has told us that it regards 23 to 25 per cent on capital employed (using the historical basis) as a reasonable return, and about the rate of profit which it requires in order to support its modernization and research programme and to enable it to raise additional money on the market. From 1945 to 1951, B.O.C. paid a dividend of 20 per cent of its ordinary capital and in the latter year made a bonus issue equal to 50 per cent of its existing ordinary stock. From 1952 to 1954 the dividend was 15 per cent (which was equivalent to $22\frac{1}{2}$ per cent on the capital before the bonus issue), and in 1954 this was about 5 per cent on its capital employed (on an historical cost basis). In 1955, B.O.C. raised £8 million of new capital by offering £1 units for 50s, which at the rate of dividend of 15 per cent would give a return to the stockholder of 6 per cent on his outlay. Thus, taking together the existing and the new capital, B.O.C. will in future need between 5 and 6 per cent on capital employed to continue to pay dividends at the existing level. To give shareholders 6 per cent at present requires a profit before taxation of just over 9 per cent from which

to pay it. Even, therefore, if B.O.C.'s contention that profit on capital employed should be calculated on a replacement basis were to be accepted, it will be seen that a substantial part of B.O.C.'s profits would remain after giving this return to the stockholders.

259. As far as its business in oxygen and dissolved acetylene is concerned, B.O.C. enjoys to a very high degree the advantages of a monopoly position. It has little to fear from competition, it is dealing with essential commodities, the cost of which is a small item in the costs of most of its customers, and it is in a position to make a very close assessment of its share of the available market. The element of risk in its operations is confined mainly to the risks involved in changes in the general level of industrial activity. Its replacement requirements are no more than normal in industry, while it can operate with lower reserves than companies which have to take a substantial measure of risk. In these respects its position is closely parallel to that of some of the recognized public utility concerns before nationalization. We are bound to confine our attention to those gases which are included in our terms of reference but in respect of its business in oxygen and dissolved acetylene it should be in a position to raise money on more favourable terms than if it were bearing normal trading risks. It seems to us indeed that it should be able to obtain a considerable part of the capital required for the expansion of its business from debentures and similar forms of borrowing which would require a somewhat lower rate of interest. In order to maintain and develop its business, a monopoly company in B.O.C.'s position does not, therefore, need to earn the same return on capital as a company in a competitive industry.

260. According to these statistics the weighted average profits during the years 1952 to 1954 in each of the 17 industry groups which are mainly manufacturing groups, were lower than those made by B.O.C. (23 to 24 per cent) except in the motors, cycles and aircraft group in 1953 and 1954, with average profit rates of respectively 25 and 27 per cent, and the newspapers, paper and printing group in 1954 only, with an average profit rate of 25 per cent. In the other manufacturing groups the average ranged from 11 per cent to 20 per cent in 1954, and the profit rates of B.O.C. in 1952 to 1954 were roughly from one-third to one-half

higher than the weighted average for all manufacturing industries. It is true of course that, as we have found in our own inquiries, there are substantial variations of profit rate as between different firms in the same industry. [. . .]

261. B.O.C. differs from firms which are in competitive industries in the extent to which it is able to set its prices at whatever levels suit it best. We note that both before and since the war B.O.C. has aimed at and secured profits in the region of 23 to 25 per cent on capital employed and that even in 1952 to 1954, which were prosperous years for industry generally, its profits were well above the average level in manufacturing industry. After making full allowance for the seller's market which has prevailed during most of the post-war period we consider that B.O.C.'s profits have been unjustifiably high for an almost complete monopoly facing a limited financial risk.

B.O.C.'s Prices

262. It follows that the prices charged by B.O.C. for oxygen and dissolved acetylene are too high. While it may be that some economies could be made, we have no evidence upon which we could base any general finding that B.O.C.'s costs are too high, but to the extent that B.O.C.'s profits are too high there is scope for reduction in the prices charged to consumers. We should not consider it any answer to this to say that it would involve B.O.C. having recourse to the market in future for a greater proportion of the capital which it may require for the extension of its business as distinct from the replacement of its existing assets. We do not think that a monopoly should take advantage of its position to charge current consumers with the cost of its future expansion as distinct from replacement. As an illustration of the scope for reduction, if the profit on capital employed had been limited to 15 per cent in 1954, prices could have been reduced on average by nearly 7 per cent. If a reduction in price of the order of 7 per cent had been uniformly applied, the average price of liquid oxygen would have fallen from 13s 4d to 12s 5d a 1,000 cubic feet; of industrial compressed oxygen from 33s 9d to 31s 6d; and of dissolved acetylene from 148s 6d to 138s 4d. [. . .]

Conclusions on Oxygen and Dissolved Acetylene

278. 'Conditions to which the Act applies' prevail in respect of oxygen and dissolved acetylene because B.O.C. has an almost complete monopoly of the supply. We have to consider whether in the manner in which, and to the extent to which, they prevail the conditions we have found to exist, or any of the 'things done' as a result of, or for the purpose of preserving, those conditions, operate or may be expected to operate against the public interest. We recognize, as we have said, that in this industry there may be substantial economies in operating as a monopoly, but, as our own inquiry has shown, there are also serious dangers in the control of virtually all the supplies by a single group which has not been content to rely on its advantages of scale and experience but has continued for many years to pursue a policy of suppressing and restricting competition. Among the 'things done' with this objective have been the control exercised over plant and equipment, the taking over of other producers, the use of fighting companies, and the incorporation of exclusivity terms in contracts. It is impossible to say how far competition would have developed if B.O.C. had not taken these steps, but we do not think that there is any doubt that B.O.C.'s policy of deliberately restricting competition has had the effect of depriving the public of the possible advantages of greater competition. We have also found that among the 'things done' as a result of the 'conditions' B.O.C. has taken advantage of the position which it has built up to charge prices which we regard as unjustifiably high, and has pursued a price policy which is in other respects open to objection. In all these circumstances we find that both the existing 'conditions' and 'things done' as a result of, or for the purpose of preserving them, operate against the public interest and that they may be expected to continue to operate against the public interest unless changes are made, and safeguards introduced, in accordance with the recommendations we have made.

Methods of Implementation

Our main recommendations have related to the prices

charged by B.O.C. for oxygen and dissolved acetylene (paragraph 263) and the pricing policy which should be followed in other respects (paragraphs 276 and 277). In addition we have recommended in connexion with these gases that B.O.C. should refrain from the use of fighting companies in future (paragraph 251) and proposed that the exclusivity clause in its contracts should be modified (paragraph 252). We have also drawn attention to the desirability of a substantial effort by B.O.C. in the field of research (paragraph 245), and to the danger which arises when a monopoly obtains a substantial measure of control over the provision of plant which might be used by its competitors or customers (paragraph 249).

280. In considering the best method of giving effect to our recommendations on prices we have paid particular attention to the importance of doing nothing which will deprive B.O.C. of adequate incentives to continued and increasing efficiency. For this reason we do not recommend that there should be any formal limitation on the profits which may be earned, and we also hope that it may be possible to avoid the detailed regulation of prices with the rigidity and the interference in day-to-day management which would be involved. The object should be to leave the company with as much freedom as is compatible with the need to safeguard the public interest.

281. This object would, we think, be best secured by an arrangement under which the Board of Trade or other competent authority was able to satisfy itself by periodical reviews that effect was being given to our recommendations. Such reviews should, we suggest, take place at intervals of two or at most three years. It would be necessary for the Board or other authority to have access to all the information relating to prices, costs, profits, capital employed and other matters which it needed to enable it to exercise its supervision of prices effectively, but the primary responsibility would rest on B.O.C. to satisfy the Board or other authority that full effect was being given to our recommendations. We have set out in paragraphs 259 to 261 the considerations which we think should be taken into account in determining the level of profit in the 'monopoly' conditions which prevail as far as oxygen and dissolved acetylene are concerned, and as we indicated in paragraph 261, we think the profit aimed at should be substantially

less than the range of 23 per cent to 25 per cent which has been aimed at in the past.

Cigarettes and Tobacco and Cigarettes and Tobacco Machinery (July 1961)

Excerpts from Chapter 16 on 'Conclusions and Recommendations'

513. Imperial has been the dominant supplier of cigarettes and tobacco in this country since the beginning of the century. In 1903, after the existing American competition had been eliminated, its share of the home trade was nearly 50 per cent. By 1920 the proportion had risen to more than 70 per cent and it has remained between 70 and 80 per cent since then except in the period around 1930, when coupon trading was at its height, and again in the last few years when the company has lost ground to Gallaher Ltd. In 1959 Imperial's share of the trade was $63\frac{1}{2}$ per cent.

514. The process of concentration in the manufacturing industry has continued fairly steadily up to the present time but has not affected Imperial's proportion which is little greater now than it was at the beginning of the 1914–18 war. The number of manufacturers has fallen from about 500 in 1900 to about 25 today. Most of the existing manufacturers have never had more than a minute share of the trade; some sell only in a small local area and some do not make cigarettes. Moreover, except for Gallaher, Imperial's larger competitors have lost ground in recent years. In 1959 Gallaher's share of the trade, at nearly 30 per cent, was larger than that of any individual competitor of Imperial throughout its history. Gallaher's advance has been made at the expense not only of Imperial but also of Imperial's other competitors.

515. The fall in the number of manufacturers may be explained to some extent by the elimination of small producers of pipe tobacco as the popularity of their products has declined; by the circumstance that a larger unit is able to effect economies in the manufacture of cigarettes as a result of quantity production; and by the increasingly onerous capital commitment required not only for plant and stocks of leaf but also for financing the duty (which the manufacturer has to pay on removal of the leaf from bond and which he does not recover until several weeks after the sale of his product). We are not convinced, however, that the pre-

sent structure of the industry is due to these factors alone. We,
see no reason why production units smaller in size than Imperials
or than Gallaher, should not be able to operate on an economic
basis if they were able to rely on a steady demand for their products. Public taste has become concentrated, however, on a few
proprietary brands of cigarettes. Demand of this kind cannot be
built up or sustained without heavy and continuing expenditure
on advertising. The experience of Imperial's competitors generally
over the past twenty-five years suggests that it is becoming increasingly difficult for the smaller or medium-sized manufacturer
to maintain a steady level of business without quite disproportionate expenditure on brand promotion. [. . .]

The Development of Imperial's Position

518. There is no evidence that those responsible for the formation
of Imperial in 1901 set out to monopolize the United Kingdom
market, but it was clearly their view that only a much larger unit
than any of the businesses which contributed to the amalgamation
could hope to offer successful resistance to the competition from
American interests which was being experienced at that time.
The agreement with the Americans which followed shortly afterwards not only eliminated that competition but also reinforced
Imperial's dominant position among British manufacturers
through the acquisition of Ogden's Ltd. Imperial says that these
early arrangements 'laid a foundation on which a powerful and
efficient enterprise could be built' but gave 'no assurance whatever
of continuing strength, and certainly no assurance of a dominant
position in the trade'. The company's dominant position is
attributable, it says, principally to its successful use of the competitive weapons open to any manufacturer.

519. Since acquiring Ogden's Imperial has not absorbed any
other substantial competitor. It has, however, acquired interests
in two tobacco manufacturers (Gallaher and Ardath Tobacco
Co. Ltd) and in a machinery manufacturer (Molins Machine Co.
Ltd); it has acquired additional interests in the distributive side
of the trade; it has developed its own leaf buying organization and
manufactures many of the other materials it requires.

521. In 1932, when Imperial bought a controlling interest in
Gallaher (see paragraphs 172 and 173) the latter company was not

Imperial's principal competitor. It had become a public company only a few years earlier and had not yet acquired the Senior Service or du Maurier brands of cigarettes or the Old Holborn brand of tobacco, all of which have played a great part in the company's subsequent success. We see no reason to believe that Imperial foresaw either the formidable nature of the competition it would have to face from Gallaher or the future value of the investment it was making. Imperial's motive was to prevent control of Gallaher passing into the hands of the American Tobacco Company, which had already gained a footing in the United Kingdom market by acquiring J. Wix & Sons Ltd and was believed by Imperial to be negotiating through that company for an interest in Gallaher. [. . .]

524. Imperial's interests in cigarette and tobacco distributing businesses (see paragraphs 141–58) appear to have little bearing on the development of the company's monopoly position. Imperial does not control, and has not at any time controlled, more than a very small proportion of the wholesale and retail channels of supply. Nor has it used those distributive outlets which it did control to discriminate against the products of other manufacturers. The shareholdings are said to have been acquired for fear that they would otherwise have fallen into the hands of competing manufacturers. [. . .]

525. The relations between Imperial and Molins have an important bearing on the Machinery reference and are discussed mainly in Part 2 of this chapter. So far as they are also relevant to the Tobacco reference we comment upon them in paragraph 552. In our view they have probably made only a limited contribution to the development of Imperial's monopoly position.

530. There remain some features of Imperial's organization and commercial policy over the years on which it is appropriate to comment. Imperial has told us that the circumstances in which it was formed 'have had a profound effect on its organization and structure'. Each of the constituent businesses had a long tradition behind it and was anxious to retain as much as possible of its individuality. Although many changes have since taken place in the company's structure and in particular the number of branches has been drastically reduced, Imperial is still organized, as it was in 1901, in a number of semi-autonomous manufacturing and

selling branches of very unequal strength. Imperial defends its branch system on the grounds that it 'reinforces the effects of outside competition in stimulating progressive increases in efficiency of manufacture and marketing and in ensuring a constant search for products which will best meet the requirements of the public'. [. . .]

531. We have noted that there were still eleven branches in 1932 and that up to 1954 this number had been reduced only by one. It is, in fact, from 1954 onwards that the more drastic action has taken place. Such evidence as we have suggests that the branches which have now been closed were making little, if any, contribution to Imperial's profits for many years before they were closed. Imperial says it has always been reluctant to close any branch, first because the branch's fortunes might revive, secondly because the transfer of brands to another branch may lead to loss of goodwill and sales, thirdly because it believes in the highest possible degree of internal competition, and fourthly because it feels responsibility towards the employees involved. It is fairly clear that in the 1930s and during and for some years after the war considerations such as these were decisive in the minds of the management. It is arguable that the speeding up of the process of closing branches which has occurred from 1954 onwards is due not so much to a change of policy as to the fact that the branches concerned were more conspicuously unsuccessful than they had been before. However this may be, we think it significant that when Imperial began to experience more determined and successful competition than it had had to meet for at least twenty years it found that it could no longer afford to maintain its branch structure in all the former diversity. [. . .]

532. As a natural corollary of the structure adopted at its formation the company continued to market the brands of the component business it absorbed. Although there was some co-ordination of policy thereafter, the withdrawal of old brands and the issue of new ones were matters primarily of branch policy. Thus the number of brands marketed by the company as a whole was very large. We are informed that in 1938 Imperial was selling 191 brands of cigarettes and 596 brands of tobacco. By 1960 the figures had been reduced to 57 and 183 respectively. This reduction in numbers is to some extent connected with the closing of

branches, many of the least successful brands being those of the least successful branches; but there has also been a considerable pruning of the brands of branches which remain in being. [. . .]

533. Although in reviewing the history and development of Imperial we have mentioned certain points of criticism, we are of the opinion that, in general, the company has shown responsibility and restraint in the use of its monopoly position. We consider, however, that at any rate from 1933, when coupon trading was brought to an end, until 1954, when the full vigour of Gallaher's competition began to be felt in a free market, the absence of any effective stimulus to efficiency was reflected in Imperial's organization and commercial policy. The episode of Walters apart, the matters arising from this review which require special consideration are the bonus arrangements and the company's shareholding in Gallaher – both of which have been of long duration and are still current – and any continuing effects on the company's efficiency of its comparative immunity from competition in the past.

The Level of Profit

534. We have calculated the profits earned in certain years by Imperial on its capital employed in producing and supplying cigarettes and tobacco in the United Kingdom, capital being computed on the basis of the historical cost of fixed assets less depreciation at Inland Revenue rates. We have made similar calculations for other leading cigarette and tobacco manufacturers, but in view of the loss of business suffered by most of them in recent years there is little purpose in comparing their results, except for Gallaher's, with Imperial's . . . In the light of these figures, after making all due allowance for difficulties of comparison, it appears that throughout the period under review, whatever method of computation is adopted, Imperial's rate of profit in relation to the capital employed in its cigarette and tobacco business has been lower than average. It is also clear that in the last few years it has earned a lower rate of profit than Gallaher. [. . .]

536. The profits on capital employed earned by Imperial are, compared with those earned by Gallaher and by manufacturing industry generally in the following table:

	Imperial	Gallaher	Average for manufacturing industries		
			By method 1(a)	By method 2(a)	By method 3(a)
	%	%	%	%	%
1949	14·7	N/A	N/A	22·4	18·7
1950	16·3	N/A	N/A	24·8	20·9
1951	15·0	9·6	19·4	25·7	22·2
1952	14·3	10·1	15·4	19·4	17·1
1953	14·4	10·1	16·6	20·2	17·6
1954	14·0	10·8	17·2	20·9	18·2
1955	13·3	12·3	17·3	20·4	18·0
1956	12·8(b)	13·0(b)	16·5	18·0	16·4
1957	11·8	14·0	15·4	16·7	15·5
1958	13·2	14 approx	14·1	N/A	N/A
1959	11·2	14 approx.	N/A	N/A	N/A

537. The fact that Imperial's rate of profit on capital has been consistently lower than the average for manufacturing industry does not in itself afford grounds for concluding that its profits are reasonable from the standpoint of the public interest. As we have mentioned, the circumstances of the tobacco industry are in some respects such as to falsify a comparison with industry at large. The proportion of net current assets to fixed assets is – principally because of payments in advance on account of duty – unusually high, and this exceptional degree of liquidity, combined with the stability of demand for the products of the tobacco trade, suggests that in the tobacco industry a return on capital employed lower than that in manufacturing industry generally might be regarded as acceptable. It might even be said that the special circumstances of the duty payments, along with the comparatively low degree of general risk, make it readily possible to finance the business to a large extent by loan capital without the need to offer the expectation of a relatively high return on equity capital, and indeed it happens to be the case that the fixed interest borrowing by Imperial approximates in amount to the sum locked up in duty. [. . .]

539. It is also possible to argue that Imperial, because of its dominant position in the industry, should be content with a lower return on capital employed than would be appropriate for a manufacturer facing more widespread competition. Imperial is not of course a monopolist in the absolute sense and is indeed at the present time exposed to vigorous and effective competition. None the less, we think that the relative security of Imperial's turnover and its present position of price leadership are factors to be taken into account in forming a judgement on the level of Imperial's profits.

540. Taking into account all the matters considered in paragraphs 536 to 539, we think that the profits achieved by Imperial are not unreasonable in today's conditions. With the recent appearance of really vigorous competition in the industry and the consequent increased exposure of Imperial's operations to the market test (on the assumption that these conditions are maintained), we see no reason to think that its rates of profit in the future are likely to be excessive.

Interests in Other Companies Engaged in the Home Tobacco Trade

541. Imperial at present owns, directly or indirectly, $42\frac{1}{2}$ per cent of Gallaher's equity, 100 per cent of Ardath (U.K.) Ltd's, Sinclair's and Bewlay's, and 49 per cent of Finlay's. Gallaher is a manufacturer, Sinclair is a wholesaler and Bewlay and Finlay are both multiple retailers of tobacco products; Ardath (U.K.) markets its own brands of cigarettes and tobacco in this country though these are manufactured by Imperial. The managements of Sinclair, Bewlay and Ardath (U.K.), which are subsidiaries of Imperial, are subject to control by the parent company. Gallaher and Finlay are under independent managements.

542. Imperial's substantial holding in Gallaher, its principal competitor, is by far the most important of these interests. As we have indicated, we accept fully the evidence which both companies have submitted to the effect that Imperial does not interfere in any way in the management of Gallaher and regards itself as bound not to do so in future. [. . .]

543. Imperial submits that the competitive position in the industry has not been and is not affected by its financial connexion with Gallaher. Gallaher's progress is not, it says, in any way a

consequence of the relationship. Nor would Imperial agree that its keenness to compete with Gallaher is blunted by the consideration that success on the part of Gallaher brings benefits to Imperial in the form of dividend income and capital appreciation of its investment; for it contends that the loss of profit when it loses trade to Gallaher outweighs the return from Gallaher. Imperial recognizes, of course, that viewed simply as an investment the holding in Gallaher has been a very profitable one; and it does not consider that the moment has yet arrived when it would be advisable from the point of view of a prudent investor to dispose of the shares. It accepts, however, that its motives are more than those of the ordinary investor and that its future actions will not necessarily be dictated solely by its judgement in that capacity. [. . .]

544. As to the possible effects of the investment on the competitive position, we think that Imperial's submissions leave a number of considerations out of account. We accept that Imperial would prefer to maintain its own turnover rather than obtain such possible higher return from its investment as a loss of trade to Gallaher might produce. But we think it is also inherent in the present situation that Imperial, if it is to lose trade, must prefer to lose it to Gallaher rather than to any other competitor. Moreover the situation of an investor whose commercial interests as an independent trader may conflict with the interests of the company whose shares he holds might well become untenable. We have no doubt that Imperial gave in good faith its undertaking not to interfere in the conduct of Gallaher's business and that the present management of Imperial intends to continue to observe it. Circumstances could, nevertheless, arise where such an undertaking might be felt to conflict with the interests of Imperial's own shareholders. While we appreciate that it would be difficult to specify the precise effects of either of the considerations we have mentioned, we believe that they must tend to minimize the pursuit of the outright competition which we think desirable. In particular we think that Imperial's investment in Gallaher has developed into a partial insurance against loss of profit due to loss of trade to Gallaher. [. . .]

547. We have indicated in paragraphs 531 to 533 our view that, before it began to experience determined competition from Gallaher, Imperial was not compelled to exert its maximum

effort. The company has lost trade to Gallaher in recent years and is now taking steps to recover its position. We consider that the stimulus to efficiency which Gallaher's competition provides might have been even greater if Imperial were not through its investment in Gallaher insured to some extent against the potential loss of profit. Imperial's interest in Gallaher renders less financially serious to Imperial the effect of any increase in Gallaher's share of the market at Imperial's expense, and this might tend to weaken Imperial's incentive to achieve the highest possible standard of competitive effort. In our opinion it is in the public interest that Imperial should be continuously exposed to the most strenuous competition and, although we see nothing improper in the company's attitude in this matter, we think for the reasons given above that the continuance of Imperial's investment in Gallaher operates and may be expected to operate against the public interest. [. . .]

Interests in Other Companies Connected with the Tobacco Industry

550. Imperial has four subsidiary companies which make packing materials and cigarette paper. As we have indicated in paragraph 520 we find no grounds for criticism of Imperial in this connexion. The other interests of Imperial which call for comment are those in the British-American Tobacco Co. Ltd and in Molins. B.A.T. manufactures cigarettes and tobacco in the United Kingdom and overseas but does not sell in the United Kingdom. Imperial owns 28½ per cent of its equity. Molins' activities as a manufacturer of machinery for the cigarette and tobacco industry are fully described in this report. Imperial owns 25 per cent of its equity, another 25 per cent being held by B.A.T.

551. Imperial's minority interest in B.A.T. derives from the arrangements made in 1902 with the American tobacco manufacturers, which also gave rise to the agreement between Imperial and B.A.T. which is still in existence (see paragraphs 51, 52 and 102–104). We think that the effects of this shareholding and of the agreement cannot properly be considered apart from one another, but we are precluded from pronouncing upon the agreement because it is registered with the Registrar of Restrictive Trading Agreements. Furthermore, B.A.T.'s trade is conducted outside

this country and is, therefore, beyond the scope of our reference. In these circumstances we are not called upon to express any opinion about the bearing upon the public interest of Imperial's holding in B.A.T.

552. Imperial's interest in Molins is a matter we have to take into account in relation to the supply of machinery (see paragraphs 600 and 601). Here we are concerned with that interest only in so far as it may be relevant to Imperial's dominant position as a supplier of cigarettes and tobacco. To the extent that it has assisted Molins to develop and supply machines which many tobacco manufacturers appear to regard as the best of their kind this financial relationship has benefited the whole of the tobacco industry. It is true that during the period of development Imperial and B.A.T. had the right to claim exclusive use of new machines produced by Molins, a right which Imperial exercised extensively until about 1945 and thereafter less freely up to 1957. During the greater part of this period, however, Molins did not occupy the position of pre-eminence in the field of machinery that it now enjoys, and there is no evidence that any competitor of Imperial has been seriously hampered through inability to buy machines from Molins. We do not think that Imperial is to be criticized for acquiring its financial interest in Molins or for taking steps to ensure that if the investment proved a successful risk it should have some priority in benefiting from the results. Nor do we think that the public interest has suffered or is likely to suffer by reason of Imperial's holding in Molins. [. . .]

Machinery

592. Sales of cigarette and tobacco machinery are naturally liable to fluctuate from year to year. Average annual sales in the United Kingdom in the eight years from 1951 to 1958 were approximately £2·1 million. The principal manufacturer, Molins Machine Co. Ltd, was responsible for about 55 per cent of these sales. About 45 per cent of the total home sales, including about 58 per cent of Molins' home sales, went to Imperial.

593. The machinery with which we are concerned covers many different types, and few manufacturers can supply the whole range. Molins makes many of the most important types, including

cigarette making and cigarette packing machines. Molins exports, on average, about three-quarters of its output and its principal competitors in its export markets are manufacturers in Western Germany and in the United States. Western Germany also exports to the United Kingdom and has enjoyed a rising percentage of total sales, amounting to about 11 per cent in 1958. Some United States machinery made under contract in the United Kingdom is also sold here. None of the other British manufacturers is a serious competitor with Molins in the field of cigarette making machines though one of them has been making such machines for its parent company, Gallaher.

594. In the light of our conclusions in paragraph 342 we have to consider whether the conditions which prevail – in the case of Molins by reason of the proportion of total supplies for which it is responsible, and in the case of Imperial by reason of the proportion which it purchases – operate or may be expected to operate against the public interest, and we must also consider the 'things done' by the two parties.

595. Molins and its predecessors have been operating in this country for more than sixty years, but it is during the past thirty years that the developments have occurred which have transformed a comparatively small business into one of the world's leading specialists in cigarette and tobacco machinery. Molins says that its present position is mainly due to its 'ability to invent and develop better machines than its competitors'. It acknowledges, however, that in building up that position it has benefited from its connexions with the Associated Companies (Imperial and B.A.T.). Through its financial and trading agreements with the Associated Companies it obtained (i) capital to proceed with development 'in a manner and at a rate which might not otherwise have been possible', (ii) facilities for production trials of its machines, and (iii) a potential though not guaranteed market if it produced good machines. Molins acknowledges that the trading agreement gave the Associated Companies certain advantages over competitors up to 1957, namely preferential terms as to prices and royalties and the right (which only Imperial exercised) to obtain exclusive use of certain machines. It contends that it was reasonable that the Associated Companies should enjoy such advantages having regard to the risks they took in investing

in a company whose inventions had still to be proved better than those of anyone else. It adds that it is a common practice to grant advantages of this kind under the terms of patent licences, and that in the present instance the competitors of the Associated Companies had access to a number of alternative sources of supply of machinery. Finally it is said by Imperial – whose arguments generally support those put forward by Molins – that although the trading agreement of 1927 remained in being until 1957 Imperial exercised its exclusive rights much less rigidly from 1945 onwards than it had done before the war.

596. We see no reason for criticizing either Molins or Imperial for the actions and arrangements which have led to Molins' present dominant position. In 1927 Molins' subsequent success could by no means have been taken for granted. It has been achieved through superior inventions and the ability to develop and apply them commercially, and through enterprising management backed by the financial resources of Imperial and B.A.T. We do not think that Molins can be blamed in any way for seizing the opportunity presented by such an association or for accepting the terms on which it was offered. It was reasonable on the part of the Associated Companies that they should expect some preferential advantages from any success Molins might achieve. It is no doubt true that some of their competitors, as they have told us (see paragraphs 425 and 426), would have bought certain Molins machines earlier than they did had not the exclusive arrangements prevented it, but none of them has alleged that this had a serious effect on their competitive position. It would be a different matter if the Associated Companies had persisted in maintaining all their advantages long after Molins had established itself as the leading manufacturer of these machines. In fact, the trading agreement of 1927 was terminated in 1957, and the residual advantages to Imperial and B.A.T. afforded by their current agreements with Molins are of a very limited nature. [. . .]

600. By the terms of the financial agreement of 1927, Imperial and B.A.T. each now owns 25 per cent of the voting shares of Molins as well as approximately 25 per cent of the rest of the share capital. The two companies have the right to nominate directors to the board of Molins, but the number so nominated must always be less than half of the total number of directors. This right has

never been exercised though representatives of Imperial and B.A.T. have been appointed alternate directors for members of Molins' board. Molins says that Imperial and B.A.T. 'have never in fact sought to influence the policy of the company'. The alternate directors, it is said, 'hold no more than a watching brief', and the board of Molins 'has exercised full and independent control of the policy and affairs of the company'. Imperial has expressed similar views, saying that it exercises no more influence on Molins' policy than 'that appropriate to a large buyer of its machinery'. [. . .]

602. The profits earned by Molins in its home trade in the eight years 1951 to 1958, expressed as percentages of capital employed (computed on the basis of the historical cost of fixed assets less depreciation at Inland Revenue rates), were as follows:

	%
1951	42·7
1952	24·6
1953	28·2
1954	39·6
1955	29·2
1956	29·0
1957	45·6
1958	43·6
Average for 8 years	36·2

There is no United Kingdom manufacturer of this machinery with a business which resembles that of Molins sufficiently to make any comparison of profits as between it and Molins worth while.

603. When we compare Molins' profits with the average for manufacturing industry generally we find that, after making all due allowance for the difficulties of comparison to which we have already referred (see paragraph 536), it is quite clear that during these eight years Molins' level of profit on its home business was much higher than the average. Molins does not dispute this but has submitted certain figures designed to show that some other specialized engineering businesses earn very high rates of profit and has put forward a number of arguments in justification of its own profits (see paragraphs 396 and 503–509). We do not necessarily accept these arguments in their entirety but deal below with those that appear pertinent.

605. Molins' high profits have been earned in the face of formidable competition because its customers have been willing to pay the price for a Molins machine; its prices, that is to say, have passed the test of the market. It is catering for the special needs of a smaller number of purchasers in a market which is world-wide and its operations in the home or any other particular market cannot be considered in isolation. Its principal competitors are overseas. It depends for its livelihood on its ability to remain ahead of its competitors in inventiveness and in practical application of inventions. The company can have no assurance that its business will remain profitable; the risks are high because the market is a narrow one and a competitor who produces a better machine can quickly obtain a great part of the potential custom.

606. A high rate of profit is not necessarily against the public interest. Molins is exposed to a high degree of risk and earns its profits in fully competitive conditions. Although exports, as such, are not within our terms of reference we cannot but have some regard to the inter-dependence of Molins' home and export business and to the benefits which the latter brings to the national economy. For all these reasons we do not find that Molins' pricing policy or the level of profit which results from it are against the public interest.

607. To a large extent our review of Molins' trading and financial agreements with Imperial and B.A.T. and of its level of profits has covered the considerations that have to be taken into account in forming a judgement upon Molins' position as a monopoly supplier. Molins says that its dominant position is due to its inventiveness and efficiency which enable it to sell at competitive prices machines which its customers consider superior to the products of its competitors. The company goes on to say that concentration of production and supply of this machinery serves the public interest 'since the research and production facilities which Molins command in part as a result of their predominant position both give rise to economies of scale and enable them to compete the more effectively in export markets'. There is, it is said, no danger that this concentration could have harmful effects in the future, since Molins is not protected from competition and can retain its dominant position only for so long as it keeps the lead in inventiveness and sells its products at competitive prices.

Summary of Conclusions: Recommendations

610. Our conclusions as to the bearing upon the public interest of the 'conditions' and the 'things done' with which we are concerned under these two references may be summarized as follows.

Cigarettes and Tobacco

Imperial's monopoly position, as such, does not operate against the public interest nor may it be expected to do so. The retention by Imperial of its shareholding in Gallaher and Imperial's practice of allowing a bonus to distributors conditional on the grant to the company of a proportion of their display facilities are both, however, things done by Imperial, in the one case for the purpose of preserving its monopoly position and in the other both as a result of and for the purpose of preserving that position; both of these things operate and may be expected to operate against the public interest (paragraphs 590 and 591). [. . .]

Machinery

Neither Molins' monopoly position nor Imperial's position as the predominant buyer nor any things done by either company operate or may be expected to operate against the public interest (paragraphs 608 and 609).

611. We are required to consider whether any, and if so what, action should be taken by way of remedy for the matters which we have found to be against the public interest in connexion with the Tobacco reference.

(a) So far as Imperial's shareholding in Gallaher is concerned we recommend that Imperial should divest itself of any direct or indirect financial interest in Gallaher.

(b) As regards the bonus arrangements we recommend that (1) Imperial should terminate its existing Bonus Agreements, (2) any bonus or allowance granted to a distributor by any tobacco manufacturer, whether by written agreement or otherwise, should in future be related solely to that distributor's turnover in the products of the manufacturer concerned, (3) any such bonus or allowance should be completely dissociated from the grant of continuing advertising or display facilities by distributors (special arrangements for 'campaign' advertising are in our view in a different category and unobjectionable), and (4) no tobacco manufacturer should in future enter into an arrangement with a distributor the effect of which is that if the distributor advertises a competing product he must also advertise that manufacturer's product.

Household Detergents (August 1965)

Excerpts from Chaper 5 on 'Conclusions and Recommendations'

90. Sales of household detergents in the United Kingdom by manufacturers in 1962 and 1964 may be summarized as follows:

	1962		1964	
	£'000	Tons '000	£'000	Tons '000
Unilever	29,492	200	30,377	195
	(46%)	(50%)	(44%)	(45%)
Proctor & Gamble	28,244	164	32,240	183
	(45%)	(41%)	(46%)	(43)%
Others	5,475	38	7,086	50
Total	63,211	402	69,703	428

There is no reason to believe that the market shares have changed since 1964 to such an extent as would be significant for our present purpose.

    91. We conclude therefore that the conditions to which the Act applies prevail because more than one-third of all the household detergents supplied in the United Kingdom is supplied by (i) Unilever and (ii) P. & G.

The Public Interest

92. Thus the public interest issues are concerned with the shares of the household detergents market enjoyed by Unilever and by P. & G. and with the things done by each of them as a result of or to preserve their respective positions. Although we have to reach conclusions about each of the companies individually it is obvious

that, from the point of view of either of them, one of the most important facts in this market is the existence of the other; and our judgement upon the public interest clearly cannot be formed by considering either 'monopoly' in isolation.

93. In practice we have found that the central interest of this inquiry has been in the methods by which the two companies compete with one another. Competition between them in advertising and sales promotion is not only one of the most striking features of the industry from the point of view of the public; it is also an extremely important element in their costs. But the issue arising from their policies in this respect is linked with others. Advertising and promotional expenditure is one, but only one, of the factors which contribute to the determination of the prices paid by the public. We have to consider what part is played by profits in this context, whether efficiency is sharpened by the methods of competition which are employed (including competition in promotion) and, if so, whether the benefits of such higher efficiency are shared with the consumer. In this connexion, too, we must ask ourselves whether the character of the competition between Unilever and P. & G., who at present have between them some 90 per cent of the household detergents market, is such as to deter other suppliers and potential suppliers from competing effectively and, if so, whether this is desirable. [. . .]

Advertising and Sales Promotion Policies

94. The main criticisms of the policies of the two leading suppliers are:

1. that their advertising matter is more concerned with emphasizing unprovable qualities and building up a 'brand image' than with informing the public about the practical attributes of the product and how the best use can be made of it;

2. that their promotional activities encourage the consumer to buy particular products for the sake of benefits (gifts, prizes) which have nothing to do with the products themselves;

3. that the effect of emphasizing the brand image is particularly uneconomic when it leads a manufacturer to market two very similar products under different brand names;

4. that this emphasis also leads the manufacturers to undertake wasteful expenditure on launching new products or changing the formulation of existing products for the sake of 'improvements' which are of little or no intrinsic value to the user;

5. that because competition between the two companies is concentrated on advertising and promotion, the expenditure of both of them in this field is unduly high;

6. that, as a result, not only does the public have to pay for costs from which it obtains no benefit but also, at least as regards powders, newcomers to the industry are deterred by the high cost of entry.

Broadly speaking, criticisms 1 to 4 may be said to concentrate on the character of the manufacturers' advertising and promotion, while criticisms 5 and 6 relate to the level of their expenditure. There is, of course, a connexion between these two general lines of attack. [. . .]

95. The manufacturers' arguments in defence of the kind of advertising and promotional methods they use may be summarized as follows:

(*a*) Clear instructions on how to use the products are in fact printed on the containers; but it is not practicable to give more advice than is already given on how a product will respond to varying degrees of hardness in the water or on such matters as the effect of detergents containing fluorescers on certain fabrics (which is a problem for the fabric maker rather than the detergent manufacturer). The purpose of advertising and promotion must in any case be much wider than this, for the public must continually be persuaded to try and to re-try the product. The methods which have to be used by mass producers to communicate with their customers for this purpose should not be judged by the standards of taste of a minority of the public. The building up of the 'brand image' is an essential part of the operation of persuading the customer to test the manufacturer's claims by buying the product. These claims are essentially factual, though expressed in simple, often colloquial, terms; meaningless or false claims would only defeat the manufacturer's purpose, which is to develop a well-founded belief in the brand.

367

(*b*) Promotional schemes involving gifts and prizes are among the most economical methods of creating interest in the brand. They provide an extra incentive to buy the brand; customers like them; and against the cost of providing them should be set not only the promotional effect so far as the manufacturer is concerned but also a real additional benefit gained by the customer. Unilever adds that the minority of customers who dislike such schemes have the option of buying one of its 'Square Deal' brands.

(*c*) No one brand image can cover all requirements. Two brands made by one manufacturer may, on occasion, be fairly similar in composition but they appeal to different sections of the market (geographically, socially, etc. or simply as a matter of personal preference) and if one were withdrawn the custom would not automatically be transferred to the other. The extra manufacturing cost of marketing two similar brands instead of one is small; in effect, the choice available is as wide as the customer is prepared to pay for.

(*d*) The manufacturer can only stay in business by finding out what the customer wants and then providing it. If, on occasion, what the customer wants appears to the manufacturer to have little or no value for washing purposes (for example, the blue tint of some powders) the cost of providing it is negligible. In general what the customer has wanted has been detergents of increasingly improved performance, and those now on the market are, in fact, demonstrably more efficient than those that were being sold ten years ago.

96. We are concerned here with the character of the advertising and promotion in this industry insofar as it may be relevant to questions of efficiency. Can it be said that any of the methods actually used are wasteful, in the sense that they represent expenditure (for which the customer ultimately pays) which could be eliminated without any compensating increase in other costs? The manufacturers' answer to this question is 'No'. They say that every promotion they undertake is designed to maintain or increase the market share of the brand concerned; that the ability to get the maximum result for the minimum expenditure is one of the skills that have been sharpened by competition between

them; and that if they did not use their skills in this way they would not be in a position to give the public the benefits of cost-saving by mass-production and by eliminating the need for sales promotion by retailers (see paragraph 100). While we accept that some expenditure on promotion may result in cost-saving elsewhere, we do not think it follows that the balance between promotion and cost-saving achieved in this industry by two manufacturers of roughly equal strength competing with each other is necessarily the ideal one. [. . .]

97. We recognize and welcome the improvements made by the two companies in the informative quality of their labelling and hope that they will continue to give this matter their attention. We do not think that there is undue multiplication of brands of household detergents, that in general the instructions given on their use are inadequate or misleading, or that there is a great deal of wasteful effort to produce qualities and characteristics which have no intrinsic merit. We think, however, that claims which might appeal to the more discriminating user give way to those which are believed to be of more general appeal; and in spite of the insistence of both Unilever and P. & G. that quality and product improvement are the first requirements for competitive success they seem ultimately to assume that the housewife will be moved to prefer one brand to another less by superior washing power than by the competing attraction of plastic daffodils as compared with whatever concomitant 'gift' may be offered with another brand. [. . .]

98. As to the level of advertising and promotion expenditure, the main arguments of Unilever and P. & G. may be expressed briefly as follows:

(a) The use of mass media of communication, supported by promotion schemes which create interest and excitement, is essential to enable the detergents manufacturer to establish and, by constant repetition, maintain that contact with the customer without which he cannot sustain a high level of demand for his product. By these means he puts himself in a position where he can (i) achieve economies of scale in production and distribution and (ii) keep the retailer's margin at a low level; and the substantial outlay on advertising and promotion which is necessary for these purposes sharpens his cost consciousness in other fields. Generally speaking, the level of advertising and promotion expenditure is higher where there are more competitors in the market; while therefore it may be true that this expenditure is higher in conditions of competition between two suppliers than it would be if there were a single monopoly (which would, however, be less cost-conscious in other respects) it is lower than it would be if there were more competitors. The existence of potential competitors (see (*b*) below) in any event sets a very real limit to the level of Unilever's and P. & G.'s expenditure, for if their costs were too high others would come into the market to sell at lower cost and lower prices.

(*b*) New entrants could minimize their costs by entering the market on a regional basis; or multiple stores could have their own brands of powders made up for them, as some of them already do with liquid detergents. New entrants are deterred, not by the necessary outlay on advertising and promotion, but by their inability to match the costs of the two leading manufacturers or their skills in identifying and meeting consumer demand.

99. It is relevant at this point to set out the following breakdown of the average retail prices charged for the two companies' household detergents:

	Unilever		P. & G.	
Factory cost		46		$43\frac{1}{2}$
Research, administration, distribution		$7\frac{1}{2}$		7
Selling:				
Advertising	11		10	
Promotions	6		$8\frac{1}{2}$	
Market research	$1\frac{1}{2}$		$\frac{1}{2}$	
Other	$4\frac{1}{2}$	23	4	23
Total manufacturer's cost		$76\frac{1}{2}$		$73\frac{1}{2}$
Manufacturer's profit		$7\frac{1}{2}$		$10\frac{1}{2}$
Manufacturer's realized price		84		84
Retailer's margin		16		16
Retail price		100		100

For our present purpose the principal point of interest is that manufacturer's selling cost accounts on average for nearly a quarter of what the customer pays for the product, the greater part of this cost – nearly one-fifth of the retail price – representing expenditure on advertising, promotion and market research. Total selling cost, including the retailer's margin, amounts to almost two-fifths of the retail price.

100. Although we have little information on which to base precise comparisons we think there can be no doubt that the level of advertising and promotion expenditure in this industry is exceptionally high. Both Unilever and P. & G. made certain comparisons with other products. P. & G.'s figures were intended to show that advertising (excluding other forms of promotion) was not responsible for as high a proportion of the price paid by the consumer for detergents as was the case with a number of other branded goods sold in quantity on a national scale. Unilever's figures, however, appeared to show that advertising and promotion expenditure, as a whole, was high in this industry by comparison with the others for which it gave estimates. The company indeed acknowledged that the household detergents industry was one of the 'advertising–intensive' industries, that is industries in which direct appeal from manufacturer to customer tends to supersede the functions of the salesmen and of the retailer. [. . .]

101. In our view the most useful figures in this connexion are the indices of selling prices and expenditure per ton of product which we prepared (see paragraphs 64 and 68 and appendix 10, paragraphs 76, 78, 82 and 84) and we select from these figures the following:

| | Unilever (year ending 31st December) | | | P. & G. (year ending 30th June) | | | |
	1954	1959	1964	1954	1959	1964	1965
Selling price	100	108	118	100	96	100	105
Selling expenses	100	70	88	100	81	96	99
Other costs	100	106	113	100	95	90	97
Total costs	100	93	103	100	91	92	97

[. . .]

102. The manufacturers claim that their expenditure in this field is not wasteful since there are compensating economies in

their production and other costs and in retailers' margins. We do not dispute that the advertising of branded goods for sale on a national scale can have these effects. We have no doubt that each company is able to make its products at a unit manufacturing cost which is lower than it would be if demand for the brands concerned had not been built up by nation-wide advertising. It also seems probable that the relatively low retail margin on these goods which is now more or less traditional is due in part at any rate to the policy of brand advertising which was pursued by Levers and other soap makers for many years before the war. It does not seem to us to follow that extra advertising and promotion, undertaken by Unilever and P. & G. to maintain their market shares against each other, result in extra economies elsewhere. So far as the retail margin is concerned we think that there has been some effective reduction, on average, in recent years because of an increase in price-cutting by retailers. This has been due mainly to the development of new, more economical methods of retailing by self-service stores. It is a fair point that the advertising of branded goods has helped to make these methods possible, but we do not think that this in itself can be taken to justify the whole of the advertising and promotion expenditure of Unilever and P. & G.

103. To a considerable extent the companies' arguments hinge upon the assertion that the existence of potential competitors must restrain both companies from undertaking wasteful expenditure. We might have been more impressed by this assertion if it were apparent that this factor was holding down prices, since this would confirm that there was an active incentive to minimize costs. It is for this reason that the issue of advertising and promotion cost, as we have said in paragraph 93, appears to us to be linked with that of prices and profits. As we show in paragraph 109, the rates of profit earned have been substantial on the part of Unilever and very high on the part of P. & G. It is by no means clear to us, therefore, that either company can be said to have been under pressure to minimize its costs. [. . .]

104. This brings us to the question of the effect upon potential new entrants to the industry of the policies pursued by the two large suppliers in relation to advertising and promotion. It is difficult to see any reason, other than that the terms of entry are too

onerous, why this profitable field should, with the exception of liquid detergents, have been left largely in the hands of the two companies. Some of the more obvious potential competitors, such as large chemical manufacturers, are probably not deterred by the mere size of the initial investment required, but they may well feel reluctant to participate in – and by participating, perhaps, to intensify – the process of competition in promotion expenditure which appears to prevail in the industry. Such consideration need not, of course, deter from making detergents for sale to independent marketing companies. Several chemical manufacturing companies do in fact operate in this way so far as washing-up liquids are concerned, but there is very little activity of this kind in the field of powder detergents. We are indeed a little surprised that multiple stores which market their own brands of liquid detergents do not as a rule market their own brands of powders. It is certainly not impossible for them to buy powder detergents, either in bulk or made up to their requirements, and when selling in their own stores they can avoid the kind of advertising and promotional costs that are incurred by Unilever and P. & G.

105. Taking into account all the considerations we have discussed in paragraphs 94 to 104 we conclude that the policies pursued by Unilever and by P. & G. on advertising and promotion, resulting as they do in very large expenditures thereon, are 'things done' by them for the purpose of preserving their respective 'monopolies'. We think that the expenditures incurred are unnecessarily high and that one effect is to keep new entrants out of the market, but before stating our conclusion as to the effects of the policies upon the public interest we think it necessary to consider the related subject of prices and profits.

Price Policies and Profits

106. The principal criticisms to be considered under this head in the light of the evidence we have obtained are:

(1) that there is little genuine price competition between Unilever and P. & G., prices for comparable products in comparable containers tending to be the same;

(2) that prices are unnecessarily high, having regard to the levels of both advertising and promotion expenditure and profits;

(3) that, in Unilever's case in particular, the prices of soap products are kept at a higher level than would be necessary if its synthetic products were more profitable.

107. The replies of Unilever and P. & G. to these criticisms are to the following effect:

(a) Each company decides its prices independently. Competition between them makes it inevitable that prices tend to be similar or the same; neither would put up its prices unless it were satisfied (as is generally the case) that the other, being subject to the same cost pressures, would be likely to follow, and neither could as a rule afford not to follow if the other reduced its prices. Price similarity, nevertheless, often disguises real differences (for example, different weights in the containers), but 'added value' attracts demand more than price-cutting.

(b) The prices charged by Unilever and P. & G. have not, according to their calculations, risen to the same extent as the cost of living and have not attracted newcomers to the industry. This shows that the prices are not too high. The amount of profit earned by either company, within the price 'ceiling' imposed by the need to discourage new competitors, is a reflection of its efficiency. Neither company accepts in its entirety our methods of calculating its profits and P. & G. disputes the validity of such comparisons as we make between its profits and the average profits of manufacturing industry. P. & G., while accepting that its rates of profit on capital employed earned on household detergents may well be much higher than any such average, says that these are justified because (i) the company has been outstandingly successful in achieving cost savings in production, distribution and utilization of capital and, though passing on the greater part of these savings to the consumer, is entitled to retain some benefit for itself, (ii) it is entitled to obtain a return for the technical services of the parent company, which are under-valued in the costs and (iii) it is a successful company conducting an expanding business in an industry where the risks are high because recoupment of the large outlay on advertising and promotion depends on maintaining maximum efficiency.

(c) According to Unilever its soap and synthetic products are priced independently. The former have been profitable because consumer acceptance makes promotion economical; the profitability of the latter has been limited so far because of the difficulty experienced in establishing them in the market, arising from the initial lead won by P. & G. in the synthetic field in the years after the war.

108. We accept in principle that, where two suppliers of comparable strength are competing for a market with similar products, neither can expect to retain for long any price advantage over the other, so that their prices may tend to come together. This ought not to mean that neither party should ever seek to obtain such an advantage. In this industry, quality differences apart, there are effective variations and differences in price from time to time, first because there is no uniformity in the quantity of product offered at a given price, and secondly because of temporary, promotional price reductions. Both companies appear in recent years to have been anxious, while making use of the technique of temporary, selective price-cutting (whether on the '3d off' basis or by giving more of the product for the same price) to give some customers an arbitrary bonus, to avoid the appearance of price competition. The practice, now abandoned, of giving one another advance information of impending price changes may, as the companies assert, have had little or no effect in bringing about price uniformity, but we think that it was symptomatic of their attitude.

109. We have already, when discussing advertising and promotion, touched upon some aspects of the more general defence of their prices and profits submitted by the companies and have indicated our doubts about the effectiveness of the price 'ceiling' which the existence of potential competitors is said to create. Our judgement on this point is very much influenced by consideration of the profits which the two companies have been able to earn while continuing to keep the field very largely to themselves. We have discussed elsewhere the two companies' objections to our methods of computing their profits and P. & G.'s objections to comparisons with average profits of manufacturing industry. Although there is room for argument on various points which could affect some of the figures marginally, we are satisfied that the following table affords a fair general comparison between the

rates of profit on capital employed earned by Unilever and P. & G. in their household detergents businesses and those earned, on average, by manufacturing industry generally:

Profits on Capital Employed

	Historic Cost Basis			Replacement Cost Basis		
	Household detergents business		Manufacturing industry average	Household detergents business		Manufacturing industry average
	Unilever	P. & G.			Unilever	P. & G.	
	%	%	%	%	%	%
1959	N/A	41·6	15·9	N/A	29·3	12·2
1960	46·8	49·1	16·6	34·3	36·2	13·1
1961	18·2	48·0	14·0	12·9	34·8	11·1
1962	20·7	60·2	12·6	14·8	42·4	9·9
1963	37·1	58·1	13·5	26·9	40·3	10·8
1964	25·1	52·0	N/A	17·6	36·9	N/A
1965	23·4	53·2	N/A	16·4	37·0	N/A

Note: 1965 figures for Unilever are estimates.

110. The indices for manufacturing industry are average figures for companies of diverse structure and interests. [. . .] We think that in the present case, . . . there can be no doubt that P. & G. over the period examined was earning rates of profit on its household detergents business which were very much above the average for manufacturing industry; and the company, indeed, has acknowledged that this is likely to be true. The rates of profit earned by Unilever on household detergents over (approximately) the same period, while varying widely from year to year, have been less than P. & G.'s but, in general, substantially above the average for manufacturing industry. Sales of household detergents in the United Kingdom account for about two-thirds of P. & G.'s total business but for less than 5 per cent of Unilever's. [. . .]

115. Generally speaking, we think that selling costs have played a more significant part than manufacturing costs in determining the movements of both companies' prices, and that, in any event, the average increase in prices since 1954 has been proportionately greater than the increase in total costs (see paragraph 101). Our

view is that competition between Unilever and P. & G. tends to result in the escalation of advertising and promotion costs and to that extent to increase the price that the public is required to pay; that in this situation neither company is under effective pressure from third parties to reduce the prices of its main products, namely washing powders; and that, with their comfortable rates of profit, neither company is under pressure from the other to reduce its prices. P. & G. seems to be in a particularly strong position relative to Unilever; its overall costs have given it, at existing prices, handsome profit margins and, at the same time, a steady increase in its share of the market. It seems that P. & G. has the initiative and, therefore, considerable room for manoeuvre downward on price, to which Unilever would have to respond if it were to maintain its relative market position; and this would, of course, bring great pressure to bear upon Unilever to minimize not only its factory costs but also its selling costs. However, as we have shown, P. & G. has not, in fact, used its advantage in this way. [. . .]

117. We further conclude, therefore, that the price policies and the policies on advertising and promotion of Unilever and P. & G. operate and may be expected to operate against the public interest in as much as, while tending to keep new entrants out of the market, they result in over-concentration of competition on advertising and sales promotion to the detriment of effective direct price competition and in unduly high profits with the consequence that the public are charged unnecessarily high prices.

The Monopoly Positions

118. Both Unilever and P. & G. belong to powerful groups operating on an international scale. The Unilever group's interests are more diverse than those of the P. & G. group, but so far as household detergents are concerned these two are undoubtedly the leading producers in the world, though in some overseas markets there are other competitors who offer them more vigorous competition than any they have to meet at present in this country. The Unilever group's base is in this country, where its position as one of the leading detergents producers has developed out of its earlier monopoly position as a soap-maker. The P. & G. group, on the other hand, originally built up a soap business in the United States, which remains its base and by far its most important

market. It first entered into competition with Unilever in this country when it acquired the Hedley business in 1930. From then on it steadily expanded its share of the United Kingdom market and since the 1950s has competed with Unilever on approximately equal terms.

119. We do not find a great deal in the history of either company which seems to have a significant bearing upon the issues on which we have to form a judgement. It is no doubt true that Unilever owes its present position in part to various acquisitions and amalgamations which took place many years ago. It is arguable that it was still pursuing a policy of acquisition for the sake of market domination when it took over a group of companies which included [. . .]

121. We have criticized the policies of both companies and found that they operate against the public interest in certain respects. In spite of the fact that these two companies have to earn their profits in competition with each other, the return on capital earned by both of them on household detergents is high, and in one case it is very high. This situation arises because the competition between them is concentrated in the field of advertising and promotion. This not only results in wasteful expenditure but also deters potential competitors who might, otherwise, provide a safeguard against excessive profits. P. & G., in justification of the level of profits it earns, has asserted that this is a high risk industry because the large outlay on advertising and promotion can be recouped only if maximum efficiency is maintained (see paragraph 107b). To the extent that this is true in existing circumstances we think that the conditions of high risk have been created by the companies themselves, and created unnecessarily. If competition can be diverted from excessive advertising and promotion to prices, we believe that the result will be not only a saving in cost but also a more effective check upon profits than in the past. We believe that there are practicable remedies which can bring about these results (see paragraphs 122 to 126) and *we do not find that the monopoly position* of either company, *as distinct from certain things that they do*, operates or may be expected to operate against the public interest. [Italics supplied.] [. . .]

Summary of Conclusions and Recommendations

127. Our conclusions and recommendations may be summarized as follows:

(1) The conditions to which the Act applies prevail as respects the supply of household detergents because more than one-third of all the household detergents supplied in the United Kingdom is supplied by (i) Unilever and (ii) P. & G. (paragraph 91).

(2) The policies pursued by Unilever and P. & G. on advertising and promotion and their price policies are things done by them as a result of or for the purpose of preserving their 'monopoly' positions which operate and may be expected to operate against the public interest (paragraphs 105, 116 and 117); but neither 'monopoly' position, as such, operates against the public interest nor may either be expected to do so (paragraph 121).

(3) By way of remedies for the matters which we have found to be against the public interest we make the following recommendations:

For Immediate Action

(*a*) Substantial percentage reductions should be made in Unilever's and P. & G.'s wholesale selling prices for household detergents.

(*b*) The appropriate reductions should be decided by the Board of Trade in consultation with the two companies.

(*c*) The Board of Trade should encourage the two companies to agree that at least a 40 per cent reduction in selling expenses should accompany the price reduction.

(*d*) In such event, price consultations with the companies might well begin on the basis of an average 20 per cent reduction in price (paragraph 125).

For the Longer Term

(*e*) The Board of Trade should consider the possibility of introducing some form of automatic sanction that would discourage excessive expenditure in the field of household detergents (for example, by disallowing it for tax purposes), and should also continue to keep a watch on prices (paragraph 126).

A Merger: British Motor Corporation and Pressed Steel Ltd (January 1966)

Excerpts from Chapters 4, 5 and 6 on 'Conclusions and Recommendations'[1]

The Case for the Merger

28. B.M.C. and Pressed Steel have said that the case for the merger is contained in the letters of 14 August 1965 that were sent to shareholders by the Chairman of B.M.C. and the Chairman of Pressed Steel, and generally in the documents that were submitted for the proposed merger. They have enlarged upon those statements at an oral hearing, claiming that the merger will have both economic and technical advantages.

29. B.M.C. explains that for the past twenty years motor manufacturers have been adopting a policy of specialized production of the various parts of a motor vehicle with plants (whether independent or forming a part of their own organization) concentrating on the manufacture of such items as gear boxes, axles and suspensions. These techniques are equally applicable to body manufacture and greater efficiency can be achieved if plants undertake the specialized production of one or more parts of the body, rather than the complete manufacture and assembly of particular types of body. In accordance with this policy one factory might undertake, say, the pressings and sub-assemblies of the various types of door and floor required, another the monosides and boots, while output of parts from these specialized press shops would be sent to another factory for final assembly. B.M.C. has, in fact, been implementing such a policy for the past four or five years and, in respect of one of its models, has adopted specialized production in collaboration with Pressed Steel. Pressed Steel built a new factory at Swindon in 1962 at a cost of £7m. from which all the monosides, roofs and other parts for this particular model are sent to B.M.C.'s body making subsidiaries for final assembly, together with other parts manufactured by B.M.C.

1. The earlier sections of the report contain a statistical account of the two companies and sketch in the background of the British motor industry.

30. B.M.C. maintains that rationalization of body production on these lines will reduce costs and enable it to take full advantage of the economies of scale obtained by 'running high volume through specialized press shops'. The bulk purchase of material will also yield economies, for apart from buying larger quantities of metal, the combined companies will be able to take coiled sheet steel direct from the steel mills instead of buying sheet steel 'cut to specific sizes to suit a specific pressing'. Specialized production of parts will enable the company to assemble bodies anywhere it wishes. This will not only reduce transport costs and the inconvenience of moving 'ballooned' or assembled bodies, but will facilitate exports in 'CKD' form to those overseas countries where local assembly is undertaken. Another advantage of specialized production will be the improvement in quality, for high volume production necessitates more accurate methods of inspection. This in turn will result in economies of assembly in those overseas countries where the number of vehicles assembled is relatively small. B.M.C. considers that Pressed Steel's other customers as well as itself will benefit from the specialization of production in separate plants.

31. The companies have also claimed that the merger will assist their operations abroad: 'We have a very much greater global requirement for our joint facilities'. Many countries have adopted policies of 'progressive manufacture' and insist on an increasing domestic content in vehicles of local production. Pressed Steel is well placed to meet the growing demand for pressings, but its establishment abroad would be facilitated if it were able to combine its initial activities with the assembly of CKD exports from Britain and, later on, the pressing abroad of parts for B.M.C. vehicles. The operations of the two companies would therefore be more successful if they were undertaken jointly rather than separately.

32. The companies also see technical advantages in the merger by pooling their resources in engineering, production planning and research thus increasing productivity.

33. B.M.C. has given us an assurance that the interests of Pressed Steel's other customers will be fully protected. It has drawn our attention to the passage in the letter of the Chairman of Pressed Steel to shareholders which reads:

B.M.C. has stated that it is its intention that Pressed Steel should continue to operate as a separate company with the greatest practicable autonomy and has given assurances that it intends to maintain the existing good-will and business relationships with Pressed Steel's other customers in the industry.

B.M.C. explains that Pressed Steel will continue to operate indefinitely as a separate company which will be obliged to forward its accounts for registration at the Companies Registration Office where they will be available for inspection by the public. Other customers of Pressed Steel will still communicate and place their orders with Pressed Steel. Supplies to these customers will be protected by the assurances given and Pressed Steel will expand its capacity to meet increased demand, as in the past. In the event of a shortage of materials, such as steel, allocations will be made to all customers on a *pro rata* basis, in accordance with the practice in the past. [. . .]

37. Pressed Steel has explained to us its reasons for accepting B.M.C.'s offer. The company was dependent for approximately 80 per cent of its business on B.M.C. and Rootes, either or both of whom might have at any time decided to build up their own body making capacity in accordance with the industry's trend towards vertical integration. It seemed possible, therefore, that Pressed Steel might not in the long term be able to retain its independence and B.M.C.'s offer was accepted in order to protect the interests of its employees and shareholders. The company points out that its body making facilities cannot be used for any other purpose; they are an investment tied to one industry. In terms of body units, B.M.C. at present absorbs about 60 per cent of Pressed Steel's output and B.M.C. is in an expansionary phase where increased body making capacity is likely to be required. Pressed Steel will also benefit from the technical and economic advantages of the merger explained above. [. . .]

Conclusions

39. This merger involves the taking over, by one of its two principal customers, of the only remaining large independent producer of motor vehicle bodies in this country, and, incidentally, of the largest remaining independent producer of such bodies in the world.

B.M.C., which is taking over Pressed Steel, is one of the 'Big Five' motor vehicle producers in this country. Like Pressed Steel it is British owned.

40. The motor industry accounts for over 90 per cent of Pressed Steel's turnover – the production of vehicle bodies being its principal activity. At the time of the merger Pressed Steel was dependent for approximately 80 per cent of its business on B.M.C. and Rootes, the value of their purchases being approximately equal. In terms of body units, however, B.M.C.'s purchases accounted for about 61 per cent of Pressed Steel's output and Rootes' purchases for 27 per cent. The unit value of body sales to Rootes was greater because the bodies were more completely finished. B.M.C. was dependent upon Pressed Steel for about a quarter of its total requirements of bodies, including commercial vehicle bodies, and for about a third of its requirements of car bodies. Rootes was almost entirely dependent on Pressed Steel for its car bodies.

41. In addition to Rootes, two other producers, Jaguar and Rover, were and still are wholly, or very largely, dependent upon Pressed Steel for their car bodies. Rolls-Royce and Standard also obtain some car bodies from Pressed Steel. The taking over of Pressed Steel by B.M.C. was bound to raise the question of continuity of supply, upon equitable terms, to these manufacturers, each of which has its own contribution to make to our overall range of production and to our export earnings. There was an obvious danger that B.M.C. might be tempted, now or in the future, to place its own needs above those of other companies which were, of course, to a greater or lesser degree, its competitors.

42. Although prior to the merger Pressed Steel was carrying on a successful business its future as an independent concern was at least precarious. Eighty-eight per cent of its output of bodies was absorbed by two powerful companies, either or both of which might ultimately undertake the manufacture of its own bodies. If one of them should do so, Pressed Steel would suffer a severe setback; if both, the effect would almost certainly be fatal. The danger of this situation for Pressed Steel was emphasized by the recent link-up between Rootes and the Chrysler Corporation of America. The possibility of a take-over of Pressed Steel arising

out of this new situation was undoubtedly very much in the minds of those controlling the destinies of B.M.C.

43. Pressed Steel's customers outside the motor industry, for example, in the fields of refrigeration equipment and aircraft, are not unimportant and, in considering the effects of the present merger, we have to bear their interests in mind, but these outside activities do not seem to have played any part in motivating the merger and any effect of the merger upon them is incidental to the purpose of the merger.

44. The trend of recent years in the car industry throughout the world, which forms a background to this merger and which in part helps to explain why it has come about, is a factor of considerable importance, having regard to the fact that British manufacturers have to compete for their business, both in the home and in export markets, with all the principal foreign manufacturers. In the United States, where three large companies dominate the market, vertical integration has reached the point where, for practical purposes, the principal producers are independent of outside body suppliers. On the Continent, although there are specialist manufacturers and independent component manufacturers, integration by the mass producers is more extensive than in this country. In this country before the B.M.C./Pressed Steel merger, B.M.C. was far from being wholly independent of outside body supplies, but three of its principal competitors were nearing that position. In this connexion, it is worth noting that a car body represents about thirty-five per cent to forty per cent of the unit value of the finished vehicle. The attraction to a major vehicle manufacturer of making his own bodies is therefore considerable.

45. It is with these facts in mind that we are called upon to consider whether the agreed merger between B.M.C. and Pressed Steel operates, or may be expected to operate, against the public interest.

46. Our inquiry has given rise to two questions. We have had first to consider whether there were such fundamental objections to the merger as to lead us to the conclusion that the merger itself was contrary to the public interest and that we ought to recommend that the *status quo* be restored. Secondly, even if we found no such fundamental objection, we had still to consider whether there were other objections of such a character that the merger

should only be accepted subject to conditions safeguarding the public interest.

47. This merger has been brought about by agreement between the parties and both parties were naturally concerned to testify in its favour. We had to look further in search of any possible objection. As we have stated in the Introduction, we got in touch with all the principal customers of Pressed Steel both in, and outside, the motor trade, and sought their views. We found that while there were expressions of regret at the passing of the independence of Pressed Steel none objected to the merger, which all were prepared to accept.

48. In this connexion, it is important to notice that the assurances to customers contained in the letter of the Chairman of Pressed Steel to shareholders, dated 14 August 1965 formed an integral part of the terms of the merger, and that these had clearly influenced the attitude of Pressed Steel's customers. We shall return to this point later. For the moment it is sufficient to say that, taking the terms of the merger as a whole, none of Pressed Steel's customers felt sufficiently strongly to oppose it. Nor did we receive any objection from the trade union confederation concerned.

49. We have therefore received no evidence of any fundamental objection which should lead us to condemn the merger and recommend a return to the *status quo*.

50. Despite the fact, however, that the parties most directly affected were all prepared to accept it, we were bound to consider whether, having regard to the public interest, there were objections of a general nature which might lead us to the conclusion that the merger might be contrary to the public interest.

51. In considering these more general aspects of the situation, we must first take account of the arguments in favour of the merger which were put forward by the parties. We have set these out in Chapter 5. It will be seen that B.M.C. has been at pains to stress the economic advantages of larger scale, integrated production. These are said to arise in two ways. The first by increased specialization in individual factories in the production of particular parts of vehicle bodies with assembly elsewhere, which we are told has already been tried successfully between B.M.C. and Pressed Steel at Pressed Steel's Swindon factory and which is said to offer both economies in the cost of production and a higher standard of

precision engineering. Secondly, it is claimed that some savings will result from the fact that production planning will no longer have to be done by two firms in consultation with each other, each to some extent going over the same ground, and that this will result in some saving of the time of highly skilled and scarce man-power.

52. We accept that some such saving and some increase in efficiency are probable although we do not think the benefits would be quite so important as is claimed.

53. It is also claimed that B.M.C., with its existing overseas interests and organization, will be able to a significant degree to assist Pressed Steel on its export side, and perhaps more especially to help it in those countries where Pressed Steel might wish to establish local production. Again, we think there are some advantages to be gained from the merger in this respect.

54. B.M.C. appears to attach special importance to the fact that the merger is one between two companies which are British owned and controlled and that any risk that there may have been of Pressed Steel becoming a wholly owned subsidiary of some foreign company has now been eliminated. There may be differing views as to the value to the British economy of investment by foreign firms in manufacturing capacity in this country. We certainly do not seek to criticize the behaviour of foreign vehicle manufacturers who have set up wholly-owned subsidiaries here, but we think that B.M.C. may be expected to show more consideration for the needs of Pressed Steel's existing customers than a foreign principal would necessarily feel obliged to do. With Pressed Steel in foreign hands questions might also have arisen about remittances abroad and perhaps about 'rationalization' of Pressed Steel's exports to fit in with a pattern which better suited the policy and the other interests of the foreign principal. On balance, therefore, we think that in this case there is some appreciable advantage in Pressed Steel being taken over by a British rather than a foreign company.

55. The main argument against the merger must be based on such risk as there may be that Rootes and important specialist producers such as Jaguar, Rover and Rolls-Royce whose individual expertise, production and goodwill make an important contribution, both to the technical side of our vehicle industry and to our export earnings, might be embarrassed or even, in the last

resort, put out of business, by some failure on the part of Pressed Steel to maintain its supply of bodies. This argument, also, bears on the question of whether if the merger is to be approved any additional conditions need to be imposed to safeguard the position of Pressed Steel's customers.

56. In considering whether the merger might be contrary to the public interest, we have also had to take into account the longer term position and prospects of Pressed Steel. In the short term, we think that it might well have been difficult for either of Pressed Steel's principal customers, B.M.C. and Rootes, to have to set up their own alternative production of vehicle bodies. In any case, on the evidence before us, this must have taken some years to organize. We cannot help feeling, as we have already mentioned (see paragraph 42) that in the longer term, one or other of them might have done so had Pressed Steel remained independent and we do not think that Pressed Steel acted unreasonably in anticipating events to some extent by accepting now an offer from their principal customer.

57. Had Pressed Steel been taken over eventually by someone other than B.M.C. and more particularly by some foreign company, B.M.C. might have been compelled to set up additional manufacturing capacity of its own, and this might have involved a wasteful duplication of national resources.

58. It remains to consider whether the merger embodies sufficient safeguards for the interests of the other customers of Pressed Steel. This is a question which has given us very serious concern.

59. In recommending the merger to shareholders, the Chairman of Pressed Steel said:

B.M.C. has stated that it is its intention that Pressed Steel should continue to operate as a separate company with the greatest practicable autonomy and has given assurances that it intends to maintain the existing good-will and business relationships with Pressed Steel's other customers in the industry.

These assurances form an integral part of the terms of the merger upon which we are asked to pass judgement. They seem to have been accepted by all those to whom they were addressed and we are satisfied that they were given in good faith.

60. We were, however, at an early stage in our inquiry, shown a

copy of an internal document, drawn up while negotiations were still in progress, which set out the terms of the merger and the assurances which were to be offered to customers, but which made arrangements negotiated by Pressed Steel Co. for the continuance of supplies of bodies or tools to customers other than B.M.C. 'subject to B.M.C.'s own requirements'. Had this document, or this qualifying clause formed any part of the final proposal for the merger, it must have seriously influenced the view which we have taken. We have, however, been assured by both B.M.C. and Pressed Steel that this was only a preparatory document and that it has been entirely superseded by the assurances contained in the letter to shareholders. We have also been assured that, if necessary, Pressed Steel will expand its capacity to meet increased demand, as it has done in the past. In the event of a shortage of materials, such as steel, allocations will be made to all customers on a *pro rata* basis in accordance with the practice followed on previous occasions. We have also received assurances with regard to the secrecy of designs and to price discrimination (paragraphs 33 and 34).

61. At our invitation B.M.C. and Pressed Steel have put in more specific terms, as set out hereunder, the undertakings intended to be conveyed by Pressed Steel's letter to shareholders, and have stated their willingness to be bound by them:

Pressed Steel shall if and to the extent that any of its customers shall request continue to perform the services and to manufacture products of the same or similar nature for its customers as Pressed Steel has done in the past and to the extent necessary to ensure supply of the future requirements of such customers under contracts to be negotiated from time to time upon such terms as are shown to be fair and reasonable for Pressed Steel and the customers respectively.

62. If the undertakings and assurances given are implemented the customers of Pressed Steel have little to fear from the change in ownership. We are satisfied that these undertakings and assurances will, for the foreseeable future, in fact be honoured and this has greatly influenced us in reaching our conclusion.

63. So far as the minor activities of Pressed Steel are concerned, we have been assured that no change of policy is intended in the field of refrigeration equipment, aircraft or railway rolling stock.

We have also received satisfactory assurances with regard to the interests of the labour force involved.

64. Accordingly, while in common with others we may regret the loss of Pressed Steel's independence, in all the circumstances we conclude that the merger does not operate and may not be expected to operate against the public interest.

A Merger: *The Times* Newspaper and the *Sunday Times* (December 1966)

An abridgement of Chapter 6 on 'The Public Interest Conclusion'

The Need of *The Times* for Outside Help

147. The essence of the problem is that, during a period in which the market for quality newspapers was growing, the circulation of *The Times* remained static, with the result that its share of the market gradually declined. The quality newspapers are even more dependent on advertising revenue than are the popular newspapers because they cannot hope to match the revenue of the latter from sales to readers. They are able to attract sufficient advertising without the enormous circulations of the popular newspapers only because, in general, the public which they reach is a public of special interest to certain classes of advertisers. But it remains necessary for quality newspapers to convince such advertisers that they are reaching a sufficient share of that market and that they can therefore offer good value. Its declining share of the quality market has put *The Times* in a weak position to attract advertising and has meant that, in terms of the number of readers reached, it has become relatively expensive to advertise in *The Times*. In consequence, although the average size of the newspaper has stayed approximately the same, the proportion of space devoted to advertising has declined from 38·9 per cent in 1961 to 33·5 per cent in 1966. [. . .]

149. To achieve a satisfactory level of profit *The Times* must obtain more advertising, but to do this it must first increase its circulation. As explained in paragraph 15, there is an inevitable time lag before increased circulation can bring benefit in the shape of increased advertising revenue; the immediate effect of an increase in circulation is a decrease in profit or an increase in loss.

389

The Times Publishing Company told us that the changes in the layout and contents of *The Times* introduced in May 1966 had led to an increase in circulation as great as it had hoped for. But this has not yet attracted additional advertising, and there is therefore little additional revenue to offset the additional costs incurred in producing a large number of copies and in mounting a publicity campaign to promote sales. This factor (no doubt now aggravated by the effects of the present recession) seems to account for the loss which the Company expects to incur in 1966.

150. Some witnesses expressed the view that the Times Publishing Company could have avoided its present difficulties if the problem of increasing the circulation of *The Times* had been tackled energetically some years ago. We see no reason to disagree. Indeed, we find it surprising that the company found it urgently necessary to look for rescue by a change of ownership at this particular stage. On the face of it the company's financial prospects do not appear desperate. The company made a profit during the period 1960–5, despite the fact that it was bearing the additional costs occasioned by the re-building of the Printing House Square premises. . . . It is true that substantial capital will be needed for further development, particularly if new printing methods are to be introduced, but it should not be unduly difficult to raise once satisfactory profits were being made. The most pressing need is probably for good management, skilled in marketing, which could make a determined and well directed effort to get the greatest advantage from the higher circulation which is already being achieved and which could be raised further. [. . .]

Advantages of a Link with the *Sunday Times*

152. We have no doubt that, as regards management and marketing, the proposed transfer has much to recommend it. The Thomson organization has an outstanding reputation among newspaper publishers in these respects and, we were told, it has built up a marketing organization much larger and more highly skilled than any company publishing a single newspaper could afford. The results of this can be seen in the success in recent years of the *Sunday Times* in taking full advantage of editorial improvement to expand circulation and so attract a very high proportion of

advertising (an average of 59 per cent of the newspaper in the first ten months of 1966). The skills and experience of this organization would be at the disposal of Times Newspapers Ltd, and this should greatly improve the commercial prospects of *The Times*.

153. As regards finance, the advantage of the proposed transfer is that the profits earned by the *Sunday Times* (see paragraph 62) would be available in full to enable Times Newspapers to sustain the losses which *The Times* is likely to incur until sufficient advertising revenue can be obtained. The transfer might also make possible some economies in editorial costs, for instance in the cost of foreign correspondence, which would further strengthen the joint position of the two newspapers. [. . .]

How the Proposed Transfer Might Affect the Public Interest

156. In assessing the implications of the proposed change in the ownership of *The Times*, we consider first the particular position which it occupies. Some witnesses argued that *The Times* is a national institution of unique importance and prestige which should not be permitted to come under the control of a company actuated by considerations of commercial profit. Others took the view that its position is not essentially different from that of competing quality newspapers. Indeed, some of these considered that its pretension to be in a quite different class from that of other newspapers had done positive harm.

157. We recognize that there was a time, in the nineteenth century, when *The Times* stood virtually alone, and even when other newspapers overtook it in popularity it still retained great influence. It no longer enjoys the same position of dominance nor the same influence on public affairs as it has done at some periods in the past, but some of the prestige arising from its historical position still clings to it and, in the minds of some people, differentiates it from other newspapers. Moreover, on occasion in the past, the editor of *The Times* allowed himself and the newspaper to be used by the Government of the day as an instrument for moulding public opinion. This may in part account for the fact that, particularly abroad, *The Times* is still sometimes believed to have an authority which it does not now possess. [. . .]

159. It is valued for two qualities. The first is the nature and

range of its news reporting. The Times Publishing Company told us that it would like to widen and improve its news coverage, but it is generally accepted that in the news that it prints it sets a high standard of accuracy and freedom from bias. Moreover *The Times* still, as a matter of course, provides a record of some matters which may not appear in any other newspaper, for example, Parliamentary reports, public and university appointments, the law reports, the obituaries and the Court Circular. The other quality that *The Times* has is freedom to express opinions on great issues of the day without regard to popularity or to political or other pressures. *The Times* is not unique in this, but there are few newspapers whose editors are completely free to express forthright views uncoloured by special or sectional interests.

160. It is against this background that we must consider whether the public interest might suffer as a result of the proposed transfer. The questions are:

(i) whether the transfer would cause an excessive concentration of newspaper power;

(ii) whether there would be a threat to the survival of other newspapers;

(iii) whether changes in the nature of *The Times* are likely to result which would rob it of the qualities which make its preservation a matter of public interest.

Concentration of Ownership

161. As regards the first question, the transfer of *The Times* would, in form, be to a company which would publish only one daily and one Sunday newspaper. Although this does not in itself suggest a serious concentration, 85 per cent of the shares of this company would be owned by The Thomson Organization, which would also have the right to buy the remaining 15 per cent if the Astor interests should wish to sell them. We cannot therefore regard the device of the creation of a separate company as effectively separating control of *The Times* and the *Sunday Times* from the rest of the Thomson interests. Thus the result of the transfer would be to add *The Times* to a group which in the United Kingdom, apart

from the *Sunday Times*, also owns the *Scotsman* and about 100 magazines and provincial newspapers and has various interests outside the newspaper industry, including Scottish television, book publishing, 'package holiday' tours and an airline. The addition of an important vehicle of opinion such as *The Times* represents a material increase in power to this group. It would be a continuation of the movement towards concentration in the ownership of the press, which must ultimately tend to stifle the expression of variety of opinion.

162. If the danger to be anticipated from such concentration is that one man or company might have an undue degree of influence on public opinion, there are factors which suggest that the present proposal need not be regarded as a matter for serious concern. The first is that The Thomson Organization does not at present own an English national daily newspaper, and even with *The Times* its share of the circulation of all national and provincial daily newspapers would be only about 7 per cent. Another factor is that, apart from the *Sunday Times* and the *Scotsman*, the other interests of The Thomson Organization do not give it much influence over public opinion; it is not permitted to control opinion expressed on Scottish television, and its provincial newspapers, although numerous, can scarcely be regarded as influential by comparison with national newspapers. Furthermore the avowed approach of The Thomson Organization to newspaper businesses is to select good editors and editorial staff and to leave the editors free to decide editorial policy. The Organization claims that it is concerned only with efficient and profitable management and does not interfere in matters of opinion, even if its various newspapers contradict one another. Ultimately of course the needs of commercial profitability may lead a management which adopts such an approach to remove an editor who expresses such unpopular opinions that the paper is commercially prejudiced, but our witnesses generally confirmed that The Thomson Organization has in practice given its editors a great deal of freedom. Although there can be no guarantee that The Thomson Organization or its successors will always abide by this policy, nevertheless the transfer of *The Times* to a company with such a policy involves little risk. It certainly involves less risk of stifling variety or of the misuse of power to influence opinion than would the transfer of *The Times*

to a proprietor who regarded newspapers as vehicles for his own views. Accordingly, we do not consider that the proposed transfer would lead to an undue concentration of newspaper power. [. . .]

Competition

164. The concentration of newspaper and other interests may not only afford power to control the expression of opinion but may also bring commercial and financial power. This leads to the second question posed in paragraph 160, whether the proposed transfer of *The Times* threatens the survival of other newspapers. If *The Times* were preserved only at the cost of losing one or more other newspapers the public interest could suffer as much as by the loss of *The Times*. The question falls into two parts: the first concerns the special position of the *Guardian* and the *Observer*, both of which would be printed by the new company, and the second concerns the effect on these and other newspapers generally of increased competition from *The Times*.

165. The *Observer* and the *Guardian* have discussed their position with The Thomson Organization and have informed us of the outcome. Both were nervous of the difficulties that could arise through being printed by the same company, if not in the same building, as their principal competitors. The *Observer* has sought to protect its position by negotiating terms on which its printing contract could, if necessary, be terminated (see paragraph 136). The *Guardian*'s negotiations are not yet completed. We hope that a satisfactory agreement will be reached covering the two points on which Lord Thomson has already offered to meet the *Guardian*'s wishes (see paragraph 141) and also mutually acceptable provisions for the extension of the printing contract for a further period after 1976. We recognize that both newspapers would be in a vulnerable position and could yet be put to considerable difficulty. But we consider that this is a matter which must be left to negotiation between the parties and we do not think it would be appropriate to suggest any special safeguards in the public interest.

166. As regards competition more generally, there is no doubt that if *The Times* is to be made commercially successful it will have to compete for readers and moreover that, supported by the marketing skill and strength of the Thomson Organization, it

would compete very strongly for advertisers. If it were successful, the circulation or advertising revenue, or both, of other newspapers would be bound to be affected adversely, although we were told that in some respects newspapers in the quality group could benefit from the competition, if for instance it enhanced the value of quality newspapers generally in the eyes of advertisers (see paragraph 143). [. . .]

Editorial Independence

172. There was considerable anxiety among our witnesses about the danger to *The Times* as a vehicle for the free expression of opinion on public issues. They were concerned about editorial freedom in two respects.

173. First, some thought that *The Times* would suffer from the fact that the avowed object of The Thomson Organization is to make profits. They feared that there might therefore be undue reluctance to express unpopular views for fear that these views would prejudice the newspaper's commercial prospects, and even that pressure might be put upon the editor to refrain from publishing opinions which might upset either readers or advertisers. We were told of instances in which an unpopular editorial line in a newspaper had led to loss of readers or to withdrawal of advertisers' custom; any editor must have this danger in mind, and he is particularly susceptible to it if either the financial position of his newspaper is weak or if the proprietor's object is to achieve the highest profits. Secondly, many witnesses were also concerned that not only would *The Times* and the *Sunday Times* be under common management but their editors would be under the control of a single editor-in-chief. It was generally thought that the editor-in-chief would be bound to influence the editorial policies of both papers, with the result that both could be expected to speak with the same voice on important issues, so that one independent voice in the Press would have been lost. We consider that there is real ground for these anxieties.

174. As regards the first point we think it likely that, under the new management, commercial considerations would play a greater part in running *The Times*. The Thomson Organization, in the interest of its shareholders, is likely to want to ensure that

the profits from the *Sunday Times* are not wholly swallowed up by *The Times*. The Thomson Organization told us that the paper would still be aimed at the same class of readers, but commercial pressures might lead the new company, in seeking higher circulation figures, to appeal to a wider class of readers. For this purpose the editor might find it necessary to make changes in the paper which could include the avoidance of provocative or controversial opinion and some blurring of the editorial voice. On the other hand, unless their papers have great financial strength, editors cannot be entirely shielded from commercial necessities, and other plans for making *The Times* more profitable might have the same result. Indeed, a proprietor who did not have the financial resources of The Thomson Organization might be even more dominated by commercial considerations. Under any new arrangement the editor of *The Times* is likely to have to pay more regard to commercial requirements than recent editors have been accustomed to; this is probably unavoidable, and it must be recognized that *The Times* would no longer speak with its accustomed voice. We do not, however, regard this in itself as a valid ground for objecting to the transfer, provided that the editor would remain free of external control in matters of opinion.

175. We are more concerned about the danger that, as a result of the editorial link with the *Sunday Times*, *The Times* might speak with the same voice on major matters as the *Sunday Times*. While it is impossible to lay down any provisions to ensure that, in the public interest, a newspaper shall speak with a particular voice, it is important to seek to preserve that diversity of opinion should, as far as possible, be reflected in the Press and any diminution in the opportunity for the expression of such diversity is a matter for concern. We therefore regard it as an important question whether the independence and integrity of *The Times* as a separate newspaper would be preserved and whether the editor would be free of external control or influence in matters of opinion. [. . .]

178. The special feature, however, of the present proposal is the appointment of a single editor-in-chief for both *The Times* and the *Sunday Times*, and in our discussions with The Thomson Organization we inquired particularly about the effect of this appointment (see paragraphs 84–8). We accept the argument of Lord Thomson and his associates that coordination of the editorial resources

available to both newspapers would be necessary if they were to be used economically, and that such coordination could be to the advantage of both *The Times* and the *Sunday Times*. We agree also that it would be desirable, if not indeed essential, that one man should be charged with the responsibility for planning in this field and should have the executive authority to allocate resources between the two newspapers and to develop such common services as might be thought necessary.

179. We were concerned, however, that centralization of administrative power in this respect should not affect the identities of *The Times* and the *Sunday Times* as separate editors in the expression of opinion on matters of public policy. We were assured by Lord Thomson (speaking also on behalf of his son) and by Mr Hamilton, the designated editor-in-chief, that they wished to maintain the separate identities of the two newspapers and that it was not intended that the office of editor-in-chief should infringe in any way either the independent responsibility of the two editors for editorial opinion or their direct authority over their editorial staffs. [. . .]

Conclusion

182. The evidence of our witnesses showed that the proposed transfer has aroused apprehensions for the public interest and our investigations have suggested that these apprehensions are not groundless. The independence of *The Times* could not be regarded as certain, and it must be recognized that if it came under the control of The Thomson Organization commercial considerations would play a greater part than they have in the past (see paragraph 174). But in the light of The Thomson Organization's assurances about its intentions for the paper's management, as recorded in this report, we think that there is every prospect that the survival of *The Times* would be assured, that the public would continue to be offered a good, and in some respects an improved, newspaper, and moreover that in matters of editorial opinion there is reasonable assurance that it would continue to speak with a separate voice. It would no longer be the same voice or the same *Times* as in the past, and it is important that it should be recognized both at home and abroad, that it would have no claim to any special

397

role or status; but we do not regard that as contrary to the public interest. The combination of *The Times* and the *Sunday Times*, backed by the commercial strength of The Thomson Organization, would present formidable competition to the other quality newspapers, some of which already face a difficult future. But we think that neither this increase in competitive strength nor the increase in concentration of newspaper ownership which would result from the proposed transfer is, of itself, cause for concern.

183. Taking into account all the relevant circumstances and having regard to the need for accurate presentation of news and free expression of opinion we conclude that the proposed transfer of *The Times* and the *Sunday Times* to a newspaper proprietor may be expected not to operate against the public interest.

Further Reading

ADELMAN, M. A., 'The measurement of industrial concentration', *Review of Economics and Statistics*, vol. 34, 1951.

ADELMAN, M. A., *A and P: A Study in Price Cost Behaviour and Public Policy*, Harvard University Press, Cambridge, Mass., 1959.

ALEXANDER, R. S., and HILL, R. H., 'What to do about the Discount House', *Harvard Business Review*, January 1955, p. 53.

ALLEN, G. C., *British Industries and Their Organization*, Longmans, London, 1959.

ALLEN, G. C., *Monopoly and Competition and Their Control*, edited by E. H. Chamberlin, Macmillan, London, 1954.

ALLEN, G. C., *The Structure of Industry in Great Britain*, Longmans, London, 1961.

American Economics Association, *Readings in Industrial Organization and Policy*, Irwin, Homewood, Illinois, 1958.

American Economics Association, *Readings in Price Theory*, Allen & Unwin, London, 1953.

American Economics Association, *Readings in Social Control of Business*, The Blakiston Company, Philadelphia, 1949.

ANDREWS, P. W. S., *Manufacturing Business*, Macmillan, London, 1949.

ANDREWS, P. W. S., and FRIDAY, F. A., *Fair Trade*, Macmillan, London, 1960.

ARNDT, H. W., *The Economic Lessons of the Nineteen-Thirties*, Oxford University Press, London, 1944.

BAIN, J. S., *Price Theory*, Holt, New York, 1952.

BAIN, J. S., *Barriers to New Competitions*, Harvard University Press, Cambridge, Mass., 1956.

BAIN, J. S., *Industrial Organization*, Wiley, London and New York, 1959.

BAIN, J. S., 'The profit rate as a measure of monopoly power', *Quarterly Journal of Economics*, vol. 55, 1941.

BAUMOL, W., *Business Behaviour, Value and Growth*, Macmillan, London, 1959.

BEACHAM, A., 'Some thoughts on the cement judgement', *Economic Journal*, June 1962.

Board of Trade, 'Acquisitions and amalgamations of quoted companies 1954–61', *Economic Trends*, no. 114, Central Statistical Office, London, April 1963.

Board of Trade, *Annual Reports on the Monopolies and Restrictive Practices Acts* 1948 and 1953, H.M.S.O., 1949–67.

Board of Trade, *Reports of the Census on Production* 1958, parts 133–5, H.M.S.O., 1962–3.

Board of Trade, *Report of the Committee on Resale Price*, Cmnd 7696, H.M.S.O., 1949.

Bow Group, *Monopolies and Mergers*, no. 270, Conservative Political Centre, 1963.

BOULDING, K., 'Welfare economics', in B. F. Haley (ed.), *A Survey of Contemporary Economics*, vol. 2, Irwin, Illinois, 1952.

BOWMAN, W. S., 'The pre-requisites and effects of resale price maintenance', *University of Chicago Law Review*, vol. 22, 1954–5, p. 825.

BRASH, D. T., *American Investment in Australian Industry*, Australian National University Press, 1966.

BROWN PHELPS, E. H., and WISEMAN, J., *A Course in Applied Economics*, Pitman, London, 1964.

BROWN, W. J., *The Prevention and Control of Monopolies*, John Murray, London, 1914.

BURN, D., *The Structure of British Industry*, two volumes, Cambridge University Press, 1958.

BURNHAM, J., *The Managerial Revolution*, Putnam, London, 1944.

BURNS, A. R., *The Decline of Competition*, McGraw-Hill, New York, 1936.

BUSHNELL, J. A., *Australian Contemporary Mergers 1946–59*, Melbourne University Press, 1965.

BYE, R. T., and HEWETT, W. W., *Applied Economics*, Allen & Unwin, London, 1960.

Canada Restrictive Trade Practices Commission, *Report on an Inquiry into Loss-Leader Selling*, Ottawa, 1955.

CARTER, C. F., and WILLIAMS, B., *Industry and Technical Progress*, Oxford University Press, London, 1958.

CARTER, C. F., and WILLIAMS, B., *Investment in Innovation*, Oxford University Press, London, 1958.

CASSADY, R., *Price Making and Price Behaviour in the Petroleum Industry*, Yale University Press, New Haven, 1954.

Central Statistical Office and Board of Trade, *Economic Trends*, April Issues nos. 102 and 114, H.M.S.O., 1962 and 1963.

CHAMBERLIN, E. H. (ed.), *Monopoly and Competition and Their Regulation*, Macmillan, London, 1954.

CHAMBERLIN, E. H., *The Theory of Monopolistic Competition*, 6th edn, Harvard University Press, Cambridge, Mass., 1950.

CLARK, J. M., *Competition as a Dynamic Process*, Brookings, 1961.

CLARK, J. M., *The Social Control of Business*, McGraw-Hill, New York, 1949.

CLARK, J. M., 'Toward a concept of workable competition', *American Economic Review*, vol. 30, June 1940.

COOK, P. L., and COHEN, R., *The Effects of Mergers*, Allen & Unwin, London, 1958.

CUTHBERT, N., and BLACK, W., 'Restrictive practices in the food trades', *Journal of Industrial Economics*, vol. 8, no. 1, 1959 and vol. 10, no. 1, 1961.

DENNISON, S. R., 'The restrictive trade practices act', *Journal of Law and Economics*, Washington, 1941.

DEWEY, D., *Monopoly in Economics and Law*, Rand McNally, Chicago, 1959.

DIRLAM, J. B., and KAHN, E. K., *Fair Competition: The Law and Economics*, Cornell University Press, Ithaca, 1958.

DOWNIE, J., *The Competitive Process*, Duckworth, London, 1958.

DOYLE, P., 'Economic aspects of advertising: a survey', *Economic Journal*, vol. 78, 1968, pp. 570–602.

DUNNING, J. H., *American Investment in British Manufacturing Industry*, Allen & Unwin, London, 1958.

DUNNING, J. H., and THOMAS, C. J., *British Industry*, Hutchinson, London, 1961.

EDWARDS, C. D., *Maintaining Competition*, McGraw-Hill, 1948.

EDWARDS, H., *Competition and Monopoly in the British Soap Industry*, Oxford University Press, London, 1962.

EDWARDS, R. S., and TOWNSEND, H., *Business Enterprise*, Macmillan, London, 1959.

ERHARD, L., *Prosperity Through Competition*, Thames and Hudson, London, 1960.

EVELY, R., and LITTLE, I. M. D., *Concentration in British Industry*, Cambridge University Press, 1960.

FELLNER, W., *Competition Among the Few*, Knopf, New York, 1949.

FLORENCE, P. S., *The Logic of British and American Industry*, Routledge and Kegan Paul, London, 1958.

FLORENCE, P. S., *Ownership, Control and Success of Large Companies*, Sweet and Maxwell, London, 1961.

FOG, B., *Industrial Primary Policies*, North Holland, Amsterdam, 1960.

FRIEDMANN, W. (ed.), *Anti-Trust Laws*, Stevens, London, 1956.

FRIEDMANN, W., *Law and Social Change in Contemporary Britain*, Stevens, London, 1951.

GALBRAITH, J. K., *American Capitalism*, 2nd edn., Hamish Hamilton, London, 1958.

GAMMELGAARD, S., *Resale Price Maintenance*, European Productivity Agency, project no. 238, O.E.E.C., Paris, 1958.

GILBERT, A. S., *Comparative Aspects of Anti-Trust Law in the U.S.A., the U.K. and the E.E.C.: A Report*, British Institute of International and Comparative Law, London, 1963.

GINSBERG, M., *Law and Opinion in England in the Twentieth Century*, Stevens, London, 1959.

GORDON, R. A., *Business Leadership in the Large Corporation*, University of California Press, Berkeley, 1961.

GRETHER, E. T., *Price Control under Fair Trade Legislation*, Oxford University Press, New York, 1939.

GROSSFIELD, K., 'The origin of restrictive practices in the cable industry', *Journal of Industrial Economics*, October 1958.

GRUNFELD, G., and YAMEY, B., *Anti-Trust Laws*, edited by W. Friedmann, R. Stevens, London, 1956.

GUENALT, P. H., and JACKSON, J. M., *The Control of Monopoly in the United Kingdom*, Longmans, London, 1960.

Further Reading

HALL, M., *Distributive Trading*, Hutchinson's University Library, London, 1948.

HALL, R. L., and HITCH, C. J., 'Price theory and business behaviour', *Oxford Economic Papers*, vol. 1, May 1939.

HALLE, E., *Trusts in the United States*, Macmillan and Co., New York, 1895.

HEATH, J. B., 'Restrictive practices and after', *Manchester School*, vol. 34, No. 2, May 1961.

HEATH, J. B., *Still Not Enough Competition*, 2nd edn, Hobart Paper No. 11, Institute of Economic Affairs, London.

HEATH, J. B., 'The restrictive practices court on competition and price restriction', *Manchester School*, vol. 28, January 1960.

HEATH, J. B., 'The *per se* rule in the light of British experience', *North Western University Law Review*, May–June 1962.

HENDERSON, J. M., and QUANDT, R. E., *Microeconomic Theory*, McGraw-Hill, New York, 1958.

HICKS, J. R., 'Foundations of welfare economics', *Economics Journal*, vol. 49, 1939, pp. 549–52.

H.M. Government, *Monopolies, Mergers and Restrictive Practices*, Cmnd 2299, H.M.S.O., March 1964.

House of Commons Library, *Bibliography No. 47: Monopolies*.

HUGHES, H., *The Australian Iron and Steel Industry*, Melbourne University Press, 1964.

HUNTER, A., and SIMONS, D., 'Collusive tending and public authorities', *Australian Quarterly*, March 1963.

HUNTER, A. (ed.), *Economics of Australian Industry*, Melbourne University Press, 1963 and 1965.

HUNTER, A., 'Competition and the Law', *Manchester School*, vol. 27, January 1959 (also November 1959).

HUNTER, A., *Competition and the Law*, Allen & Unwin, London, 1966.

HUNTER, A., 'Notes on countervailing power', *Economic Journal*, vol. 65, 1958.

HUNTER, A., 'Product differentiation and welfare economics, *Quarterly Journal of Economics*, vol. 69, November 1955, pp. 533–52.

HUNTER, A., 'Restrictions of competition in New Zealand', *Economic Record*, November 1963.

HUNTER, A., 'Restrictive practices and monopolies in Australia', *Economic Record*, vol. 37, March 1961, and reprinted in H.W. Arndt and M. W. Corden, *The Australian Economy*, Cheshire, 1963.

HUNTER, A., 'The monopolies commission and price fixing', *Economic Journal*, vol. 66, December 1956.

HUNTER, A., 'Tribulations of a tribunal', *Australian Economic Papers*, vol. 7, June 1968.

HUTBER, P., *Wanted – A Monopoly Policy*, Fabian Society, No. 219, 1960.

INCORPORATED COUNCIL OF LAW REPORTING, *Law Reports: Restrictive Practices* vols. 1–4, 1957–64.

JEFFERYS, J. B., *The Distribution of Consumer Goods*, Cambridge University Press, 1950.

JEWKES, J., 'British Monopoly and Policy 1944–56', *Journal of Law and Economics*, October 1958.

JEWKES, J., 'The Size of factory', *Economic Journal*, vol. 62, 1952.

JEWKES, J., SAWERS, D., and STILLERMAN, R., *The Sources of Invention*, Macmillan, London, 1958.

KAHN, R. F., 'Some notes on ideal output', *Economic Journal*, vol. 45, 1935, pp. 1–35.

KALDOR, M., 'The Economic Aspects of Advertising', *Review of Economic Studies*, vol. 28, 1949–50.

KARMEL, P., and BRUNT, M., *The Structure of the Australian Economy*, Cheshire, Melbourne, 1963.

KAYSEN, C., *United States v. United Shoe Machinery Corp.*, Harvard University Press, Cambridge, Mass., 1956.

KAYSEN, C., and TURNER, D. F., *Anti-Trust Policy*, Harvard University Press, Cambridge, Mass., 1959.

KNIGHT, F. H., *Risk, Uncertainty and Profit*, London School of Economics, 1933.

LABINI, S. P., *Oligopoly and Technical Progress*, Harvard University Press, Cambridge, Mass., 1962.

LERNER, A. P., SINGER, H. W., and EDWARDS, H., 'Some notes on duopoly and spatial competition', *Journal of Political Economy*, vol. 45, 1937.

LERNER, A. P., 'The concept of monopoly and the measurement of monopoly power', *Review of Economic Studies*, June 1934, pp. 157–75.

LERNER, A. P., *The Economics of Control*, McGraw-Hill, New York, 1944.

LETWIN, W. J., 'The origins of the anti-trust policy', *Journal of Political Economy*, vol. 64, April 1956, p. 158.

LEVY, H., *Monopoly and Competition*, Macmillan, London, 1911.

LEVY, H., *Monopolies, Cartels and Trusts in British Industry*, Macmillan, London, 1927.

LEWIS, W. A., 'Competition in the retail trade', *Economica*, vol. 12, 1945.

LEWIS, W. A., *Overhead Costs*, Allen & Unwin, London, 1949.

LEWIS, W. A., *The Principles of Economic Planning*, Allen & Unwin, London, 1949.

LITTLE, I. M. D., *A Critique of Welfare Economics*, 2nd edn, Oxford University Press, London, 1957.

LITTLE, I. M. D., *The Price of Fuel*, Oxford University Press, London, 1953.

LLOYD, D., *Public Policy*, Athlone Press, London, 1953.

LORD CHANCELLOR, *Restrictive Practices Court Rules*, Statutory Instrument no. 603, 1957.

LUCAS, A. F., *Industrial Reconstruction and the Control of Competition*, Longmans, London, 1937.

MACDONALD, T. A., *Resale Price Maintenance*, Butterworth, London, 1964.

MACHLUP, F., *The Basing Point System*, Blackiston, Philadelphia, 1949.

Further Reading

MACHLUP, F., *The Political Economy of Monopoly*, Johns Hopkins Press, Baltimore, 1952.

MACROSTY, H. W., *The Trust Movement in British Industry*, Longmans, London, 1907.

MARRIS, R., *The Economics of Managerial Capitalism*, Macmillan, London, 1964.

MARSHALL, A., *Industry and Trade*, Macmillan, London, 1927.

MARTIN, A., *Restrictive Trade Practices and Monopolies*, Routledge and Kegan Paul, London, 1954.

MASTERMAN, G. G., and SOLOMON, E., *The Australian Trade Practices Law*, Butterworth, Sydney, 1967.

MCLEAN, J. G., and HAIGH, R. W., *The Growth of Integrated Oil Companies*, Harvard Business School, Boston, 1954.

MCLELLAND, W. G., *Studies in Retailing*, Blackwell, Oxford, 1963.

MEANS, G., *Pricing Power and the Public Interest*, Horner and Bros., New York, 1962.

MILLER, J. P. (ed.), *Competition Cartels, and their Regulation*, North Holland, Amsterdam, 1962.

MISHAN, E. J., 'A survey of welfare economics, 1939–45', *Economic Journal*, vol. 70, 1960, pp. 197–265.

MONOPOLIES COMMISSION, *Collective Discrimination*, Cmnd 9504, H.M.S.O., 1955.

MONOPOLIES COMMISSION, *Dental Goods*, H.M.S.O., 1950.

MONOPOLIES COMMISSION, *Cast Iron Rainwater Goods*, H.M.S.O., 1951.

MONOPOLIES COMMISSION, *Electric Lamps*, H.M.S.O., 1951.

MONOPOLIES COMMISSION, *Insulated Electric Wires and Cables*, H.M.S.O., 1952.

MONOPOLIES COMMISSION, *Insulin*, H.M.S.O., 1952.

MONOPOLIES COMMISSION, *Matches and Match-Making Machinery*, H.M.S.O., 1953.

MONOPOLIES COMMISSION, *Imported Timber*, H.M.S.O., 1953.

MONOPOLIES COMMISSION, *The Process of Calico Printing*, H.M.S.O., 1954.

MONOPOLIES COMMISSION, *Buildings in the Greater London Area*, H.M.S.O., 1954.

MONOPOLIES COMMISSION, *Semi-Manufacturers of Copper and Copper Based Alloys*, H.M.S.O., 1955.

MONOPOLIES COMMISSION, *Collective Discrimination*, H.M.S.O., 1955.

MONOPOLIES COMMISSION, *Pneumatic Tyres*, H.M.S.O., 1955.

MONOPOLIES COMMISSION, *Sand and Gravel in Central Scotland*, H.M.S.O., 1956.

MONOPOLIES COMMISSION, *Fibre Cordage*, H.M.S.O., 1956.

MONOPOLIES COMMISSION, *Linoleum*, H.M.S.O., 1956.

MONOPOLIES COMMISSION, *Certain Rubber Footwear*, H.M.S.O., 1956.

MONOPOLIES COMMISSION, *Certain Industrial and Medical Gases*, H.M.S.O., 1956.

MONOPOLIES COMMISSION, *Electrical and Allied Machinery and Plant*, H.M.S.O., 1957.

MONOPOLIES COMMISSION, *Electronic Valves and Cathode Ray Tubes*, H.M.S.O., 1956.

MONOPOLIES COMMISSION, *Supply of Tea*, H.M.S.O., 1956.

MONOPOLIES COMMISSION, *Standard Metal Windows and Doors*, H.M.S.O., 1956.

MONOPOLIES COMMISSION, *Imported Timber*, H.M.S.O., 1958.

MONOPOLIES COMMISSION, *Chemical Fertilizer*, H.M.S.O., 1959.

MONOPOLIES COMMISSION, *Cigarettes and Tobacco and of Cigarette and Tobacco Machinery*, H.M.S.O., 1961.

MONOPOLIES COMMISSION, *Electrical Equipment for Mechanically Propelled Land Vehicles*, H.M.S.O., 1963.

MONOPOLIES COMMISSION, *Wallpaper*, H.M.S.O., 1964.

MONOPOLIES COMMISSION, *Petrol (Supply to Retailers)*, H.M.S.O., 1965.

MONOPOLIES COMMISSION, *Films: Supply for Exhibition*, H.M.S.O., 1966.

MONOPOLIES COMMISSION, *Household Detergents*, H.M.S.O., 1966.

MONOPOLIES COMMISSION, *British Motor Corporation and the Pressed Steel: Proposed Merger*, H.M.S.O., 1966.

MONOPOLIES COMMISSION, *Electrical Wiring Harnesses*, H.M.S.O., 1966.

MONOPOLIES COMMISSION, *Colour Film*, H.M.S.O., 1966.

MONOPOLIES COMMISSION, *Ross Group and Associated Fisheries: Proposed Merger*, H.M.S.O., 1966.

MONOPOLIES COMMISSION, *The Times and Sunday Times Newspaper: Proposed Merger*, H.M.S.O., 1966.

MONOPOLIES COMMISSION, *Dentist Supply Co. of New York and Amalgamated Dental Co: Proposed Merger*, H.M.S.O., 1966.

MONOPOLIES COMMISSION, *British Insulated Callendar's Cables and Pyrotenox Ltd: Proposed Merger*, H.M.S.O., 1967.

MONOPOLIES COMMISSION, *Guest, Keen and Nettlefolds Ltd, and Birfield Ltd: Proposed Merger*, H.M.S.O., 1967.

MONOPOLIES COMMISSION, *Infant Milk Foods*, H.M.S.O., 1967.

MONOPOLIES COMMISSION, *Aluminium Semi-Manufacturers*, H.M.S.O., 1967.

NATIONAL BUREAU OF ECONOMIC RESEARCH, *Business Concentration and Price Policy*, Princeton University Press, 1955.

NEALE, A. D., *The Anti-Trust Laws of the U.S.A.*, Cambridge University Press, 1960.

NELSON, R. L., *Merger Movements in American Industry* 1895–6, Princeton University Press, 1959.

NEUMANN, J. von, and MORGENSTERN, O., *Theory of Games and Economic Behaviour*, Princeton University Press, 1944.

PAPANDREOU, A. G., 'Market structure and monopoly power', *American Economic Review*, vol. 39, 1949.

PENROSE, E., *The Theory of the Growth of the Firm*, Oxford University Press, London, 1959.

P.E.P., *Industrial Trade Associations*, Political and Economic Planning, London, 1959.

Further Reading

PIGOU, A. C., *Aspects of British Economic History 1918–25*, Macmillan, London, 1947.

PLANT, A., 'The economic theory concerning patents for inventions', *Economica*, vol. 1, February 1934.

POOLE COMMITTEE, *Monopoly and the Public Interest*, Conservative Political Centre, no. 273, 1963.

PRAIS, S. J., and HART, P. E., 'The analysis of business concentration: a statistical approach', *Journal of the Royal Statistical Society*, Series A, vol. 119, 1956.

RESTRICTIVE PRACTICES COURT, *Law Reports: Restrictive Practices*, Incorporated Society of Law Reporting: London, vols. 1–6, 1957–67.

REDER, M. W., *Studies in the Theory of Welfare Economics*, Columbia University Press, New York, 1947.

REES, J. M., *Trusts in British Industry*, King and Son, London, 1923.

Registrar of Restrictive Trading Practices, *Reports 1959, 1961, 1963, 1965 and 1967*, H.M.S.O.

RICHARDSON, G., *Information and Investment*, Oxford University Press, London, 1960.

RICHARDSON, J. E., *The Australian Trade Practices Act*, Hicks Smith, Sydney, 1967.

ROBERTSON, D. H., *Lectures on Economic Principles*, Fontana, London, 1963.

ROBINSON, E. A. G., *Monopoly*, Nisbet and Cambridge University Press, 1946.

ROBINSON, J., *Economics of Imperfect Competition*, Macmillan, New York, 1935.

ROSENBLUTH, G., *Concentration in Canadian Manufacturing Industry*, Princeton University Press, 1959.

ROSTOW, E. V., 'Comparative developments in restrictive practices legislation', *Modern Law Review*, vol. 23, 1960.

ROTHSCHILD, K. W., 'The Degree of monopoly', *Economica*, vol. 9, 1942.

ROWLEY, C. K., *The British Monopolies Commission*, Allen & Unwin, London, 1966.

SCHUMPETER, J. A., *A History of Economic Analysis*, Allen & Unwin, London, 1961.

SCHUMPETER, J. A., *Capitalism, Socialism and Democracy*, Allen & Unwin, London, 1947.

SCHUMPETER, J. A., *The Theory of Economic Development*, Harvard University Press, Cambridge, Mass., 1949.

SCITOVSKY, T., *Welfare and Competition*, Allen & Unwin, London, 1952.

STELZER, I. M., *Selected Anti-Trust Cases*, Irwin, Illinois, 1955.

STEVENS, B., and YAMEY, B. S., *The Restrictive Practices Court*, Weidenfeld and Nicolson, London, 1965.

STEVENS, R., 'Justiciability: the Restrictive Practices Court re-examined', *Public Law*, Autumn 1964.

STEVENS, R. 'The intentional arousing of expectation in others and the

Registrar of Restrictive Trading Practices', *Modern Law Review*, vol. 26, September 1963.

STIGLER, G. J., *Five Lectures on Economic Problems*, Macmillan, London, 1950.

STIGLER, G. J., 'The statistics of monopoly and merger,' *Journal of Political Economy*, vol. 64, February 1956.

STIGLER, G. J., 'An economist plays with blocs', *American Economic Review: Proceedings*, vol. 44, May 1954.

STOCKING, G. W., and WATKINS, M. W., *Cartels in Action*, Twentieth Century Fund, New York, 1947.

STOCKING, G. W., *Cartels in Competition*, Twentieth Century Fund, New York, 1947.

SWEEZY, P., 'Demand under conditions of oligopoly', *Journal of Political Economy*, vol. 47, 1939.

TENNANT, R. B., *The American Cigarette Industry*, Yale University Press, New Haven, 1950.

TRIFFIN, R., *Monopolistic Competition and General Equilibrium Theory*, Harvard University Press, Cambridge, Mass., 1941.

U.S. Government, *The Attorney General's National Committee to Study the Anti-Trust Laws*, U.S. Government Printing Office, Washington, 1955.

U.S. Government, Temporary National Economic Committee, *Monograph No. 21 on Competition and Monopoly in American Industry*, Washington, 1941.

U.S.A.: Federal Trade Commission, *Report on Resale Price Maintenance*, Washington, 1941.

WALKER, G. de Q, *Australian Monopoly Law*, Cheshire, Melbourne, 1967.

WESTON, J. F., *The Role of Mergers in the Growth of Large Firms*, University of California Press, Berkeley, 1953.

WILBERFORCE, R. O., CAMPBELL, A., and ELLES, N. P. M., *The Law of Restrictive Trade Practices and Monopolies*, Sweet and Maxwell, London, 1957.

WILCOX, C., *Public Policies Towards Business*, Irwin, Illinois, 1955.

WILES, P., *Price, Cost and Output*, Oxford University Press, London, 1956.

WILSON, T., *Modern Capitalism and Economic Progress*, Macmillan, London, 1950.

WORSWICK, G. D. M., 'On the benefits of being denied the opportunity to "go shopping"', *Bulletin of Oxford Statistics*, August 1961.

YAMEY, B. S., *The Economics of Resale Price Maintenance*, Pitman, London, 1951.

YAMEY, B. S., *Resale Price Maintenance and Shopper's Choice*, Hobart Paper no. 1, 3rd edn, Barrie and Rockcliff, 1964.

YAMEY, B. S., (ed.), *Resale Price Maintenance*, Weidenfeld and Nicolson, London, 1966.

Acknowledgements

Permission to reprint the papers published in this volume is acknowledged from the following sources.

Reading 1   Richard D. Irwin Inc.
Reading 2   K. W. Rothschild and the Royal Economic Society
Reading 3   George Allen & Unwin Ltd
Reading 4   George Allen & Unwin Ltd and Harper & Row Inc.
Reading 6   George Allen & Unwin Ltd
Reading 7   J. K. Galbraith, Hamish Hamilton Ltd and Houghton Mifflin Company
Reading 8   B. S. Yamey and George Weidenfeld & Nicolson Ltd
Reading 9   E. V. Rostow
Reading 10 R. B. Stevens, B. S. Yamey and George Weidenfeld & Nicolson Ltd
Reading 11 Cambridge University Press

Author Index

References to bibliographies are printed in italics.

Author Index

Subject Index

Penguin Modern Economics Readings

Other volumes available in this series are:

**Economics of
Education 1**
Ed. M. Blaug
X56 9s.

The Labour Market
*Ed. B. J. McCormick and
E. Owen Smith*
X55 9s.

Managerial Economics
Ed. G. P. E. Clarkson
X57 9s.

Public Enterprise
Ed. R. Turvey
X59 9s.

Regional Analysis
Ed. L. Needleman
X60 9s.

Transport
Ed. Denys Munby
X58 9s.

Volumes published simultaneously with Monopoly and Competition
are:

Inflation
Ed. R. J. Ball and Peter Doyle

Since the Second World War our thinking about inflation has
changed considerably. Several different strains of the disease,
including 'creeping inflation', have been identified and the literature
on this topic, central to economists, politicians and businessmen
alike, is now enormous.

The feat of the editors of this key volume of Penguin Modern
Economics readings is to make the interplay of theoretical and
applied thinking on inflation not only crystal clear but also a
fascinating story in its own right: they take the reader from Keynes
in 1940 ('There is no difficulty whatever in paying for the cost of the
war out of voluntary savings provided we put up with the
consequences') to the continuing controversies (*per* Machlup: 'The
galloping inflation of literature on the creeping inflation of price')
focused on cost push and demand pull.
X32 9s.

International Finance
Ed. R. N. Cooper

Balance-of-payments problems, their causes and remedies are compelling and perennial issues. This volume starts with the superb analysis of the specie-flow mechanism by David Hume – a tribute to the power of classical economics. Various forms of balance-of-payments adjustment under fixed exchange rates are then considered, followed by several selections on the consequences of altering exchange rates. The difficulties of reconciling domestic and foreign policies are explored and the readings end with an examination of international liquidity.
X34 9s.

International Trade
Ed. Jagdish Bhagwati

The pure theory of international trade, one of the oldest branches of economics, deals with the causes of trade between nations, the gains from trade and the effects of commercial policy. The readings in this volume explore the theoretical foundations of the celebrated Heckscher–Ohlin model and the associated empirical literature on the 'Leontief Paradox'. The gains from free trade and, more importantly, trade in the presence of tariffs and rigid wages also receive attention. The final section explores the inter-relations of trade and growth.
X63 9s.